to accompany
McConnell *Economics* AP® Edition

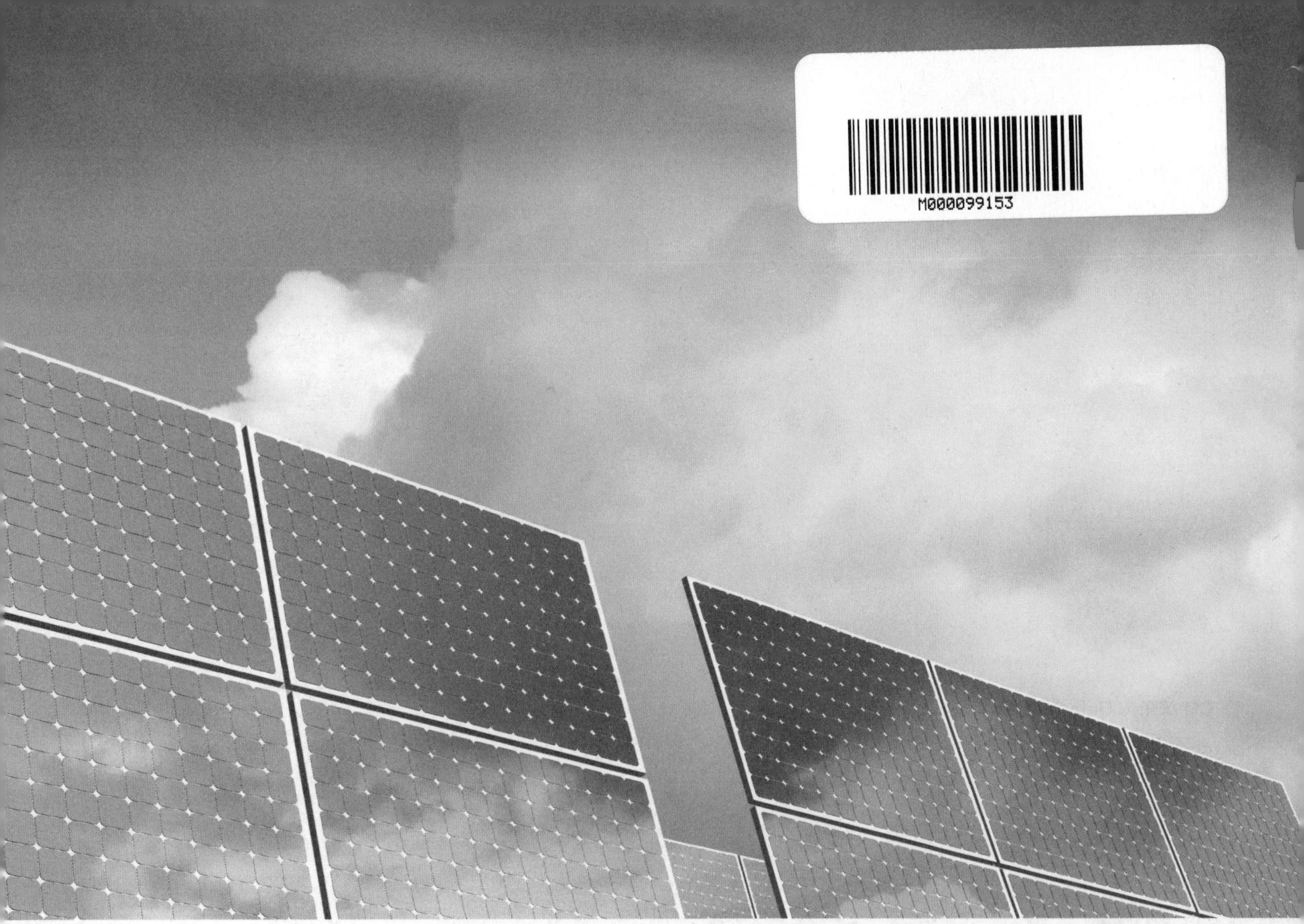

COVER: © Getty Images/Kativ.

mheducation.com/prek-12

Send all inquiries to:
McGraw-Hill Education
8787 Orion Place
Columbus, OH 43240

ISBN: 978-0-07-900260-0
MHID: 0-07-900260-9

Printed in the United States of America.

1 2 3 4 5 6 7 8 9 QVS 23 22 21 20 19 18 17

About the Author

Lisa C. Herman Ellison taught AP Micro/Macroeconomics, AP US Government, and College-Prep, Applied, and Consumer Economics at Kokomo High School (Kokomo, IN) for 26 years before retiring in 2014. In addition to serving as a reader for the College Board's AP Economics exams, she has served as the teacher representative to the Indiana Council for Economic Education's Executive Committee and worked on the teams that wrote the Indiana Economics Standards and the Indiana Economics teaching license exams. Currently, she is a member of the Board of School Trustees for the Kokomo School Corporation.

During her distinguished career, Ellison received numerous awards, including the Olin W. Davis Award for Exemplary Teaching of Economics from the Indiana Council for Economic Education and the Jasper P. Baldwin Award for Excellence in Undergraduate Teaching from the University of Oklahoma. She has received the US Department of Education Excellence in Economic Education Award, the National Association of Regulatory Utility Commissioners' Excellence in Education Award, was one of five national finalists for the NASDAQ National Teaching Award for Teachers of Excellence and Innovation, and was the third place winner for the Council for Economic Education's National Award for the Teaching of Economics.

She has written or co-authored more than three dozen lessons and articles for the National and Indiana Councils for Economic Education, the Federal Reserve, the Indiana Department of Education, and the Indiana Historical Society.

Acknowledgements

This book would not have been possible without the help of friends and family. My deepest gratitude goes to my husband Brett and our sons Andrew and Cameron for their unwavering encouragement and support. Deepest thanks also go to my Mom, Judy Herman, for instilling in me the passion to help kids understand the world around them. I also appreciate the friendship, advice, and support of Vanessa Marsh, Tom Richardson, and Susan Stouse. Special thanks to Dr. Jeff Sanson and the staff at the Indiana Council for Economic Education for providing so many opportunities for me to grow. I am grateful to Juyong Pae, my editor at McGraw-Hill, for her guidance and patience throughout this project, and to Sally Meek, for her helpful reviews and suggestions for improvement.

—Lisa Ellison

CONTENTS

For ease-of-use we have color coded our guide.

Microeconomics Parts and Chapters are indicated with green

Macroeconomics Parts and Chapters are indicated with purple

Parts and Chapters that **cover both content** are indicated with combined green and purple

This *Focus Review Guide* works hand in hand with the *Economics* Student Edition!

Sections in the *Economics* Student Edition marked with the AP icon AP indicates that there is additional support material available in our *Focus Review Guide.*

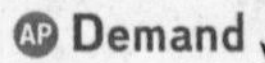

LO3.2 Describe *demand* and explain how it can change.

Demand is a schedule or a curve that shows the various amounts of a product that consumers are willing and able to purchase at each of a series of possible prices during a specified period of time.[1] Demand shows the quantities of a product that will be purchased at various possible prices, *other things equal*. Demand can easily be shown in table form. The table in Figure 3.1 is a hypothetical **demand schedule** for a *single consumer* purchasing bushels of corn.

The table reveals the relationship between the various prices of corn and the quantity of corn a particular consumer would be willing and able to purchase at each of these
We say "willing and able" because willingness alo
effective in the market. You may be willing to buy
television set, but if that willingness is not backed by
essary dollars, it will not be effective and, therefore,
be reflected in the market. In the table in Figure 3
price of corn were $5 per bushel, our consumer w
willing and able to buy 10 bushels per week; if it wer
consumer would be willing and able to buy 20 bus
week; and so forth.

Demand

Refer to pages 48–53 of your textbook.

A CLOSER LOOK The Demand Curve

The **demand** curve shows the quantity of products consumers are willing and able to buy at various prices. It is a downward-sloping curve, showing the inverse relationship between the price and the quantity demanded. According to the **Law of Demand,** when the price falls, the quantity demanded increases; when the price rises, the quantity demanded falls. You know this to be true from purchases you have made. If you had a choice of paying $100 or $75 for the very same pair of shoes, which price would you be more willing and able to pay?

So what makes the Law of Demand operate as it does? Three factors create this effect. The first is **diminishing marginal utility.** As a consumer gets more and more of a product, the satisfaction he gets from each additional product falls; therefore, he is not willing to pay as much for additional products. A pencil is very useful for school work, and if you really need one, you might be willing to pay $1 for it. A second pencil is still useful, but not as much as that first one was, so you might only be willing to pay 50¢ for it. In order to entice you to buy more, the producer must lower the price for additional products.

The second factor is the **income effect.** At a lower price, a consumer can afford to buy more of the product. Say you go to the store, expecting to pay $2 for a box of pencils. But you find that the store is having a sale, with a price of only $1 for the box of pencils. You now have a dollar left over, which you might use to buy a second box of pencils. When the price falls, people are able to buy more.

The third factor is the **substitution effect.** At a lower price, a customer may choose to substitute one product for another. If you went to the store planning to pay $2 for a box of pens, but saw the box of pencils on sale for $1, you might be willing to buy the pencils instead of the pens. When the price falls, people are willing to buy more.

To draw a demand curve, you must first create a demand schedule, showing how many products the consumer is willing and able to buy at each price. Then you can plot the points into the graph and connect those points to draw the curve.

A Closer Look provides additional information and explanation to ensure complete understanding.

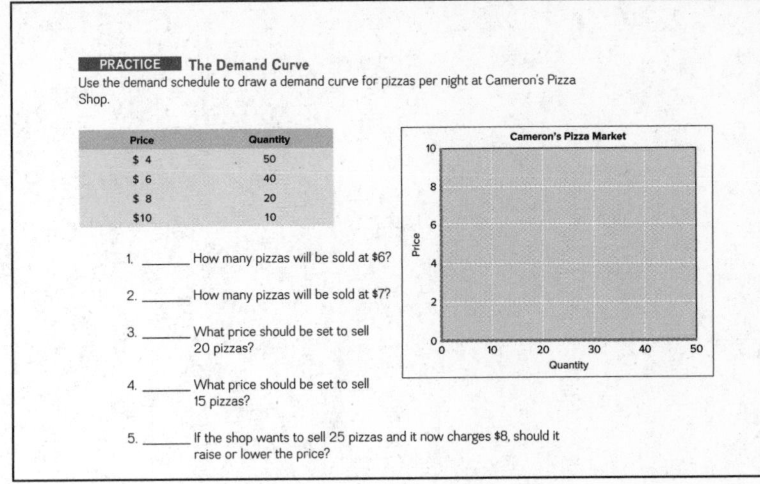

PRACTICE **The Demand Curve**

Use the demand schedule to draw a demand curve for pizzas per night at Cameron's Pizza Shop.

Price	Quantity
$ 4	50
$ 6	40
$ 8	20
$10	10

1. _______ How many pizzas will be sold at $6?
2. _______ How many pizzas will be sold at $7?
3. _______ What price should be set to sell 20 pizzas?
4. _______ What price should be set to sell 15 pizzas?
5. _______ If the shop wants to sell 25 pizzas and it now charges $8, should it raise or lower the price?

Practice sections include questions and graphing exercises that allow students additional practice in applying AP concepts.

Valuable features, such as **Caution, Graphing Guidance, Keep in Mind,** and **Economically Speaking** give students tips, advice, and study tools to help them avoid common mistakes and earn high scores on the AP Exams.

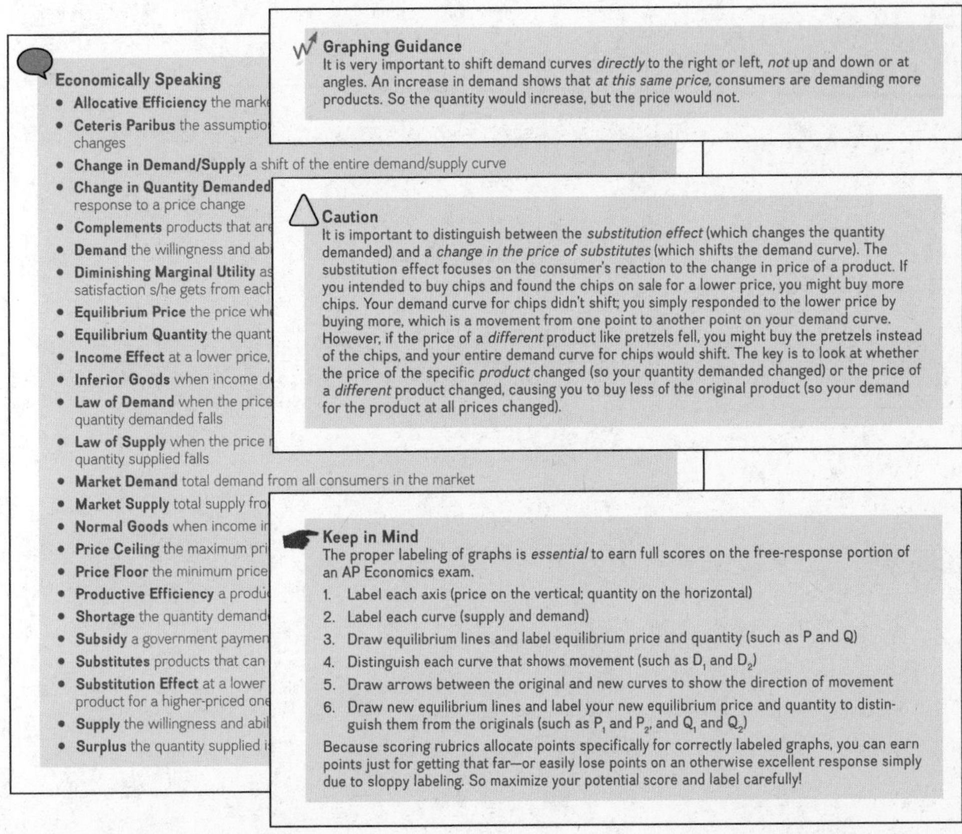

Economically Speaking

- **Allocative Efficiency** the mark
- **Ceteris Paribus** the assumptio changes
- **Change in Demand/Supply** a shift of the entire demand/supply curve
- **Change in Quantity Demanded** response to a price change
- **Complements** products that ar
- **Demand** the willingness and ab
- **Diminishing Marginal Utility** a satisfaction s/he gets from each
- **Equilibrium Price** the price wh
- **Equilibrium Quantity** the quant
- **Income Effect** at a lower price,
- **Inferior Goods** when income d
- **Law of Demand** when the price quantity demanded falls
- **Law of Supply** when the price quantity supplied falls
- **Market Demand** total demand from all consumers in the market
- **Market Supply** total supply fro
- **Normal Goods** when income i
- **Price Ceiling** the maximum pri
- **Price Floor** the minimum price
- **Productive Efficiency** a produ
- **Shortage** the quantity demand
- **Subsidy** a government paymen
- **Substitutes** products that can
- **Substitution Effect** at a lower product for a higher-priced one
- **Supply** the willingness and abil
- **Surplus** the quantity supplied i

Graphing Guidance

It is very important to shift demand curves *directly* to the right or left, *not* up and down or at angles. An increase in demand shows that *at this same price*, consumers are demanding more products. So the quantity would increase, but the price would not.

Caution

It is important to distinguish between the *substitution effect* (which changes the quantity demanded) and a *change in the price of substitutes* (which shifts the demand curve). The substitution effect focuses on the consumer's reaction to the change in price of a product. If you intended to buy chips and found the chips on sale for a lower price, you might buy more chips. Your demand curve for chips didn't shift; you simply responded to the lower price by buying more, which is a movement from one point to another point on your demand curve. However, if the price of a *different* product like pretzels fell, you might buy the pretzels instead of the chips, and your entire demand curve for chips would shift. The key is to look at whether the price of the specific *product* changed (so your quantity demanded changed) or the price of a *different* product changed, causing you to buy less of the original product (so your demand for the product at all prices changed).

Keep in Mind

The proper labeling of graphs is *essential* to earn full scores on the free-response portion of an AP Economics exam.

1. Label each axis (price on the vertical; quantity on the horizontal)
2. Label each curve (supply and demand)
3. Draw equilibrium lines and label equilibrium price and quantity (such as P and Q)
4. Distinguish each curve that shows movement (such as D_1 and D_2)
5. Draw arrows between the original and new curves to show the direction of movement
6. Draw new equilibrium lines and label your new equilibrium price and quantity to distinguish them from the originals (such as P_1 and P_2, and Q_1 and Q_2)

Because scoring rubrics allocate points specifically for correctly labeled graphs, you can earn points just for getting that far—or easily lose points on an otherwise excellent response simply due to sloppy labeling. So maximize your potential score and label carefully!

Chapter 1

Limits, Alternatives, and Choices

At the heart of economics is the simple but very real prospect that we cannot have it all. We don't have enough resources to meet all of our wants and needs, so we are forced to make choices. Chapter 1 identifies this problem and introduces the first in a series of models economists use to describe decision making by individuals, firms, governments, and societies. The principle of "tradeoffs" takes both numeric and graphic form and provides the foundation for the rest of the economics course.

Material from Chapter 1 appears in several multiple-choice questions on both the AP Microeconomics and AP Macroeconomics exams and occasionally appears in free-response questions.

Key Concepts

Below is a summary of the chapter's concepts important to AP coursework. Upon completing the lessons that follow, return to these concepts to make sure you understand them and how the practice exercises you completed relate to them.

- Because resources are scarce, an economy cannot produce as many goods as society wants.
- Economics is the study of how society fulfills unlimited wants with scarce resources.
- Opportunity cost is the next best alternative given up when a choice is made.
    - Think of it this way: you have to choose between buying a hat and buying gloves, and you choose the hat. Your opportunity cost for the hat is the gloves—that is, you *gave up* the gloves.
    - Opportunity cost is the other choice, not the price or the resource used to obtain your first choice. If you spend $20 to buy a game rather than a T-shirt, your opportunity cost for the game is the T-shirt, not the $20, which you would have spent either way.
    - Opportunity cost is only the *next* best choice, not every available alternative.
    - Costs that are incurred regardless of which choice you make are not opportunity costs. If you drove to school to go to a band concert or a basketball game, you would have spent the same amount for gas to drive to school, so that gas or the cost of the gas is not an opportunity cost.
    - Opportunity cost only involves costs, not benefits.
- Microeconomics is the study of decisions made by individual consumers or firms.

- Macroeconomics is the study of the economy as a whole.
- The factors of production are land, labor, capital, and entrepreneurship.
- The production possibilities curve illustrates the maximum amount of products that can be produced in an economy, if it is using all available resources and technology.
- Then, in order to produce more of one good, the economy must produce less of another. The reduction in the production of this other good is the opportunity cost of producing more of the first good.
- The Law of Increasing Opportunity Costs illustrates that as production of one good increases, the opportunity cost of producing each additional unit increases, because resources are not perfectly adaptable in producing different products.
- Marginal analysis is used to determine the optimal allocation of products, which occurs where the marginal benefit equals the marginal cost.
- Points inside the production possibilities curve represent unemployment of resources and inefficient production of goods. The short-run goal of the economy is to move onto the curve to produce at full-employment output.
- Points outside the production possibilities curve are currently unattainable due to limits on resources and technology. The long-run goal of the economy is to pursue economic growth, shifting the curve outward through improved resources and technology.
- International trade allows a country to reach production possibilities beyond its own limits.

Caution

You must be able to recognize that every choice involves another alternative that was given up, even if the choice made the person better off. Keep in mind that you're looking for what was given up in making the decision, and that will help you identify what is – and what is not – an opportunity cost.

Now, let's examine more closely the following concepts from your textbook:

- **Production Possibilities Model**
- **Unemployment, Growth, and the Future**

These sections were selected because they require the ability to both create and interpret graphs likely to appear on the AP exams.

Production Possibilities Model

Refer to pages 9–13 of your textbook.

A CLOSER LOOK Production Possibilities Table and Curve

The **production possibilities curve (PPC)** shows the maximum amount of products an economy can produce with its resources. Recall that scarce resources limit how many products an economy can make. So if a society chooses to make more of one product, it must produce less of another (the **opportunity cost**). The production possibilities curve allows us to move beyond discussion of individual choices, as have been discussed in the earlier examples of opportunity cost thus far, to analyze opportunity costs across an entire economy.

The production possibilities curve starts with several assumptions. These assumptions suspend reality a bit, but they will help you to more easily see the concepts involved. These assumption are,

1. The economy can only produce two products. It can use all of its resources to produce Product A, it can produce only Product B, or it can produce some combination of Products A and B.
2. All of the economy's resources are being used, which is known as **full employment** of resources.
3. The quantity and quality of resources and technology do not change during the analysis.

Now let's assume our economy can only produce corn or wheat. Let's also assume we have five possible combinations of tons of wheat or corn that our economy can produce. They are as follows:

	Tons of Corn	Tons of Wheat
Point A	0	80
Point B	10	60
Point C	20	40
Point D	30	20
Point E	40	0

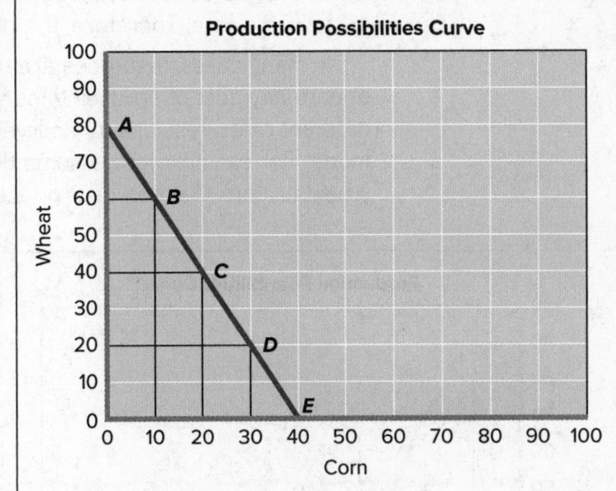

We can then put these five data points on a graph to show how many tons of corn and wheat our economy can produce with its limited resources and technology.

From the data in both the graph and table, you can see the opportunity cost our economy bears each time it produces products. If we start at Point A, where no corn is being produced but 80 tons of wheat are being produced, and then move to Point B, where 10 tons of corn and 60 tons of wheat are being produced, we can see that the economy at Point B is producing 10 additional units of corn—but with the opportunity cost of 20 fewer tons of wheat. Moving from Point B to Point C, our economy can produce 10 additional tons of corn, again with an opportunity cost of 20 tons of wheat, and so on. To sum up then, for every ton of corn our economy produces, the opportunity cost is 2 tons of wheat. Moving in the other direction on the curve, for every ton of wheat the economy produces, the opportunity cost is ½ ton of corn.

PRACTICE Production Possibilities Table and Curve

Now let's assume another economy can only produce apples or oranges in these combinations:

	Tons of Apples	Tons of Oranges
Point A	30	0
Point B	20	30
Point C	10	60
Point D	0	90

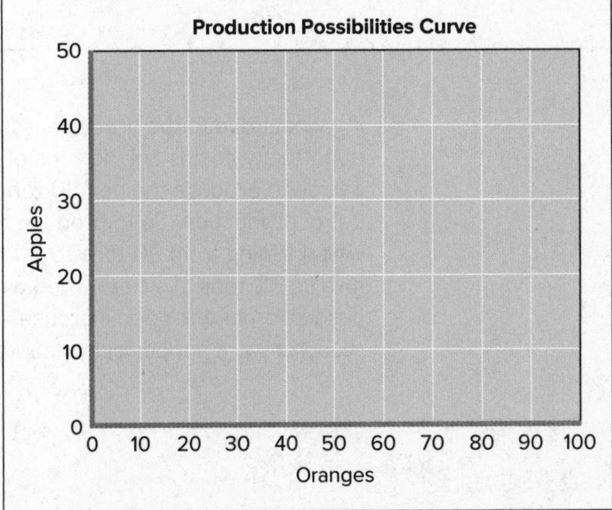

Draw the production possibilities curve for this economy in the blank graph on page 3 and answer the questions below:

1. _______ What is the opportunity cost to produce 10 tons of apples?

2. _______ What is the opportunity cost to produce 1 ton of apples?

3. _______ What is the opportunity cost to produce 1 ton of oranges?

A CLOSER LOOK Law of Increasing Opportunity Costs

Up to this point, we have assumed that productive resources are perfectly interchangeable in producing the two products. Land, labor, capital, and technology are used equally efficiently in producing wheat or corn. As a result, opportunity costs have remained constant—that is, for every product produced, the opportunity cost in terms of the other product changes at the same rate. Therefore, the production possibilities curve is a straight line.

In many cases, resources are not perfectly adaptable or interchangeable. As a result, the opportunity cost of producing more of a product does not remain constant, but changes at different rates, resulting in a curve rather than a straight line in the production possibilities model. For example, let's assume the following are the five possible combinations tons of wheat or corn that can be produced in our economy:

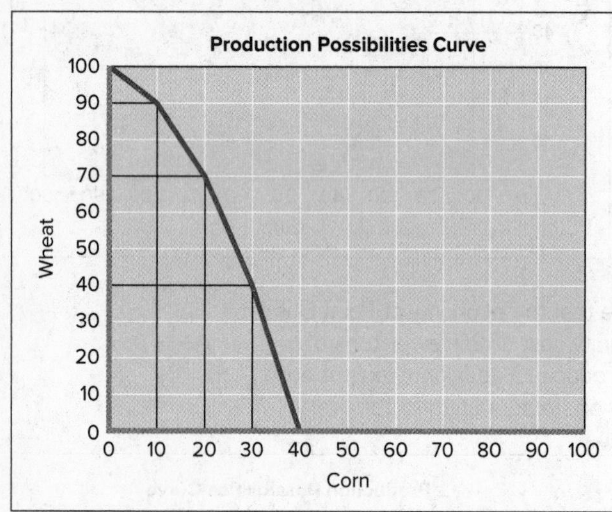

	Tons of Corn	Tons of Wheat
Point A	0	100
Point B	10	90
Point C	20	70
Point D	30	40
Point E	40	0

See how the curve bends? Opportunity costs change at different rates when productive resources are not perfectly adaptable. For example, not all farmland is equal. Let's assume some farmland has drainage problems, and wheat is more sensitive than corn to standing water. Let's start at the production possibility of 100 tons of wheat and no corn. If we decide to begin producing corn, we would choose to produce that corn on the land that is least productive in producing wheat due to the drainage issues. So when we increase corn production to 10 tons, the opportunity cost is only 10 tons of wheat (falling from 100 tons to 90 tons). But when we decide to produce the next 10 tons of corn, we begin taking better wheat-producing land out of production. So to produce the next 10 tons of corn, the opportunity cost is 20 tons of wheat (falling from 90 tons to 70 tons). To produce the next 10 tons of corn, society must give up 30 tons of wheat. The **Law of Increasing Opportunity Costs** explains that as production of one good increases, the opportunity cost increases. This occurs when resources are not perfectly adaptable.

PRACTICE Law of Increasing Opportunity Costs

Draw two production possibilities curves using points from the tables below and answer the questions for each curve.

PPC 1	
Good A	Good B
0	12
1	10
2	8
3	6
4	4
5	2
6	0

PPC 2	
Good A	Good B
0	12
1	10
2	6
3	0

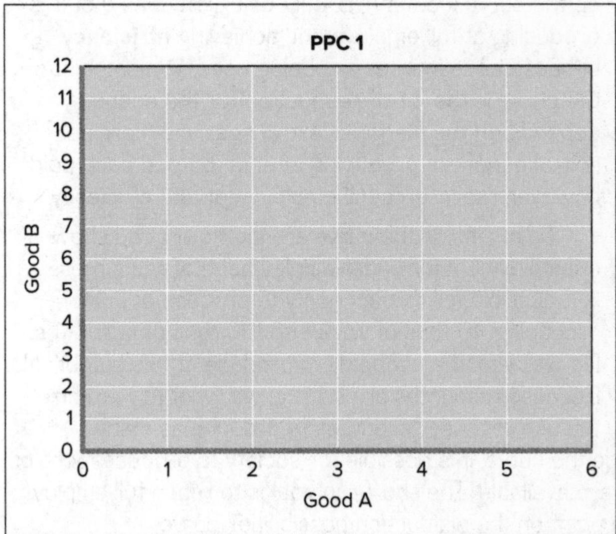

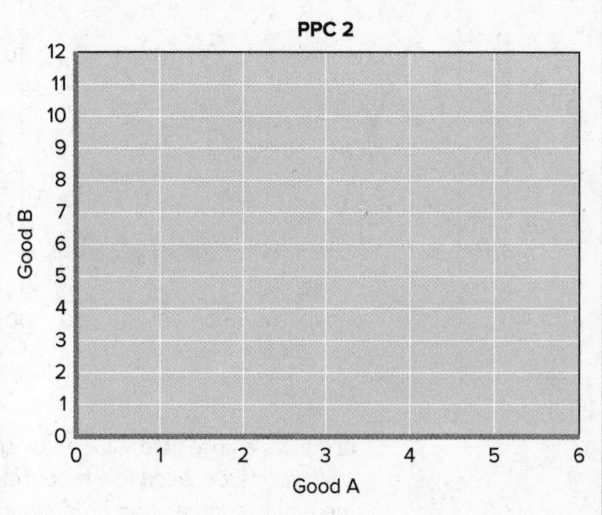

Assume these economies are currently producing 0 units of Good A and 12 units of Good B.

1. The opportunity cost of increasing production of Good A from 0 to 1 is the loss of how many units of Good B?

   __________ for PPC 1 __________ for PPC 2

2. The opportunity cost of increasing production of Good A from 1 to 2 is the loss of how many units of Good B?

   __________ for PPC 1 __________ for PPC 2

3. The opportunity cost of increasing production of Good A from 2 to 3 is the loss of how many units of Good B?

   __________ for PPC 1 __________ for PPC 2

4. Is this graph an example of a constant or increasing opportunity cost?
_________ for PPC 1 _________ for PPC 2

5. Why do production possibilities curves generally show increasing costs?
____
____

Unemployment, Growth, and the Future

Refer to pages 13–15 of your textbook.

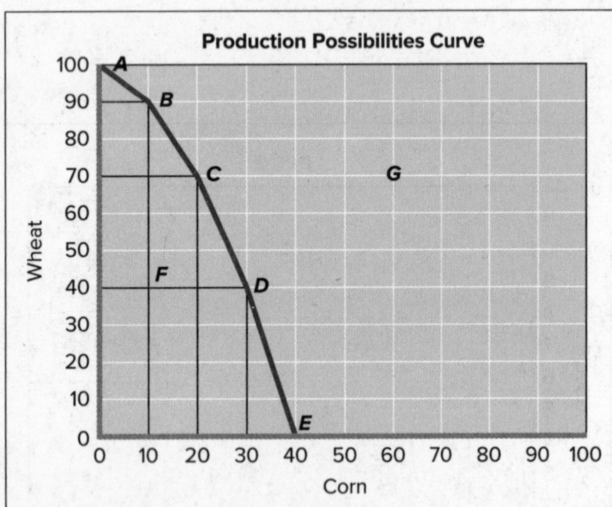

A CLOSER LOOK A Growing Economy

Let's look more broadly at what points on the PPC graph mean. If an economy is producing at any point on the curve (Points A, B, C, D, or E), it means that it is producing at full employment, achieving **efficiency** because all resources are being used. Which point on the curve is the "best" production for the economy depends on the marginal (extra) cost and marginal (extra) benefit of producing at each output. Each point, however, represents full employment and efficiency.

Points inside the curve are inefficient and show unemployment (or under-employment) of resources. Is it possible for this economy to produce at Point F, producing 40 tons of wheat and 10 tons of corn? Yes. Do we *want* the economy to produce at this output? No. Because resources are scarce, we want to maximize the use of those resources to produce as many products as possible. At a point inside the curve, it is possible for society to produce more of *both* goods, because idle resources are available. The short-run goal is to reach full employment of resources and produce at a point on the production possibilities curve.

Points outside the curve are unattainable, due to limited resources and technology. It is not possible for this economy to produce at Point G, making 70 tons of wheat and 60 tons of corn. However, the long-run goal for an economy is economic growth. Growth can occur, if, for example, the working-age population increases, or a better quality of seed is created, or better harvesting technology is developed. Such developments will make it possible, then, for this society to produce more products. When the quantity or quality of resources and technology are improved, the entire production possibilities curve shifts outward, allowing this society to produce *both* more wheat *and* more corn. This shifting outward of the curve reflects economic growth.

PRACTICE A Growing Economy

Refer to the graph shown here on the right.

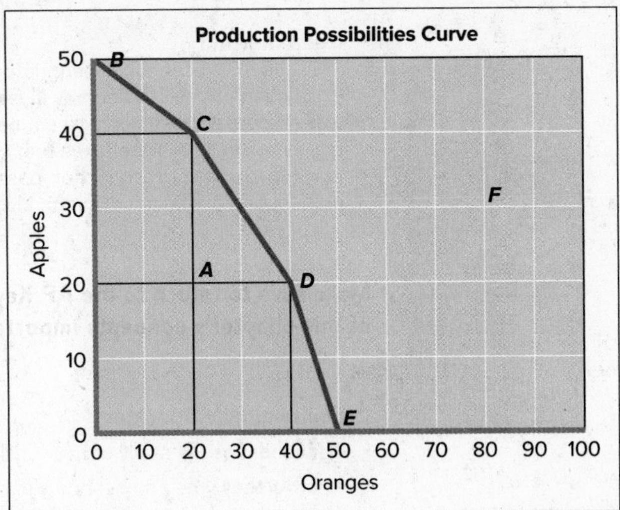

1. _______ Which letters illustrate points of efficient, full employment output?

2. _______ Which letter illustrates a point of unemployment (inefficiency)?

3. _______ Which letter illustrates a point that is unattainable right now?

4. In general terms, what are the two factors that limit the ability of an economy to produce beyond its production possibilities curve?

____

____

5. Draw a new curve representing economic growth in the graph above

6. Provide two examples of a way in which an economy might achieve economic growth.

____

____

A CLOSER LOOK Present Choices and Future Possibilities

Another point to consider about the production possibilities curve is the tradeoff between consumer goods for current consumption and capital goods, the equipment producers buy in order to produce even more products. If a society chooses to produce more consumer goods, it has fewer resources available to produce capital goods. This can reduce potential output in the long run, so societies must consider the tradeoff between current consumption and future production.

It is important to note that it is possible for only one end of the production possibilities curve to shift outward while the other end remains anchored in place. For example, perhaps a more insect-resistant variety of corn is developed, so that it is possible to produce a maximum of 60 tons of corn, rather than 40 tons. (Refer to the above graphs for wheat and corn production.) Or maybe the society of this economy is choosing to engage in international trade with a country that produces wheat more efficiently. In summary, some changing conditions can result in the movement of only one end of the curve.

We will revisit these concepts later and put the concepts into practice with exercises.

Keep in Mind

Previous free-response questions, particularly on the AP Macroeconomics exam, have included production possibilities curves illustrating tradeoffs before and after international trade. Other free-response questions have connected increased labor productivity or investments in technology (or lower corporate taxes that would allow firms to invest in technology) to the effect on long-run changes in production possibilities. You may be asked to draw a correctly-labeled production possibilities curve to illustrate those changes through shifts in the curve.

Make sure to return to the AP Key Concepts section above to check your understanding of this chapter's concepts important to AP coursework.

Economically Speaking

- **Economics** the study of how society fulfills unlimited wants with scarce resources
- **Efficiency** when an economy is producing products without any waste of resources
- **Full Employment** represented as any point *on* the production possibilities curve, where all of a society's resources and technology are being used to produce the greatest possible amount of products
- **Law of Increasing Opportunity Costs** the rule that as production of one good increases, the opportunity cost of producing each additional unit of that good increases, because resources are not perfectly adaptable
- **Macroeconomics** the study of the economy as a whole
- **Marginal Analysis** comparing the marginal benefit and marginal cost in making a decision
- **Microeconomics** the study of the individual consumer or firm
- **Opportunity Cost** the most valuable thing given up in order to get something else
- **Production Possibilities Curve** illustrates the maximum amount of products that can be produced using all available resources and technology

The Market System and the Circular Flow

The problem of scarcity forces societies to make choices about what to produce, how to produce those goods, and who will receive the goods that are produced. But societies must first decide who will have the power to make those decisions: the government, the people, or both. In doing so, societies set up economic systems. Chapter 2, then, examines the three types of economic system constructs—laissez-faire capitalism, the command system, and the market system—and takes a more in-depth look at the market system.

Material from Chapter 2 could appear in a multiple-choice question on either exam. A question about who makes decisions in a particular economic system is likely to appear on the AP Microeconomics exam. A question about a simple model of the market system (the circular flow model) is likely to appear on the AP Macroeconomics exam.

Key Concepts

Below is a summary of the chapter's concepts important to AP coursework. Upon completing the lesson that follows, return to these concepts to make sure you understand them and how the practice exercise you completed relates to them.

- Economic systems answer the questions of what, how, and for whom to produce goods, how to accommodate change, and how to promote progress.
- In laissez-faire capitalism, markets direct nearly all economic activity, and government intervention is minimal.
- In a command economy, government directs nearly all economic activity.
- In market (or mixed market) economies, markets are responsible for most economic decisions, but some government intervention exists.
- Characteristics of a market economy include private property; free enterprise; self-interest; competition; the guiding function of prices and profits; advanced technology and capital goods; specialization; extensive use of money; and active, but limited, government.
- Consumer sovereignty determines which products will be produced.
- The market system uses changes in prices and profits to signal consumers and businesses to make changes in purchases and production.
- Adam Smith identified self-interest as the "invisible hand" that guides a market system.
- The term *resource* (or *factor*) *markets* refers to the understanding that households provide resources (factors of production: land, labor, capital, and entrepreneurial ability) to businesses in return for money (wages, rents, interest for capital, and profits for entrepreneurial ability).

- The term *product markets* refers to the understanding that businesses provide goods and services in return for money (revenue).

Now, let's examine more closely the following concept covered in your textbook:

- **Circular Flow Model**

We are examining this model more closely, because it is easy to confuse the actions taking place in the resource (factor) market and the product market.

The Circular Flow Model

Refer to pages 28–39 of your textbook.

A CLOSER LOOK The Circular Flow Model

A **market** is a mechanism that allows buyers and sellers to make an exchange. It is important to keep in mind that markets are not limited to brick-and-mortar stores. For example, eBay is a market. A Girl Scout selling cookies to her neighbor is a market. A restaurant hiring a server is a market. The market allows buyers and sellers to engage in voluntary exchange, with each willing to make a trade, because both of them gain from the trade.

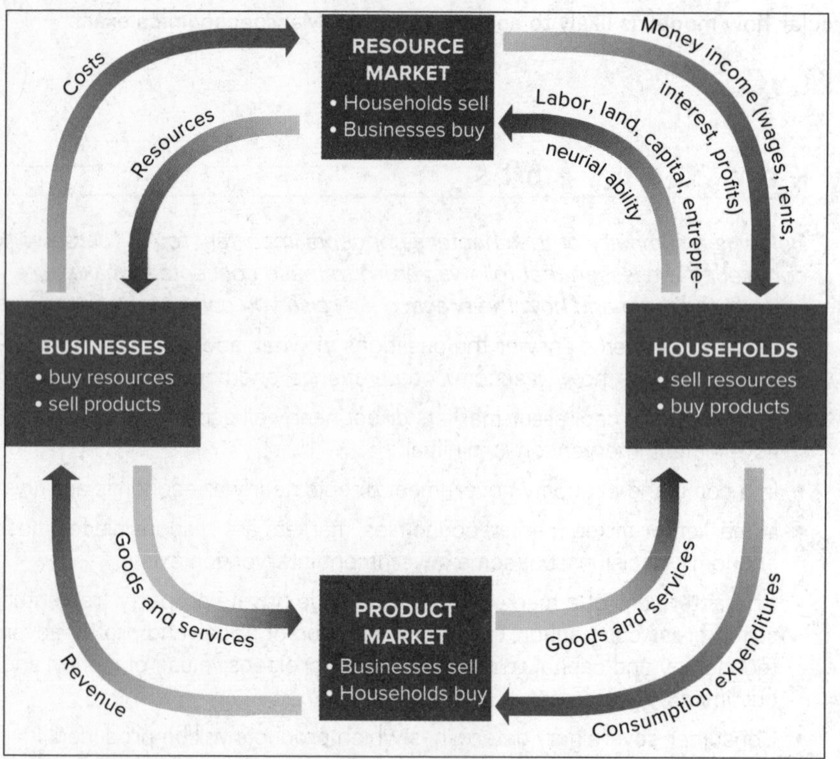

The **circular flow model** illustrates the flow of resources, goods and services, and money in the *resource (factor)* and *product markets* of a market economy. It is a simplified model of the entire economy, avoiding the illustration of government activity, imports, exports, savings, and other complicating factors. In later chapters, you will be introduced to a more complicated model.

In the **resource (factor) market,** resources are bought and sold. In this market, households sell the factors of production (land, labor, capital, and entrepreneurial ability) to businesses, which use those resources to create products. Money flows in the other direction, as businesses pay for the use of these resources: rent for land, wages for labor, interest for capital, and profits for entrepreneurial ability. Most people—like you and me—participate in the resource market by selling their labor to a business in return for a paycheck (form of income).

In the **product market,** goods and services are bought and sold. In this market, businesses sell products to households, which use their incomes to purchase the products. As in the resource (factor) market, products flow one direction, while money flows the other. Most people—like you and me—participate in the product market by buying products, whether at a brick-and-mortar store, online, or in a direct face-to-face encounter.

Caution

It can be confusing to remember what is sold in each market and what each actor is doing in that market. In one market, households are buying, while businesses are selling, and in the other market, the reverse occurs. To remember what is being sold, just look at the name of the market. In the resource (factor) market, resources (factors of production) are being sold. In the product market, products are being sold. To remember what each actor is doing in the market, think about what each actor has the incentive to do. In the resource (factor) market, resources are being sold. Who has resources to sell? Households. Who needs to buy resources to make products? Businesses. In the product market, the two actors take on opposite roles, as households buy products from the businesses that are selling them. If you can keep straight what is being sold in each market, the actions of the actors will follow.

Adam Smith, known as the father of economics, explained the operation of market systems in his 1776 book *The Wealth of Nations*. He described how the "invisible hand" of self-interest leads businesses and households to act in ways that benefit themselves as well as society. For example, to earn more profit, businesses produce products consumers want, and they produce those products as efficiently as possible, reducing waste of limited resources, which, in turn, can be used to produce other goods. On the other hand, the desire for higher income encourages people to seek higher education and job training to command that higher wage. That education, in turn, benefits society by improving worker productivity and reducing production costs.

In a **command economy,** the government makes the decisions about what to produce, what prices to charge, and how to distribute the products. In a **market economy,** the circular flow model operates without the need for government planning. Households earn income in the factor market and use that money to buy products in the product market. Companies earn revenue in the product market and then use that money to buy even more resources in the resource (factor) market. Households and businesses both have the incentive to take action that benefits them as well as society.

PRACTICE The Circular Flow Model

For each question about markets below, identify the answer as **resource** or **product.**

1. _________ In which market would a company sell its services?

2. _________ In which market would a household be the seller?

3. _________ In which market would a corporation hire an accountant?

4. _________ In which market would a consumer buy a new truck?

5. _________ In which market would a business earn money?

6. __________ In which market would farmers buy land from retiring farmers?

7. __________ In which market would a worker earn her wages?

8. __________ In which market would a person buy a computer?

Keep in Mind

While a question or two on the AP Microeconomics and AP Macroeconomics multiple-choice exams are likely to come from this chapter, a good understanding of the incentives and motivations involved in the market system is important to understand the decisions of consumers, workers, firms, and governments explored in later chapters. No free-response questions have been based specifically on material from this chapter.

Make sure to return to the AP Key Concepts section to check your understanding of the chapter's concepts important to AP coursework.

Economically Speaking

- **Circular Flow Model** illustrates the flow of resources, goods and services, and money in the resource (factor) and product markets of a market economy
- **Command Economy** an economic system in which government directs nearly all aspects of the economy
- **Economic System** a set of institutional arrangements a society uses to determine *what* will be produced, *how* those products will be produced, and *who* gets the products
- **Laissez-Faire Economy** an economic system in which markets direct economic activity and government plays little to no role in the economy
- **Market** a mechanism that brings buyers and sellers together to make exchanges
- **Market (Mixed Market) Economy** an economic system in which the markets direct most of the economic activity, but some government intervention exists
- **Product Market** where households buy products produced by businesses
- **Resource (Factor) Market** where businesses buy resources provided by households

Demand, Supply, and Market Equilibrium

Supply and demand are mechanisms that help our market economy run efficiently. Changes in supply and demand affect prices and quantities of goods and services produced, which in turn affect profit, employment, wages, and government revenue. Chapter 3 introduces models to explain the behavior of consumers and producers in markets, as well as the effects of government policies on market activity. The concepts of supply and demand reappear throughout the economics course to explain how wages, interest rates, currency values, and other values are determined.

Material from Chapter 3 is heavily covered on the multiple-choice and free-response sections of both AP Economics exams. The AP Microeconomics exam is likely to feature questions about changes in the supply and demand for either products or labor. The AP Macroeconomics exam is likely to test the concepts of supply and demand as they apply in money markets, loanable funds markets and currency markets.

Key Concepts

Below is a summary of the chapter's concepts important to AP coursework. Upon completing the lessons that follow, return to these concepts to make sure you understand them and how the practice exercises you completed relate to them.

- Demand shows the willingness and ability of a consumer to buy a product at a particular price. Willingness is not enough; the consumer must also *be able* to buy for demand to exist.
- A demand schedule, which is used to draw a demand curve, lists a series of prices for a product and the quantity of it that a consumer is willing and able to buy at each price.
- It is critical to remember *ceteris paribus:* when we are conducting an analysis, we assume that nothing else is changing. If we study how a consumer reacts to a price change, we assume that the consumer's income and tastes are not changing, in order to keep a clean analysis.
- The Law of Demand states that when the price falls, the quantity demanded increases; when the price increases, the quantity demanded falls. This is an inverse relationship, meaning that price and quantity demanded move in opposite directions.
- Causes of the Law of Demand:
    - Diminishing marginal utility—as a consumer gets more and more of a product, the satisfaction he gets from each additional product falls.
    - Income effect—at a lower price, a consumer can afford to buy more of the product.
    - Substitution effect—at a lower price, a customer may choose to substitute one product for another.

- The income and substitution effects combine to make consumers more willing (substitution effect) and able (income effect) to buy more at lower prices.
- Market demand is the total demand from all consumers in the market; the quantities demanded from each individual consumer are summed horizontally.
- A change in *quantity* demanded occurs when a customer responds to a change in price. The curve hasn't moved; movement is along the curve to a different point.
- A change in demand occurs when the entire demand curve shifts. Increases shift the curve directly to the right, while decreases shift the curve directly to the left.
- The non-price determinants of demand (or demand shifters, which can cause a change in demand) are consumer tastes (preferences), the number of consumers, consumer incomes, the prices of substitutes and complements, and consumer expectations.
- Supply shows the willingness and ability of a producer to sell a product at a particular price.
- The Law of Supply states that when the price rises, the quantity supplied increases; when the price falls, the quantity supplied falls. This is a direct relationship, meaning that price and quantity supplied move together in the same direction.
- Causes of the Law of Supply:
  - Greater revenue entices producers to increase production.
  - At some point, the cost to produce each product increases, so the producer must charge a higher price to cover those increased costs of production.
- Market supply is the total supply from all producers in the market; the quantities supplied by each individual producer are summed horizontally.
- A change in *quantity* supplied occurs when a producer responds to a change in price. The curve hasn't moved; movement is along the curve to a different point.
- A change in supply occurs when the entire supply curve shifts. Increases shift the curve directly to the right, while decreases shift the curve directly to the left.
- The non-price determinants of supply (or supply shifters, which can cause a change in supply) are resource prices, technology, taxes and subsidies, the prices of other goods, producer expectations, and the number of producers.
- Market equilibrium occurs where the quantity supplied equals the quantity demanded; this point determines the equilibrium price and equilibrium quantity.
- If the price is set too high, a surplus develops; the price will fall, causing the quantity demanded to increase and the quantity supplied to decrease until equilibrium is reached.
- If the price is set too low, a shortage develops; the price will rise, causing the quantity demanded to fall and the quantity supplied to rise until equilibrium is reached.
- Productive efficiency occurs when a product is produced in the least costly way.
- Allocative efficiency occurs when a market produces the mix of products most valued by society.
- Increases in demand increase both equilibrium price and equilibrium quantity; decreases in demand decrease both equilibrium price and equilibrium quantity.
- Increases in supply lower the equilibrium price but increase the equilibrium quantity; decreases in supply increase the equilibrium price and lower the equilibrium quantity.
- When both supply and demand change, the effect on equilibrium price or quantity can be determined by what the individual supply and demand changes have in common; the effect on the other (price or quantity) is indeterminate.

- When government places an effective price ceiling below equilibrium price, a shortage develops.
- When government places an effective price floor above equilibrium price, a surplus develops.

Now, let's examine more closely the following concepts from your textbook:

- **Demand**
- **Supply**
- **Market Equilibrium**
- **Changes in Supply, Demand, and Equilibrium**
- **Government-Set Prices**

These sections were selected because these concepts can be confusing, and because the ability to graph supply and demand is critical to success on both the AP Microeconomics and AP Macroeconomics exams. Supply and demand serve as the basis of markets throughout the economy, and the principles learned in this chapter will be central to understanding almost every other chapter throughout the AP Economics course.

Demand

Refer to pages 48–53 of your textbook.

A CLOSER LOOK The Demand Curve

The **demand** curve shows the quantity of products consumers are willing and able to buy at various prices. It is a downward-sloping curve, showing the inverse relationship between the price and the quantity demanded. According to the **Law of Demand,** when the price falls, the quantity demanded increases; when the price rises, the quantity demanded falls. You know this to be true from purchases you have made. If you had a choice of paying $100 or $75 for the very same pair of shoes, which price would you be more willing and able to pay?

So what makes the Law of Demand operate as it does? Three factors create this effect. The first is **diminishing marginal utility.** As a consumer gets more and more of a product, the satisfaction he gets from each additional product falls; therefore, he is not willing to pay as much for additional products. A pencil is very useful for school work, and if you really need one, you might be willing to pay $1 for it. A second pencil is still useful, but not as much as that first one was, so you might only be willing to pay 50¢ for it. In order to entice you to buy more, the producer must lower the price for additional products.

The second factor is the **income effect.** At a lower price, a consumer can afford to buy more of the product. Say you go to the store, expecting to pay $2 for a box of pencils. But you find that the store is having a sale, with a price of only $1 for the box of pencils. You now have a dollar left over, which you might use to buy a second box of pencils. When the price falls, people are able to buy more.

The third factor is the **substitution effect.** At a lower price, a customer may choose to substitute one product for another. If you went to the store planning to pay $2 for a box of pens, but saw the box of pencils on sale for $1, you might be willing to buy the pencils instead of the pens. When the price falls, people are willing to buy more.

To draw a demand curve, you must first create a demand schedule, showing how many products the consumer is willing and able to buy at each price. Then you can plot the points into the graph and connect those points to draw the curve.

Graphing Guidance

Economists draw supply and demand graphs with the price on the vertical axis and quantity on the horizontal axis. It is *critically* important to use this convention, or your graphs will be upside-down. Do not worry about the math conventions of placing the dependent variable on one axis and the independent variable on the other; economics graphs do not operate that way. It is important to remember that zero is a point on the axes; don't create a separate quantity point for zero.

It is also *critically* important to space your price and quantity values equally and move in uniform units (quantities of 5, 10, 15, 20 or prices of $2, $4, $6, $8) to determine the correct shape of the curve. If your demand schedule shows quantities of 10, 25, 40, and 100, your quantity values across the bottom of the graph should *not* be equally spaced and then labeled with these numbers. Instead, the quantity values should be equally spaced and labeled with uniform units (such as 20, 40, 60, 80, 100), with the data points placed appropriately within that grid.

As a rule of thumb, economists usually draw graphs with a price or cost on the vertical axis and a quantity of a product on the horizontal axis. You will see exceptions to this rule, but in general, money is on the vertical axis and products are on the horizontal axis.

Let's look at Mike's demand for steak at the grocery store. His demand schedule is below:

Price per Pound	Quantity of Pounds
$10	0
$ 8	1
$ 5	2
$ 4	3
$ 2	4

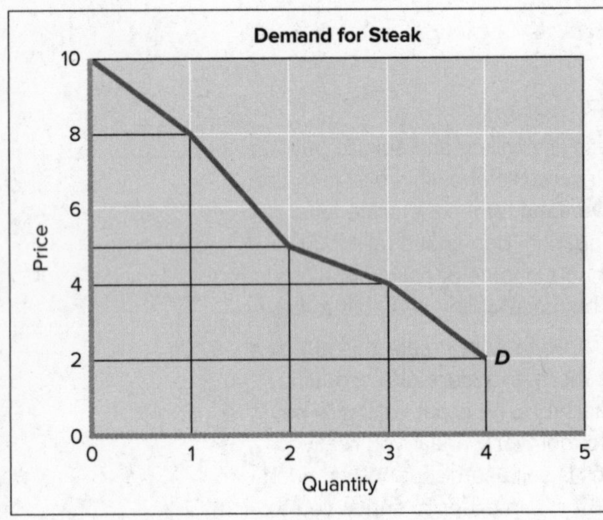

We can then plot these points on the graph to show Mike's demand curve for steak.

With your graph in place, you can also estimate values that are not listed in the demand schedule by using points on the curve. For example, how many pounds of steak would Mike buy if the price were $3 per pound? By drawing a line across from $3 on the vertical axis to the curve, and then drawing a line down to the quantity, you can see that Mike would buy about 3½ pounds of steak at a price of $3.

A **change in quantity demanded** is a movement from one point to another point on the demand curve. The curve has not moved. A customer is simply responding to a change in price. In the example above, at a price of $5 per pound, Mike will buy two pounds of steak. But if the price of steak falls to $4 per pound, Mike will buy three pounds of steak. Only a change in the price of the product will cause a change in the quantity demanded.

PRACTICE The Demand Curve

Use the demand schedule to draw a demand curve for pizzas per night at Cameron's Pizza Shop.

Price	Quantity
$ 4	50
$ 6	40
$ 8	20
$10	10

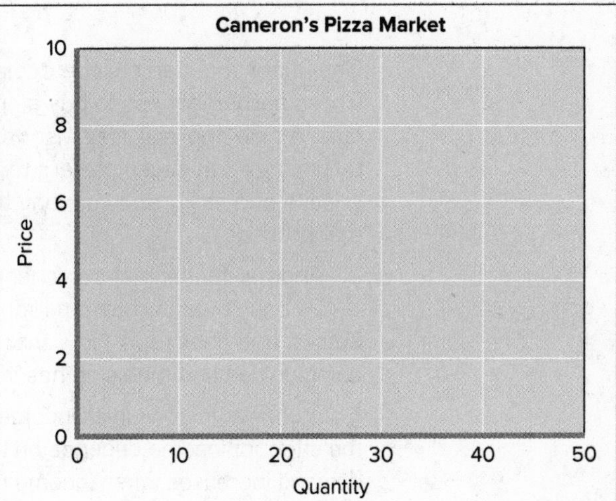

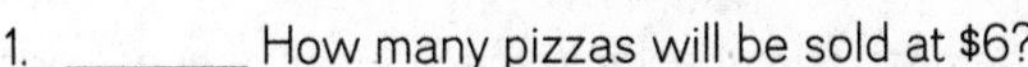

1. _______ How many pizzas will be sold at $6?
2. _______ How many pizzas will be sold at $7?
3. _______ What price should be set to sell 20 pizzas?
4. _______ What price should be set to sell 15 pizzas?
5. _______ If the shop wants to sell 25 pizzas and it now charges $8, should it raise or lower the price?

A CLOSER LOOK Changes in Demand

A **change in demand** occurs when the entire demand curve shifts. An increase in demand is shown by a shift to the right; a decrease in demand is shown by a shift to the left.

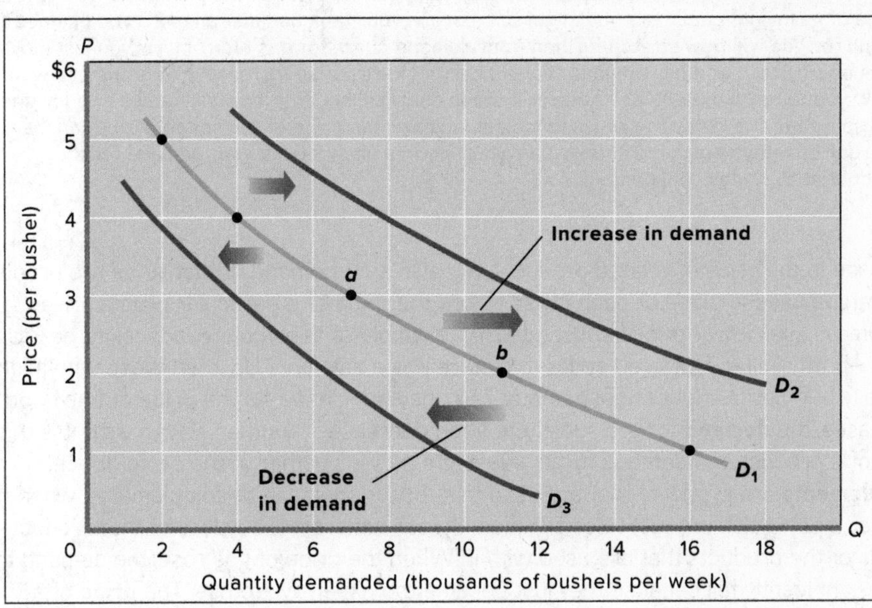

Graphing Guidance

It is very important to shift demand curves *directly* to the right or left, *not* up and down or at angles. An increase in demand shows that *at this same price,* consumers are demanding more products. So the quantity would increase, but the price would not.

One factor that can change demand is a change in consumer tastes or preferences. Consumer willingness to buy a product is often fueled by advertising, recommendations, or fads. A new pop star may inspire fans to buy music and concert tickets. A new gaming technology can cause players to abandon their old systems in favor of the new one. The release of a study documenting the dangers of using a product will decrease demand for that product.

Another factor that can change demand is a change in the number of consumers. The 1940s baby boom created millions of new parents who increased the demand for diapers, bottles, and baby food. Now that those baby boomers are retiring, demand for retirement communities and medicine has increased.

A change in consumer income affects the ability of consumers to buy products. However, the effect of income depends on the type of product. Most goods are **normal goods,** for which demand increases when income rises and demand falls when income falls. Most products, such as cars, televisions, and shirts are normal goods. Other products, known as **inferior goods,** have the reverse relationship. When income falls, consumers *increase* demand for inferior goods. For example, if income falls, consumers will tend to buy more generic food rather than name-brand food; they buy more hamburger than steak. It is important to understand that consumers aren't actually buying *more* because their incomes fell; they are buying lower-priced *substitutes* for the products they would have purchased with a higher income.

Caution

It is important to understand the difference between the *income effect* (which changes the quantity demanded) and a *change in income* (which shifts the demand curve). The income effect refers to the consumer's reaction to a change in the price of the product. If you saw the price of gas significantly fall, you might put more in your tank because the $20 you planned to spend for gas will now stretch further. Your demand curve for gas didn't move; you just moved from one point to another on your demand curve. However, an increase in your income would allow you to buy more gas at whatever price is charged, because your demand curve for gas has shifted to the right. The key is to look at whether the price of the specific *product* changed (so your quantity demanded changed) or your *income* changed (so your demand for the product at all prices changed).

A change in the price of related products can also shift demand. **Substitutes** are products that can be used in place of each other. When the price of a particular product rises, consumers seek lower-priced substitutes. An example of substitute goods might be 7-Up and Sprite—both similarly flavored sodas. If a store has a sale on 7-Up, then those who might normally buy Sprite might choose to buy 7-Up instead. Hence, as the **price** of one good decreases, the **demand** for the substitute good decreases. Another way to view it is that the price of a product and demand for its substitute move together, in the same direction. **Complements** are products that are used together. In the case of complements, when the price of a particular product rises significantly, consumers will buy less of that product—as well as of the products that are used with it. When the price of gas rose, the demand for SUVs significantly fell because they just became too expensive to use. The **price** of a product and **demand** for its complement move in opposite directions. That is, if the price of a product increases or decreases, the demand for its complement will shift the opposite way.

Caution

It is important to distinguish between the *substitution effect* (which changes the quantity demanded) and a *change in the price of substitutes* (which shifts the demand curve). The substitution effect focuses on the consumer's reaction to the change in price of a product. If you intended to buy chips and found the chips on sale for a lower price, you might buy more chips. Your demand curve for chips didn't shift; you simply responded to the lower price by buying more, which is a movement from one point to another point on your demand curve. However, if the price of a *different* product like pretzels fell, you might buy the pretzels instead of the chips, and your entire demand curve for chips would shift. The key is to look at whether the price of the specific *product* changed (so your quantity demanded changed) or the price of a *different* product changed, causing you to buy less of the original product (so your demand for the product at all prices changed).

Consumer expectations also have important effects on the demand for products. If consumers expect the prices of products to increase soon, they will hurry out to buy those products before the price hike. On the other hand, if consumers are worried about the possibility of losing their jobs in a recession, they are less likely to buy new homes and cars, and their demand falls for those products at every price.

Caution

It is very, very important to remember the difference between a *change in quantity demanded* (moving along a stationary curve) and a *change in demand* (shifting the entire curve). If the price of the product changes, it will cause a change in quantity demanded. Changes in tastes, the number of consumers, income, the prices of related goods (complementary and substitute goods), and expectations will cause the entire curve to shift.

PRACTICE Changes in Demand

1. _______ If research shows that eating strawberries helps to prevent cancer, which will increase: the *demand* for strawberries or *quantity* of strawberries demanded?

2. _______ If your income falls and your demand for noodles increases, are the noodles normal or inferior goods?

3. _______ If a rise in the price of Good A causes a decrease in demand for Good B, are these two goods substitutes or complements?

4. _______ If grapes and oranges are substitutes, and grape prices rise, what will happen to the demand for oranges?

5. _______ If consumers are worried a recession is coming and they might lose their jobs, what happens to the demand for new cars?

6. _______ If the price of phones increases and consumers buy fewer phones as a result, which changed: the *demand* for phones or *quantity* of phones demanded?

Supply

Refer to pages 53–56 of your textbook.

A CLOSER LOOK The Supply Curve and Changes in Supply

The **supply** curve shows the quantity of products producers are willing and able to produce at various prices. It is an upward-sloping curve, showing the direct relationship between the price and the quantity supplied. According to the **Law of Supply,** when the price rises, the quantity supplied rises; when the price falls, the quantity supplied falls. You know this to be true from experiences when someone has asked you to do something for pay. If you had a choice of being paid $5 an hour or $10 an hour to babysit or mow lawns, which wage would make you more willing and able to provide those services?

How does the Law of Supply work? When a producer can charge more for a product, an incentive exists to produce more. At some point, however, the producer's cost to produce subsequent units of the product increases. For example, the producer most likely will have to buy more materials and equipment, or hire more workers, or get a larger facility in order to increase production further. To cover these increased per unit costs, the producer must raise the price of the product.

Caution

Supply is the producer's decision of how many products to produce. It's very important *not* to think about supply as the quantity of products for sale on a shelf. The products on the shelf represent previous output, not current production decisions, and looking at supply that way will cause errors in your analysis. If an increase in consumer demand causes the price of products to increase, that higher price serves as an incentive to produce more products, so the quantity supplied would increase. However, if you look at supply as "products on the shelf," you might see the higher demand resulting in consumers buying those products off the shelf, leaving fewer products on that shelf, so you might conclude that the quantity supplied fell. Keep in mind that you're focusing on the producer's *decision* about production, and you'll be more likely to reach the correct conclusions in your analysis.

To draw a supply curve, you must first create a supply schedule, showing how many products the producer is willing and able to sell at each price. Then you can plot the points into the graph and connect those points to draw the curve.

Graphing Guidance

The supply curve will eventually appear on the same graph as the demand curve, so the same rules apply for drawing both graphs.

1. Price is on the vertical axis and quantity is on the horizontal axis.
2. Zero is a point on the axes; don't create a separate quantity point for zero.
3. Space your price and quantity values equally and move in uniform units.

Let's look at Susan's supply of high-quality pens for sale at her shop. Her supply schedule is below:

Price	Quantity
$ 2	10
$ 4	20
$ 5	30
$ 8	40
$10	50

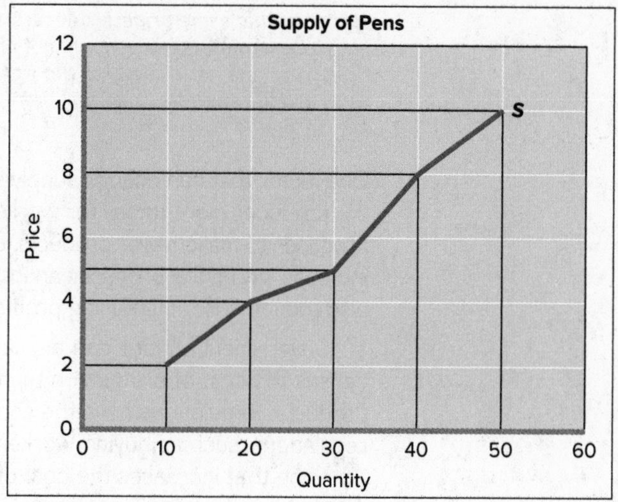

We can then plot these points on the graph to show Susan's supply curve for pens.

Just as with demand, you can estimate values on a supply curve. For example, to estimate the quantity of pens Susan would supply at a price of $6, draw a line across from $6 on the vertical axis to the curve, and then draw a line down to the quantity. Susan would supply about 33 pens at a price of $6.

A **change in quantity supplied** is a movement from one point to another point on the supply curve. The curve has not moved; the producer is just responding to a change in price. In the example above, at a price of $4, Susan will supply 20 pens. But if the price of pens rises to $5, Susan will supply 30 pens. Only a change in the price of the product will cause a change in the quantity supplied.

A **change in supply** occurs when the entire supply curve shifts. An increase in supply is shown by a shift to the right; a decrease in supply is shown by a shift to the left.

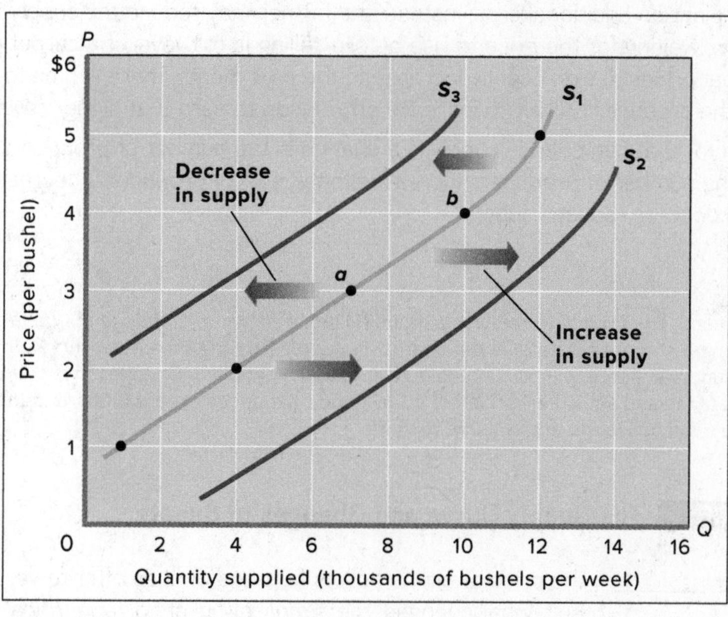

Graphing Guidance

As with the demand curve, it is very important to shift supply curves *directly* to the right or left, *not* up and down or at angles. An increase in supply, or a shift of the curve to the right, shows that *at this same price,* producers are willing to supply more products. So the quantity would increase, but the price would not change. If you were to show an increase in supply as a shift *upward* and not *directly to the right,* it would have the same effect as shifting it to the left, and all of your answers, then, will be reversed.

One factor that can change supply is the cost of resources used by the producer. If it costs the producer more to pay for workers or materials, the reduction in profit will cause the producer to make fewer products. But if the producer can find lower-cost materials, profit will increase, giving the producer an incentive to increase supply. Improvements in technology can also reduce costs, increasing profits and encouraging the producer to increase supply.

Government actions can also affect supply. An increase in corporate income taxes causes the cost of production to increase, leading producers to reduce the supply of products. Regulations have the same effect because it costs producers money to meet new regulations, such as buying workers safety equipment or installing pollution-control devices. Anything that increases the cost of production will encourage producers to reduce supply. A **subsidy,** which is a government payment to reduce production costs, has the opposite effect, leading producers to increase supply.

Another factor that can change supply is a change in the price of other goods. When ethanol companies sprang up after 2000, their increased demand for corn to produce ethanol caused a spike in corn prices. When farmers saw that they could earn more profit from growing corn than from growing soybeans, many switched crops to produce corn, reducing the supply of soybeans.

Producer expectations about the future price of a product can also affect supply, although a producer's reaction may depend on the ability to quickly respond to that price change. If a rice farmer expects rice prices to significantly increase in the next month, there is no time to plant an additional crop; instead, the farmer may reduce the supply of rice for sale right now, waiting for the price to rise before selling it. However, if a carpet producer expects carpet prices to significantly increase in the next month, there is time to make more carpet, and the producer is likely to increase production to earn that higher revenue.

A final factor that can change supply is a change in the number of producers. An increase in the number of producers increases the supply of products; a decrease in the number of producers reduces supply.

Caution

As with demand, it is critical to remember the difference between a *change in quantity supplied* (moving along a stationary curve) and a *change in supply* (shifting the entire curve). If the price of the product changes, it will cause a change in quantity supplied. Changes in resource prices, technology, taxes and subsidies, prices of other goods, producer expectations, and the number of producers will cause the entire curve to shift.

PRACTICE The Supply Curve and Changes in Supply

1. __________ If the price of airline tickets falls and airlines offer fewer flights as a result, what changed: the *supply* of tickets or *quantity* of tickets supplied?

2. __________ If an increase in wages in the bicycle industry causes the cost of production to increase, what will happen to the supply of bicycles?

3. __________ If an improvement in technology increases the productivity of steelworkers, what will happen to the supply of steel?

4. __________ If the government places a tax on the production of fireworks, what will happen to the supply of fireworks?

5. __________ If the government places new pollution-reducing regulations on factories that produce lab chemicals, what will happen to the supply of lab chemicals?

6. __________ If several new car producers have entered the industry, which has changed: the *supply* of cars or the *quantity* of cars supplied?

Market Equilibrium

Refer to pages 56–58 of your textbook.

A CLOSER LOOK Equilibrium Price and Quantity

Market equilibrium occurs where the supply curve and the demand curve intersect. The **equilibrium price** is the price where the quantity supplied equals the quantity demanded. The **equilibrium quantity** is the quantity at which the quantity supplied equals the quantity demanded.

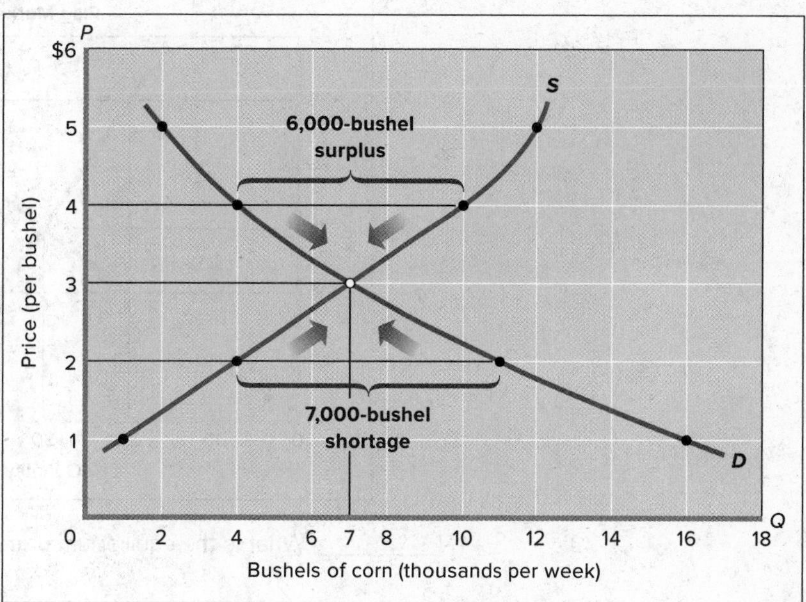

In the graph here, the equilibrium price is $3 and the equilibrium quantity is 7,000 bushels of corn. At the market-clearing price, producers are supplying the precise amount of the product that consumers are demanding. It is important to remember that the market is *always* seeking equilibrium, and market forces will keep working until they reach that equilibrium.

If farmers tried to set a price of $4 per bushel, producers would supply 10,000 bushels, while consumers would only demand 4,000 bushels, resulting in a **surplus** of 6,000 bushels. If the market is left to resolve the problem, the price will begin to fall. The farmers who are left with all of that surplus corn will lower the price in order to sell the excess inventory. At the lower price, consumers are more willing and able to buy the corn, so they move to the right along the demand curve and the quantity demanded increases. At the same time, farmers realize that they will make less profit at the lower prices, so they move to the left along the supply curve and the quantity supplied falls. Eventually the market will reach the $3 equilibrium price and become stable.

On the other hand, if farmers tried to set a price of $2 per bushel, producers would only supply 4,000 bushels, while consumers would demand 11,000 bushels. This would create a 7,000 bushel **shortage.** If the market is allowed to fix the shortage, the price will begin to rise. Consumers who cannot get the corn they need will begin to offer producers higher prices in order to obtain it. At the higher price, fewer consumers are willing and able to buy the corn, so they move to the left along the demand curve and the quantity demanded decreases. At the same time, farmers will see that they can make more profit at the higher price, so they move to the right along the supply curve and the quantity supplied will increase. Eventually the market will reach the $3 equilibrium price and stabilize.

Caution

Note that in the case of a surplus or shortage, as the market works toward achieving equilibrium, neither the supply curve nor the demand curve is moving. It is a change in *quantity* supplied and *quantity* demanded (moving *along* the curves) that moves the market to equilibrium.

When the market reaches equilibrium, the economy will achieve both productive and allocative efficiency. **Productive efficiency** occurs when producers are producing their products at the lowest per-unit cost. When production is efficient, more resources are left available to produce other products. **Allocative efficiency** means that the markets are producing the *mix* of goods most valued by society. Markets help to determine how much plastic is devoted to the production of food wrap, toys, pipes, and containers. Because products are scarce, we don't want to waste the resources required to make them.

PRACTICE Equilibrium Price and Quantity

Use the graph below to answer the questions.

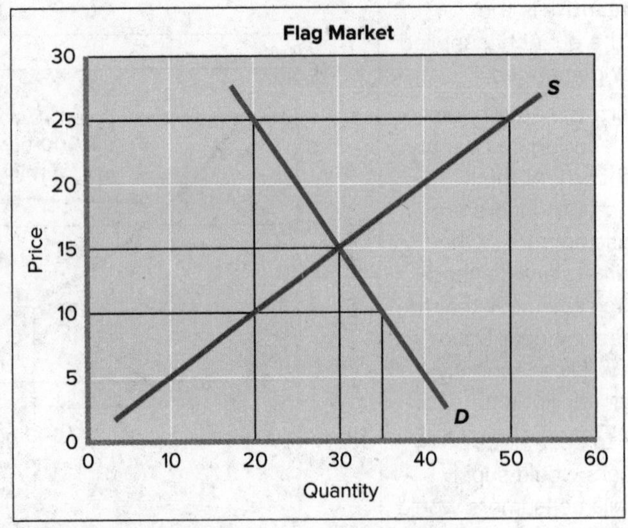

1. __________ What is the equilibrium price for flags?

2. __________ What is the equilibrium quantity of flags?

3. __________ If the price of a flag is set at $10, will a surplus or shortage develop?

   A. __________ What is the quantity of the surplus or shortage?

   B. __________ What must happen to the price to resolve the surplus or shortage?

   C. __________ When the price changes, what will happen to quantity demanded?

   D. __________ When the price changes, what will happen to quantity supplied?

4. __________ If the price of a flag is set at $25, will a surplus or shortage develop?

A. __________ What is the quantity of the surplus or shortage?

B. __________ What must happen to the price to resolve the surplus or shortage?

C. __________ When the price changes, what will happen to quantity demanded?

D. __________ When the price changes, what will happen to quantity supplied?

Changes in Supply, Demand, and Equilibrium

Refer to pages 58–60 of your textbook.

A CLOSER LOOK Changes in Demand and Supply

Shifts in supply and demand curves cause changes in the equilibrium price and quantity of a product sold in the market. When demand increases, the new equilibrium is higher and to the right of the original equilibrium; therefore, increases in demand result in a higher price and higher quantity. On a cold night at a high school football game, you would expect demand for coffee to rise. Entrepreneurs in the concession stand could raise the price and still sell more coffee due to the increased demand. A decrease in demand causes the opposite result, with the new equilibrium showing a lower price and quantity. When consumer demand for SUVs fell because of high gas prices, the quantity sold fell, and dealerships lowered prices in an attempt to draw consumers into the market.

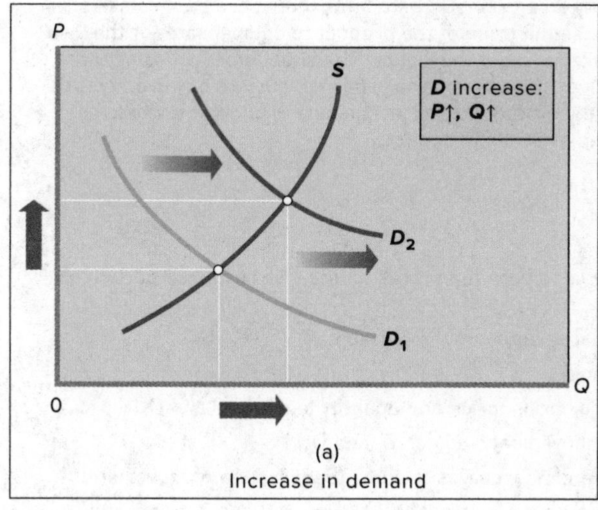

(a)
Increase in demand

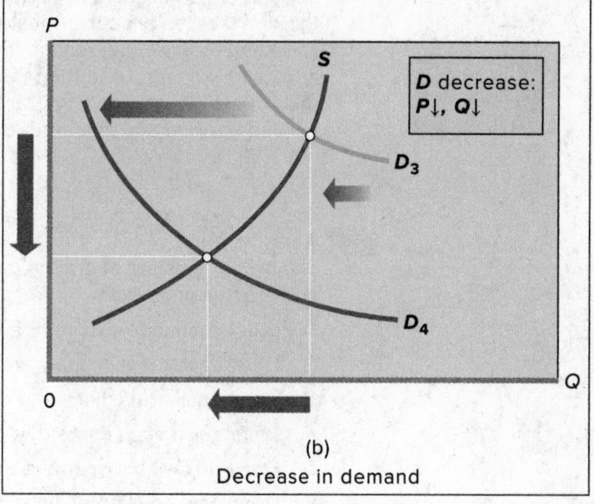

(b)
Decrease in demand

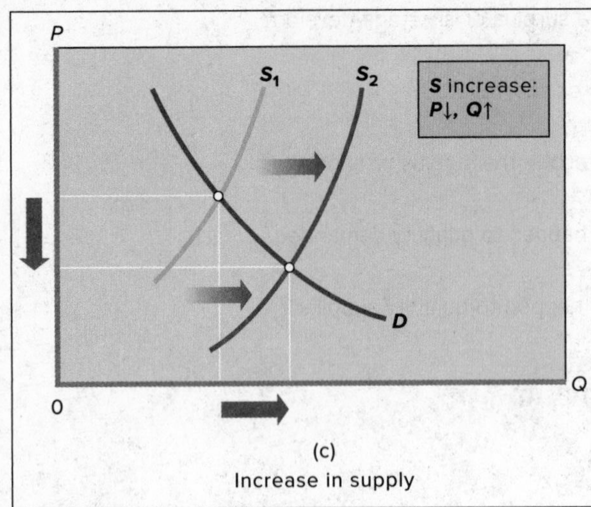

(c)
Increase in supply

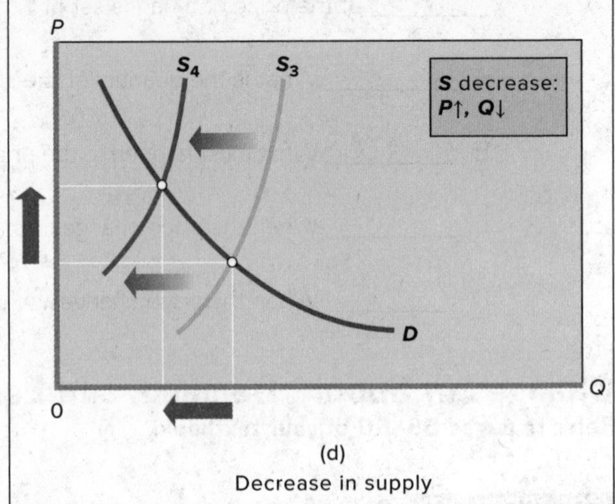

(d)
Decrease in supply

When supply increases, the new equilibrium shows a lower price and a higher quantity sold. If farmers produce a large crop of tomatoes this year, the quantity increases, forcing the price per tomato down. If supply instead decreases, the equilibrium price rises, while the equilibrium quantity falls. When a hurricane damaged oil refineries, the supply of gas fell, reducing the quantity of gas in the market and causing the price to increase.

Caution

Let the graph tell you what will happen to price and quantity. Students commonly make the mistake of worrying about the producer's revenue rather than the market analysis. For example, when demand falls, the quantity sold falls. Many students then make the mistake of thinking that the producer must then raise the price of the product to compensate for the lost sales and to "make up" for the lower revenues. But think about the situation: if consumers are already buying less, and then the producer *raises* the price, won't consumers buy even *less* of the product? Keep drawing graphs for each situation and let the curves show you what will happen to price and quantity, so you can avoid such mistakes.

Keep in Mind

The proper labeling of graphs is *essential* to earn full scores on the free-response portion of an AP Economics exam.

1. Label each axis (price on the vertical; quantity on the horizontal)
2. Label each curve (supply and demand)
3. Draw equilibrium lines and label equilibrium price and quantity (such as P and Q)
4. Distinguish each curve that shows movement (such as D_1 and D_2)
5. Draw arrows between the original and new curves to show the direction of movement
6. Draw new equilibrium lines and label your new equilibrium price and quantity to distinguish them from the originals (such as P_1 and P_2, and Q_1 and Q_2)

Because scoring rubrics allocate points specifically for correctly labeled graphs, you can earn points just for getting that far—or easily lose points on an otherwise excellent response simply due to sloppy labeling. So maximize your potential score and label carefully!

Caution

It is at this point that you can begin to understand why the distinction between a change in *supply* and a change in *quantity supplied* (or a change in *demand* and a change in *quantity demanded*) is so important. Let's take the situation of an increase in demand. The demand curve shifts to the right, causing the price to increase. But did the *supply increase?* No. The *quantity supplied* increased when the producer responded to the higher price by moving to another point higher up the supply curve.

Most multiple-choice and free-response questions on the AP Microeconomics Exam involve the movement of only one curve at a time. Yet one of the most common mistakes students make is to confuse the situation and shift both curves ("Now that the price is higher because of increased demand, the producer will produce more, and so I'll shift the supply curve to the right . . . ."). Keep in mind the factors that cause shifts in supply and demand, and determine which factor is at work—a demand factor or a supply factor. Then only move *that* curve and watch what happens. The other actor (the consumer or producer) will simply *react* to the change in price by adjusting the quantity bought/sold at that new equilibrium point; a second curve shift doesn't happen!

PRACTICE Changes in Demand and Supply

For each scenario, state which curve (*Demand* or *Supply*) moves. Then state whether the curve shift is an *Increase* or *a Decrease*. Next, state whether the equilibrium price and equilibrium quantity increased or decreased. For example: Higher Gasoline Prices Affect Pickup Truck Sales

Curve **Demand** Change **Decrease** Price **Decrease** Quantity **Decrease**

1. Consumer Fears of Recession Hurt Housing Sales
   Curve ______ Change _______ Price _______ Quantity _______

2. Congress Raises Tax on Cigarettes
   Curve ______ Change _______ Price _______ Quantity _______

3. Grape Juice Market Affected by Orange Juice Price Increase
   Curve ______ Change _______ Price _______ Quantity _______

4. Consumer Incomes Rise; Market for Cars (a normal good) Responds
   Curve ______ Change _______ Price _______ Quantity _______

5. New Robots Improve Productivity in Local Factory
   Curve ______ Change _______ Price _______ Quantity _______

6. Kids Lose Interest in Hoverboards
   Curve ______ Change _______ Price _______ Quantity _______

7. Costs of Meat and Vegetables Rise for Local Restaurants
   Curve ______ Change _______ Price _______ Quantity _______

A CLOSER LOOK Complex Cases

In our examples to this point, we have assumed *ceteris paribus* – nothing else is changing during our analysis. Unfortunately, the models don't always reflect real world conditions, where many changes occur at the same time. When both the supply curve and the demand curve are shifting at the same time, the analysis can become complicated. While we can determine what will happen to *either* equilibrium price *or* quantity, we cannot know what will happen to the other.

Assume we start at initial equilibrium, then increase demand and increase supply, and find the new equilibrium from the new supply and demand curves. We know for sure that quantity will increase, because both the increases in supply and demand will cause an increase in quantity. But we cannot know for sure whether the equilibrium price will rise or fall because that depends on how far the two curves shifted. If supply increased a lot but demand only increased a little, the price would fall; if supply only increased a little but demand increased a lot, the price would rise. If both curves shifted by the same amount, the price would remain the same. Therefore, the change in price is indeterminate.

Assume phone producers develop new technology, allowing them to produce at a lower cost. At the same time, consumer incomes fall. Supply would increase while demand would fall. Because both curve shifts would result in a lower equilibrium price, we know for sure that the price of phones would fall. But because the higher supply increases the quantity and the lower demand reduces the quantity, the equilibrium quantity is indeterminate; we cannot know what will happen to the quantity.

Caution

For questions involving double shifts, it is better to find the answer without drawing the graphs. Instead, consider each of the shifts independently and then find out what they have in common. For example, suppose that consumers are buying more iPads (increase in demand), but workers in iPad-producing factories have gone on strike (decrease in supply). Generally, we know that an increase in demand causes both equilibrium price and equilibrium quantity to go *up*. Further, we know that, generally, a decrease in supply causes equilibrium price to go *up* and equilibrium quantity to go *down*. In our scenario, then, since both events have in common the increase in price, we know equilibrium price will rise. Equilibrium quantity is indeterminate; we need more information to know whether it will rise, fall, or remain the same.

Keep in Mind

A couple of questions about double shifts have appeared fairly consistently on the multiple-choice portion of the AP Microeconomics exam. Double shift questions will clearly demonstrate that two separate events are occurring at the same time.

Sometimes the exam will pose a double shift question in reverse, with the stem of the question telling you that price and quantity both fell and the question asking which curve(s) must have moved which direction. The process of elimination may be your best tactic to deal with these questions. The key is to look very carefully at the wording of the question. If the question asks which curve shift(s) would *definitely* lead to a particular result that could be achieved by moving only one of the curves, and that option is one of the answers, that single curve movement is correct. If the question asks which curve shift(s) *could* lead to a particular result, start the process of elimination. If the result of both shifts is an increase in price, a combination of lower demand and higher supply could not create that result, so rule that answer out. Continue that process until you have only one answer left.

PRACTICE **Complex Cases**

These questions involve shifts in *both* supply and demand. A and B each involve one curve. C involves changes after *both* curves have moved. For a change that cannot be determined, write "Indeterminate."

1. In the cotton market, boll weevils have damaged crops *and* consumer incomes have risen.

   A. How will cotton supply change? ____ Price change? ____ Quantity change? ____

   B. How will cotton demand change? ____ Price change? ____ Quantity change? ____

   C. How will equilibrium price change? ____ How will equilibrium quantity change? ____

2. In the bat market, new technology reduces production costs *and* consumers play more baseball.

   A. How will bat supply change? ____ Price change? ____ Quantity change? ____

   B. How will bat demand change? ____ Price change? ____ Quantity change? ____

   C. How will equilibrium price change? ____ How will equilibrium quantity change? ____

Choose the letter(s) of the correct events that would create each result. In some cases, more than one combination can create the result. For each question, the number of correct combinations is indicated.

3. ________ One correct answer

   What *combination* of supply and demand shifts would *definitely* cause the quantity sold to fall?

   A. Demand rises and supply rises B. Demand falls and supply rises
   C. Demand rises and supply falls D. Demand falls and supply falls

4. ________ One correct answer

   What *combination* of shifts in supply and demand would *definitely* cause the price to fall?

   A. Demand rises and supply rises B. Demand falls and supply rises
   C. Demand rises and supply falls D. Demand falls and supply falls

5. ________ One correct answer

   What is the *only* combination that could cause quantity sold to fall *and* price to stay the same?

   A. Demand rises and supply rises B. Demand falls and supply rises
   C. Demand rises and supply falls D. Demand falls and supply falls

6. ________ One correct answer

What *combination* of events would *definitely* cause *both* the price and quantity sold to fall?

A. Demand rises and no change in supply

B. Demand falls and no change in supply

C. Supply rises and no change in demand

D. Supply falls and no change in demand

7. _____ _____ Two correct answers

What *combination* of shifts in supply and demand *could* cause price to rise *and* quantity to rise?

A. Demand rises and supply rises

B. Demand falls and supply rises

C. Demand rises and supply falls

D. Demand falls and supply falls

8. _____ _____ Two correct answers

What *combination* of shifts in supply and demand *could* cause price to rise *and* quantity to fall?

A. Demand rises and supply rises

B. Demand falls and supply rises

C. Demand rises and supply falls

D. Demand falls and supply falls

9. ________ One correct answer

What *combination* of events would cause the quantity of cars to fall with an indeterminate impact on the price of cars?

A. The cost of production rises and consumer incomes fall

B. Gas prices fall and worker productivity improves

C. Taxes on producing cars fall and consumers begin to prefer motorcycles over cars

D. More companies produce cars and consumer incomes rise

Government-Set Prices

Refer to pages 60–64 of your textbook.

A CLOSER LOOK Price Ceilings and Price Floors

Supply and demand generally set prices and quantities in markets. Sometimes government officials identify goals that are more important than efficiency, so they create policies to intervene in markets.

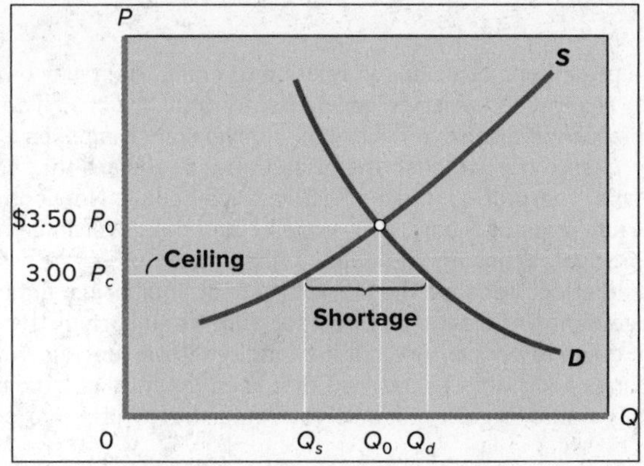

When the government sets a **price ceiling,** it sets a maximum price producers are allowed to charge. When the government places that price ceiling below the equilibrium price, it helps consumers by lowering the price. In the graph above, the equilibrium price is $3.50, but the government has set a price ceiling of $3.00. The ceiling lowers the price; however, it creates a shortage because the quantity demanded is greater than the quantity supplied at the lower price. Remember that the market *always* tries to reach equilibrium. But because the price is capped by law, the shortage persists. Sometimes consumers resort to black markets to buy products illegally at a higher price, just to get a product at all.

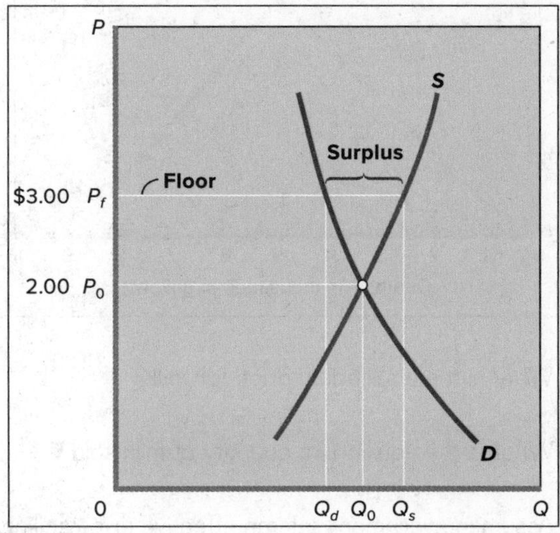

A **price floor** is a minimum price set by a government. A price floor set above the equilibrium price helps producers by increasing the price. In the graph above, the equilibrium price is $2.00, but the price floor is set at $3.00. While the floor raises the price, it also creates a surplus because the quantity supplied is greater than the quantity demanded. If there were no price floor, market pressures would reduce the price back to equilibrium. But because the price cannot fall, the surplus will continue.

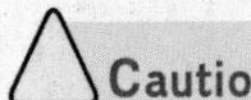

Caution

The placement of the price floor or ceiling in relation to equilibrium may be confusing until you think about what they really mean. A price ceiling *below* equilibrium? Isn't a ceiling high? Think about the market, which *always* seeks equilibrium. If government imposes a price ceiling below equilibrium, market pressure tries to push the price upward—toward that equilibrium—but the price cannot legally rise. Therefore, it is an *effective* price ceiling. Now consider what would happen if the equilibrium price of the product were $7 and the government established a price ceiling of $8 on the product. What would happen? Absolutely nothing. A price ceiling higher than equilibrium has no effect because the market rests at equilibrium until something disturbs it. Conversely, if the government places a price floor above equilibrium, the market pressure tries to pull the price down to equilibrium, but it cannot go lower because of the floor. If you think about price ceilings and floors as barriers that keep the market from reaching equilibrium, where it naturally wants to go, it can help you remember where a price floor or ceiling belongs in the graph.

PRACTICE Price Ceilings and Price Floors

Use the graph below to answer the questions.

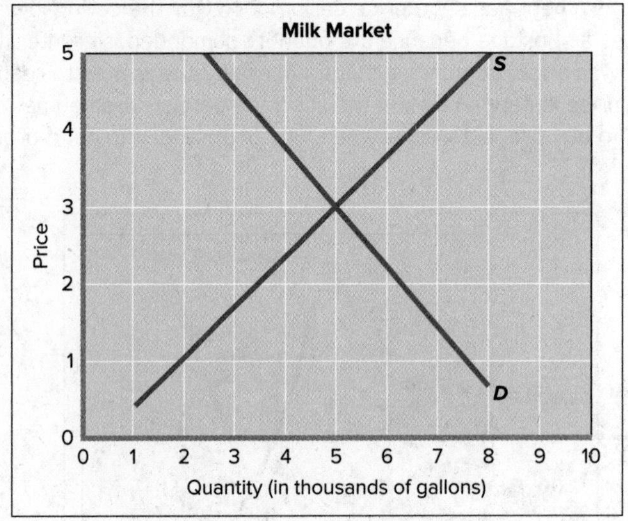

1. ________ What is the equilibrium price for milk?

2. ________ What is the equilibrium quantity of milk sold?

3. ________ Assume government sets an effective price ceiling $1 away from the equilibrium price. What is the new price? (Draw the price ceiling on the graph.)

4. ________ Is the price ceiling designed to help producers or consumers?

5. ________ Will the price ceiling create a surplus or a shortage?

6. ________ What is the quantity of the surplus or shortage with the price ceiling in place?

7. ________ If government sets a price ceiling of $5, at what price will milk be sold? Explain.

Keep in Mind

Previous free-response questions on the AP Microeconomics exam have included changes in supply and demand, the effects of changes in the cost of an input, the effects of changes on substitutes and complements, implementation of price floors and ceilings, and applications of tax changes, labor markets, and international trade. On the AP Macroeconomics exam, free-response questions have included applications of supply and demand in macroeconomic markets, money markets, loanable funds markets, and exchange rates. Understanding supply and demand is critically important to grasping the rest of the material throughout the AP Economics course.

Make sure to return to the AP Key Concept section above to check your understanding of this chapter's concepts important to AP coursework.

Economically Speaking

- **Allocative Efficiency** the market produces the mix of products society values most highly
- **Ceteris Paribus** the assumption that when we are conducting an analysis, nothing else changes
- **Change in Demand/Supply** a shift of the entire demand/supply curve
- **Change in Quantity Demanded/Supplied** movement along the demand/supply curve in response to a price change
- **Complements** products that are used together
- **Demand** the willingness and ability of a consumer to buy a product at a particular price
- **Diminishing Marginal Utility** as a consumer gets more and more of a product, the satisfaction s/he gets from each additional product falls
- **Equilibrium Price** the price where the quantity supplied equals the quantity demanded
- **Equilibrium Quantity** the quantity where the quantity supplied equals the quantity demanded
- **Income Effect** at a lower price, a consumer can afford to buy more of the product
- **Inferior Goods** when income decreases, demand for inferior goods increases
- **Law of Demand** when the price falls, the quantity demanded rises; when the price rises, the quantity demanded falls
- **Law of Supply** when the price rises, the quantity supplied rises; when the price falls, the quantity supplied falls
- **Market Demand** total demand from all consumers in the market
- **Market Supply** total supply from all producers in the market
- **Normal Goods** when income increases, demand for normal goods increases
- **Price Ceiling** the maximum price government allows a producer to charge
- **Price Floor** the minimum price government allows a producer to charge
- **Productive Efficiency** a product is produced in the least costly way
- **Shortage** the quantity demanded is greater than the quantity supplied
- **Subsidy** a government payment to a producer which reduces the cost of production
- **Substitutes** products that can be used in place of each other
- **Substitution Effect** at a lower price, a customer may choose to substitute a lower-priced product for a higher-priced one
- **Supply** the willingness and ability of a producer to sell a product at a particular price
- **Surplus** the quantity supplied is greater than the quantity demanded

Chapter 4

Market Failures: Public Goods and Externalities

Our market economy is based on the private sector interaction of businesses and households. But in our mixed market economy, government can also shape how those markets work and provide public sector solutions when the market fails. Chapter 4 describes market failures and remedies.

The material in Chapter 4 is almost exclusively part of the AP Microeconomics exam. While perhaps one multiple-choice question about public goods and two about externalities will appear, it is common to see a free-response question providing a scenario and asking students to graph and explain externalities and policy solutions.

Key Concepts

Below is a summary of the chapter's concepts important to AP coursework. Upon completing the lessons that follow, return to these concepts to make sure you understand them and how the practice exercises you completed relate to them.

- Market failure occurs when the market fails to allocate resources correctly.
    - A demand-side market failure occurs when the demand curve does not show the full amount consumers are willing and able to pay for a product.
    - A supply-side market failure occurs when the supply curve does not show the full cost of producing a product.
- Consumer surplus is the difference between the maximum price a consumer is willing to pay for a product and the actual price the consumer pays for the product.
    - Consumer surplus is the area of the triangle above equilibrium price and below the demand curve. Consumer Surplus = ½ (Difference in Prices) × Quantity
- Producer surplus is the difference between the minimum price a producer is willing to accept for a product and the actual price the producer charged for the product.
    - Producer surplus is the area of the triangle below equilibrium price and above the supply curve. Producer Surplus = ½ (Difference in Prices) × Quantity

- At equilibrium:
    - The market achieves productive efficiency (producers making products at the lowest per-unit cost, represented by the supply curve).
    - The market achieves allocative efficiency (the mix of goods most valued by society, represented by the fact that the quantity supplied equals the quantity demanded).
    - The marginal benefit (demand curve) equals the marginal cost (supply curve).
    - The total surplus (consumer surplus + producer surplus) is maximized.
- If fewer than the equilibrium quantity of products are produced, a deadweight loss of consumer surplus and producer surplus exists, illustrated by a triangle to the left of equilibrium.
- If more than the equilibrium quantity of products are produced, a deadweight loss of consumer surplus and producer surplus exists, illustrated by a triangle to the right of equilibrium.
- Private goods have characteristics of rival consumption (only one consumer at a time can use it) and excludability (those who won't pay for it can be prevented from having it).
- Public goods are non-rival and non-excludable, so consumers become "free riders." Producers cannot force consumers to pay; without profit, producers stop producing and the market fails.
- Government must provide public goods and require consumers to pay through taxes.
- Using cost-benefit analysis, government should provide goods until the marginal cost equals the marginal benefit of producing the last unit of the public good.
- An externality occurs when part of the cost or benefit of a product "spills over" to someone other than the buyer or the seller.
- With a negative externality like pollution, a producer passes off some costs to society; because it does not consider all of its costs, it overproduces the product and creates a deadweight loss.
- Government can resolve negative externalities by limiting the action or imposing a tax.
- In the case of a positive externality like vaccinations, consumers only consider the benefits to themselves, not society; consumers demand too few of the product, creating a deadweight loss.
- Government can resolve positive externalities by subsidizing either the producer or the consumer or by providing the product itself.
- Using cost-benefit analysis, government should correct externalities until the marginal cost equals the marginal benefit of the last unit of correction.

Now, let's examine more closely the following concepts from your textbook:

- **Efficiently Functioning Markets**
- **Public Goods**
- **Externalities**

These sections were selected because public goods and externalities provide exceptions to the assumptions of effective markets. Market failure requires government correction, and it is important to understand the appropriate measures to correct the market failure.

Efficiently Functioning Markets

Refer to pages 77–82 of your textbook.

A CLOSER LOOK Consumer Surplus and Producer Surplus

Consumer surplus shows the difference between the maximum price a consumer is *willing* to pay for a product and the price that consumer was *actually* charged. Say you went into a shoe store, willing to pay $30 for a pair of shoes, but found the store was selling the shoes for $25. Your consumer surplus is $5. Will you explain to the clerk, "But I was *willing* to pay $30 for these, so just go ahead and charge me $30?" Of course not! You're charged the same $25 every other customer is being charged, and so you now have an additional $5 that you can use to buy something else.

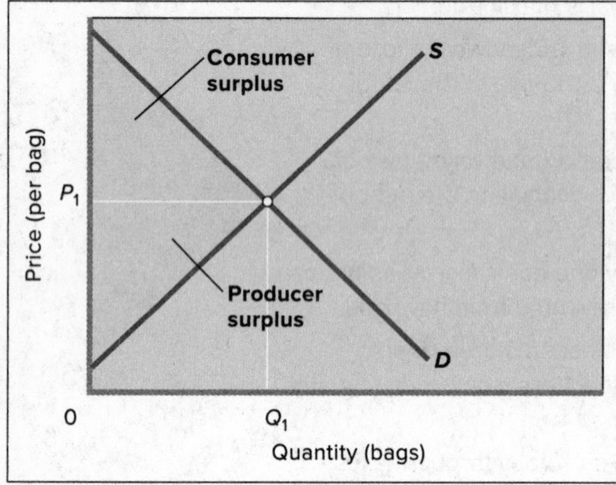

Differences in consumer surplus also illustrate the Law of Demand, showing why the demand curve slopes downward. If Lauren was only willing to pay $25 for those shoes, but Nikki was willing to pay $35, each of the three consumers will have a different level of consumer surplus ($10 for Nikki, $5 for you, and $0 for Lauren), but all three of you will buy the shoes because you are willing and able to do so. But if the store chooses to raise the price of the shoes to $30, only Nikki and you will be willing to buy the shoes, because $30 is more than Lauren is willing and able to pay. At the higher price, the quantity demanded fell.

Producer surplus shows the difference between the minimum price a producer is *willing* to accept for a product and the price that producer *actually* charged. Back at that shoe store, the owner was willing to accept just $10 to sell that first pair of shoes, but the equilibrium price he actually could charge was $25. So his producer surplus is $15. Will the store owner tell customers that he would have been willing to accept only $10 for those shoes? Of course not! But he is happy to keep that producer surplus.

Differences in producer surplus also illustrate the Law of Supply, demonstrating why the supply curve slopes upward. The minimum price the producer will accept is the company's cost to produce one more product. As output increases, the producer must buy more resources and equipment, and encounters diminishing returns, so the cost to produce each additional product rises. The producer will only supply more products if the price he earns from selling them can cover his production costs. So at the higher price, the quantity supplied rises.

Caution

It can be easy to forget which triangle represents consumer surplus and which triangle represents producer surplus. Just remember that consumer surplus is measuring the willingness of consumers, which will be on the demand curve, which is above equilibrium. The producer surplus measures the willingness of producers, which will be on the supply curve, which is below equilibrium.

Refer to the example *Shoe Market* graph on the following page. Calculating the total consumer surplus in the market is as easy as calculating the area of a triangle. On the supply and demand graph, the area of consumer surplus is the right triangle *above* the equilibrium price and *below* the demand curve. The formula to find the area of a triangle is ½ Base × Height. So if you tilt your head to see the price axis as the base and quantity axis as the height, the formula is:

$$\text{Consumer Surplus} = \tfrac{1}{2}(50 - 25) \times 50 = \tfrac{1}{2}(25) \times 50 = 12.5 \times 50 = 625$$

When the price increases, total consumer surplus falls; when the price falls, total consumer surplus rises.

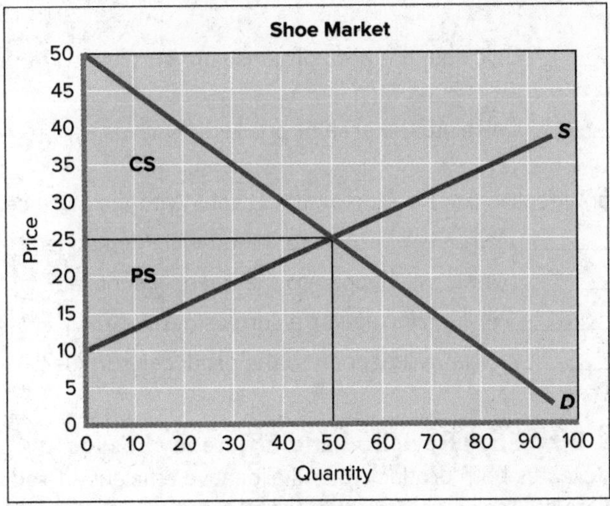

To find the total producer surplus, use the same formula to calculate the area of the right triangle *below* the equilibrium price and *above* the supply curve. Using the graph above, again tilting your head to see the price axis as the base and the quantity axis as the height, apply the ½ Base × Height formula:

$$\text{Producer Surplus} = \tfrac{1}{2}(25 - 10) \times 50 = \tfrac{1}{2}(15) \times 50 = 7.5 \times 50 = 375$$

When the price increases, total producer surplus rises; when the price falls, total producer surplus falls.

PRACTICE Consumer Surplus and Producer Surplus

Use the graph below to answer the questions.

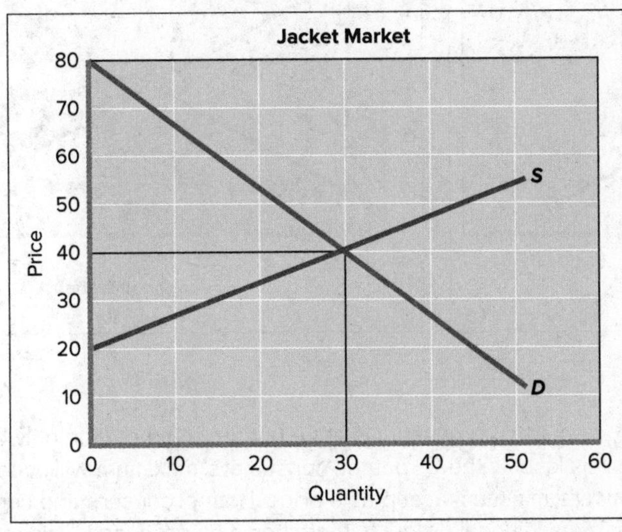

1. Label the area of consumer surplus with vertical lines.

2. Label the area of producer surplus with horizontal lines.

3. __________ Calculate the area of consumer surplus.

4. __________ Calculate the area of producer surplus.

5. Draw an effective price ceiling on the graph. With the price ceiling in place:
   A. __________ What will happen to the quantity demanded?
   B. __________ What will happen to the quantity supplied?
   C. __________ Will a shortage or a surplus develop?
   D. __________ What will happen to the producer surplus?

A CLOSER LOOK Efficiency Revisited and Efficiency Losses

Market equilibrium creates both productive and allocative efficiency. **Productive efficiency** means that producers are making products at their lowest **marginal cost** (per-unit cost). Competition pressures producers to create products in the most efficient way. The supply curve represents marginal cost.

Allocative efficiency means that the market is producing the right mix of products most valued by society. At equilibrium, the **marginal benefit** to society equals the marginal cost to society. At no other output would society be better off than at equilibrium. At equilibrium, the quantity supplied equals the quantity demanded, so no surplus or shortage exists. Also at equilibrium, the total surplus (consumer surplus + producer surplus) is maximized.

What happens if the market produces at an output other than at equilibrium? Efficiency is lost.

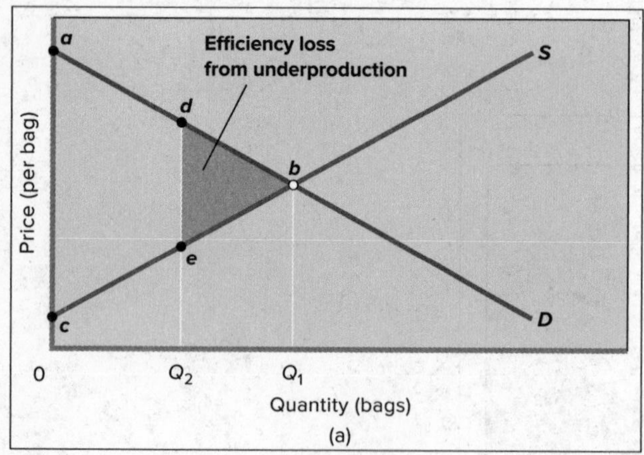

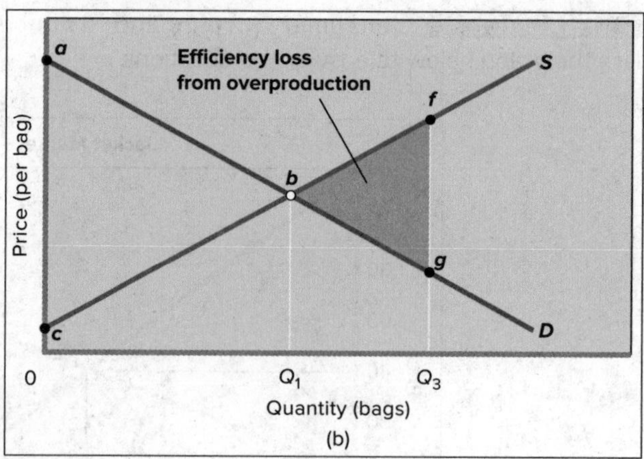

In Graph (a) above, if equilibrium quantity is at Q_1, but for some reason only Q_2 products are produced, efficiency is lost. At the Q_2 output, consumers' maximum willingness to pay is greater than producers' minimum acceptable price. Both producers and consumers are losing benefit from the additional products that should be produced. This efficiency loss, called a **deadweight loss,** represents the lost producer and consumer surplus caused by not producing at equilibrium. It is illustrated by the triangle to the left of equilibrium.

In Graph (b), if the market overproduces Q_3 output rather than the Q_1 equilibrium output, efficiency is again lost. At the Q_3 output, the minimum price producers will accept is higher than the maximum price consumers are willing to pay, so those products should not be produced. When they are produced, resources are drawn away from producing some other product that would be more valuable to society. This is again a deadweight loss, this time illustrated by a triangle to the right of equilibrium.

Keep in Mind
Free-response questions on the AP Microeconomics exam have frequently asked students to draw a graph of a particular situation and then shade the area of deadweight loss. Students sometimes find it difficult to remember which side of equilibrium represents the deadweight loss. Think of the triangle as an arrow. It is always pointing toward equilibrium, the quantity the market *should* be producing. If the market is *under*producing, the deadweight loss will be to the left, pointing toward equilibrium; if the market is *over*producing, the deadweight loss will be to the right, pointing toward equilibrium.

Public Goods

Refer to pages 82–88 of your textbook.

A CLOSER LOOK Private and Public Goods Characteristics

Most products in our economy are considered private goods, which have characteristics of rival consumption and excludability. If you buy an airline ticket, no one else can use your seat at the same time you are using it, and it is easy for the airline to exclude people from the flight if they haven't bought tickets. The market works well for private goods.

Public goods, however, are non-rival and non-excludable. Many people can use the same national defense protection at the same time, and if a citizen refuses to pay his taxes, there is no reasonable way to exclude him from protection while still providing national defense to everyone else. This is a case of demand-side market failure. The demand curve doesn't reflect how much consumers are willing and able to pay for public goods, because even though consumers clearly want the public good, they don't report the full amount they are willing and able to pay.

Because of these unique characteristics, public goods suffer from a "free rider" problem, as consumers want to enjoy the benefits without paying for them. In an unregulated market, private producers can't force consumers to pay for the goods; therefore, producers cannot earn a profit. So private producers simply refuse to produce the product and the market fails. In the case of small, low-cost public goods like a fireworks display, producers could privately pay for the public good or accept donations.

In the case of very important public goods like national defense and fire protection, the government intervenes by providing public goods and collecting mandatory taxes to pay for them. Governments also provide quasi-public goods like public education and libraries. While it would be possible to exclude non-paying customers, the benefits extend beyond the consumer to the rest of society, so it is in the public interest for government to provide them.

How much of the public good should the government provide? Every resource used to produce a public good has an opportunity cost; those resources could have been used by private producers to make products. Theoretically, using **cost-benefit analysis,** as long as the marginal benefit to society is greater than the marginal cost, government should keep increasing output, until the marginal benefit equals the marginal cost for the last unit produced. In reality, it is very difficult to determine the marginal benefit to society for a public good.

PRACTICE Private and Public Goods Characteristics

1. __________ What are the two characteristics of public goods (such as national defense, highways, and fireworks displays) that make them different __________ from private goods (such as houses, cars, and computers)?

2. __________ What is the term for consumers not being willing to pay for public goods?

3. __________ In an unregulated market, would the private sector produce *more* or *less* than the efficient quantity of public goods?

4. __________ How can government ensure that consumers pay for the use of public goods?

5. __________ If the marginal social benefit increases for a public good, should the government provide *more* or *less* of the public good?

Externalities

Refer to pages 88–91 of your textbook.

A CLOSER LOOK Negative and Positive Externalities

An **externality** occurs when either the costs or benefits of producing or consuming a product "spill over" onto someone other than the buyer or seller. In these cases, the market again fails, because all of the costs of production are not captured in the supply curve or all of the benefits of consumption are not captured in the demand curve. As a result, the unregulated market under- or overproduces the product.

A **negative externality** occurs when producers are able to shift some of their costs of production onto outsiders. The classic example of a negative externality is pollution. If a producer can send its pollution up the smokestack rather than disposing of it properly, those who live around the plant pay the cost in the form of medical treatment for lung issues and lower property values. The lower production cost allows the producer increase production. In Graph (a) on the following page, in a market with no government regulation, the supply curve shifts to the right, from S_t to S. The vertical distance between S_t and S is the amount of the negative externality. The increase in output creates an overallocation of resources to production of the product. As a result, a deadweight loss develops, shown by the triangle to the right of socially optimal quantity.

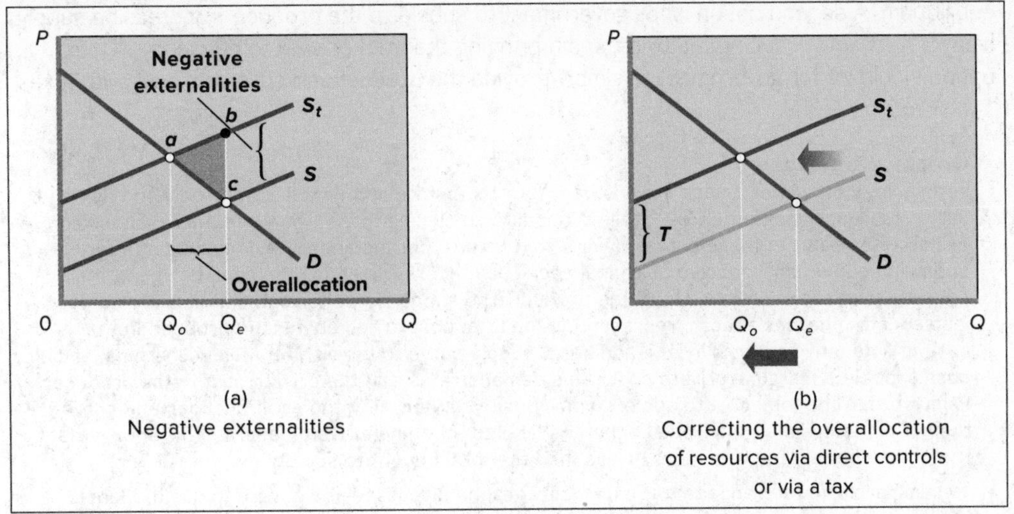

Because the marginal cost to society is greater than the marginal benefit at Q_e, the government must intervene in the market to restore efficiency. To force producers to absorb all of their costs, government can limit pollution by requiring producers to buy pollution control equipment. Government also has the option to impose taxes on the producer. Both actions increase the producer's cost of production and shift supply to the left, from S to S_t, returning the market to socially optimal output.

In the case of a **positive externality,** some of the benefits of an economic decision "spill over" onto others outside of the market. A classic example of a positive externality is vaccinations. When people consider the costs and benefits of a vaccination, they do not take into account the benefit their friends, neighbors, and others in society gain by also avoiding disease. As a result, demand is lower than it would be if all benefits were considered. In the graph below, in a market with no government regulation, the demand curve is too far to the left, at D rather than D_t. The vertical distance between D and D_t is the amount of the positive externality. Because resources are underallocated, a deadweight loss develops, shown by the triangle to the left of socially optimal equilibrium.

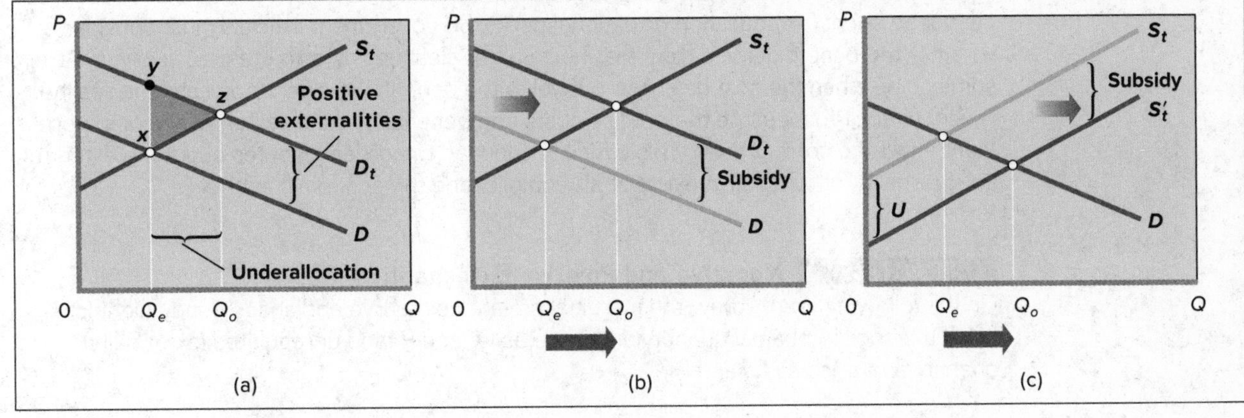

At Q_e, the marginal benefit to society is greater than the marginal cost, so the government must intervene to improve efficiency. A positive externality can be eliminated in three ways. Government could subsidize the price consumers pay for the product, increasing demand from D to D_t and eliminating the deadweight loss to restore the market to socially optimal equilibrium. A second option is for government to subsidize the producers, increasing supply from S_t to S'_t and reducing the price, again bringing the market back to efficiency. A third option would be for government to simply provide the product and cover the cost with taxes.

Graphing Guidance

Terminology can differ among economists. Your textbook's author relies on supply and demand curves to illustrate externalities. Other economists, including those who write the AP Economics exams, often refer to these curves by different names. For instance, the demand curve for optimum equilibrium is labeled "marginal social benefit," representing the complete benefit all consumers in society receive from the product. The supply curve for optimum equilibrium is labeled "marginal social cost," representing the total cost to society for the product. In the case of a negative externality, the additional supply curve to the right of (below) marginal social cost is labeled "marginal private cost." This demonstrates that the private cost to the producer is lower than the total cost to society. For a positive externality, the additional demand curve to the left of (below) marginal social benefit is labeled "marginal private benefit." This shows that the private benefit to consumers is less than the total benefit to society.

To summarize, in reference to our externality graphs discussed, if we were to use the labels and terms the AP Economics exam uses, then the labels and terms would be as follows:

For the negative externality graphs,

D = MSB S = MPC S_t = MSC

For the positive externality graphs,

D = MPB (except the 3rd graph, where D = MSB)

D_t = MSB

S_t = MSC (except the 3rd graph, where S_t = MPC)

S'_t = MSC

MSB stands for *marginal social benefit*, MSC stands for *marginal social cost*, MPB stands for *marginal private benefit*, and MPC stands for *marginal private cost*.

If the government intervenes, how far should it go to correct an externality? The simple answer, theoretically, is that government should intervene just until the marginal cost of the intervention equals the marginal benefit of that intervention. This explains why, after an oil spill, government does not keep cleaning until it reaches every duck and every grain of sand. Every resource government spends on cleanup has an opportunity cost, as those resources cannot be spent for education or national parks. So government officials must consider whether the benefit derived from that next unit of cleanup is worth the cost involved. At some point, when the cost begins to outweigh the benefit, the cleanup will stop. In reality, it is very difficult to measure the precise costs and benefits of either externalities or government efforts to correct them. This difficulty can lead to political debates about the extent of an externality, or whether it exists at all, complicating the economic analysis.

PRACTICE Negative and Positive Externalities

On the following graph, draw the marginal private cost curve and shade deadweight loss. Label the socially optimal quantity and price as Q_o and P_o and unregulated (externality) quantity and price as Q_e and P_e.

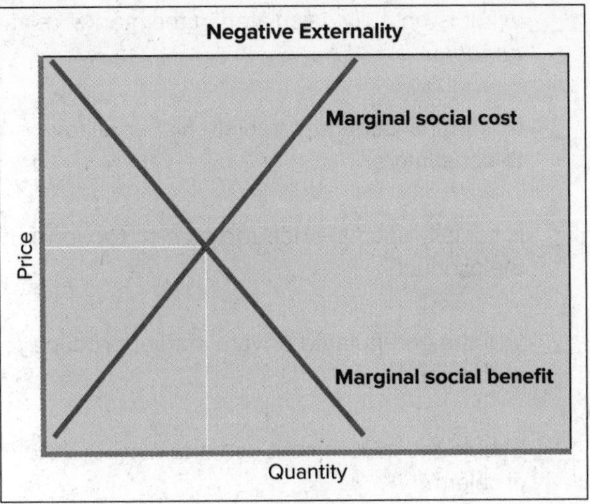

1. ________ What is not fully calculated in the market relationship: *costs* or *benefits*?

2. ________ Is marginal cost to society *higher* or *lower* than marginal cost to producers?

3. ________ Will the unregulated private market charge a price that is *too high* or *too low*?

4. ________ Will the unregulated private market produce *too many* or *too few* of the good?

5. ________ Should the government use a *tax* or a *subsidy* to correct the problem?

6. ________ Will the government action in #5 make the market *more* or *less* efficient?

On the graph below, draw the marginal private benefit curve and shade deadweight loss. Label socially optimal quantity and price as Q_o and P_o and unregulated (externality) quantity and price as Q_e and P_e.

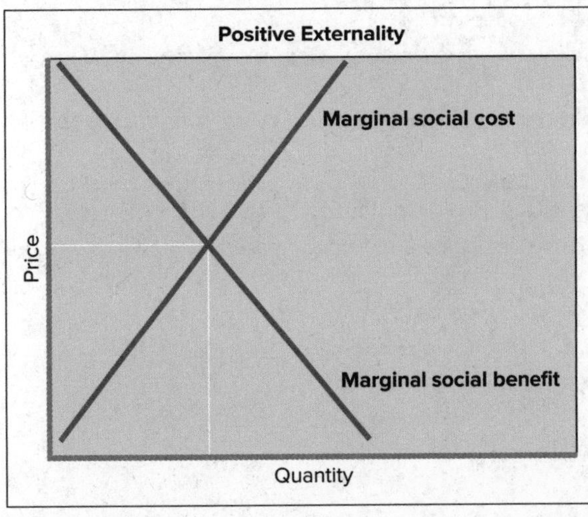

7. __________ What is not fully calculated in the market relationship: *costs* or *benefits*?

8. __________ Is marginal benefit to society *higher* or *lower* than marginal benefit to consumers?

9. __________ Is socially optimal price *too high* or *too low* for consumers to buy the product?

10. __________ Will the unregulated private market produce *too many* or *too few* of the good?

11. __________ Should the government use a *tax* or a *subsidy* to correct the problem?

12. __________ Will the government action in #11 make the market *more* or *less* efficient?

Make sure to return to the AP Key Concepts section above to check your understanding of this chapter's concepts important to AP coursework.

Economically Speaking

- **Allocative Efficiency** the economy is producing the mix of goods most valued by society
- **Consumer Surplus** the difference between the highest price a consumer is *willing* to pay for a product and the actual price the customer *does* pay for it
- **Cost-Benefit Analysis** comparing the marginal cost and marginal benefit of producing a product
- **Deadweight Loss** the loss of consumer surplus and producer surplus resulting from producing a quantity of output different from socially optimum output
- **Externality** costs/benefits of producing/consuming a product "spill over" onto someone other than the buyer or seller
- **Marginal Benefit** the increase in total satisfaction received from consuming one more product
- **Marginal Cost** the increase in total cost resulting from the production of one more product
- **Market Failure** the market fails to allocate resources correctly because demand does not show the full value of what consumers are willing and able to pay, or because supply does not show the full cost of production
- **Negative Externality** some costs of production are imposed on people who are not buyers or sellers of the product
- **Positive Externality** some benefits of production spill over onto people who are not buyers or sellers of the product
- **Producer Surplus** the difference between the lowest price a producer is *willing* to charge for a product and the actual price the producer *does* receive for it
- **Productive Efficiency** producers are producing products at the lowest cost of production

Government's Role and Government Failure

While our market economy relies primarily on private sector transactions, government intervenes to correct market failures, provide public goods, regulate industries, redistribute income, and stabilize the economy. Chapter 5 describes the role government plays in improving our mixed market economy.

The AP Microeconomics exam may include a question about the role of government, and the AP Macroeconomics exam may ask for a definition of fiscal or monetary policy, but questions are likely to involve related information covered in further chapters.

Key Concepts

Below is a summary of the chapter's concepts important to AP coursework.

- Government has the power to tax and make regulations.
- Government corrects for market failure of public goods by providing them.
- Government corrects for market failure of positive externalities by subsidizing production or consumption.
- Government corrects for market failure of negative externalities by taxing or fining producers.
- Government reduces risk for producers and consumers by establishing copyrights and patents, and by making coercion, deception, discrimination, price-fixing, and violation of contracts illegal.
- Government may choose to undertake some policies even when the marginal cost exceeds the marginal benefit because it is pursuing goals other than efficiency.
- Fiscal policy is the use of taxes and government spending to stabilize the economy.
- Monetary policy is the use of the money supply and interest rates to stabilize the economy.

PRACTICE Government's Economic Role

1. ________ Government provision of a product, such as traffic lights, would solve which market failure: *public good, positive externality*, or *negative externality*?

2. ________ What is one way government reduces risk in the marketplace?

Economically Speaking

- **Fiscal Policy** the use of taxes and government spending to stabilize the economy
- **Monetary Policy** the use of the money supply and interest rates to stabilize the economy

6 Chapter

Elasticity

Elasticity explains consumer responses to changes in price, income, and the prices of related products. Businesses and governments use knowledge of elasticity to determine how to raise revenue. Chapter 6 introduces formulas to calculate elasticity and interprets the meaning for product demand and supply.

Material from Chapter 6 consistently appears on the AP Microeconomics exam in a few multiple-choice questions and often as part of a free-response question.

Key Concepts

Below is a summary of the chapter's concepts important to AP coursework. Upon completing the lessons that follow, return to these concepts to make sure you understand them and how the practice exercises you completed relate to them.

- Price elasticity of demand tells us how sensitive consumers are to a change in price of a product.
  - Demand is elastic when a change in price causes a large change in quantity demanded.
  - Demand is inelastic when a price change causes a small change in quantity demanded.
- Price Elasticity of Demand Formula: E = % Change in Quantity Demanded / % Change in Price
- Economists use the absolute value of price elasticity of demand, so ignore the minus sign.
- The elasticity quotient indicates the percentage change in quantity demanded that results from a 1% change in price.
- The total revenue test ($TR = P \times Q$) is a shortcut for determining elasticity by noting what happens to the total revenue of a business or government when the price changes.
- Perfectly elastic demand occurs when a change in price causes a complete change in quantity demanded; if the price rises at all, consumers completely stop buying.
  - Elasticity: $E = \infty$ (a 1% change in price causes an infinite change in quantity).
- Elastic demand occurs when a change in price causes a larger change in quantity demanded; consumers are very sensitive to price changes.
  - Elasticity: $E > 1$ (a 1% change in price causes a more than 1% change in quantity).
  - Total revenue test: when price falls, total revenue increases.

- Unit elastic demand occurs when a change in price causes a proportional change in quantity demanded.
    - Elasticity: E = 1 (a 1% change in price causes a 1% change in quantity).
    - Total revenue test: when price falls, total revenue remains the same.
- Inelastic demand occurs when a change in price causes a smaller change in quantity demanded; consumers are not very sensitive to price changes.
    - Elasticity: E < 1 (a 1% change in price causes a less than 1% change in quantity).
    - Total revenue test: when price falls, total revenue falls.
- Perfectly inelastic demand occurs when a change in price causes absolutely no change in quantity demanded; consumers buy exactly the same quantity, regardless of the price.
    - Elasticity: E = 0 (a 1% change in price causes no change in quantity).
- Determinants of price elasticity of demand:
    - Substitutability—the more substitutes a product has, the more elastic is demand.
    - Proportion of income—the higher the product price is (compared to consumer income), the more elastic is demand.
    - Luxury versus necessity—the less necessary the product is, the more elastic is demand.
    - Time—the more time consumers have to adapt to price, the more elastic is demand.
- How producers use knowledge of elasticity:
    - If product demand is elastic, the producer can earn more revenue by lowering the price. Consumers are so sensitive to price that when price falls only slightly, they demand a much larger quantity of products.
    - If product demand is inelastic, the producer can earn more revenue by raising the price. Consumers are not sensitive to price changes, so when the price rises, the producer will not lose many customers.
- How government uses knowledge of elasticity:
    - Government earns more revenue by placing an excise tax on products with inelastic demand.
    - Consumers will largely continue to buy products with inelastic demand, such as gasoline, cigarettes, and liquor, even at the higher price.
- Price elasticity of supply tells us how sensitive *producers* are to a change in price of a product.
    - Supply is elastic when a change in price causes a large change in quantity supplied.
    - Supply is inelastic when a price change causes a small change in quantity supplied.
- Price Elasticity of Supply Formula: E = % Change in Quantity Supplied / % Change in Price
- The determinant of the price elasticity of supply is how quickly producers can shift resources to alternative uses. The more time the producer has available, the more elastic is the supply.
    - The immediate period is the period of time in which a producer cannot change production; supply is perfectly inelastic (vertical).
    - The short run is the period of time too short for the producer to change plant capacity, but long enough to change production to some extent; supply is more elastic.
    - The long run is the period of time in which the producer can change the plant size and new competitors can enter the industry; supply is even more elastic.

- Cross elasticity (or cross-price elasticity) of demand measures how sensitive consumers are to a change in price of *related* products.
- Cross-Price Elasticity of Demand Formula: E = % Change in Quantity of Good X / % Change in Price of Good Y
    - If the answer is positive, the products are substitutes.
    - If the answer is negative, the products are complements.
- Income elasticity of demand measures how sensitive consumers are to a change in *income*.
- Income Elasticity of Demand Formula: E = % Change in Quantity Demanded / % Change in Income
    - If the answer is positive, the product is a normal good.
    - If the answer is negative, the product is an inferior good.

Now, let's examine more closely the following concepts from your textbook:

- **Price Elasticity of Demand**
- **The Total Revenue Test**
- **Price Elasticity of Supply**
- **Cross Elasticity and Income Elasticity of Demand**

These sections were selected because the elasticity formulas are very similar and easy to confuse, and it is important to understand how elasticity explains consumer, producer, and government behavior.

Price Elasticity of Demand

Refer to pages 122–124 of your textbook.

A CLOSER LOOK The Price-Elasticity Coefficient and Formula

The Law of Demand explains that consumers buy more at lower prices and less at higher prices. But we know that consumers are more responsive to changes in the price of some products and not as responsive to others. **Price elasticity of demand** measures how sensitive consumers are to price changes by calculating the change in quantity demanded from two points on the demand curve.

The formula to measure price elasticity of demand is:

$$E = \frac{\text{Percentage Change in Quantity Demanded}}{\text{Percentage Change in Price}}$$

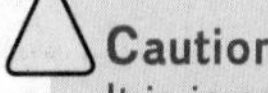

Caution

It is important to note that while the formulas for elasticity and slope look similar, they are not the same. The slope of a curve measures how tall or flat a line is. The slope for a straight line is constant, regardless of which points one chooses on the curve. But elasticity measures how *responsive* the quantity demanded is, to a change in price. The elasticity of demand is different between every two points on a straight line, because the bases are different. At the top of the demand curve, percentage changes in price are small, while percentage changes in quantity are large; at the bottom of the demand curve, the opposite is true. So it is important to calculate elasticity between two specific points on the demand curve to determine how sensitive consumers are to specific price changes.

If you have specific data, in order to avoid calculation issues, the midpoint formula is the best to use:

$$E = \frac{\dfrac{(\text{Quantity 1} - \text{Quantity 2})}{(\text{Quantity 1} + \text{Quantity 2})/2}}{\dfrac{(\text{Price 1} - \text{Price 2})}{(\text{Price 1} + \text{Price 2})/2}}$$

For example, at a price of $5, a consumer will buy 10 products, and at a price of $3, the consumer will buy 20 products. Using the elasticity formula:

$$E = \frac{\dfrac{(10 - 20)}{(10 + 20)/2}}{\dfrac{(5 - 3)}{(5 + 3)/2}} = \frac{\dfrac{-10}{15}}{\dfrac{2}{4}} = \frac{-0.67}{0.50} = -1.34$$

Economists use the absolute value of the elasticity coefficient. Because the demand curve is downward sloping, elasticity of demand must be a negative number. But we ignore the minus sign because we are simply looking at the *strength* of the relationship between price and quantity demanded.

So what does this number mean? It is the percentage change in quantity demanded that results from a 1% change in price. In this case, if the price rises by 1%, the quantity demanded will fall by 1.34%.

Caution

The midpoint formula may look intimidating at first. But notice that the formula for the numerator is exactly the same as the formula for the denominator. The only difference is that quantity is in the numerator and price is in the denominator.

Keep in Mind

Some multiple-choice and free-response questions on the AP Microeconomics exam have asked students to calculate elasticity and interpret the meaning of the number. Sometimes the question gives percentage changes, making it easy to use the percentage change formula. Other times, it is necessary to use the midpoint formula. But it is far more common for questions to deal with applications of elasticity in specific circumstances or to identify whether demand is elastic or inelastic when consumers or total revenues respond to price changes in a particular way.

Five levels of price elasticity exist: perfectly elastic, elastic, unit elastic, inelastic, and perfectly inelastic.

Perfectly elastic demand occurs when a change in price causes a *complete* change in quantity demanded. If price rises even slightly, the quantity demanded falls to zero; at the equilibrium price, consumers will demand an infinite quantity of the product. This occurs when $E = \infty$. Using the midpoint formula, infinity occurs when the denominator is zero. In economics, anything divided by zero is infinity. It is a perfectly horizontal curve. As you can imagine, this is an extremely rare circumstance. Consider a farmer's market, where 30 farmers are selling identical bags of corn, with 12 ears in each bag. You see that 29 of the farmers are selling corn at a price of $3 per bag, while one farmer is selling the identical corn for $4 per bag. How many consumers will buy the $4 corn? None. In later chapters about perfectly competitive markets, you will see a perfectly elastic demand curve again.

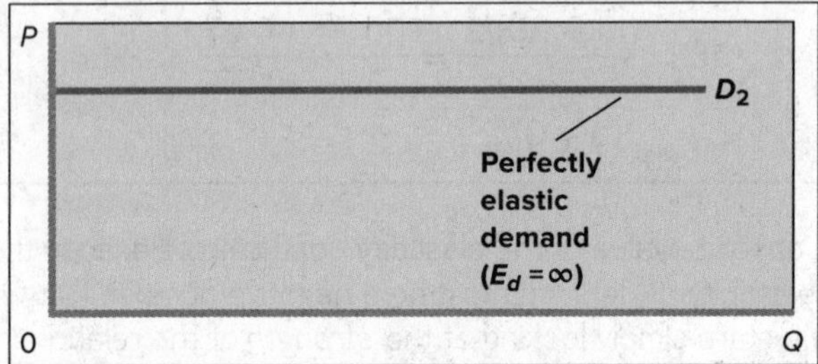

Elastic demand occurs when a change in price causes a *larger* change in quantity demanded. If the price rises even slightly, consumers are *very* sensitive to the change in price. This occurs when $E > 1$, meaning that a 1% change in price will cause *more* than a 1% change in quantity demanded. Products with elastic demand are common, including expensive products like homes and cars, and products with many substitutes such as soft drinks and candy.

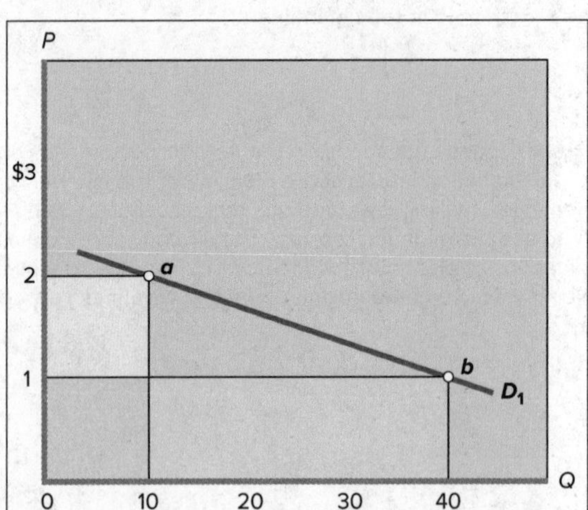

Unit elastic demand occurs when a change in price causes a proportional change in quantity demanded. If the price rises by 10%, the quantity demanded falls by exactly 10%. This occurs when E = 1. This is a specific elasticity on demand curves that results from the selection of particular points. No specific type of product exhibits unit elastic demand.

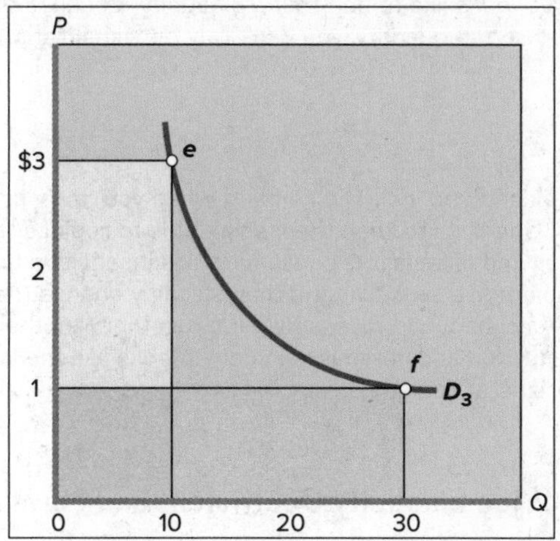

Inelastic demand occurs when a change in price causes a *smaller* change in quantity demanded. Even if the price rises sharply, consumers are *not* very sensitive to the change in price. This occurs when E < 1, meaning that a 1% change in price will cause *less* than a 1% change in quantity demanded. Products with inelastic demand are common, including necessities like gasoline and toilet paper, and things people think they can't do without, like morning coffee.

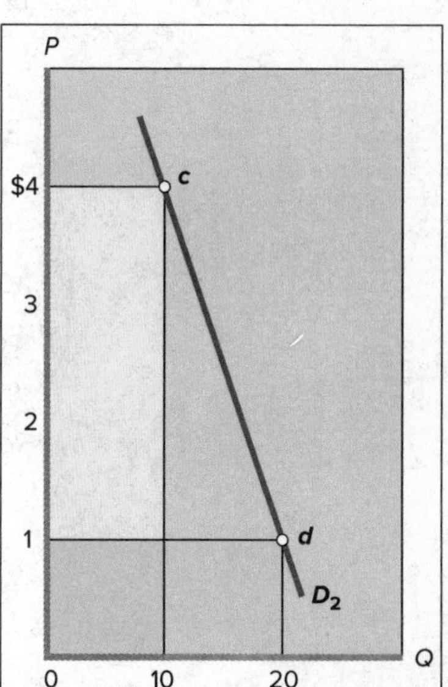

Perfectly inelastic demand occurs when a change in price causes *zero* change in quantity demanded. Consumers buy exactly the same amount of the product, no matter what the price. This occurs when E = 0. Using the midpoint formula, this occurs when the numerator is zero. It is a perfectly vertical curve. Again, this is an extremely rare circumstance. Examples are limited to extreme medical interventions, such as insulin for a diabetic or a heart transplant to save a patient's life. No one will ask when the hospital will have a clearance sale or buy a second heart if the price is low enough. In later chapters about the supply of certain resources like land, you will see a perfectly inelastic demand curve again.

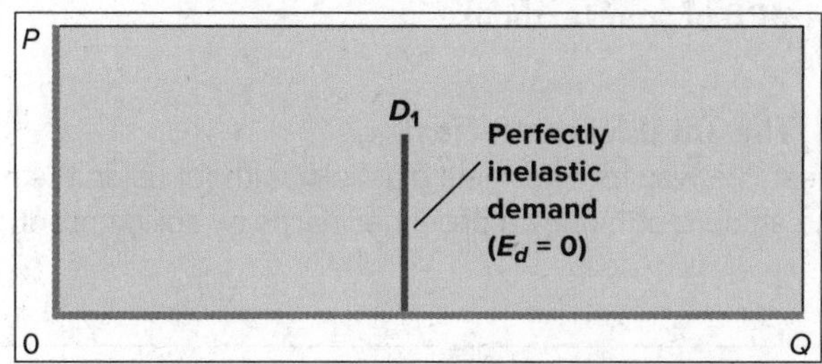

Graphing Guidance

Notice that in the example price elasticity graphs just discussed, as you move from one level of elasticity to the next, the curve becomes taller and taller. At the same time, the elasticity coefficient falls from infinity to zero. This is because the level of elasticity is on a continuum, not in discrete categories. You can see the difference in these examples, but it is important not to rely on what a curve *looks* like to determine elasticity. Because elasticity depends on *percentage* changes in price and quantity, you can't rely on visualization.

Caution

It can be easy to mix up elastic and inelastic demand when you're trying to remember the term for a particular situation. One trick to keep them straight is to replace the word "elastic" with the word "sensitive." If demand is inelastic, consumers are insensitive to price change; when demand is elastic, consumers are sensitive and they strongly change the quantity bought when price changes. The "in"s—*in*elastic and *in*sensitive—go together. Another trick is to remember that the perfectly "I"nelastic demand curve is vertical—it looks like the letter "I". Perfectly elastic demand is the horizontal curve.

PRACTICE The Price-Elasticity Coefficient and Formula

1A. __________ If the price of a lily increases by 5% and the quantity demanded falls by 2%, calculate the elasticity of demand for lilies.

B. __________ Is the demand for lilies elastic, unit elastic, or inelastic?

2A. __________ If the price of a car increases by 10% and the quantity demanded falls by 20%, calculate the elasticity of demand for cars.

B. __________ Is the demand for cars elastic, unit elastic, or inelastic?

3A. __________ At a price of $4, the quantity of coffee demanded is 15 cups. At a price of $5, the quantity demanded is 12 cups. Calculate the elasticity of demand for coffee.

B. __________ Is the demand for coffee elastic, unit elastic, or inelastic?

The Total Revenue Test

Refer to pages 124–128 of your textbook.

A CLOSER LOOK The Total Revenue Test

The total revenue test is a way to determine elasticity without using the midpoint formula. **Total revenue** is the amount of money a producer earns by selling products. The formula for total revenue is:

$$\text{Total Revenue} = \text{Price} \times \text{Quantity}$$

After calculating the amount of total revenue a producer can earn at each of two points on the demand curve, you can determine whether demand is elastic, inelastic, or unit inelastic.

If demand is elastic, a decrease in price will cause an increase in total revenue. Assume total revenue at Point A is $20 ($2 × 10), while total revenue at Point B is $40 ($1 × 40). In this case, when the price falls, the producer actually earns *more* revenue. This is possible because consumers are very sensitive to price changes. A small change in price causes a large change in quantity demanded. In short, if price and total revenue move in opposite directions, demand is elastic.

If demand is inelastic, a decrease in price will cause a decrease in total revenue. Assume total revenue at Point C is $40 ($4 × 10), while total revenue at Point D is $20 ($1 × 20). In this case, when the price falls, the producer earns *less* revenue. This is possible because a lower price just doesn't attract very many more consumers. A large change in price causes very little change in quantity demanded. In short, if price and total revenue move together in the same direction, demand is inelastic.

If demand is unit elastic, when the price decreases, total revenue will remain the same. Total revenue at Point E is $30 ($3 × 10), and total revenue at point F is also $30 ($1 × 30). In short, if total revenue does not change when the price changes, demand is unit elastic.

Caution

It is important to note that the total revenue test only reflects the change in *income* to the producer. It tells us nothing about the change in *profit*, because costs of production are not part of the analysis.

An understanding of elasticity is important to producers. If a producer wants to increase total revenue and demand for the product is *inelastic*, the producer should *increase* the price of the product. Because consumers are not very sensitive to the change in price, the quantity demanded will decrease by little. A higher price with little loss in quantity demanded will result in more revenue for the producer.

On the other hand, if the producer wants to increase total revenue but faces an *elastic* demand curve, the producer should *decrease* the price of the product. It may sound wrong to lower prices in order to raise revenue, but remember that when demand is elastic, consumers are very sensitive to changes in price. Even when the price falls relatively little, the quantity demanded rises relatively more. A slightly lower price with a larger increase in quantity demanded will result in more revenue for the producer.

The government also uses knowledge of elasticity when deciding which products to subject to an **excise tax.** If government places a tax on a product with elastic demand, consumers will be very sensitive to the price increase and significantly reduce the quantity they buy. The government will not earn much revenue, and the producer will be hurt by a serious reduction in product sales. But if the government instead taxed a product with inelastic demand, the increase in price would have little effect on the quantity demanded. Government earns more revenue, and the producer only sees a small decrease in quantity demanded. The government places excise taxes on inelastic demand products like cigarettes, gasoline, alcohol, utilities, and other products consumers tend to buy even when the price increases.

Because of the math involved, each specific section of the demand curve has a different level of elasticity. In general, as the price falls, demand becomes less and less elastic. The upper left end of the demand curve is more elastic than the lower right end of the demand curve.

Graphing Guidance

This only reinforces the warning to *not* judge elasticity by just looking at the curve; it would appear that demand becomes more and more elastic while moving from point to point down the curve—but it does not. Trust the math, not your eyes.

PRACTICE **The Total Revenue Test**

1. Complete the table.

Price	Quantity	Total Revenue	When price rose, did total revenue rise or fall?	Is demand elastic or inelastic?
$ 4	50			
$ 6	40			
$ 8	20			
$10	10			

2. __________ When the price of a car increases by 5%, the quantity demanded decreases by 15%. What will happen to the producer's total revenue?

3. __________ When the price of corn rises, if farmers' revenue rises, is demand elastic, inelastic, or unit elastic?

4. __________ If a producer's product demand is elastic and the producer wants to increase its revenue, what should it do to the price?

5. __________ If government wants to increase its revenues, should it tax products with elastic or inelastic demand?

6. __________ If demand is perfectly inelastic and the government imposes a 3% tax, what will happen to the quantity demanded?

Price Elasticity of Supply

Refer to pages 130–133 of your textbook.

A CLOSER LOOK Price Elasticity of Supply: The Immediate Period, the Short Run, and the Long Run

Price elasticity of supply tells us how sensitive producers are to a change in the price of a product. **Elastic supply** occurs when a change in price causes a large change in quantity supplied; **inelastic supply** exists when a price change causes a small change in quantity supplied.

The formula to calculate price elasticity of supply is virtually the same as for demand, except measuring the change in quantity *supplied* rather than quantity *demanded*.

$$E = \frac{\text{Percentage Change in Quantity Supplied}}{\text{Percentage Change in Price}}$$

What determines the elasticity of supply is how quickly producers can shift resources to alternative uses. The more time the producer has available, the more elastic is the supply.

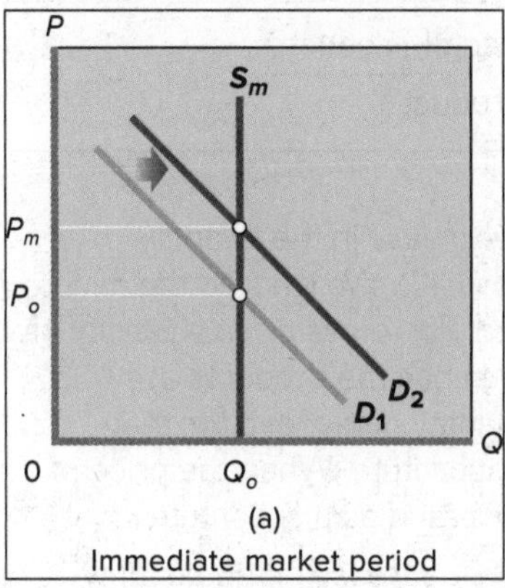

(a)
Immediate market period

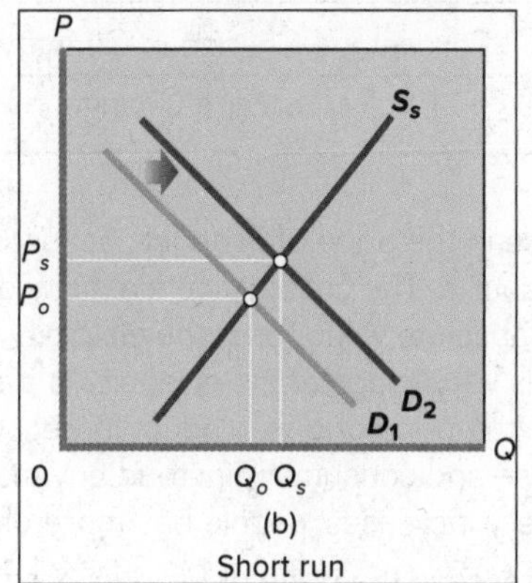

(b)
Short run

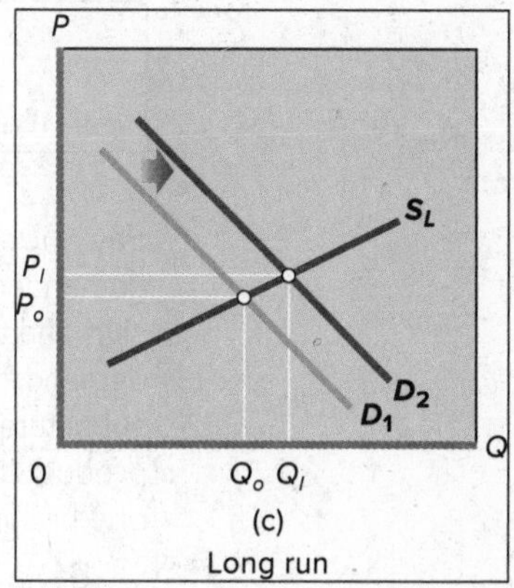

(c)
Long run

The **immediate period** is the period of time in which a producer cannot change production. Have you ever placed an order at the fast food drive-thru, only to have the worker ask you to pull into a parking space and wait? In the immediate period, the restaurant cannot provide any more of the product. Even if you offered the worker $100 for the hamburger, it simply cannot cook any more quickly. In the same way, producers simply cannot instantly increase output when the price increases. It takes time to put resources into place, so output is fixed. As shown in Graph A above, supply is perfectly inelastic. The supply curve is vertical; regardless of how much price increases, quantity supplied does not change.

The **short run** is the period of time too short for the producer to change plant capacity, but long enough to change production to some extent. The producer doesn't have enough time to build a new factory or add equipment, but there is time to hire more workers, work overtime, and put on additional shifts of workers. As a result, the producer can increase output somewhat in response to a price increase. As shown in Graph B above, supply is more elastic than in the immediate period, sloping upward.

The **long run** is the period of time long enough for producers to change plant size and new competitors to enter the industry. If the price increases enough and producers believe the additional demand will be sustained for a long time, producers will build larger factories, buy higher-capacity equipment, and make other long-term investments that take time to implement. Entrepreneurs will also start up new businesses in the industry. As a result, producers can increase output even more significantly. As shown in Graph C above, supply is even more elastic than in the short run, still sloping upward, but flatter.

Cross Elasticity and Income Elasticity of Demand

Refer to pages 133–135 of your textbook.

A CLOSER LOOK Cross Elasticity of Demand and Income Elasticity of Demand

Cross elasticity (or cross-price elasticity) **of demand** measures how sensitive consumers are to a change in the price of *related* products. The formula to calculate cross-price elasticity is similar to the formula for price elasticity of demand, except measuring the change in quantity demanded for *one* product because of the change in price of a *different* product:

$$E = \frac{\text{Percentage Change in Quantity Demanded of Product X}}{\text{Percentage Change in Price of Product Y}}$$

Say a 10% increase in the price of Product Y causes a 20% *increase* in the quantity demanded of Product X. The cross-price elasticity of demand is +2. We ignored the minus sign and took the absolute value for *price* elasticity of demand. For *cross-price* elasticity of demand, the sign is very important. If elasticity is a *positive* number, the products are substitutes. When the price of one product increases, the quantity demanded for that product decreases—and consumers instead buy more of its substitute. When the price of one brand of battery increases, people buy more of the other brand as a substitute.

Say a 10% increase in the price of Product Y causes a 15% *decrease* in the quantity demanded of Product X. The cross-price elasticity of demand is −1.5. Because the elasticity is a *negative* number, the two products are complements. When the price of one product increases, the quantity demanded for that product decreases—and consumers buy less of the complement that is used with it. If the price of hot dogs increases, leading consumers to buy fewer hot dogs, they will also buy fewer hot dog buns.

Say a 10% increase in the price of Product Y causes *no change* in the quantity demanded of Product X. A cross-price elasticity of demand of zero or near zero means the two products are not related. An increase in the price of shoes will not affect the quantity demanded of shampoo.

So, in short, if the cross-price elasticity of demand is positive, the products are substitutes. If it is negative, the products are complements. And if it is zero, the products are not related.

Income elasticity of demand measures how sensitive consumers are to a change in *income*. The formula to calculate cross-price elasticity is virtually the same as for demand, except measuring the change in quantity demanded because of a change in *income*:

$$E = \frac{\text{Percentage Change in Quantity Demanded}}{\text{Percentage Change in Income}}$$

Say a 10% increase in income causes a 7% *increase* in the quantity demanded. The income elasticity of demand is +0.7. While we ignored the minus sign and took the absolute value for *price* elasticity of demand, for *income* elasticity of demand, the sign is very important. If the elasticity is a *positive* number, the product is a normal good. A positive number indicates that when income increases, the quantity demanded for that product increases. The vast majority of products, including cars, electronics, and vacations are normal goods. When income increases, people buy more normal goods.

Say a 10% increase in income causes a 13% *decrease* in the quantity demanded. The income elasticity of demand is −1.3. When elasticity is a *negative* number, the product is an inferior good. If income rises, the quantity demanded of that product falls. If income increases, people will buy fewer packages of bologna and more pork chops; they'll buy fewer cross-country bus tickets and more airline tickets.

If a 10% increase in income causes *no* change in the quantity demanded, the product is a necessity not related to income. Consumers must buy some products regardless of income, such as toothpaste, toilet paper, medicine, and soap. When income falls, consumers may switch to generic brands, but will not stop buying the product. When income rises, consumers are not likely to buy more of the product.

So, in short, if income elasticity of demand is positive, the product is a normal good. If it is negative, the product is an inferior good. And if it is zero, demand for the product is not related to income.

Caution

It can be very easy to confuse the different types of elasticity, what they measure, and what the measures of elasticity mean. What they all have in common is that they are measuring how sensitive a producer or consumer is when some factor changes. A summary of elasticities:

Price elasticity of demand—measures how sensitive *consumers* are to *price* changes

If $E > 1$, demand is elastic; if $E < 1$, demand is inelastic

Price elasticity of supply—measures how sensitive *producers* are to *price* changes

If elastic, producers are responsive; if inelastic, producers cannot respond

Cross-price elasticity of demand—measures how sensitive demand for *one* product is when the price of a *different* product changes

If positive, the products are substitutes; if negative, the products are complements

Income elasticity of demand—measures how sensitive *consumers* are to changes in *income*

If positive, the product is a normal good; if negative, the product is an inferior good

PRACTICE Cross Elasticity of Demand and Income Elasticity of Demand

1. ________ If cross-price elasticity of demand for two products is positive, are the goods substitutes or complements?

2. ________ When the price of peanuts increases by 5%, the quantity demanded of jelly beans falls by 2%. Are peanuts and jelly beans substitutes or complements?

3. ________ Assume the cross-price elasticity of demand for Jello and cottage cheese is –2.5. Are Jello and cottage cheese substitutes or complements?
   - A. ________ Assume that cows become more productive. If the supply of cottage cheese increases, what will happen to the price of cottage cheese?
   - B. ________ If the price of cottage cheese changes as you indicated in #3A, what will happen to the demand for Jello?

4. ________ If peanut butter is an inferior good, when Thanh's income increases, what will happen to the quantity of peanut butter Thanh demands?

5. ________ When Emily's income increases by 5%, the quantity of movie tickets she demands increases by 2%. Calculate Emily's income elasticity of demand.

A. ________ Given the income elasticity of demand you determined in #5, are movie tickets a normal good or an inferior good for Emily?

B. ________ With the same 5% income increase, Emily's demand for lemonade falls by 10%. Is lemonade a normal good or an inferior good for Emily?

Make sure to return to the AP Key Concepts section above to check your understanding of this chapter's concepts important to AP coursework.

Economically Speaking

- **Cross Elasticity** (or Cross-Price Elasticity) **of Demand** the sensitivity of consumers to a change in the price of *related* products
- **Elastic Demand** a change in price causes a large change in quantity demanded
- **Elastic Supply** a change in price causes a large change in quantity supplied
- **Excise Tax** a tax placed on a specific product
- **Immediate Period** a period of time so short that a producer cannot change output
- **Income Elasticity of Demand** the sensitivity of consumers to a change in income
- **Inelastic Demand** a change in price causes a small change in quantity demanded
- **Inelastic Supply** a change in price causes a small change in quantity supplied
- **Long Run** a period of time long enough that producers can change plant size and new competitors can enter the industry
- **Perfectly Elastic Demand** a change in price causes a complete change in quantity demanded
- **Perfectly Inelastic Demand** a change in price causes no change in quantity demanded
- **Price Elasticity of Demand** the sensitivity of consumers to a change in product price
- **Price Elasticity of Supply** the sensitivity of producers to a change in product price
- **Short Run** a period of time too short to change plant capacity, but long enough to use resources to increase output
- **Total Revenue** the total income a producer receives from selling products
- **Unit Elastic Demand** a change in price causes a proportional change in quantity demanded

Chapter 7

Utility Maximization

Understanding how consumers make purchasing decisions is the key to understanding demand. Chapter 7 explains how consumers maximize utility through purchases and how that knowledge can be used to determine product demand. The Law of Diminishing Marginal Utility takes numeric and graphic form to show why consumers respond as they do in markets.

Material from Chapter 7 appears consistently in one or two multiple-choice questions on the AP Microeconomics exam and occasionally as an entire free-response question.

Key Concepts

Below is a summary of the chapter's concepts important to AP coursework. Upon completing the lessons that follow, return to these concepts to make sure you understand them and how the practice exercises you completed relate to them.

- The Law of Diminishing Marginal Utility says that as a person consumes more of a product, the satisfaction gained from each additional product decreases.
- Total utility is the total amount of satisfaction a consumer receives from all of the products together.
- Marginal utility (MU) is the extra satisfaction a consumer receives from one more unit of a product, which is the increase in total utility.
- Marginal utility decreases from the very first unit consumed. At some point, marginal utility becomes negative.
- Total utility increases at first, because each additional unit adds to total utility. But when marginal utility becomes negative, total utility begins to fall.
- The utility maximizing rule: to maximize satisfaction, a consumer should allocate income so that the last dollar spent on each of two products yields the same marginal utility per dollar.
- To achieve consumer equilibrium, compare the marginal utility per dollar of two products. Select the product with the larger marginal utility per dollar until income is exhausted. When the last dollar spent on Product A yields the same marginal utility per dollar as the marginal utility per dollar spent on Product B, consumer equilibrium (maximum utility) is achieved.
- Consumer equilibrium: MU of Product A / Price of A = MU of Product B / Price of B
- The demand curve slopes downward for three reasons:
  - Marginal utility decreases with each additional product, so consumers are not willing to pay as much for the next product.

- The income effect—a decrease in price increases a consumer's real income, increasing the quantity demanded; at a lower price, consumers can buy more.
- The substitution effect—a decrease in price causes a product to become relatively less expensive than its substitute; at a lower price, consumers are willing to buy more.

Now, let's examine more closely the following concepts from your textbook:

- **Law of Diminishing Marginal Utility**
- **Theory of Consumer Behavior**

These sections were selected because practice is required to fully understand how to determine consumer equilibrium. Similar total/marginal graphs will appear in later chapters, so understanding the relationship now will help to make it easier to recognize the relationships later.

Law of Diminishing Marginal Utility

Refer to pages 139–141 of your textbook.

A CLOSER LOOK Total Utility and Marginal Utility

As we learned in Chapter 3, the Law of Diminishing Marginal Utility explains the downward slope of the demand curve. According to the **Law of Diminishing Marginal Utility,** as a consumer gets more and more of a product, the satisfaction he gets from each additional product falls; therefore, he is not willing to pay as much for additional products.

Economists attempt to quantify utility by measuring the units of satisfaction in terms of "utils." **Total utility** is the total amount of satisfaction a consumer receives from total consumption of the product. **Marginal utility** is the increase in satisfaction (the increase in total utility) the consumer receives from consuming one more unit of the product.

Products have different levels of utility, demonstrating differences among consumers and differences among products. Lobster holds a high level of utility for Chris, and he is willing to pay a high price to buy a lobster dinner. But Kim does not like the taste of lobster, so it holds no utility at all for her. As a result, she has no demand for lobster at any price.

Products also exhibit different levels of marginal utility. The marginal utility you gain from reading a newspaper can bring you satisfaction. How much satisfaction will you gain from reading a second copy of the same newspaper? Virtually none. Newspaper publishers understand this concept, which explains why many newspaper boxes on street corners completely open when you insert money. A stack of ten or more newspapers may be lying in the box, but customers only take one. Cans of soda are different. One can of soda holds a certain level of utility for a consumer, and a second can of soda still holds some utility, though less. This is why you won't find vending machines for soda that allow you to insert your money and just open up to offer you a large number of cans of soda. Consumers would take them! Differences in marginal utility can even lead to differences in the way some products are sold.

Why does marginal utility diminish? If you have taken a long walk on a hot day, a bottle of water holds a great deal of utility for you. You may be willing to pay a premium price for that bottle of water. Once you've consumed that bottle of water, how useful is a second bottle of water? A second bottle may still bring you some satisfaction, but not as much as the first one. How about a third bottle? The sixth? The 54th bottle of water? As you gain satisfaction by consuming bottles of water, the satisfaction you gain from the next one will be less. At some point, say after the third bottle of water, your marginal utility falls to zero. You're full, and another bottle of water holds no utility for you. What happens if you drink that third bottle of water and you're offered a fourth bottle? At that point, you'll experience *negative* marginal utility. You won't pay for an additional bottle of water; someone would have to pay *you* to accept it! You simply would not buy that water, and your quantity demanded would fall to zero.

(1) Tacos Consumed per Meal	(2) Total Utility, Utils	(3) Marginal Utility, Utils
0	0	
1	10	10
2	18	8
3	24	6
4	28	4
5	30	2
6	30	0
7	28	−2

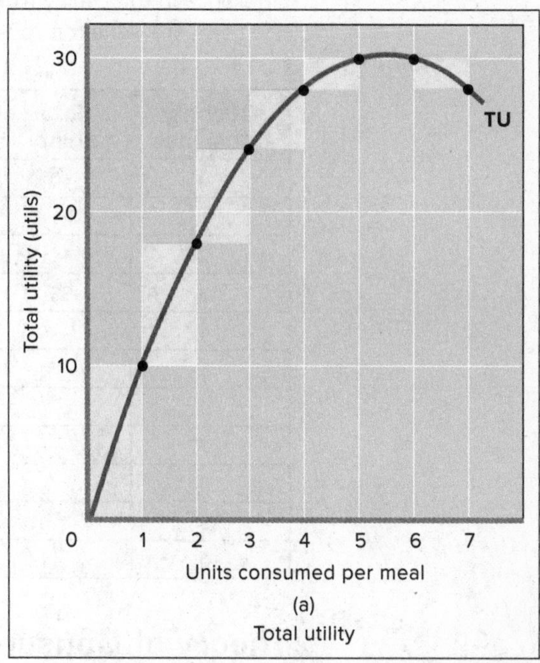

(a)
Total utility

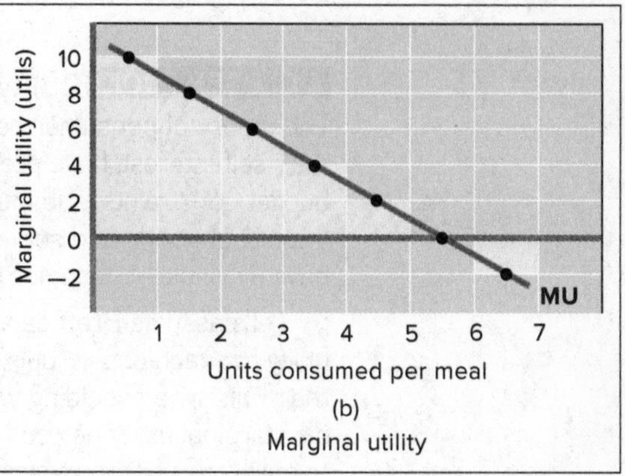

(b)
Marginal utility

How are marginal utility and total utility related? When given the total utility, you find the marginal utility by measuring the change in total utility from consuming each unit of a product. Refer to the graph and table. Consuming the first taco brings you a total of 10 utils. In moving from zero to one taco, total utility increases by 10 utils. So marginal utility is 10. When you eat two tacos, your total utility is 18 utils. The second taco increased your total utility from 10 to 18 utils, so your *marginal* utility—the *increase* in utility you received just for eating the second taco—is 8 utils.

Marginal utility, shown in Graph (b), begins to fall from the very first unit consumed. At some point, marginal utility falls below zero and becomes negative. But the total utility, in Graph A above, increases at first, because each additional product you consume has some positive level of utility. When you consumed the second taco, the marginal utility fell from 10 to 8 utils. But the total utility increased from 10 to 18, because the 8 utils from the second taco were added. But at the point that marginal utility reaches zero, total utility reaches its peak. For every unit of the product consumed after that point, the marginal utility is negative, so that takes away from total utility, pulling the total utility curve downward. In the scenario above, consuming the sixth taco brought you no marginal utility at all, and the total utility peaked at 30 utils. If you consume the seventh taco, which brings you a marginal utility of −2 utils, the total utility falls from 30 to 28 utils.

PRACTICE **Total Utility and Marginal Utility**

In the first three columns, use marginal utility to calculate total utility. Add the marginal utility from consuming the 4th product (15) to the total utility already received from consuming 3 products (59). In the next three columns, use total utility to calculate marginal utility. Find the difference in total utility from consuming 3 products and consuming 4 products. The first few rows are done for you.

Quantity Consumed	Total Utility	Marginal Utility		Quantity Consumed	Total Utility	Marginal Utility
0	0	—		0	0	—
1	21	21		1	13	13
2	41	20		2	23	10
3	59	18		3	31	8
4		15		4	37	
5		11		5	42	
6		6		6	45	
7		0		7	47	
8		−7		8	47	
9		−15		9	44	
10		−24		10	36	

Theory of Consumer Behavior

Refer to pages 142–144 of your textbook.

A CLOSER LOOK **Utility-Maximizing Rule**

The theory of consumer behavior begins with the assumptions that people act rationally in their self-interest, have preferences for some products over others, are limited by their budget constraints, and must pay to buy products. Given those assumptions, consumers find the mix of goods and services that bring them the greatest utility within the budget they have available—consumer equilibrium.

Let's assume Brett can buy either orange juice or coffee. He measures his marginal utility for each cup in "utils," or units of utility. Of course people don't sit down to calculate their utils when deciding what to buy. But they act as though they do! Once Brett has found his marginal utility per cup of each drink, he needs to divide that utility by the price per cup to make the units comparable. In this case, orange juice costs $2 per cup, while coffee costs $4 per cup. Therefore, Brett's table looks like this:

Number of Goods	Marginal Utility of Orange Juice	MU per Dollar of Orange Juice	Marginal Utility of Coffee	MU per Dollar of Coffee
1	10	5	24	6
2	8	4	20	5
3	6	3	12	3
4	4	2	4	1

If Brett has $18 of income to spend, how much orange juice and coffee should he buy to maximize his utility? According to the utility maximizing rule, consumers maximize their satisfaction by consuming products in such a way that the last dollar spent on each of two products brings the consumer the same amount of marginal utility per dollar spent.

Step 1: Brett would start by comparing the amount of marginal utility *per dollar* he could receive from the first cup of orange juice with the marginal utility *per dollar* he would get from the first cup of coffee. The first cup of juice would bring Brett 5 utils per dollar, while the first cup of coffee yields 6 utils per dollar. Brett is better off buying a cup of coffee first, which earns him 24 utils at a cost of $4.

Step 2: Next, Brett must choose between buying the first cup of juice for 5 utils per dollar or buying a second cup of coffee, which will also bring 5 utils per dollar. He is indifferent between them, so he will buy one of each. The cup of juice adds 10 utils for a total utility of 34 utils with $6 spent. The second coffee adds 20 utils, for a total utility of 54 utils, with the $4 price of coffee added to total $10 spent.

Step 3: Brett's next choice is between a second cup of juice for 4 utils per dollar or a third cup of coffee for 3 utils per dollar. He is better off buying a second juice for 8 additional utils, bringing total utility to 62 utils for the $12 spent.

Step 4: Next, Brett must decide between buying a third cup of juice for 3 utils per dollar or a third cup of coffee for 3 utils per dollar. He is again indifferent between the two choices, so he buys one of each, exhausting his $18. He adds 6 utils from the juice and 12 utils from the coffee to his total. Brett maximizes is utility by buying the 3 cups of juice and 3 cups of coffee for a total utility of 80 utils. He has reached consumer equilibrium, because the marginal utility per dollar received from the last cup of juice equals the marginal utility per dollar received from the last cup of coffee.

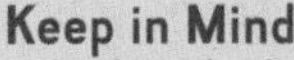

Keep in Mind

In both multiple-choice and free-response questions, you will need to be able to construct this table. Given the quantities, total utilities, and prices of two products, you must be able to calculate marginal utilities and MU per dollar. Be sure to read the column headings *very* carefully. Some questions may give you the marginal utility, rather than total utility, so that you only have to calculate the MU per dollar. You must also be able to recalculate these numbers if the price of one product changes and determine the resulting change in demand. You will not be allowed to use a calculator on the AP Economics exams, but the numbers are chosen to keep the math simple.

Caution

One common mistake is to try to determine whether a consumer should buy a product by comparing the marginal utility of products, rather than the marginal utility *per dollar* of products. It is crucial that you calculate *that* column in order to take relative prices into consideration.

Another common mistake when calculating the total utility of all of the purchases is to add up the marginal utilities *per dollar* rather than the marginal utilities. One way to avoid this mistake is to complete your analysis and determine how many of each product the consumer will buy, and after that, add up the marginal utilities of those purchases to find the total utility.

Utility-maximizing consumer equilibrium can also be expressed as an equation:

$$\frac{\text{MU of Product A}}{\text{Price of Product A}} = \frac{\text{MU of Product B}}{\text{Price of Product B}}$$

To maximize utility, a consumer should buy Products A and B until the ratios are equal and the consumer's income is spent. If the ratios are unequal, the consumer would be better off reallocating purchases to increase total utility. In our example, Brett could have bought 2 cups of juice and 4 cups of coffee, but he would only have gained 78 units of total utility, compared to the 80 utils he received by maximizing his utility. Using the equation, had Brett bought 2 juices and 4 cups of coffee, the equation would have looked like this:

$$\frac{8}{2} > \frac{4}{4}$$

Because the marginal utility per dollar spent for orange juice is clearly larger than the marginal utility per dollar spent for coffee, Brett would be better off buying more orange juice and less coffee until the marginal utilities per dollar become equal.

We can see the Law of Diminishing Marginal Utility in the downward-sloping demand curve; when consumers get less marginal utility from consuming the next unit of a product, they will only buy it if the price is lower. We can also see the income effect at work; when the price lowers, the consumer has income left with which to buy more products. With the substitution effect, when the price of one product falls, consumers buy more as a substitute for higher-priced products. In the utility maximization formula, you can see that a lower price reduces the denominator, increasing the marginal utility per dollar and increasing the consumer's utility.

PRACTICE **Utility-Maximizing Rule**

The table below shows the total utility (in utils) you receive from consuming strawberries and grapes. Strawberries cost $1 per bowl, grapes cost $2 per bowl, and you spend your entire income of $6 on strawberries and grapes.

Strawberry Quantity	Total Utility	Marginal Utility	Strawberry MU/$		Grape Quantity	Total Utility	Marginal Utility	Grape MU/$
0	0				0	0		
1	10				1	14		
2	16				2	24		
3	18				3	32		
4	19				4	34		

Which would you buy first or next?	How many units of marginal utility would you gain?	What would be your total utility from all units?	How much did you spend for this purchase?	How much do you have left to spend?

1. After exhausting your income:

   A. __________ How many bowls of strawberries did you buy?

   B. __________ How many bowls of grapes did you buy?

   C. __________ How much total utility did you gain from your purchases?

2. _______ Assume that instead of the numbers in the table above, you gained 10 units of marginal utility from the last bowl of strawberries you purchased at a price of $1, and you gained 12 units of marginal utility from the last bowl of grapes you purchased for $2. Which is true?

   A. You should have purchased more strawberries and fewer grapes.

   B. You should have purchased more grapes and fewer strawberries.

   C. You have achieved consumer equilibrium.

Make sure to return to the AP Key Concepts section above to check your understanding of this chapter's concepts important to AP coursework.

Economically Speaking

- **Law of Diminishing Marginal Utility** as a person consumes more of a product, the satisfaction gained from each additional product decreases
- **Marginal Utility** the extra satisfaction a consumer receives from one more unit of a product
- **Total Utility** the total amount of satisfaction a consumer receives from all of the products together

Chapter 8

Businesses and the Costs of Production

Now that we have studied consumer behavior, it is time to look at firm decision making. Production costs help to determine efficiency and profit maximization. We will learn about short-run and long-run costs of production and the mathematical and graphical models that illustrate these concepts.

These concepts usually appear in several multiple-choice questions on the AP Exam and combine with later concepts to form the basis for free-response questions about firm output and pricing decisions.

Key Concepts

Below is a summary of the chapter's concepts important to AP coursework. Upon completing the lessons that follow, return to these concepts to make sure you understand them and how the practice exercises you completed relate to them.

- An economic cost is a payment a firm must make to obtain a resource.
  - Explicit costs require payment for resources a firm doesn't own, so it must buy them.
  - Implicit costs are the opportunity costs of using resources a firm already owns.
  - Economic Costs = Explicit Costs + Implicit Costs
- Profit:
  - Accounting Profit = Total Revenue − Explicit (Accounting) Cost
  - Normal profit is the income an entrepreneur would have earned by engaging in a different industry (the opportunity cost); economists consider it a cost of production.
  - Economic Profit = Total Revenue − Economic Cost (explicit *and* implicit costs)
  - Economic profit improves allocative efficiency; firms earning profits expand, and firms facing economic losses close.
- In the short run, time is too short to change plant capacity, but output can change somewhat.
- In the long run, firms can change plant capacity and enter or leave the industry.
- Diminishing Returns:
  - Total product is the total quantity of products produced.
  - Marginal product is the extra output produced when one more unit of labor is hired.
  - Average product (labor productivity) is the output per unit of labor input.

- The Law of Diminishing Returns says that as units of a variable resource (like labor) are added to a fixed resource (like capital), beyond some point, the marginal product falls.

- Short-Run Production Costs:
  - Fixed cost does not change when output changes (mortgage, rent, and debt interest).
  - Variable cost changes when output changes (labor, materials, and utilities).
  - Total cost is the sum of all of the fixed and variable costs of production.
  - Graphically, the difference between the total cost and variable cost is the fixed cost.
  - Average Costs:
    - Average Fixed Cost = Fixed Cost/Output; AFC falls as output increases.
    - Average Variable Cost = Variable Cost/Output; due to increasing and diminishing returns, AVC falls and then rises, creating a U-shaped curve.
    - When average product is at its maximum, AVC is at its minimum.
    - Average Total Cost = Total Cost/Output; also ATC = AFC + AVC.
    - Because ATC is the vertical sum of AFC and AVC curves, it is a U-shaped curve.
  - Marginal cost is the additional cost to produce one more product; MC = Change in Total Cost/Change in Output.
    - Marginal cost falls, then increases, because of the Law of Diminishing Returns.
    - The marginal cost and marginal product curves are mirror images.
    - Marginal cost crosses both AVC and ATC at their minimums. If MC > AVC or ATC, it pulls the average up; if MC < AVC or ATC, it pulls the average down.
  - Shifts in Cost Curves:
    - If a fixed cost or lump-sum tax increases, AFC and ATC increase.
    - If a variable cost or per-unit tax increases, AVC, ATC, and MC increase.
- Long-Run Production Costs:
  - In the long run, firms can change plant size; all costs are variable.
  - The long-run ATC curve is made up of all of the minimum points of ATC curves for each possible plant size; it is a U-shaped curve.
- Economies and Diseconomies of Scale:
  - Economies of scale (or increasing returns to scale) occur when, as plant size increases, long-run ATC decreases; the larger the plant becomes, the more efficient it becomes.
    - It is located on the downward-sloping portion of the long-run ATC curve.
    - A 10% increase in resources will yield a *more*-than-10% increase in output.
    - It is caused by labor and management specialization and efficient use of capital.
  - Constant returns to scale occur when, as plant size increases, long-run ATC is the same.
    - It is located along the lowest points on the long-run ATC curve.
    - A 10% increase in resources will yield *exactly* a 10% increase in output.
  - Diseconomies of scale (or decreasing returns to scale) occur when, as plant size increases, long-run ATC rises; the larger the plant becomes, the less efficient it becomes.
    - It is located on the upward-sloping portion of the long-run ATC curve.
    - A 10% increase in resources will yield a *less*-than-10% increase in output.
    - It is caused by difficulty controlling a large plant, communication issues between management and workers, the cost of management, and worker alienation.

- Minimum efficient scale is the output at which a firm can minimize long-run ATC; it is the lowest point on the long-run ATC curve.
- A natural monopoly occurs when the long-run ATC continues to fall over a long range of plant sizes, so that ATC is minimized when only one firm makes the product.

Now, let's examine more closely the following concepts from your textbook:

- **Economic Costs**
- **Short-Run Production Relationships**
- **Short-Run Production Costs**
- **Long-Run Production Costs**

These sections were selected because understanding production costs is essential to understanding business decisions. Changes in costs affect profit, output, pricing, and shutdown decisions. The ability to graph and interpret these graphs is critical to success on the AP Microeconomics exam.

Economic Costs

Refer to pages 160–163 of your textbook.

A CLOSER LOOK Explicit and Implicit Costs, Accounting and Normal Profit, and Economic Profit

Scarce resources have alternative uses, so when a resource is used for one product rather than another, a cost occurs. **Economic costs** include all of the firm's costs to make a product. **Explicit** (accounting) **costs** are money payments for resources. **Implicit costs** are the firm's opportunity costs for resources that could have gone to other uses. If you gave up another job and used your own savings to start a business, your opportunity costs are the wages you gave up and the interest or dividends you could have earned on the savings that you instead invested in your firm. These implicit costs are not captured in accounting costs, but are still an important cost of business. **Normal profit** is the payment required to keep the entrepreneur working for that firm. It equals the cost of the entrepreneur's best alternative choice of career. If the entrepreneur is not paid, she will leave the firm to look for other opportunities.

Economic Cost = Explicit Cost + Implicit Cost

Accounting Profit = Total Revenue – Accounting Cost

Economic Profit = Total Revenue – Economic Cost

Accounting profit, total revenue minus total explicit cost, is the kind of profit we typically hear about in the news. Economists understand the importance of recognizing *all* costs of production, so **economic profit** takes into account normal profit and other implicit costs necessary for production. Because accountants don't consider the implicit costs, accounting profit is generally higher than economic profit.

Visualize how accounting and economic profit are calculated. An accountant and an economist who are looking at the firm's books would recognize the same accounting (explicit) costs, such as rent and wages. An accountant would subtract those costs from total revenue and call the difference accounting profit. But an economist would go one step further, subtracting normal profit (implicit costs) from that area of accounting profit, because economists consider normal profit a part of the cost of production. The economist would subtract the explicit *and* implicit costs to find the *economic* profit.

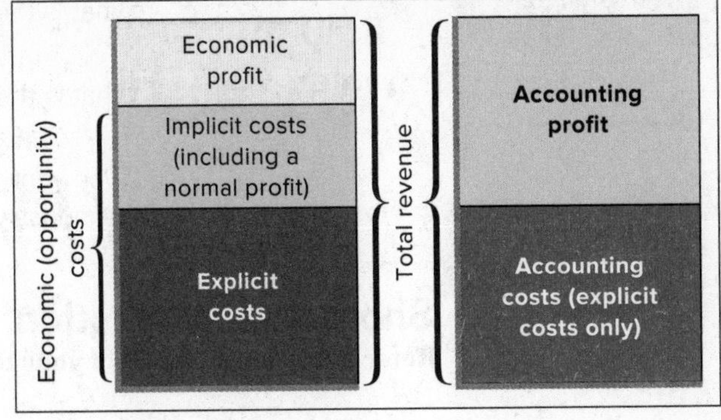

In economics, it is important to consider *economic* profit, because *that* is the number business owners use to determine whether to enter or exit an industry. If entrepreneurs see that firms are making an economic profit—earning *more* than enough to cover all explicit costs *and* the opportunity cost of entering the industry—those entrepreneurs will be enticed to enter the industry. But even if current firms in the industry can cover all of their explicit costs, if they can't also cover their *implicit* costs, they will have an incentive to leave the industry. This is why you will sometimes see a firm that is earning accounting profit eventually go out of business.

Caution

Recognizing the difference between accounting and economic profit will become very important in later chapters, when we consider how economic profits and losses draw firms into and out of industry. When a firm is making zero economic profit, the industry is in long-run equilibrium, and there is no incentive for firms to enter or exit the industry. Students often ask why a firm would remain in business if it is making no profit. It is important to remember that a firm earning zero *economic* profit is still covering all of its explicit costs, as well as paying the entrepreneur a normal profit. So a firm that shows no *economic* profit may still have a large *accounting* profit in the traditional way we've understood profit.

PRACTICE Explicit and Implicit Costs, Accounting and Normal Profit, and Economic Profit

Below are the costs per day for ABC Corporation. Is each cost an explicit cost or an implicit cost?

1. __________ Building rent: $100

2. __________ Workers' wages: $160

3. __________ Income the entrepreneur could have earned working elsewhere: $200

4. __________ Materials: $120

Total revenue for ABC Corporation is $600 per day.

5. __________ What is the total accounting (explicit) cost per day?

6. __________ What is the accounting profit per day?

7. __________ What is the total economic cost per day?

8. __________ What is the economic profit per day?

9. __________ Given your answer to #8, would firms eventually *enter* or *exit* the industry?

Short-Run Production Relationships

Refer to pages 163–166 of your textbook.

A CLOSER LOOK Law of Diminishing Returns

As we learned in Chapter 6, a firm's ability to respond to a change in demand depends on how much time is available. In the short run, plant capacity (factory size and large equipment) is fixed, but production can be increased to some extent by hiring more workers and increasing work hours.

In the short run, with plant size and equipment fixed, production can be measured in three ways. **Total product** is the total output from all of the workers together. **Average product** (productivity) measures the output per worker. **Marginal product** is the extra output produced when one more worker is hired.

Average Product = Total Product/Number of Workers
Marginal Product = Change in Total Product/Change in the Number of Workers

To measure the effect on output as the number of workers increases, we assume that all workers are equal in terms of education, experience, and motivation; each worker is identical. Of course that isn't realistic, but it will help you to understand the effect that occurs with the hiring of additional workers. These models generally focus on labor, but the concepts hold true for any variable resource.

(1) Units of the Variable Resource (Labor)	(2) Total Product (TP)	(3) Marginal Product (MP), Change in (2)/ Change in (1)		(4) Average Product (AP), (2)/(1)
0	0			—
		10	Increasing marginal returns	
1	10			10.00
		15		
2	25			12.50
		20		
3	45			15.00
		15	Diminishing marginal returns	
4	60			15.00
		10		
5	70			14.00
		5		
6	75			12.50
		0	Negative marginal returns	
7	75			10.71
		−5		
8	70			8.75

Given total product, you can calculate marginal product by measuring the change in total product from hiring the next worker. In the table above, the first three workers bring increasing returns, because due to specialization, the next worker adds even more to production than the worker before him. Because specialization increases efficiency and workers save time by not having to switch from task to task, all of the workers become more efficient by virtue of that next worker being there.

In the table on p. 70, workers 4-7 bring diminishing returns. Each worker adds to total product, but less than the worker before him. Specialization wears off until the seventh worker adds no output. After that, each additional worker actually reduces production. In negative returns, each worker's marginal product is negative as workers overwhelm the fixed capital, so production falls.

Caution

It is important to understand that marginal product doesn't change due to differences in the quality of the workers. Students commonly make the mistake of thinking the firm hires high quality workers first, resulting in high marginal product, but then marginal product falls as the firm begins to hire lower quality workers. Remember, we assume all workers are equal. The marginal product falls because more workers are using a fixed amount of capital, and increases in production will become more limited.

The **Law of Diminishing Returns** explains that as more units of a variable resource (like labor) are added to a fixed resource (like capital), marginal product falls. This concept recognizes the limit on production when a plant and equipment are fixed in the short run. Note in Graph (a) to the right—the total product graph—that during increasing returns, total product rises quickly. During diminishing returns, when marginal product declines but is still positive, total product increases, but at a slower rate. When marginal product is zero, total product is at its maximum. In negative returns, when marginal product is negative, total product falls.

The relationship between marginal and average product is also important. In Graph (b)—the marginal product graph—when the marginal product is higher than average product, the marginal product pulls up the average, so average product rises. If marginal product i s lower than average product, average product falls. Marginal product equals average product where the average product is at its maximum. It is very similar to your grade point average (GPA). If your Economics grade is higher than your GPA, that marginal grade will help pull up your GPA; if your Econ grade is lower than your GPA, it will pull your GPA down.

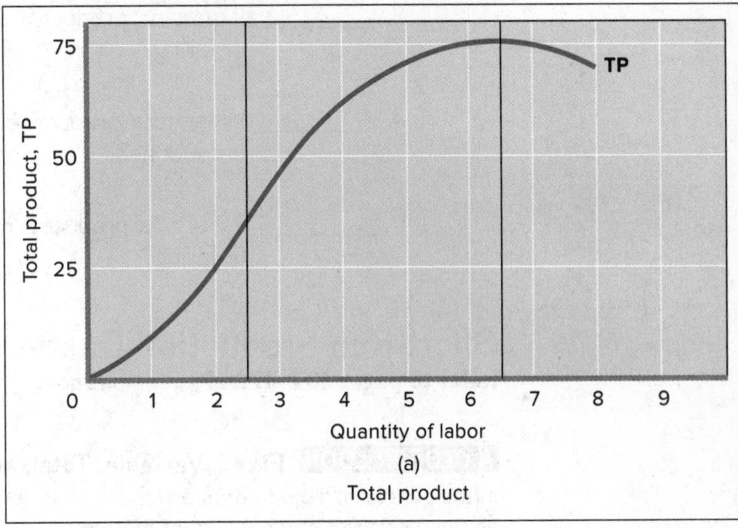

(a)
Total product

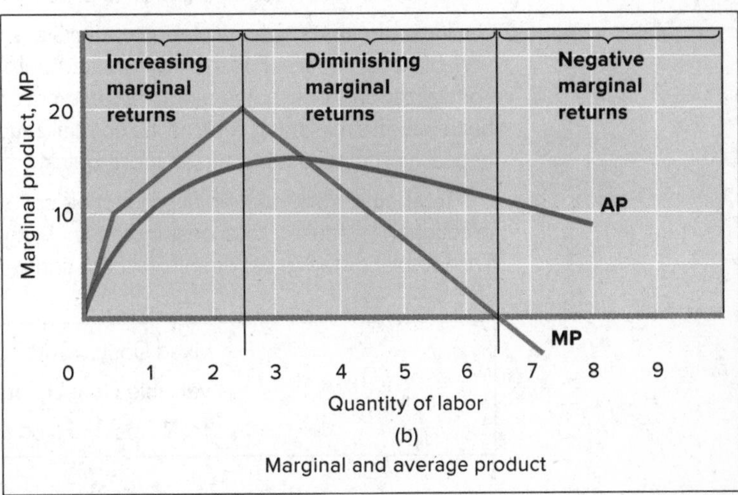

(b)
Marginal and average product

Keep in Mind

The Law of Diminishing Returns may sound vaguely familiar. In some ways, it is similar to the Law of Diminishing Marginal Utility. In both cases, the more you have of something, the less you get out of each additional one. It is important to keep these terms straight, as they frequently appear together as options on multiple-choice questions. Marginal utility measures the utility you gain from consuming one more product. Marginal returns measures the output a firm gains from hiring one more worker. You must be able to calculate marginal product; identify the ranges of increasing, diminishing, and negative returns; and interpret those portions of the graphs for the AP exam.

PRACTICE Law of Diminishing Returns

1. __________ Why is the marginal product of a second worker higher than that of the first?

2. __________ Why does marginal product eventually fall?

3. __________ If marginal product > average product, is the average product rising or falling?

4. __________ When total product reaches its peak, what must the marginal product be?

5. __________ If marginal product is negative, are total and average product rising or falling?

Short-Run Production Costs

Refer to pages 167–172 of your textbook.

A CLOSER LOOK Fixed, Variable, Total, and Marginal Costs

In the short run, **fixed costs** are those that do not change with the amount of output, such as the mortgage and equipment bought on contract with monthly payments. These costs remain the same, whether the firm is producing a million products or no products at all.

Variable costs, such as labor, materials, and utilities, change with output. At zero output, variable cost is zero. For the first units of output, the rate of increase is small because of specialization. After some point, variable cost begins to increase at an increasing rate because of diminishing returns; as specialization wears off and workers overwhelm fixed capital, variable cost increases more quickly.

Total cost is the sum of all production costs. At zero output, total cost is the fixed cost. As production increases, total cost increases by the amount of the variable cost at each output. The vertical distance between total cost and variable cost on the graph is the fixed cost.

Fixed Cost = Total Cost at Zero Output
Variable Cost = Total Cost − Fixed Cost
Total Cost = Fixed Cost + Variable Cost

Average costs are calculated by dividing the cost by output. Fixed cost does not change with output, so as the fixed cost is spread over more and more output, the **average fixed cost** (AFC) continuously falls.

> Average Fixed Cost = Fixed Cost/Output
> Average Variable Cost = Variable Cost/Output
> Average Total Cost = Total Cost/Output
> Marginal Cost = Change in Total Cost/Change in Output

Total-Cost Data				Average-Cost Data			Marginal Cost
(1) Total Product (Q)	(2) Total Fixed Cost (TFC)	(3) Total Variable Cost (TVC)	(4) Total Cost (TC) TC = TFC + TVC	(5) Average Fixed Cost (AFC) $AFC = \frac{TFC}{Q}$	(6) Average Variable Cost (AVC) $AVC = \frac{TVC}{Q}$	(7) Average Total Cost (ATC) $ATC = \frac{TC}{Q}$	(8) Marginal Cost (MC) $MC = \frac{\text{change in TC}}{\text{change in Q}}$
0	$100	$ 0	$ 100				$ 90
1	100	90	190	$100.00	$90.00	$190.00	80
2	100	170	270	50.00	85.00	135.00	70
3	100	240	340	33.33	80.00	113.33	60
4	100	300	400	25.00	75.00	100.00	70
5	100	370	470	20.00	74.00	94.00	80
6	100	450	550	16.67	75.00	91.67	90
7	100	540	640	14.29	77.14	91.43	110
8	100	650	750	12.50	81.25	93.75	130
9	100	780	880	11.11	86.67	97.78	150
10	100	930	1,030	10.00	93.00	103.00	

Keep in Mind
Given specific data, you must be able to calculate total, fixed, variable, marginal, and average costs in a variety of ways. You may be given total costs and then asked to calculate the marginal cost at a specific output. Or you may be given the fixed and marginal costs and then asked to calculate the total cost at a particular output. Be familiar with different ways to calculate each cost, because such questions have appeared on both the multiple-choice and free-response portions of the AP Microeconomics exam.

Average variable cost (AVC) is a U-shaped curve due to diminishing returns. As the first few workers specialize, the firm raises output using few workers, so AVC falls. But during diminishing returns, more workers and other resources are required to produce each product, so the AVC begins to rise again.

Average total cost (ATC) is found by vertically adding the AFC and AVC curves. It is also U-shaped and above both the AFC and AVC. The distance between the ATC and AVC is the AFC, and as more and more units of output are produced, ATC and AVC get closer and closer together as the AFC continues to fall.

Marginal cost is the extra cost to produce one more unit of output. It is the increase in total or variable cost to produce one more product. Because fixed cost doesn't change, changes in total and variable costs will be identical. The marginal cost curve looks like a checkmark. Marginal cost falls with the first few workers hired because of increasing returns; as marginal product per worker increases, the marginal cost of producing each additional product actually falls. But as specialization wears off and diminishing returns set in on production, the marginal cost of producing the next unit begins to rise quickly.

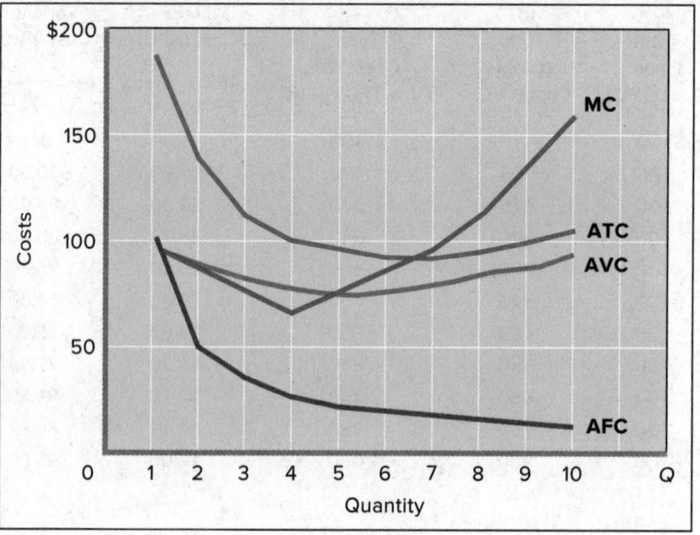

As shown in the graph above, the marginal cost curve crosses both AVC and ATC at their lowest points. Just as with marginal and average product, when marginal cost is lower than AVC or ATC, it pulls down the average; when marginal cost is higher than AVC or ATC, it pulls up the average. Again, a similar example is how your marginal grade in Economics affects your GPA. Because the fixed cost does not change with the amount of output, the AFC continues to fall as output rises.

Keep in Mind

It is essential that you understand the relationships between the marginal and average cost curves and be able to draw them from memory. Questions about these relationships consistently appear on the multiple-choice portion of the AP Microeconomics exam, and almost every AP Microeconomics exam contains at least one free-response question that requires you to draw a graph for a specific type of market. All of those markets use cost curves in the relationships shown in this chapter.

PRACTICE Fixed, Variable, Total, and Marginal Costs

1. ________ Give one example of a fixed cost.

2. ________ Give one example of a variable cost.

This table refers to Questions 3–5.

Output	Total Cost
0	20
1	27
2	32
3	35
4	45
5	61
6	83

3. ________ According to the table, what is the marginal cost to produce the 4th unit of output?

4. ________ According to the table, what is the average total cost to produce 2 units of output?

5. ________ According to the table, what is the average fixed cost to produce 5 units of output?

This table refers to Questions 6–8.

Output	Marginal Cost	Fixed Cost
0	—	40
1	20	
2	10	
3	15	

6. ________ According to the table, what is the total cost of producing 3 units of output?

7. ________ According to the table, what is the variable cost of producing 2 units of output?

8. ________ According to the table, what is the average total cost of producing 2 units of output?

9. ________ A firm's fixed cost is $100 per day. Four workers each earn a wage of $30 per day. If the firm produces 10 products per day, what is the ATC per day?

10. ________ What is represented by the distance between the ATC and AVC curves?

11. ________ If ATC and AVC are the same at every point on the curve, what must AFC be?

12. ________ Where does the MC curve cross both the ATC and AVC curves?

13. ________ At a given output, if MC is higher than ATC, must ATC be rising or falling?

A CLOSER LOOK Shifts of the Cost Curves

Changes in the cost of production shift cost curves directly up and down. But *which* cost has changed will determine which curves move. If a fixed cost such as a property tax increases, the firm's total cost will also increase, so AFC and ATC will increase. But no variable cost changed, and the additional cost to produce the next product did not change, so the AVC and MC curves will not shift.

If, instead, a variable cost such as the wage increases, the firm's total cost of production will also increase. The marginal cost to produce each additional product increases, as well. But the fixed cost has not changed. So if a variable cost increases, ATC, AVC, and MC increase, but AFC does not change.

Changes in taxes and subsidies can affect either the fixed or variable cost, depending on how they are implemented. A lump-sum tax or subsidy is unrelated to output; the firm is simply required to pay the amount of the tax, such as a property tax. Therefore, it acts as a fixed cost, causing only AFC and ATC to shift. A per-unit tax or subsidy, however, acts as a change in variable cost because it affects each individual product produced, causing ATC, AVC, and MC to change, while AFC does not change.

Keep in Mind
It is vital for you to be able to illustrate curve shifts. Free-response questions frequently ask you to draw the graph for a market, and then ask you to shift the curves based on a scenario. It is important to know whether that situation shifts the marginal cost curve (if it is a variable cost) or not (if it is a fixed cost), because that decision will determine whether the firm changes its output to maximize profit.

PRACTICE Shifts of the Cost Curves

Changes in fixed cost only affect AFC and ATC. Changes in variable cost only affect MC, AVC, and ATC. Show the changes with arrows for each situation. One or more curves will *not* shift in each scenario.

1. Show how an improvement in technology affects: MC __ ATC __ AFC __ AVC __
2. Show how an increase in workers' wages affects: MC __ ATC __ AFC __ AVC __
3. Show how an increase in annual factory rent affects: MC __ ATC __ AFC __ AVC __
4. Show how an increase in a per-unit tax affects: MC __ ATC __ AFC __ AVC __
5. Show how a lump-sum government subsidy affects: MC __ ATC __ AFC __ AVC __
6. Show how a lump-sum property tax on a firm affects: MC __ ATC __ AFC __ AVC __

Long-Run Production Costs

Refer to pages 172–177 of your textbook.

A CLOSER LOOK Economies and Diseconomies of Scale

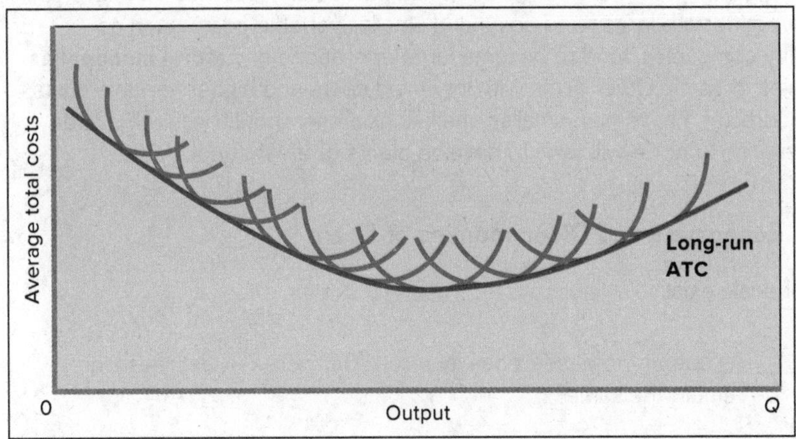

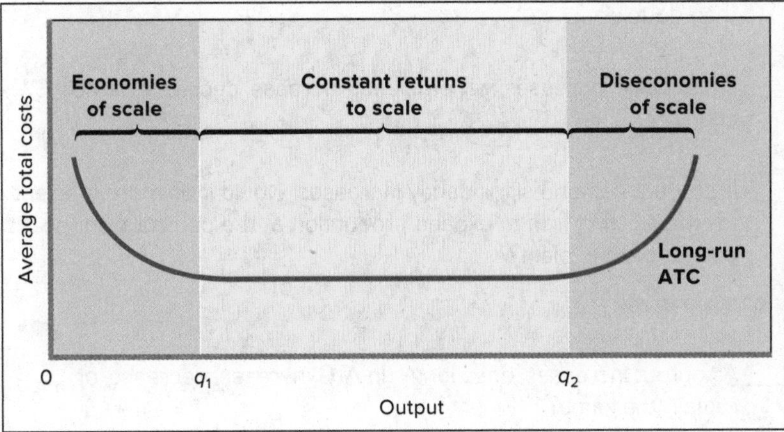

In the **short run,** firms are constrained by limitations in plant size and equipment, and fixed costs result from those constraints. But in the **long run,** all costs are variable. The firm can change the plant size or equipment, and firms have time to enter or leave the industry. Therefore, the firm's long-run decisions focus on plant size. As shown in the graph to left, the long-run average total cost curve is U-shaped, made up of the minimum points of all of the short-run ATC curves for all of the potential plant sizes.

For the first units of production, long-run ATC falls. With **economies of scale,** the larger the plant, the lower its ATC. Economies of scale result from specialization and more efficient capital. If resource inputs are doubled, the firm's output more than doubles; therefore, ATC falls. If a firm is producing output in the range of economies of scale, it would improve efficiency by operating a larger plant.

At some point, long-run ATC rises. With **diseconomies of scale,** the larger the plant, the higher its ATC. Diseconomies of scale result from larger management, communication issues, and worker alienation. If inputs are doubled, the firm's output less than doubles; therefore, ATC rises. If a firm is producing output in the range of diseconomies of scale, it would improve efficiency by operating a smaller plant.

Between economies and diseconomies of scale is a range of production called **constant returns to scale.** In this range, ATC does not change with the size of the plant. When resource inputs are doubled, the firm's output doubles. Firms maximize efficiency with a plant size in this range.

Minimum efficient scale is the output where a firm minimizes its long-run ATC. Because long-run ATC curves can vary so much in shape, firms in particular industries can have very different plant sizes. Firms with large fixed costs and smaller variable costs, such as automakers and utility companies, tend to become large operations or **natural monopolies** because of economies of scale. Other firms with low fixed costs and higher variable costs, such as hotdog vendors, tend to remain smaller operations. Other industries with a wide range of constant returns to scale will tend to develop plants of a variety of sizes.

PRACTICE Economies and Diseconomies of Scale

When economies of scale exist:

1. _________ As output increases, does long-run ATC increase, decrease, or remain the same?

2. _________ If input is doubled, does output double, more than double, or less than double?

3. _________ If plant size increases, will efficiency increase, decrease, or not change?

4. _________ If product demand significantly increases, would it be more efficient for the existing firm to expand production at the current plant or open a second plant?

When diseconomies of scale exist:

5. _________ As output increases, does long-run ATC increase, decrease, or remain the same?

6. _________ If input is doubled, does output double, more than double, or less than double?

7. _________ If plant size increases, will efficiency increase, decrease, or not change?

Make sure to return to the AP Key Concepts section above to check your understanding of this chapter's concepts important to AP coursework.

Economically Speaking

- **Accounting Profit** the firm's total revenue minus explicit costs
- **Average Fixed Cost** fixed cost divided by output
- **Average Product** output per unit of labor
- **Average Total Cost** total cost divided by output
- **Average Variable Cost** variable cost divided by output
- **Constant Returns to Scale** as plant size increases, long-run average total cost stays the same
- **Diseconomies of Scale** as plant size increases, long-run average total cost increases
- **Economic Cost** a payment a firm must make to obtain a resource
- **Economic Profit** the profit earned in excess of all (explicit and implicit) costs of production
- **Economies of Scale** as plant size increases, long-run average total cost decreases
- **Explicit Cost** monetary payment for resources a firm must buy
- **Fixed Cost** a cost that does not change when output changes
- **Implicit Cost** the opportunity cost of using resources a firm already owns
- **Law of Diminishing Returns** as more units of a variable resource (like labor) are added to a fixed resource (like capital), beyond some point, the marginal product will decline
- **Long Run** a long enough time for firms to change plant capacity and enter or leave the industry
- **Marginal Cost** the extra cost of producing one more unit of output
- **Marginal Product** the extra output produced with the addition of one more unit of a resource
- **Minimum Efficient Scale** output at which a firm can minimize long-run average total cost
- **Natural Monopoly** long-run average total cost is minimized when one firm makes a product
- **Normal Profit** the profit an entrepreneur would have earned by engaging in a different industry
- **Short Run** a time period too short to change plant capacity, but long enough to change output
- **Total Cost** the total cost of production, adding the fixed and variable costs
- **Total Product** the total quantity produced
- **Variable Cost** a cost that changes when output changes

9 Chapter

Pure Competition in the Short Run

In Chapters 9-13, we reach the heart of microeconomics, the concepts which comprise more than a quarter of the AP Microeconomics exam. With a fuller understanding of revenues and costs, we bring them together to see how the firm makes price and output decisions. A firm's ability to control product price highlights differences among market structures. Chapter 9 describes pure (perfect) competition, explaining how firms make profit-maximizing, loss-minimizing, and shutdown decisions. The principles developed in this chapter carry through to decision making by firms in other market structures, as well.

Material from Chapter 9 is the basis for a large number of multiple-choice questions, and a free-response question about decision making in at least one of the market structures is part of nearly every AP Microeconomics exam.

Key Concepts

Below is a summary of the chapter's concepts important to AP coursework. Upon completing the lessons that follow, return to these concepts to make sure you understand them and how the practice exercises you completed relate to them.

- Market structures identify characteristics of industries that explain the behavior of firms.
    - Pure (perfect) competition is a market structure in which a large number of firms produce identical products; firms can freely enter and exit the industry.
    - Monopolistic competition is a market structure in which a large number of firms produce slightly differentiated products.
    - An oligopoly is a market structure in which only a few firms produce a product.
    - A monopoly is a market structure in which only one firm is the sole seller of a product.
- Perfectly competitive firms are price takers which have no control over prices; they must accept the price set by supply and demand in the industry.
- In perfectly competitive markets, industry demand is downward-sloping, but because the individual firm is a price taker, the individual firm's demand curve is perfectly elastic.
- For a perfectly competitive firm, demand, marginal revenue, price, and average revenue are equal.
- Because perfectly competitive firms cannot control price, they maximize profit based on output.
- For the perfectly competitive firm, total revenue slopes upward at a constant rate because the price to sell each additional unit does not change.

- Using the total-revenue—total-cost approach, the break-even point indicates the output where total cost equals total revenue; the firm makes normal profit, but not economic profit.
- Using the total-revenue—total-cost approach, the firm maximizes profit by producing output at the point where total revenue is the greatest vertical distance above the total cost.
- Using the marginal-revenue—marginal-cost approach, a firm should produce a product if MR is greater than or equal to MC; it should *not* produce a product if MR is less than MC.
- The MR = MC Rule: a firm maximizes profit (or minimizes loss) by producing where MR = MC.
- The MR = MC Rule applies to *all* firms, regardless of market structure.
- Because MR = P for perfectly competitive firms, the MR = MC rule can also be stated as P = MC.
- Profit per Unit = Price – Average Total Cost; Total Profit = Profit per Unit × Output
- At the output where MR = MC:
    - If ATC < P, the firm should produce and earns economic profit.
    - If ATC = P, the firm should produce and earns zero economic profit (but earns normal profit).
    - If ATC > P, the firm incurs a loss.
        - If AVC < or = P, the firm should continue producing to minimize losses in the short run.
        - If AVC > P, the firm should shut down in the short run.
- The part of the MC curve above the AVC curve is the firm's supply curve.

Now, let's examine more closely the following concepts from your textbook:

- **Four Market Models**
- **Profit Maximization in the Short Run: Total-Revenue – Total-Cost Approach**
- **Profit Maximization in the Short Run: Marginal-Revenue – Marginal-Cost Approach**

These sections were selected because it is critically important to be able to draw and interpret the perfectly competitive market model. This model also serves as the foundation for the other market structure models, so understanding the concepts of this chapter will set you up for success on the exam.

Four Market Models

Refer to pages 182–183 of your textbook.

A CLOSER LOOK Four Market Models

Industries are classified by their **market structure,** the characteristics of an industry that explain the behavior of firms within that industry. **Pure (perfect) competition** involves a large number of firms which produce identical products and can easily enter or exit the industry. The other three market structures are considered imperfect competition. **Monopolistic competition** is similar to perfect competition in that a large number of firms compete and can easily enter or exit the industry, but the products are slightly different and firms heavily advertise those non-price differences. Only a few firms compete in an **oligopoly,** which exhibits significant barriers to entry by new firms. Oligopolies are unique in that each firm is affected by its rivals' decisions. In a **monopoly,** one firm is the only producer of a product, and barriers to entry by competitors are complete.

Characteristic	Market Model: Pure Competition	Monopolistic Competition	Oligopoly	Pure Monopoly
Number of firms	A very large number	Many	Few	One
Type of product	Standardized	Differentiated	Standardized or differentiated	Unique; no close substitutes
Control over price	None	Some, but within rather narrow limits	Limited by mutual interdependence; considerable with collusion	Considerable
Conditions of entry	Very easy, no obstacles	Relatively easy	Significant obstacles	Blocked
Nonprice competition	None	Considerable emphasis on advertising, brand names, trademarks	Typically a great deal, particularly with product differentiation	Mostly public relations advertising
Examples	Agriculture	Retail trade, dresses, shoes	Steel, automobiles, farm implements, many household appliances	Local utilities

Perfectly competitive markets are rare but provide a foundation for understanding profit maximization and efficiency. Four characteristics define perfectly competitive markets. First, a large number of independent sellers produce the product, so decisions of one firm have no effect on competitors. Second, goods produced by all of the firms are identical, so consumers do not care which firm's product they buy. Third, perfectly competitive firms are **price takers,** meaning they have no control over the product price; they must accept the price set in the industry by supply and demand. Fourth, firms can freely enter and exit the industry without significant barriers to entry. Products like corn, wheat, milk, beef, stocks, and currencies are sold in perfectly competitive markets.

Keep in Mind

It will be important to memorize the characteristics of each market structure. As each new market structure is introduced in a subsequent chapter, you will clearly see the differences in industries. It is common to see a question or two on the AP Microeconomics exam that asks you to identify a market structure from the characteristics or to compare the characteristics of two or more market structures.

PRACTICE Four Market Models

Identify the market structure which exhibits the characteristic listed in each statement.

1. ________ The industry has many firms and differentiated products

2. ________ The industry has blocked entry to any new firms

3. ________ Individual firms in the industry have no control over price

4. ________ The few firms in the industry base their decisions on what their rivals might do

5. ________ All firms in the industry produce identical products

Profit Maximization in the Short Run: Total-Revenue – Total-Cost Approach

Refer to pages 185–186 of your textbook.

A CLOSER LOOK Profit Maximization in the Short Run: Total-Revenue – Total Cost Approach

Because a perfectly competitive firm cannot control its price, it must maximize profit based on output. The plant and equipment are fixed in the short run, so the firm can only change its variable costs and then determine the most profitable output. Firms can determine profit-maximizing output by studying total revenue and total cost or marginal revenue and marginal cost. First, we look at totals.

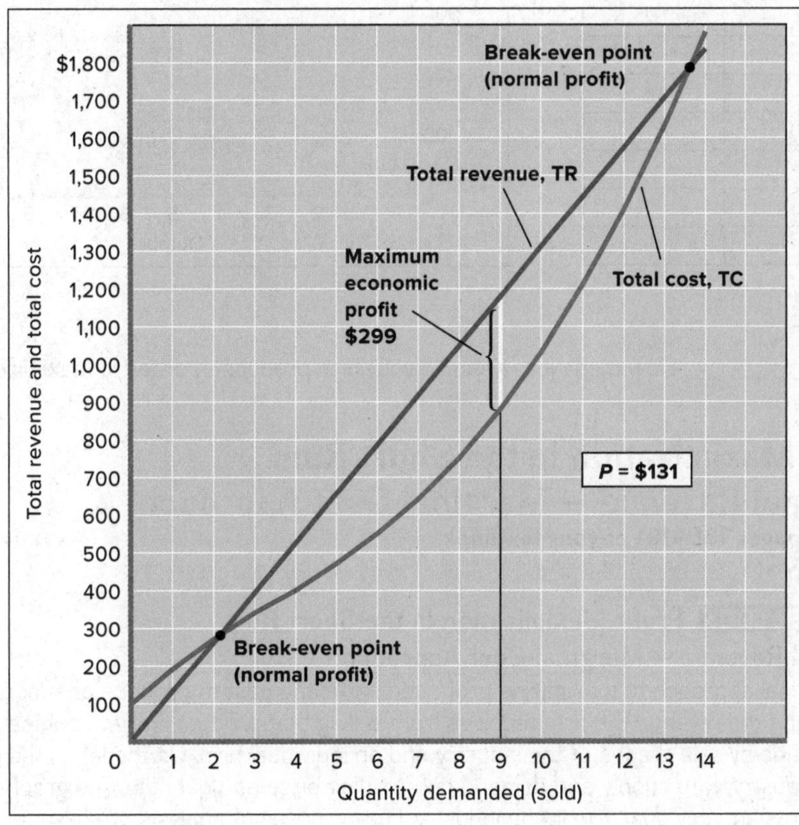

Total revenue (price × quantity sold) for a perfectly competitive firm slopes upward at a constant rate because it increases by the product price with each unit sold. **Total cost** includes all explicit and implicit costs. In the example above, for the first two units of output, total cost exceeds total revenue, so the firm would make a loss by producing at those output levels. After the second unit of output is the **break-even point,** where total cost equals total revenue and the firm achieves a normal profit, but not economic profit. After the 13th unit of output is a second break-even point. Output beyond that point again brings the firm a loss. Between those two break-even points, total revenue is greater than the total cost at each output, and the area between the total revenue and total cost represents economic profit. To maximize profit, the firm produces output at the point where total revenue is the *greatest vertical distance* above the total cost—in this case, at nine units, where total revenue is $1,179 and total cost is $880. The distance between the curves is the economic profit, in this case $299 ($1,179 – $880).

PRACTICE Profit Maximization in the Short Run: Total-Revenue – Total Cost Approach

You own Awesome Fashions, a firm that manufactures designer jeans. You sell the jeans for $50 each. Complete the table, graph the total revenue and total cost, and identify the profit-maximizing output.

Output	Total Cost	Total Revenue	Total Profit or Loss
0	20		
1	50		
2	60		
3	80		
4	110		
5	150		
6	210		
7	275		
8	375		
9	480		
10	600		

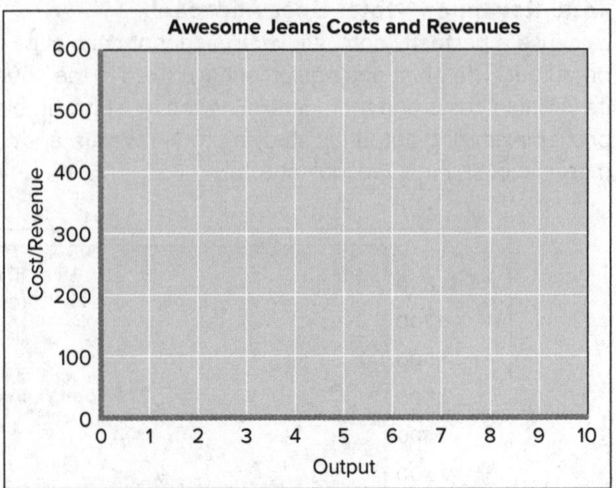

_________ How many jeans should your firm produce in order to maximize profit?

Profit Maximization in the Short Run: Marginal-Revenue – Marginal-Cost Approach

Refer to pages 186–191 of your textbook.

A CLOSER LOOK Profit Maximization in the Short Run: Marginal-Revenue – Marginal-Cost Approach

The marginal approach to maximizing profit compares the cost to produce one more product and the revenue the firm receives from selling that product. Perfect competition requires side-by-side graphs of the industry and an individual firm. On the left is the graph for the *industry*, with supply and demand determining price and quantity. The graph on the right depicts an *individual firm* in the industry. For purposes of analysis, we assume all firms have identical costs. In a perfectly competitive industry, each individual firm produces such a small fraction of the industry's output that one firm has no effect on the price or industry output. Therefore, the individual firm is a "price taker," accepting the equilibrium market price determined by industry supply and demand. To represent this relationship, a dotted line extends from the equilibrium price in the industry graph to the price in the individual firm graph. The demand curve for the individual firm is horizontal, perfectly elastic at the market equilibrium price. The firm can sell everything it produces at the industry price and will lose all customers if it raises the price.

Keep in Mind

Multiple-choice questions asking about the difference between the downward-sloping industry demand curve and the individual firm's perfectly elastic demand curve are frequently part of the exam.

The individual firm's revenue is the price times the quantity sold. Because the firm is a price taker, it sells each product for the same price, so average revenue equals price. **Marginal revenue** is the change in total revenue from selling one more unit of the product. Because the perfectly competitive firm sells every product for the same price, the marginal revenue, price, and average revenue are all equal, graphed on the horizontal demand curve. **Marginal cost** is the cost to produce one more product.

Graphing Guidance

Although the types of revenue are calculated differently, marginal revenue, price, average revenue, and demand are equal for perfectly competitive firms. For imperfectly competitive firms, marginal revenue will separate from the others. It is critical to correctly label graphs to earn all available points. This includes titling your graphs to correctly identify the industry and individual (single) firm graphs, such as shown in the graphs below. One common error is to reverse the labels on the industry graph (on the left) and the individual firm graph (on the right). Look carefully at the question to determine whether you should draw both side-by-side graphs, or just one of the graphs.

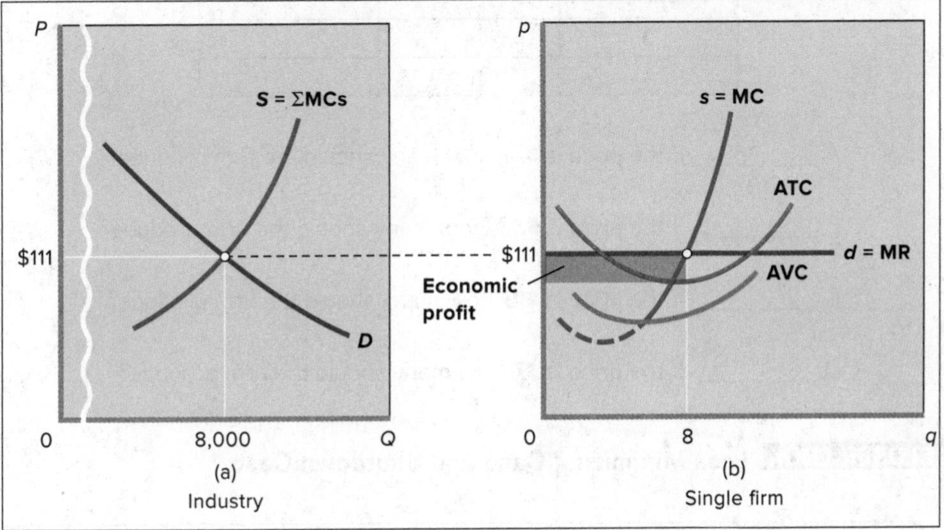

Firms find profit-maximizing output by comparing marginal revenue to marginal cost. The **MR = MC Rule** says firms *always* maximize profit by producing where MR = MC. If the firm can earn more income than it costs to make the next unit, the firm should produce it; if marginal revenue is less than marginal cost, the firm should not produce it. If the average total cost is lower than price at the profit-maximizing output, as shown in the graph above, the firm makes a profit.

Profit per Unit = Price – Average Total Cost

Total Profit = Profit per Unit × Output

Caution

Many students look at the graph and wonder why the firm wouldn't maximize profit by producing where MC is at its minimum, because the difference between MR and MC is greatest at that output. But consider what happens when you increase output by one unit from that point. The marginal revenue the firm earns from producing that next unit is greater than the marginal cost to produce that unit. It is a smaller difference, but still a gain for the firm. Remember, the firm is trying to maximize *total* profit, not profit *per unit*, so if the firm can bring in even a little more profit by producing one more product, it will. The MR = MC rule is true for *every* market structure, from perfect competitors to monopolies.

PRACTICE Profit Maximization in the Short Run: Marginal-Revenue – Marginal-Cost Approach

1. To maximize profit, firms should produce where marginal __________ equals marginal __________.

2. __________ At a firm's current level of output, P < MC. In order to maximize profit, should the firm increase production or reduce production?

3. Assume a firm faces these costs. Complete the table for marginal cost.

Output	Total Cost	Marginal Cost
0	8	—
1	17	
2	38	
3	67	
4	100	

A. __________ If the price is $21, how many should the firm produce?

B. __________ If the price is $33, how many should the firm produce?

C. __________ If the price is $18, how many should the firm produce?

D. __________ If the price is $7, how many should the firm produce?

A CLOSER LOOK Loss-Minimizing Case and Shutdown Case

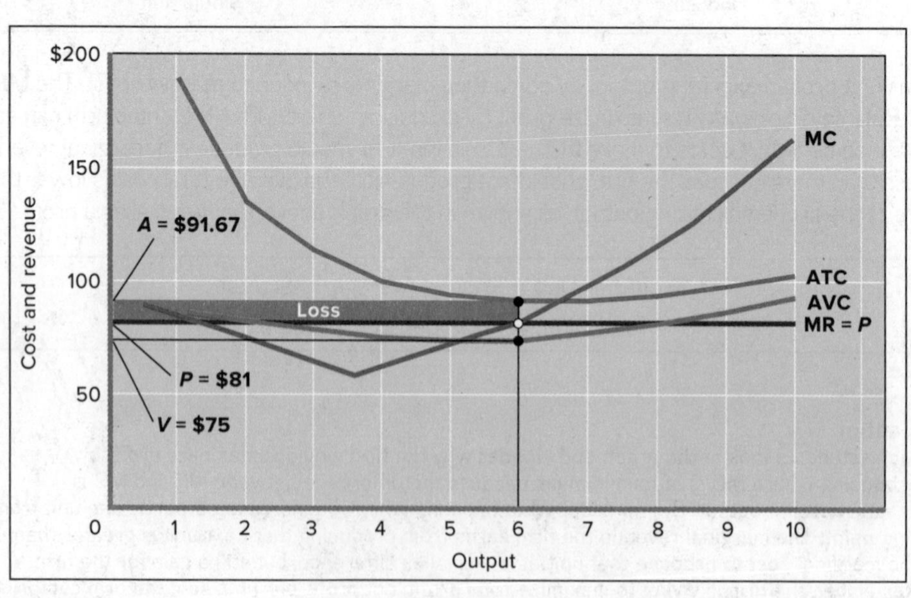

In this case, the MR = P = AR = D curve for the firm again extends from the price set by industry supply and demand. The firm, as always, should produce at the output where MR = MC. But notice that this time, ATC is *higher* than price, showing that the firm is suffering an economic loss. Loss is calculated the same way as profit (P – ATC); a negative number is a loss. So if the firm is losing money, should it shut down? Not necessarily. Remember, the firm still has fixed costs it must pay in the short run, even if the firm closes. So we need to determine whether the firm will lose more money by shutting down or staying open in the short run. Assume these are the firm's short-run costs at a particular level of output:

Fixed Cost	$100
Variable Cost	$150
Total Cost	$250
Total Revenue	$200

In this case, when the firm is in operation, it has a loss of $50 because the total cost ($250) is greater than total revenue ($200). However, if the firm shuts down, it would incur a loss of $100 because it still must pay its fixed costs even though it has no revenue. Therefore, this firm should remain in business in the short run, because its losses are lower if it remains open than if it shuts down. If the firm's marginal revenue is greater than or equal to average variable cost, the firm should remain in business in the short run, because any additional revenue earned beyond the variable cost can be put toward the fixed cost. You can see this in the loss-minimizing graph on the previous page. The MR = P curve is *above* the AVC curve at the loss-minimizing output, so the firm should remain in business in the short run.

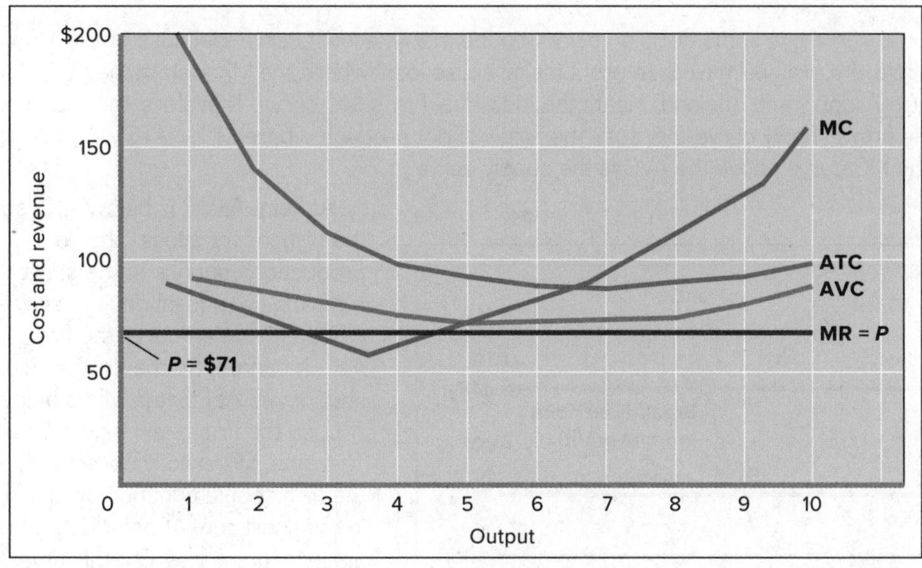

The graph above looks very similar to the loss-minimizing case, except that both the ATC and AVC curves are above the MR = P curve. Even if the firm produces at the output where MR = MC, it cannot cover its variable costs. Therefore, the firm should shut down. Let's look at numbers, using the same costs as the loss-minimizing case, but lower total revenue:

Fixed Cost	$100
Variable Cost	$150
Total Cost	$250
Total Revenue	$100

In this case, the firm is incurring a loss of $150 while operating. Should the firm remain in business in the short run? If it stays in business, it loses $150, but if it shuts down, it loses $100. In this case, the firm is better off shutting down. The firm cannot even cover the variable costs of the labor and materials to create the output it is selling, so it should shut down.

These kinds of decisions are quite common for businesses. Consider a small ice cream shop that makes an economic profit in the summer. When winter comes and demand for ice cream significantly drops, the shop can reduce its number of employees and how many ice cream supplies it buys. But the owner is still responsible for the same amount of rent, property tax, and equipment lease payments the shop had in the summer. In the winter, the ice cream shop incurs a loss, and the owner must decide whether to remain open for the winter. If the shop brings in enough revenue to cover the costs of the workers, ice cream supplies, utilities, and other variable costs, it is worth it to stay open in hopes of making a little money toward those fixed costs. But if the owner can't even cover the costs of workers and supplies, and will actually *lose* more money by remaining open, it is better to close.

So we have a series of points to determine production. At the output where MR = MC:

- If ATC < P, the firm should produce and earn economic profit in the short run
- If ATC = P, the firm should produce and earn zero economic profit (but earn normal profit)
- If ATC > P, the firm incurs a loss:
    - If AVC < or = P, the firm should produce to minimize losses in the short run
    - If AVC > P, the firm should shut down

We can see these same decision points on the marginal cost curve. Because of the MR = MC rule, the firm will maximize profit (or minimize loss) where the MR (determined by industry supply and demand) meets the individual firm's MC curve. Therefore, the MC curve is the firm's supply curve. Because the firm will not produce where MC < AVC, only the part of the MC curve above the AVC is the supply curve.

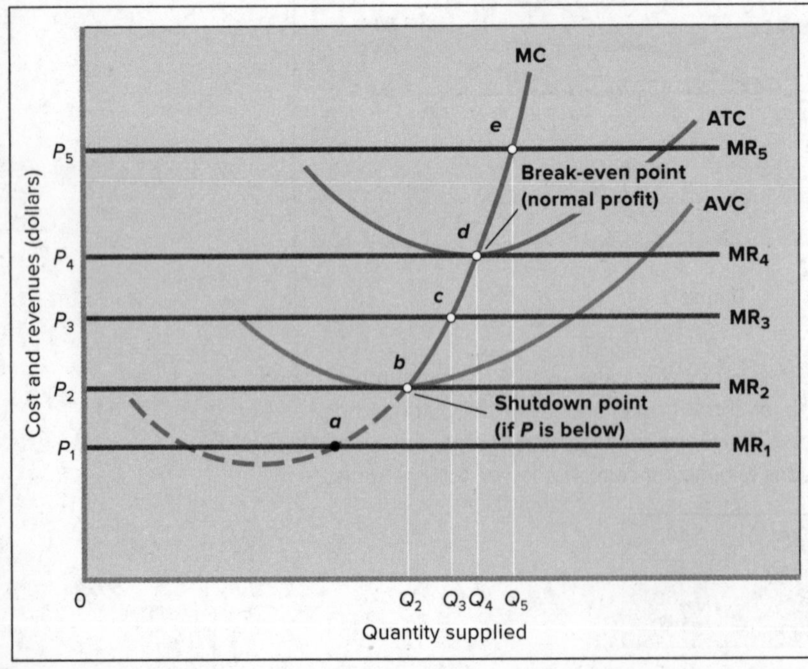

At Point A, MR is below ATC, so the firm incurs a loss. Should production continue in the short run? The next question is to see whether MR can cover the firm's AVC. It cannot. So the firm should shut down. At Point B, MR is below ATC, so the firm again incurs a loss. This time, MR exactly covers AVC, so the firm should continue producing in the short run. At point C, the firm again incurs a loss. But this time, MR more than covers AVC, so some revenue can go toward the fixed cost. The firm should continue to produce in the short run. At Point D, MR equals ATC, so the firm earns normal profit, but no economic profit. At Point E, MR is greater than ATC, so the firm is earning an economic profit.

PRACTICE Loss-Minimizing Case and Shutdown Case

1. __________ At profit-maximizing output, P = $10, ATC = $15, and AVC = $13. Should the firm continue to produce in the short run?

2. __________ At profit-maximizing output, P = $10, ATC = $15, and AVC = $9. Should the firm continue to produce in the short run?

3. Assume a firm is facing these costs and revenues at a particular output:

Total Revenue	$100
Total Cost	$150
Fixed Cost	$60
Variable Cost	$90

A. __________ Is this firm earning a profit or a loss?

B. __________ Is the firm covering its average variable cost?

C. __________ Given your answer in 3B, should the firm keep producing or shut down?

4. Assume a firm is facing these costs and revenues at a particular output:

Total Revenue	$100
Total Cost	$150
Fixed Cost	$30
Variable Cost	$120

A. __________ Is this firm earning a profit or a loss?

B. __________ Is the firm covering its average variable cost?

C. __________ Given your answer in 4B, should the firm keep producing or shut down?

Make sure to return to the AP Key Concepts section above to check your understanding of this chapter's concepts important to AP coursework.

Economically Speaking

- **Break-Even Point** output where a firm makes no economic profit (total revenue = total cost)
- **Marginal Cost** change in total cost to produce one more product
- **Marginal Revenue** change in total revenue earned by selling one more product
- **Market Structure** characteristics of an industry that explain the behavior of firms
- **Monopolistic Competition** market structure in which a large number of firms produce slightly differentiated products
- **Monopoly** market structure in which only one firm is the sole seller of a product
- **MR = MC Rule** a firm maximizes profit (or minimizes loss) by producing where MR = MC
- **Oligopoly** market structure in which only a few firms produce a product
- **Price Taker** a firm must accept the market price set by supply and demand; it can't affect price
- **Pure (Perfect) Competition** market structure in which a large number of firms produce identical products
- **Total Cost** sum of all of the costs of production
- **Total Revenue** income to the firm from all products sold (price × quantity sold)

10 Chapter

Pure Competition in the Long Run

The previous chapter illustrated how the perfectly competitive firm maximizes profit or minimizes loss in the short run. Because plant and equipment are fixed in the short run, the firm has to use an output decision to maximize profit or minimize loss. But in the long run, firms in perfectly competitive market structures can enter or exit the industry. Chapter 10 introduces the causes and effects of these long-run adjustments in the market and the effects of such changes on allocative and productive efficiency.

Material from Chapter 10 appears on the AP Microeconomics exam in several multiple-choice questions, and a free-response question about the perfectly competitive firm's long-run decision making is common.

Key Concepts

Below is a summary of the chapter's concepts important to AP coursework. Upon completing the lessons that follow, return to these concepts to make sure you understand them and how the practice exercises you completed relate to them.

- In long-run equilibrium:
    - Industry supply equals demand, so no shortage or surplus exists.
    - The individual firm is a price taker, accepting the industry's equilibrium price.
    - The individual firm provides so little output that it cannot affect price.
    - The individual firm's price curve represents four measures: MR = P = AR = D.
    - The firm maximizes profit by producing at the output where MR = MC.
    - The firm earns no economic profit, because P = ATC at profit-maximizing output.
    - The market is "at rest," with no incentive for firms to enter or exit the industry.
- If industry demand increases:
    - In the short run:
        - Increased industry demand pushes up the price, which transfers to the firm.
        - The firm's MR = P = AR = D curve shifts upward to the new price.
        - The firm increases output to where the new MR = MC.
        - The firm earns an economic profit, because P > ATC.
    - In the long run:
        - Profit draws new firms into the industry, increasing supply and lowering price.
        - The price cut transfers to the firm, causing MR = P = AR = D to shift downward.

        - The firm reduces output to where the new MR = MC.
        - The firm earns no economic profit when P = ATC; long-run equilibrium returns.
- If industry demand decreases, the above scenario works in reverse, with firms exiting.
- Allocative efficiency is achieved in long-run equilibrium, because industry supply equals demand; no shortage or surplus exists and consumer and producer surplus are maximized.
- Productive efficiency is achieved in long-run equilibrium, because output is produced at minimum ATC (where MC intersects ATC); the firm is producing at lowest per-unit cost.
- If the firm's cost of production increases:
    - An increase in a variable cost causes the firm's MC, AVC, and ATC curves to shift up.
        - Output decreases because MR = MC to the left of the original output.
        - In the short run, the firm incurs a loss because P < ATC.
        - In the long run, firms exit the industry; supply falls and price rises.
    - An increase in per-unit tax or a reduction in per-unit subsidy has the same effect as an increase in variable cost.
    - An increase in a fixed cost causes the firm's ATC and AFC to shift upward.
        - Output does not change because MR and MC did not change.
        - In the short run, the firm incurs a loss because P < ATC.
        - In the long run, firms exit the industry; supply falls and price rises.
    - An increase in lump-sum tax or reduction in lump-sum subsidy has the same effect as an increase in fixed cost.
- If an individual firm can reduce its costs while the rest of the industry cannot, the firm can sustain economic profit for an extended period of time.

Now, let's examine more closely the following concepts from your textbook:

- **The Long-Run Adjustment Process in Pure Competition**
- **Pure Competition and Efficiency**
- **Technological Advance and Competition**

These sections were selected because the movement of multiple curves for short-run and long-run adjustments for industry and the firm can be complicated. Additional explanations and practice will help you fully understand the step-by-step processes involved in these adjustments.

The Long-Run Adjustment Process in Pure Competition

Refer to pages 201–203 of your textbook.

A CLOSER LOOK Long-Run Equilibrium

In Chapter 9, we examined profit maximization in the short run, when firms could not change plant size and the time frame was too short for firms to enter or leave the industry. Because firms could not affect the product price set in the industry, they maximized profit through output decisions.

Now we consider the long-run situation, where firms can enter or exit the industry. To simplify the analysis, we assume that firms in the industry are not changing plant size, that all firms in the industry have identical costs, and that this is a **constant-cost industry,** meaning that the entry or exit of firms does not change resource prices (due to changes in demand for those resources).

In long-run equilibrium, as shown in the graphs below, supply equals demand in the industry, so no shortage or surplus exists. The individual firm is a price taker, accepting the price set in the industry. The perfectly elastic demand curve for the firm is also the marginal revenue, price, and average revenue. The firm maximizes profit by producing where marginal revenue equals marginal cost. Marginal cost intersects average total cost at its minimum point, illustrating productive efficiency. In long-run equilibrium, MR = MC = ATC. At this output, the firm has minimized its average total cost and maximized its profit. While the firm is not earning an economic profit (P – ATC = 0), it is earning a normal profit, because the firm is earning as much profit as it could expect to earn in any other industry. In long-run equilibrium, the market is "at rest"; firms have no incentive to enter or leave the industry. The market maintains this equilibrium until industry supply or demand or costs of production change.

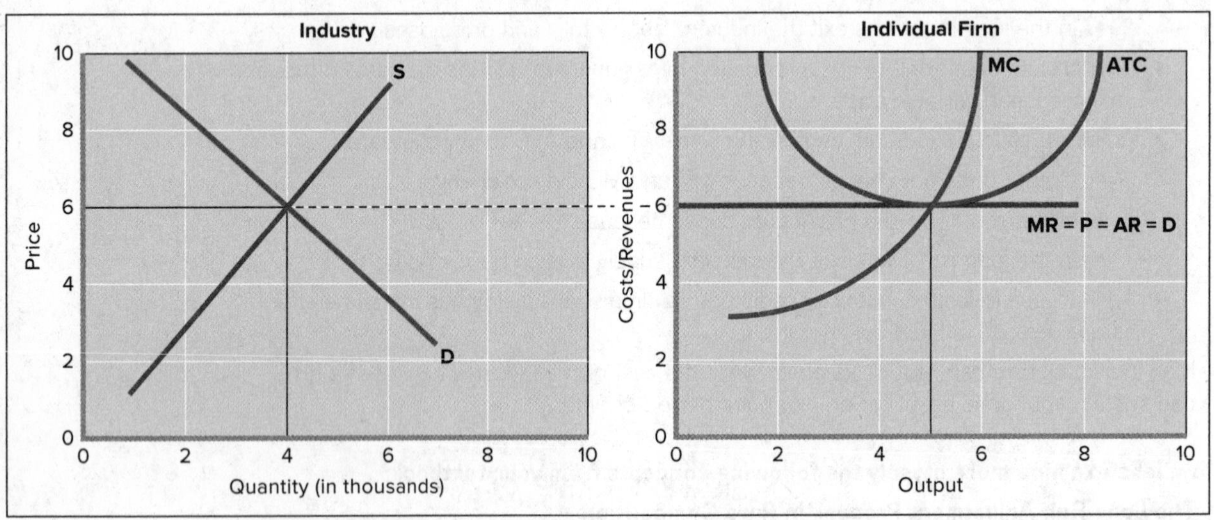

Keep in Mind

Some questions on the AP Microeconomics exam may give you details about a firm's costs and revenues at a particular output. Sketch the firm's cost and revenue curves as explained in the question, so you can see the relationships among the curves, and the answer may be more obvious.

Graphing Guidance

The graph for the perfectly competitive firm commonly appears on the AP Microeconomics exam. In some cases, you may be asked to draw the market in long-run equilibrium. In other cases, you may be asked to show a market out of equilibrium, with the firm making an economic profit or loss. Remember that the firm will *always* produce where MR = MC. You will need to position the ATC curve correctly to show the firm making a profit (P > ATC) or a loss (P < ATC). Be sure to completely label your graph!

Now let's assume that the market moves out of long-run equilibrium. If consumer income increases, demand for normal products increases from D_1 to D_2, as shown in the industry graph below. The increase in demand pushes the price in the industry up from \$50 to \$60. Because the individual firm is a price taker, the price to the firm also increases to \$60 by shifting the entire MR = P = AR = D curve directly upward. The individual firm is now out of long-run equilibrium. Using the MR = MC rule to determine profit-maximizing output, you can see that the new MR crosses the MC curve at a higher price—and a higher output. So the individual firm will increase its output in the short run. At the same time, the individual firm is earning economic profit, because P > ATC.

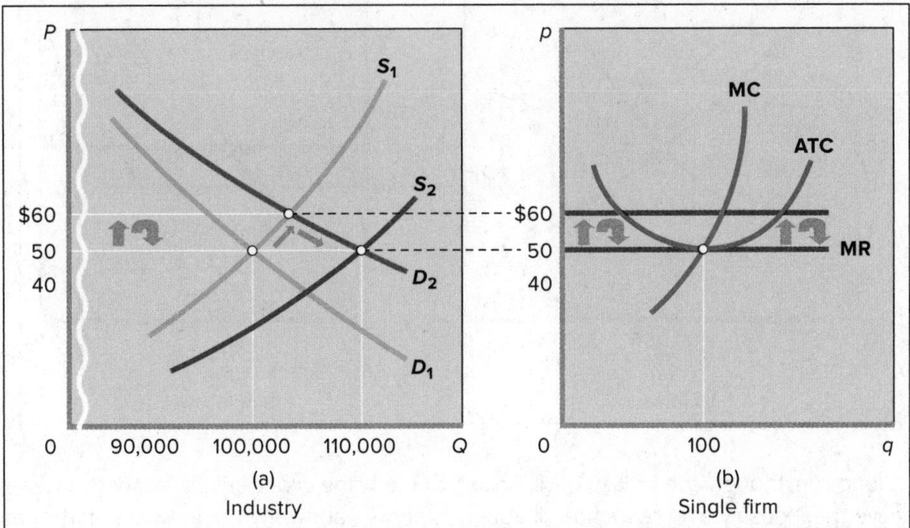

But in the long run, the industry adjusts. Economic profit draws new firms into the industry. As firms enter, supply increases from S_1 to S_2, as shown in the industry graph above. The increase in supply causes price to fall to $50 and MR falls back to $50 for the individual firm, as shown by the arrows turning back down. The firm again maximizes profit by producing where MR = MC, with economic profit falling to zero. The industry returns to long-run equilibrium, with the price at the original $50 and the output increased from 100,000 to 110,000 because more firms are producing the product.

Graphing Guidance

In the AP Exam, you may be asked to shade specific areas of your graph to indicate economic conditions and behavior in relation to long-run adjustment in pure competition. Refer to the individual firm graph above as you follow along the bulleted points below.

- Profit Per Unit: PPU = P – ATC. If MR has increased to $60 and the firm is producing at MR = MC, the profit per unit is the vertical distance between MR and ATC at the quantity produced. (Loss per unit follows the same formula, except the distance would be *above* the MR curve.)
- Total Profit: Profit = PPU × Output, so total profit is the area between the vertical profit per unit line and the dollar amounts of each on the left side of the graph. (Total loss follows the same formula, except the area would be *above* the MR curve.)
- Total Revenue: TR = P × Output, so total revenue is the area of the price, taken from the vertical axis to MR = MC, and then down to the horizontal axis.
- Total Cost: TC = ATC × Output, so total cost is the area of the ATC at profit-maximizing output, taken from the vertical axis to ATC, and then down to the horizontal axis.

Now let's assume the opposite situation occurs, with demand decreasing because consumer tastes change. Demand decreases from D_1 to D_3, as illustrated in the industry graph below. The decrease in demand pulls the industry price down from $50 to $40. Because the individual firm is a price taker, its MR = P = AR = D curve shifts directly down to $40, as well. The individual firm is again out of long-run equilibrium. Using the MR = MC rule, the firm now maximizes output at a lower price and lower output. The firm now experiences an economic loss, because the price does not cover the average total cost.

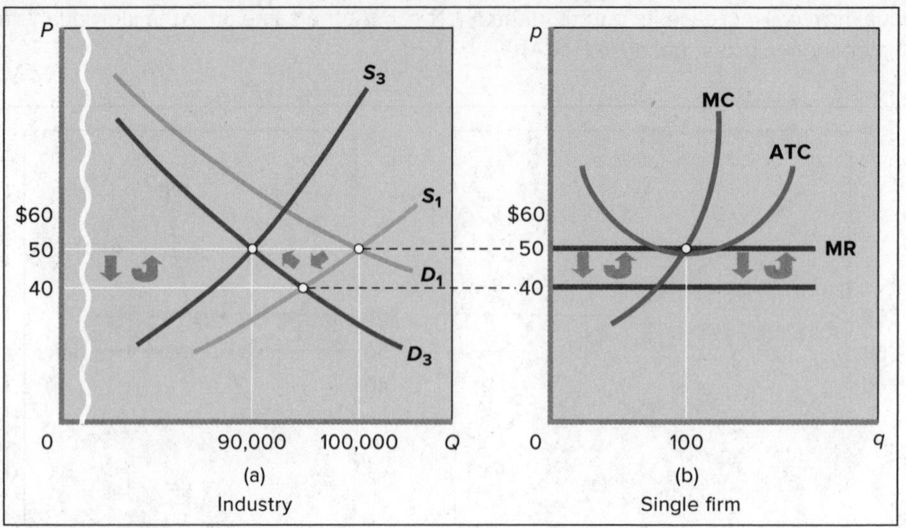

In the long run, though, the industry will adjust. Some firms experiencing economic losses will leave the industry. The reduction of supply is shown above by the leftward shift of the industry supply curve from S_1 to S_3. The decrease in supply causes price to increase, while industry output declines because fewer firms are in the industry. The increase in price from \$40 to \$50 carries over to the individual firm. The firm restores output to where MR = MC, and economic profit falls to zero because P = ATC.

PRACTICE Long-Run Equilibrium

1. In the blank graphs below, draw side-by-side graphs of the industry and firm in long-run equilibrium. For this exercise, assume that for the product you are graphing, researchers have discovered that the product offers significant health benefits. Draw the short-run changes for the industry and firm on your graph and answer the questions.

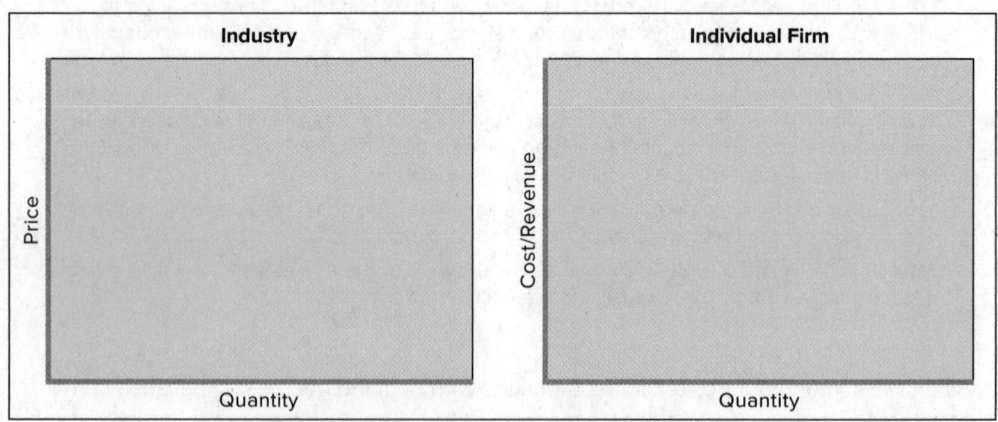

A. _________ Will industry demand increase, decrease, or remain the same?

B. _________ Will the market price increase, decrease, or remain the same?

C. _________ Will marginal revenue increase, decrease, or remain the same?

D. _________ Will the firm's output increase, decrease, or remain the same?

E. _________ Will the firm earn a short-run economic profit or loss?

Now draw the long-run adjustments in the industry and individual firm graphs above. Then answer the questions below about what will happen in the long run.

F. _________ Will firms enter or exit the industry?

G. _________ Will industry supply increase, decrease, or remain the same?

H. _________ Will the market price increase, decrease, or remain the same?

I. _________ Will marginal revenue increase, decrease, or remain the same?

J. _________ Will the firm's output increase, decrease, or remain the same?

K. _________ After long-run adjustment, what is the firm's economic profit?

2. In the blank graphs below, draw side-by-side graphs of the industry and the individual firm, with the firm incurring an economic loss. Then show how the industry and firm will adjust to long-run equilibrium and answer the questions.

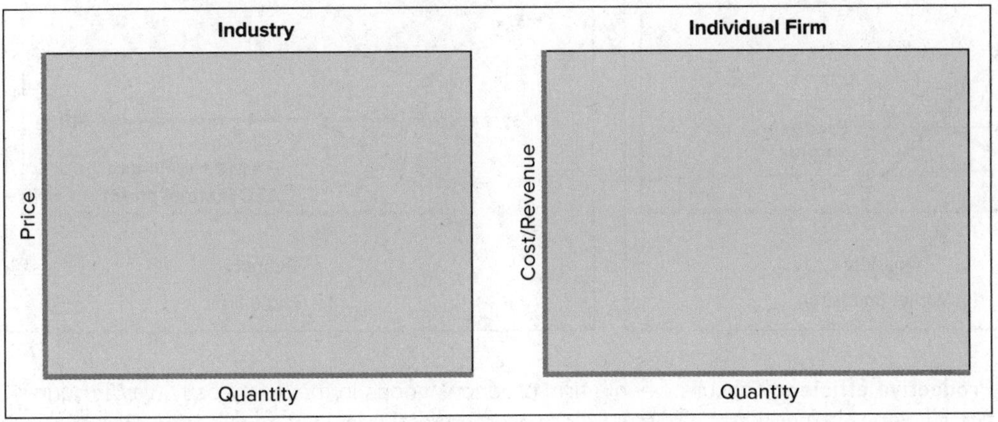

A. _________ Will firms enter or exit the industry?

B. _________ Will industry supply increase, decrease, or remain the same?

C. _________ Will the market price increase, decrease, or remain the same?

D. _________ Will marginal revenue increase, decrease, or remain the same?

E. _________ Will the firm's output increase, decrease, or remain the same?

F. _________ After long-run adjustment, what is the firm's economic profit?

Pure Competition and Efficiency

Refer to pages 205–208 of your textbook.

A CLOSER LOOK Allocative Efficiency and Productive Efficiency

In long-run equilibrium, the individual firm maximizes profit by producing where price (and marginal revenue) = marginal cost = minimum average total cost. While a firm may experience an economic profit or loss in the short run, the long-run movement of firms in and out of the industry reduces economic profit (or loss) to zero. The firm still earns a normal profit, but no economic profit.

Allocative efficiency occurs when society's scarce resources are used to produce the mix of products consumers most want. Allocative efficiency is found at the output where supply equals demand on the industry graph below. At the equilibrium price, every product produced is sold; no surplus or shortage exists. At this point, consumer and producer surplus are maximized. Remember, **consumer surplus** is the difference between the maximum price the consumer is willing to pay and the price charged (the green area of the graph). **Producer surplus** is the difference between the minimum price the producer is willing to accept and the price charged (the blue area of the graph). If the industry produced at any output other than equilibrium, a deadweight loss would result and efficiency would be lost.

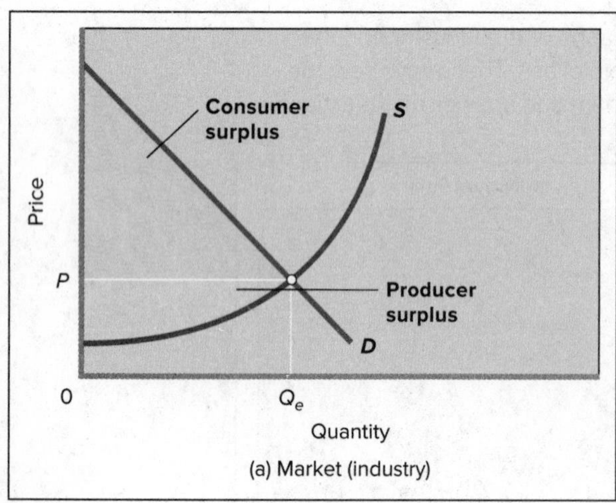

(a) Market (industry)

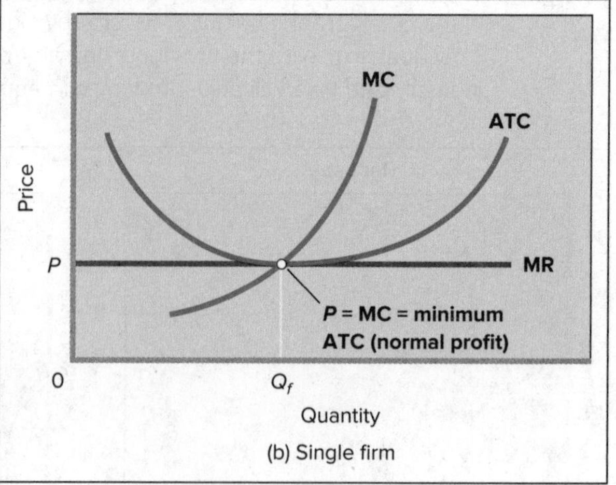

(b) Single firm

Productive efficiency occurs when a firm produces goods in the least costly way. Productive efficiency is found at the output where average total cost is at its minimum. Remember that the marginal cost curve intersects the average total cost at its minimum, because if the marginal cost is lower than the average, it pulls the average down, and if the marginal cost is higher than the average, it pulls the average up. In the graph for the individual firm above, you can see that in long-run equilibrium, MR = MC = ATC, so a perfectly competitive firm in long-run equilibrium achieves productive efficiency.

Economists consider perfect competition to be the perfect model of the "invisible hand" at work. Firms freely enter and exit the industry and determine profit-maximizing output. Productive and allocative efficiency are achieved, keeping prices down for consumers and ensuring that resources are used to produce the mix of goods society desires. When changes occur in the market, firms respond to profits and losses in the short run by changing output, and the industry changes in the long run as firms enter or exit, until long-run equilibrium and productive and allocative efficiency are once again achieved.

PRACTICE Allocative Efficiency and Productive Efficiency

1. __________ Is allocative efficiency shown on the industry or individual firm graph?

2. Allocative efficiency occurs where the __________ curve intersects the __________ curve.

3. __________ Is productive efficiency shown on the industry graph or individual firm graph?

4. Productive efficiency occurs where the __________ curve intersects the __________ curve.

5. __________ If industry demand significantly increases, will the firm maintain productive efficiency in the short run?

6. __________ After long run adjustments occur, will the firm achieve productive efficiency?

Technological Advance and Competition

Refer to pages 208–211 of your textbook.

A CLOSER LOOK Technological Advance and Competition

Changes in production costs can also change the firm's output and cause short-run profits or losses. If a variable cost such as wage increases, the MC, AVC, and ATC all shift upward. MC crosses MR to the left of the firm's original output, so the firm reduces its output in the short run to where MR = MC. Because ATC is higher than price at that output, the firm incurs a loss in the short run, but continues to produce as long as the price is higher than AVC. In the long run, industry supply decreases as a result of lower output by firms and some firms exiting the industry. As supply decreases, marginal revenue for each firm rises and the market returns to long-run equilibrium, with firms producing where MR = MC = ATC at the higher price, and the industry at a new equilibrium at a higher price and lower quantity. An increase in **per-unit tax** or a reduction in **per-unit subsidy** has the same effect as an increase in variable cost.

Changes in fixed costs, such as property taxes or operating licenses, affect only AFC and ATC. Because these costs do not affect marginal cost, the MC curve does not shift, and output does not change in the short run. However, the increase in cost causes ATC to shift upward, so the firm incurs a short-run loss. In the long run, industry supply will decrease as firms exit the industry. The market price and thus marginal revenue to the firm will increase, and the firm will again return to long-run equilibrium to produce at the output where MR = MC = ATC, earning zero economic profit. An increase in a **lump-sum tax** or reduction of a **lump-sum subsidy** has the same effect as an increase in fixed cost.

Up to this point, we have assumed that every firm in the industry has identical costs and revenues. But what happens if just one firm in an industry discovers a way to produce the product at a lower cost? Perhaps a technician discovers an innovation to increase production speed. Or a systems engineer changes the production process. Or management institutes a rewards program or inspires workers to produce at a faster pace. What if that one firm could manage to keep its innovation a secret? The firm could actually reduce its MC and ATC, maximizing profit at a higher output and earning economic profit. If the firm can keep its secret, it can actually sustain economic profit for an extended length of time.

Caution

Although firms may make economic profit or suffer loss in the short run, the long-run entry or exit of firms in the industry eventually returns the market to equilibrium, where firms earn zero economic profit. It is important to remember the difference between normal and economic profit. The firm's accountant is still showing a normal profit, which covers the firm's opportunity costs. But beyond that normal profit, there is no economic (or excess) profit to draw other firms into the industry.

Keep in Mind

It is very important to be able to distinguish the effects of changes in *per-unit* and *lump-sum* production costs. Changes in per-unit costs affect variable cost and ATC. Changes in these costs also shift marginal cost, so the firm's output changes to produce at MR = MC. Changes in lump-sum costs affect fixed cost and ATC. However, changes in these costs do *not* affect the firm's marginal cost curve, so the firm will continue to produce at the same output in the short run. Free response questions have asked students to make this distinction to correctly explain the effects of changes in production costs.

PRACTICE Technological Advance and Competition

In the space below, draw side-by-side graphs of the industry in long-run equilibrium. Now assume the government increases the minimum wage, and all firms in the industry face an increase in labor costs. Draw the short-run changes for the firm on your graph and answer the questions below.

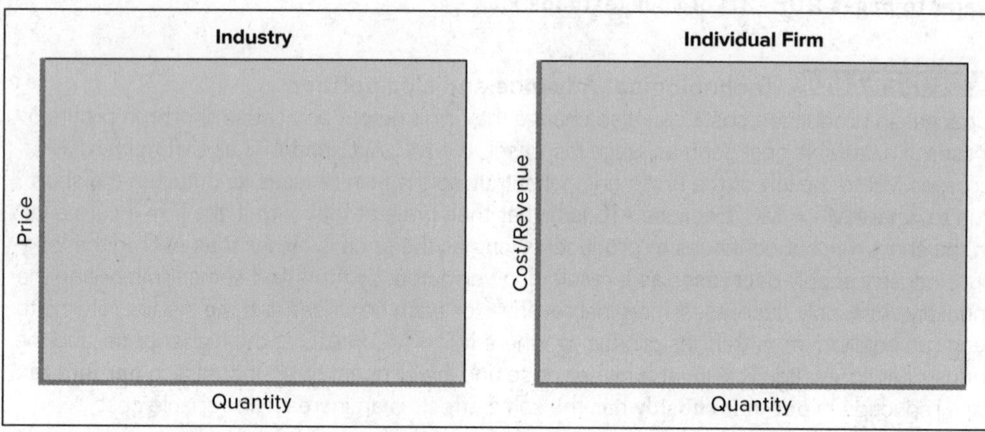

1. __________ Will average fixed cost increase, decrease, or remain the same?

2. __________ Will average variable cost increase, decrease, or remain the same?

3. __________ Will average total cost increase, decrease, or remain the same?

4. __________ Will marginal cost increase, decrease, or remain the same?

5. __________ Will marginal revenue increase, decrease, or remain the same?

6. __________ Will output increase, decrease, or remain the same?

7. __________ Will the firm experience a short-run profit or a short-run loss?

Given your answers above, answer the following questions about what will happen in the long run.

8. __________ Will firms enter or exit the industry?

9. __________ Will industry supply increase, decrease, or remain the same?

10. __________ Will the market price increase, decrease, or remain the same?

11. __________ Given your answer to #10, will marginal revenue rise, fall, or remain the same?

12. __________ Given your answer to #11, will the firm's output rise, fall, or remain the same?

13. __________ After adjustment to long-run equilibrium, what is the firm's economic profit?

Answer the questions below about specific scenarios for firms in a perfectly competitive industry.

14. __________ If one firm is able to lower its costs in a way that its competitors cannot, can that firm sustain the economic profit, or will new firms enter the industry?

15. __________ If the government wanted to provide a subsidy in a way that would not change output for each firm, should it use a per-unit or lump-sum subsidy?

16. __________ If the government wanted to lower taxes in a way that would increase output for firms and the industry, should it use a per-unit or lump-sum tax cut?

Make sure to return to the AP Key Concepts section above to check your understanding of this chapter's concepts important to AP coursework.

Economically Speaking

- **Allocative Efficiency** society's scarce resources are used to produce the mix of products consumers most want to consume
- **Constant-Cost Industry** the entry or exit of firms does not affect the price of resources
- **Consumer Surplus** the difference between the maximum price the consumer is willing to pay and the market price of the product
- **Lump-Sum Subsidy** government makes a one-time payment to a firm, not related to output
- **Lump-Sum Tax** government imposes a one-time tax on a firm, not related to output
- **Per-Unit Subsidy** government pays a firm a certain amount for each product produced
- **Per-Unit Tax** government imposes a specific tax on a firm for each product produced
- **Producer Surplus** the difference between the minimum price the producer is willing to accept and the market price of the product
- **Productive Efficiency** the minimum average total cost of production

11 Chapter

Pure Monopoly

While the perfectly competitive firm has no control over price, the monopoly has the power necessary to determine both the price and output of its product. The monopoly model also shows us important differences from perfect competition in terms of efficiency and effects on producer and consumer surplus. Chapter 11 focuses on the ways monopolies develop, how output and price are determined, the effects of monopoly behavior, and government regulation. The monopoly model is important to understanding the oligopoly and monopolistic competition, which will be covered in Chapters 12 and 13.

Material from Chapter 11 appears on the AP Microeconomics exam in a large number of multiple-choice questions, and a free-response question about decision making in at least one of the market structures is part of nearly every AP Microeconomics exam.

Key Concepts

Below is a summary of the chapter's concepts important to AP coursework. Upon completing the lessons that follow, return to these concepts to make sure you understand them and how the practice exercises you completed relate to them.

- A monopoly is an industry with one producer, no close substitutes, and total barriers to entry.
- Barriers to entry allow monopolies to hold market power; as price makers, they set prices.
- Natural monopolies use economies of scale as their barrier to entry by competitors.
- Because a monopoly is the only firm in the industry, the industry demand is the firm's demand.
  - Monopoly's demand is downward-sloping; average revenue and price are on this curve.
  - Marginal revenue is lower than the demand curve, because for the firm to sell more products, it must lower the price for all of the products it sells.
  - When marginal revenue is positive, total revenue rises; when MR is negative, TR falls.
  - The firm sets its price in the elastic portion of the demand curve.
- The monopolist maximizes profit by producing where marginal revenue = marginal cost.
  - To set the price, draw a vertical line from MR = MC up to the demand curve.
  - The profit per unit is price (on the demand curve) minus average total cost.

- The total profit is profit per unit times the quantity sold.
- The total revenue is the area below and to the left of the point where price is set (P × Q).
- The total cost is the area below and to the left of ATC where quantity is set.
- The total profit is the area above total cost within the total revenue area.

- A monopoly cannot charge any price it wants; it is constrained by the demand curve.
- A monopoly can sustain long-run economic profit because barriers to entry prevent competitors from entering the industry; the perfectly competitive firm cannot sustain economic profit.
- A monopoly incurs economic loss when ATC is greater than price at profit-maximizing output.
    - If P > AVC and the monopolist sees the loss as a short-run issue, the firm can operate.
    - If P < AVC or the monopolist foresees a long-run loss, the firm should shut down.
- If a variable (per-unit) cost increases, MC, AVC, and ATC increase; output falls and price rises.
- If a fixed (lump-sum) cost increases, AFC and ATC increase; output and price are unchanged.
- The monopoly does not achieve allocative or productive efficiency.
- The monopoly restricts output to raise the price; a deadweight loss of consumer and producer surplus develops in a triangle to the left of allocative efficiency.
- Monopolists can use price discrimination, selling the same product at different prices; perfect price discrimination eliminates consumer surplus and the firm produces at allocative efficiency.
- Governments may choose to regulate monopolies to improve the outcome for society.
    - Setting a price ceiling at socially optimal price (MC = D) causes the monopoly to produce at allocative efficiency—more output at a lower price. The firm may incur an economic loss at this price, so government may have to subsidize the firm to keep it in business.
    - Setting a price ceiling at fair-return price (ATC = D) allows the firm a normal profit, but not economic profit. The firm produces less at a higher price than at socially optimal price, but avoids the problem of needing a subsidy to keep the firm in business.

Now, let's examine more closely the following concepts from your textbook:

- **Monopoly Demand**
- **Output and Price Determination**
- **Economic Effects of Monopoly**
- **Regulated Monopoly**

These sections were selected because it is critically important to be able to draw and interpret the monopoly market model. This model is the basis for the oligopoly and monopolistic competition models and can help you to understand the firm's behavior in words and in graphs.

Monopoly Demand

Refer to pages 217–220 of your textbook.

A CLOSER LOOK MR is Less Than Price and the Monopolist Sets Prices in the Elastic Region of Demand

A **monopoly** is a market structure with only one producer, no close substitutes, and complete barriers to entry. Unlike a perfectly competitive firm, a monopoly is a price maker that determines its own output and market price. Because the monopoly faces a downward-sloping demand curve, it can restrict output in order to raise the market price. Monopolies include local electric, water, and natural gas companies, as well as pharmaceutical companies and other firms that hold patents on their products.

Monopolies hold **market power,** the power to determine market prices, because of **barriers to entry**—factors that prevent other firms from entering the industry. One important barrier is economies of scale; the larger the firm, the more efficient it becomes. A **natural monopoly** achieves economies of scale, with ATC continuing to fall over such a large range of output that it is more cost-effective to have only one firm in the industry. New firms face higher costs of production and cannot compete.

The government creates barriers by granting patents, protecting ownership rights to support investment in research and development. Government also creates barriers by licensing producers, from teachers to cosmetologists to electricians. Firms create barriers by controlling resources necessary to produce the product, lowering prices to undercut the competition, making deals with retailers to reinforce their monopoly status, and finding ways to make a competitor's product more expensive or less desirable. In studying the monopoly model, we assume that barriers keep out all competitors, government does not regulate the firm, and the monopoly charges all consumers the same price for the product.

The most important difference between a perfectly competitive firm and a monopoly is the demand curve. Remember, the perfectly competitive firm was a price taker, accepting the price set in the industry. So the firm had a perfectly elastic, horizontal demand curve, with the marginal revenue equal to price. Because it is the only firm in the industry, a monopoly has only one graph, unlike the side-by-side graphs for perfect competition. Because a monopoly is the only producer, industry demand *is* the firm's demand. Therefore, a monopoly faces a downward-sloping demand curve; quantity demanded increases as price falls. This difference has important ramifications for price and output decisions, most significantly that the monopoly is a **price maker** with the power to determine the market price.

The marginal revenue curve is lower than the demand (price) curve. For the firm to sell more products, it must lower the price for *all* the goods it sells, not just the last one. Therefore, the **marginal revenue**—the change in total revenue from selling one more product—will be *lower* than the price charged for that product. Say a firm sells 5 T-shirts for $10 each, for total revenue of $50. If the firm wants to sell the 6th T-shirt, it must lower its price of T-shirts to $9—for all of them. Now the firm sells 6 T-shirts for $9 each, for total revenue of $54. So while the price of the T-shirt is $9, the marginal revenue to the firm is just $4 (total revenue increased from $50 to $54). The marginal revenue is less than the price. Average revenue, price, and demand are all represented on the higher curve for the monopoly.

Keep in Mind

The concept of marginal revenue being lower than demand has frequently appeared on the multiple-choice and free-response sections of the AP Microeconomics exam. It is important to understand and be able to explain the reason for this relationship: in order for the firm to sell more products, it must lower price for *all* of the products sold. It is also important to remember that MR = P = AR = D *only* for perfectly competitive firms. Marginal revenue separates from demand in all other market structures.

As illustrated in the graph below, as marginal revenue falls, the growth in total revenue slows. While marginal revenue is positive, the sale of additional products adds to the total revenue of the firm, but each additional sale adds less and less revenue. At the point where the marginal revenue of the next product is zero, crossing through the bottom axis of the graph, total revenue is maximized, reaching its peak. So if, for some reason, the firm wanted to maximize its total revenue, it would produce output at the point where marginal revenue is zero. After that point, each additional product sold results in a negative marginal revenue. The product price is positive, but the reduction in price for all of the earlier units overwhelms that price, so marginal revenue becomes negative and the total revenue of the firm begins to fall. You may remember a similar relationship from Chapter 7; when marginal utility fell below zero, it caused total utility to fall. In Chapter 8 we saw the same relationship; when marginal product became negative, total product fell.

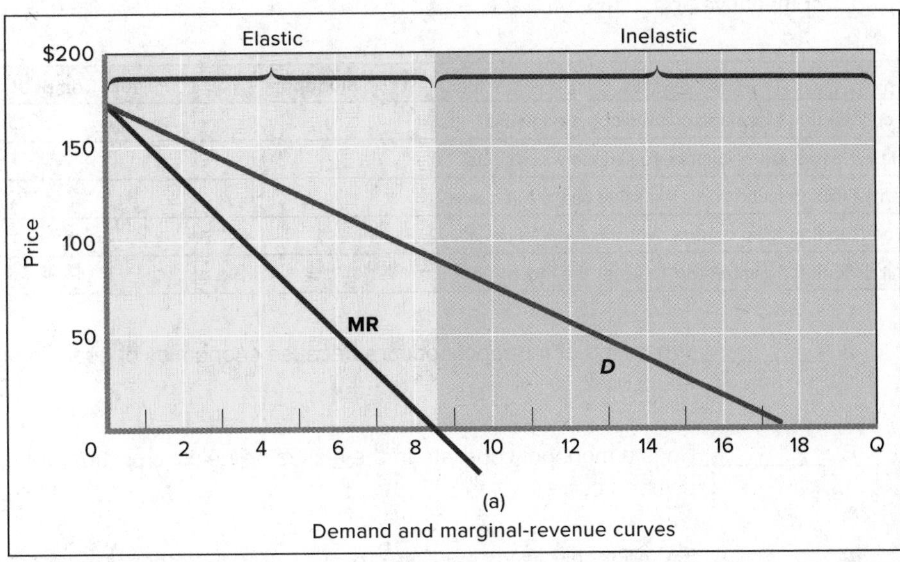

(a)
Demand and marginal-revenue curves

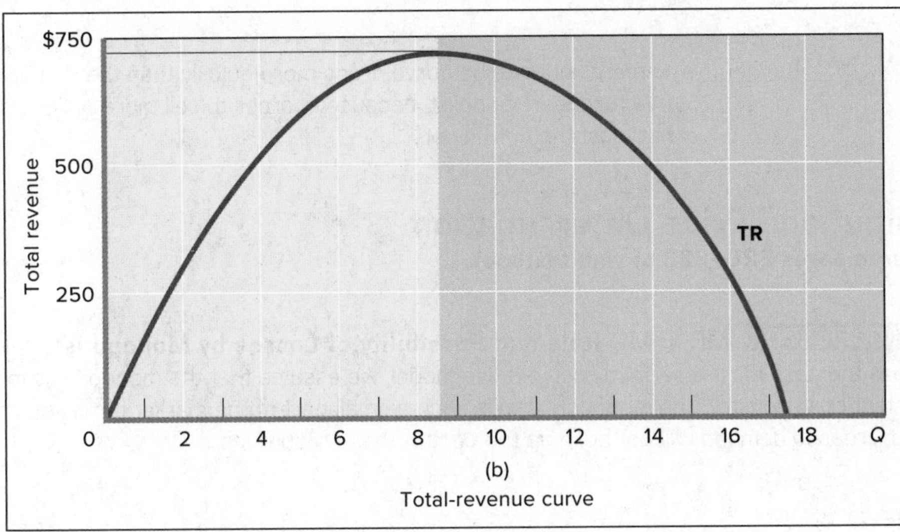

(b)
Total-revenue curve

Another effect of a downward-sloping demand curve is that the firm will set its price in the elastic portion of the demand curve, as shown in the first graph on the previous page. The firm will never choose to produce where the marginal revenue is negative, because the output would result in a lower total revenue for the firm at the same time that total cost is rising; therefore, the firm would experience lower profit in that range of production. Because the monopoly seeks to maximize profit, the firm will set its output in the elastic portion of the demand curve, to the left of where marginal revenue falls to zero.

PRACTICE MR is Less Than Price and the Monopolist Sets Prices in the Elastic Region of Demand

1. Complete this comparison table for the monopoly firm and the perfectly competitive firm.

	Monopoly	Perfect Competition
A. Does the firm's demand curve slope downward?		
B. Must the firm lower its price to sell more products?		
C. Is the firm's demand curve the same as the MR curve?		
D. Does the firm have control over the product price?		
E. Is it difficult for competitors to enter the industry?		

2. __________ What kind of monopoly occurs because economies of scale improve efficiency?

3. __________ Does a monopoly operate in the elastic or inelastic portion of its demand curve?

4. __________ If a monopoly earns economic profit, why don't other firms enter the industry?

5. __________ The marginal revenue curve drops more quickly than the demand curve for the monopolist, because in order to sell more products, what must the firm lower?

Output and Price Determination

Refer to pages 220–223 of your textbook.

A CLOSER LOOK MR = MC Rule and Possibility of Losses by Monopolist

As was the case for the perfectly competitive model, we assume that the monopoly is in a constant-cost industry. The monopoly firm is such a small part of the market for resources that increased demand will not push up the cost of those resources.

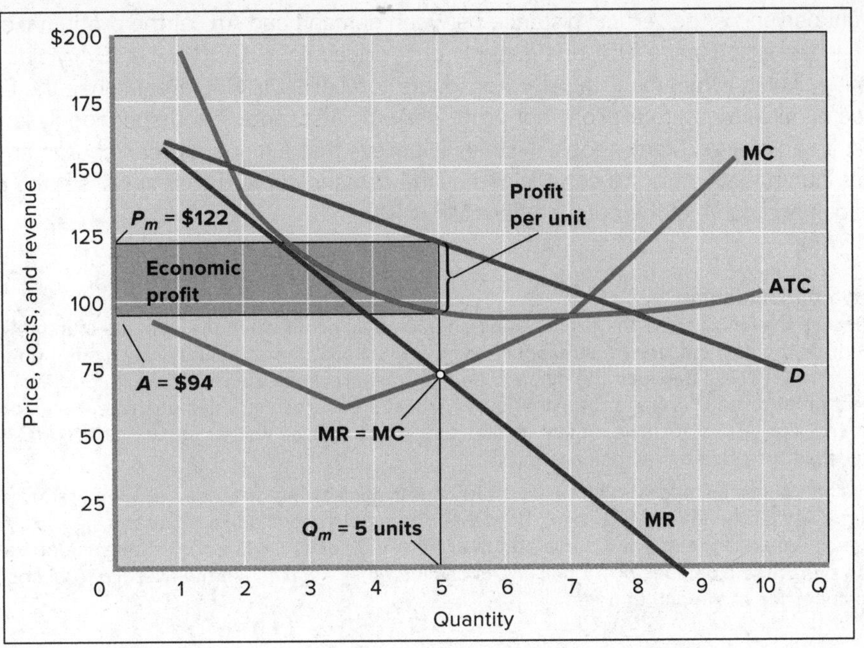

Using the same **MR = MC rule** as a perfectly competitive firm, the monopolist maximizes profit at the output where marginal revenue equals marginal cost. As long as the firm receives revenue greater than or equal to the cost of producing the next unit of output, the firm should produce it. In the graph above, the firm maximizes profit where MR = MC, at 5 units of output. To find the price, extend the line at the selected output up to the demand curve. Because consumers are willing and able to pay that price, that is the price the firm will charge. In this case, the firm charges a price of $122 for its products.

Graphing Guidance
When determining the monopoly price, be very careful to go all the way up to the demand curve. Students often make the mistake of treating the MR = MC point similarly to a supply and demand equilibrium, setting the price at that same point. Consumers are willing and able to pay the higher price, and charging that higher price maximizes the firm's profit.

To calculate profit, you must compare the price to the average total cost at the MR = MC output. Just as was the case for the perfectly competitive firm, you can calculate the profit two different ways:

Profit = Total Revenue – Total Cost
Total Revenue = Price × Output
Total Cost = ATC × Output
Profit = Profit per Unit × Output
Profit per Unit = Price – Average Total Cost

The total revenue ($122 × 5) is the area below and to the left of the profit-maximizing price point in the graph above. Total cost ($94 × 5) is the portion of that area below and to the left of ATC at that output. Economic profit ($28 × 5 = $140) is the portion of that area above and to the left of ATC at that output.

Profit per unit is the vertical distance between demand and ATC at the profit-maximizing output. In the graph (page 105), at a quantity of 5, price minus ATC ($122 – $94) yields $28 of profit per unit. When the firm sells 5 products, total profit is $140. Remember, the firm is focused on maximizing *total* profit, not profit *per unit*. Also, note that the monopoly is limited in what it can charge. Many people mistakenly believe that a monopoly can charge any price it wants, but in reality, it is still constrained by the demand curve. The firm will set the price on the demand curve at the output where MR = MC.

Graphing Guidance

To ensure that you'll show the firm earning an economic profit when drawing the monopoly, first draw the demand, marginal revenue, and marginal cost curves. Then draw a point on the marginal cost curve between the demand and marginal revenue curves. Make that point the lowest point on your average total cost curve. This tip ensures you'll demonstrate marginal cost crossing ATC at its lowest point (productive efficiency), as well as show that the ATC is lower than the price on the demand curve.

When determining profit, be very careful to only look at the distance between the price and the ATC at the MR = MC output. Students often make the mistake of measuring the distance between the demand curve and the MR = MC point, viewing *that* difference as the profit per unit. Remember, profit per unit is calculated by subtracting the average total cost from the price at the output point.

Keep in Mind

You must be able to draw a monopoly graph to determine profit-maximizing output, the price, and the area of economic profit. The AP Microeconomics exam includes several multiple-choice questions involving the monopoly, as well as almost always asking a free-response question requiring you to draw a graph for a firm in one of the four market structures. Sketching a graph can help you to visualize the market and improve your chance of success in correctly answering the questions.

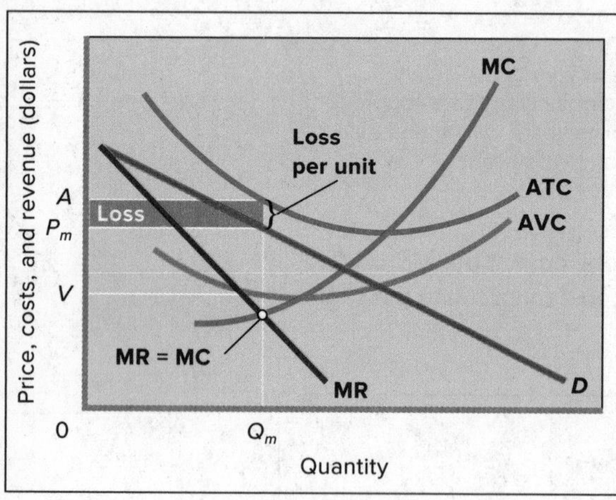

A perfectly competitive firm can earn short-run economic profit. But in the long run, the profit motive draws other firms into the industry, lowering the price and marginal revenue to the firm until economic profit is reduced to zero. A monopolist, however, can sustain economic profit due to barriers to entry. Because no new firms are able to enter the industry, no long-run adjustment occurs for monopolies.

While the monopoly can earn a profit, it can also sustain a loss, as shown in the graph. A loss occurs when the firm's ATC is greater than the price (on the demand curve) at the MR = MC output. If a firm incurs a loss, should it remain in operation? The rule for perfect competition is the same for all four market structures. If price is greater than or equal to the firm's average variable cost, the firm should remain in operation in the short run. But if the firm cannot even recover its variable costs to produce the additional output, the firm should shut down. It is important to note that because there is no long-run adjustment of other firms leaving the industry, the firm has to make its own decision of whether to shut down in the long run. If the firm is convinced that losses will persist in the long run, the firm will likely shift its resources to a more profitable opportunity or shut down altogether.

As with the perfectly competitive firm, cost changes for the monopoly shift the cost curves directly up and down, because the curves represent the costs at each output. If a variable (per-unit) cost increases, MC, AVC, and ATC all increase. Because the new MC = MR at a lower output, the firm produces less output at the higher cost. Price, set on the demand curve above where MR = MC, is higher as a result of the lower output. If a variable (per-unit) cost decreases, MC, AVC, and ATC all shift downward, the firm increases output, and the price falls. If a fixed (lump-sum) cost increases, only AFC and ATC increase. Because MC did not change, output and price do not change. With a higher ATC, the firm's profit decreases, but nothing else changes. If a fixed (lump-sum) cost decreases, AFC and ATC shift downward. While output and price remain the same, the firm's profit increases.

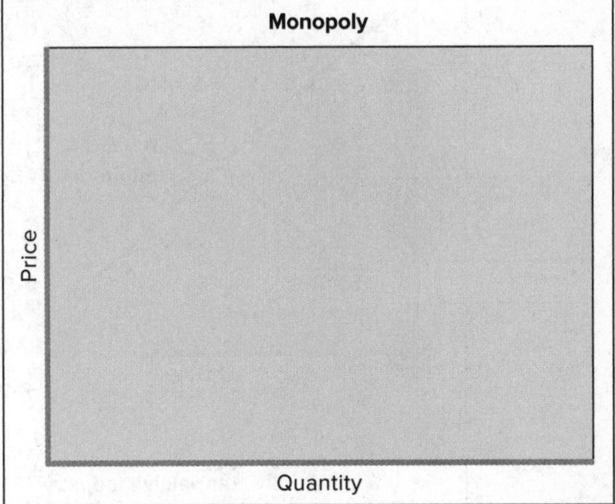

PRACTICE MR = MC Rule and Possibility of Losses by Monopolist

1. Draw a graph showing a monopoly earning long-run economic profit.
   A. Indicate the profit-maximizing quantity of output.
   B. Indicate the price the monopoly would charge consumers.
   C. Shade and label the area of economic profit.

2. Complete this comparison table for the monopoly firm and the perfectly competitive firm.

	Monopoly	Perfect Competition
A. Does the firm have a U-shaped ATC curve?		
B. Does MC = ATC at the lowest point on the ATC curve?		
C. Does the firm maximize profit at MR = MC?		
D. At the profit-maximizing output, does P = MR?		
E. In the long run, does the firm earn economic profit?		

3. Complete this comparison table for loss-minimizing monopolies receiving a subsidy.

	Lump-Sum Subsidy	Per-Unit Subsidy
A. What will the subsidy do to marginal cost?		
B. Given (A), what happens to the firm's output?		
C. Given (A), what happens to the deadweight loss?		
D. Given (A), what happens to the consumer surplus?		
E. With a subsidy, what happens to ATC and losses?		

Economic Effects of Monopoly

Refer to pages 223–227 of your textbook.

A CLOSER LOOK Price, Output, and Efficiency

The perfectly competitive model and the monopoly model, the extremes of the four market structures, demonstrate significant differences in efficiency, output, and price.

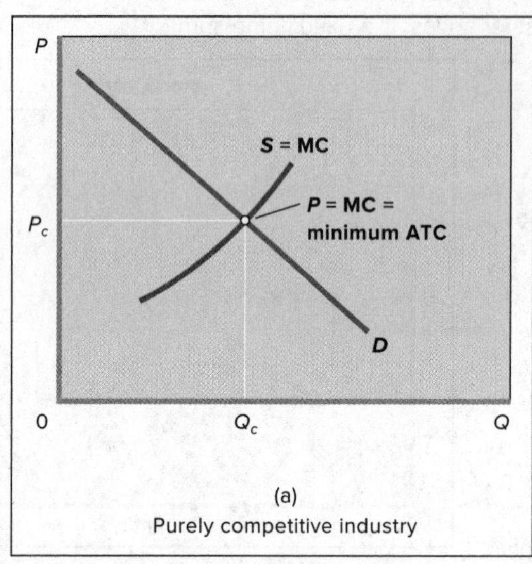

(a)
Purely competitive industry

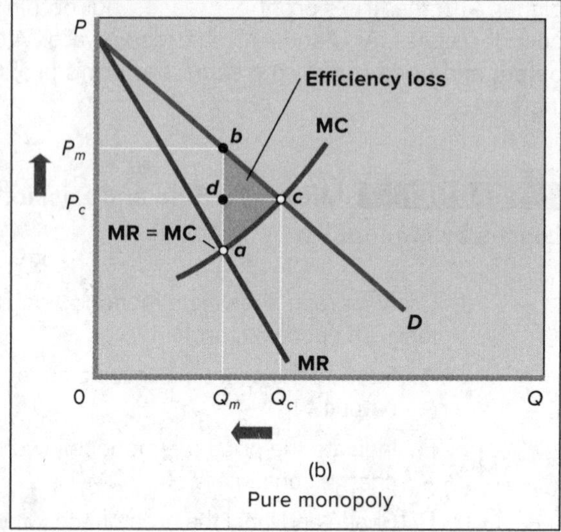

(b)
Pure monopoly

First, allocative and productive efficiency are achieved in perfect competition. As shown in the left graph above, the industry produces output where supply equals demand, and firms produce where MC = ATC. The monopoly does not achieve either efficiency. It maximizes profit by producing where MR = MC, at an output lower than that required to achieve allocative efficiency. **Deadweight loss,** the loss of consumer and producer surplus due to the monopoly output decision, is illustrated by the triangle to the left of the point of allocative efficiency (where MC = D) in the right graph above. Price exceeds both MC and minimum ATC at profit-maximizing output, so productive efficiency is not met by the monopoly.

Second, a monopoly produces fewer products and charges a higher price than a perfectly competitive industry. Monopolists maximize profit at MR = MC, less than allocative efficiency at MC = D. The monopolist then sets price on the demand curve, higher than a perfectly competitive firm would charge.

Third, a monopoly can sustain long-run profit because price > ATC and barriers prevent firms from entering the industry. Perfectly competitive firms may enjoy short-run profit, but in the long run, firms enter and lower the price, lowering the firm's marginal revenue until economic profit returns to zero.

Keep in Mind

Questions comparing the perfectly competitive and monopoly models are a standard feature of both the multiple-choice and free-response portions of the AP Microeconomics exam. It is important to be able to correctly graph and label both models, including the area of deadweight loss for the monopoly.

Graphing Guidance
Deadweight loss is the area of the vertical distance between MR and D at profit-maximizing output (MR = MC), over to allocative efficiency (MC = D). The market always seeks equilibrium, and for the monopoly, that equilibrium is where MC = D. The arrow of deadweight loss points to that equilibrium.

Up to this point, we have assumed that a monopoly charges all consumers the same price for a product. But the monopolist is able to engage in **price discrimination,** selling a product at more than one price when price differences are not justified by differences in the cost of production. You have likely seen price discrimination, such as a special price for movie tickets for children and senior citizens, or discount cards for frequent shoppers at a store. Airlines charge lower fares for tickets purchased well in advance, when people have more elastic demand. But airlines charge higher prices to last-minute travelers with inelastic demand. If a monopolist were able to engage in perfect price discrimination, rather than setting price above MR = MC on the demand curve for all consumers, the firm would set individual prices for each individual consumer, based on her willingness and ability to pay. Consumer surplus would be eliminated, and the firm would increase output to allocative efficiency. Price discrimination is common and legal in the United States, as long as it is not used to prevent firms from entering the industry.

PRACTICE Price, Output, and Efficiency

1. Draw a graph for a monopoly earning long-run economic profit.
   A. Indicate the profit-maximizing quantity of output.
   B. Indicate the price the monopoly would charge consumers.
   C. Indicate the quantity at the point of allocative efficiency.
   D. Indicate the quantity at the point of productive efficiency.
   E. Shade and label the area of economic profit.
   F. Stripe and label the area of deadweight loss.

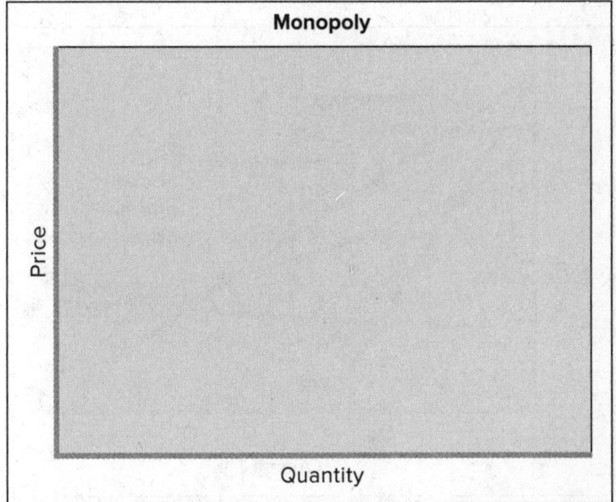

2. Complete this comparison table for the monopoly firm and the perfectly competitive firm.

	Monopoly	Perfect Competition
A. In the long run, is allocative efficiency achieved?		
B. In the long run, is productive efficiency achieved?		
C. Which firm has a higher price; which has a lower price?		
D. Which firm has more output; which has less output?		
E. Can the firm practice price discrimination?		

3. ________ Does a monopoly underallocate or overallocate resources to make products?

4. ________ If the firm produced at allocative efficiency, rather than profit-maximizing output, would consumer surplus increase, decrease, or remain the same?

5. ________ If perfect price discrimination occurs, what would happen to consumer surplus?

6. ________ If perfect price discrimination occurs, will a firm's output increase or decrease?

Regulated Monopoly

Refer to pages 229–232 of your textbook.

A CLOSER LOOK Socially Optimal Price and Fair-Return Price

Natural monopolies, such as public utilities, are regulated by state and local governments to limit prices and ensure product quality. Because the monopolist reduces output and raises price to maximize profit, and does not achieve productive or allocative efficiency, governments attempt to improve the outcome for society through regulation.

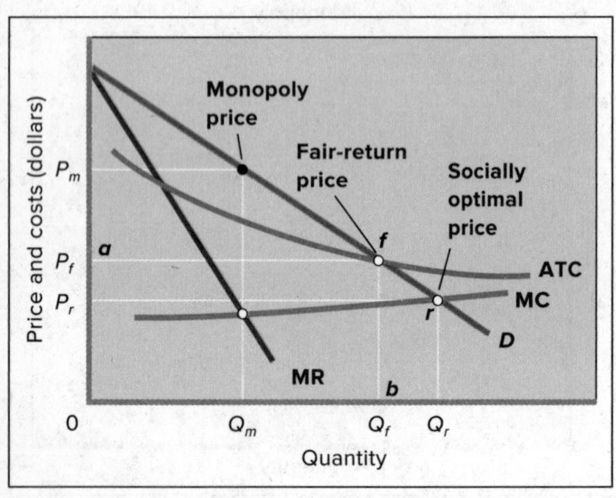

As shown in the graph, an unregulated monopoly maximizes profit by setting output at Q_m (MR = MC) and price at P_m (on the demand curve above MR = MC). In order to achieve allocative efficiency (MC = D), the government may set a price ceiling at the **socially optimal price,** P_r. At that price ceiling, the marginal revenue curve becomes the price (as we saw for perfect competition), so the monopoly will produce Q_r units of output, at a lower price and higher output than it would have produced as an unregulated monopoly. MC = P at this output, signifying allocative efficiency.

But notice that this arrangement leaves this particular firm producing at a price lower than ATC at this output. The firm incurs a loss and will have to decide whether to even stay in business in the short run. In the long run, if the firm cannot raise its price or lower its costs, it will not remain in business. To encourage the firm to remain in operation, the government could offer the firm a subsidy to cover those costs. Or perhaps the government could allow the firm to engage in price discrimination to charge a higher price to those consumers with the most inelastic demand for the product.

Often, regulatory commissions instead set the price ceiling at the **fair-return price,** where ATC = D. At that output, as shown in the graph above, the monopoly achieves a normal profit, but not an economic profit. The price is lower and the output higher than it would be under an unregulated monopoly, but not as much as if the regulators set the price ceiling at the socially optimal price of P = MC. But this solution avoids the need for a subsidy to keep the firm in business.

PRACTICE Socially Optimal Price and Fair-Return Price

1. Use the graph from the previous page to complete this comparison table for monopoly regulation.

	Monopoly Price	Fair-Return Price	Socially Optimal Price
A. Is the firm producing at allocative efficiency?			
B. Is the firm producing at productive efficiency?			
C. Is the firm earning an economic profit?			
D. Is the firm earning a normal profit?			

2. __________ If the government sets a ceiling at a price forcing the monopoly to incur a loss, what must the government provide in order to keep the firm in business?

Make sure to return to the AP Key Concepts section above to check your understanding of this chapter's concepts important to AP coursework.

Economically Speaking

- **Barriers to Entry** factors that prevent other firms from entering the industry
- **Deadweight Loss** the loss of consumer and producer surplus due to a firm restricting output
- **Fair-Return Price** the price ceiling set by government which leads a monopolist to produce where it achieves normal profit, but not economic profit (ATC = Demand)
- **Marginal Revenue** the change in total revenue from selling one more product
- **Market Power** a firm's ability to determine market prices
- **MC = MR Rule** a firm maximizes profit by producing where marginal revenue = marginal cost
- **Monopoly** a market structure with only one producer
- **Natural Monopoly** a firm which achieves economies of scale over a long range of output, so that it is more efficient to have only one producer
- **Price Discrimination** selling a product at more than one price when price differences are not justified by differences in the cost of production
- **Price Maker** a firm that can determine the market price of a product
- **Socially Optimal Price** the price ceiling set by government which leads a monopolist to produce at the allocatively efficient output (Marginal Cost = Demand)

12

Chapter

Monopolistic Competition

While perfect competition and monopoly represent the extremes of market structures, most American firms are found in the two market structures between those extremes. Monopolistic competition is very similar to perfect competition, though the firm has a small amount of market power. Oligopoly, which will be examined in Chapter 13, is very similar to monopoly. Chapter 12 introduces monopolistic competition, its characteristics, its operation, price and output determination, and efficiency.

Material from Chapter 12 commonly appears on the AP Microeconomics exam in a few multiple-choice questions and as a whole free-response question.

Key Concepts

Below is a summary of the chapter's concepts important to AP coursework. Upon completing the lessons that follow, return to these concepts to make sure you understand them and how the practice exercises you completed relate to them.

- Monopolistic competition is a market structure in which a large number of firms produce differentiated products, and firms can easily enter or exit the industry.
- Firms focus on product differentiation, making slight changes in the product and heavily advertising those differences with nonprice competition to attract customers from competitors.
- Brand loyalty serves as a strong barrier to entry for firms new to the industry.
- Demand slopes downward because the firm must lower its price to sell more products.
    - Marginal revenue is below demand, because the firm must lower price for all units.
    - Demand and marginal revenue are much more elastic than for the monopoly because of competition and the ease with which firms can enter the industry.
- Like all other firms, the monopolistic competitor maximizes profit by producing where MR = MC.
    - The firm sets the price on the demand curve directly above the MR = MC output.
    - In long-run equilibrium, ATC is tangential to demand at the price point where MR = MC.
- In long-run equilibrium, a monopolistic competitor makes normal profit, but no economic profit.

- If a firm makes short-run economic profit, firms enter the industry until profit returns to zero.
  - Profit per Unit = Price − ATC; Total Profit = Profit per Unit × Output.
  - If firms enter, demand becomes more elastic (because of increased competition) and shifts to the left (because the existing firm has a smaller market share).
- If a firm makes a short-run economic loss, firms will exit the industry until the loss falls to zero.
  - Loss per Unit = ATC − Price; Total Loss = Loss per Unit × Output.
  - When a firm incurs an economic loss, if P > AVC, the firm should keep operating in the short run; if the firm cannot cover its variable costs, it should shut down.
- If a variable (per-unit) cost changes, ATC and MC change, causing output to change.
- If a fixed (lump-sum) cost changes, only ATC changes, so output will not change.
- The monopolistically competitive firm does not achieve productive or allocative efficiency.
- Excess capacity occurs because the firm produces less output than is productively efficient.

Now, let's examine more closely the following concepts from your textbook:

- **Monopolistic Competition**
- **Price and Output in Monopolistic Competition**

These sections were selected because although the graphs look similar, subtle differences illustrate how monopolistically competitive firms are very different from monopolies.

Monopolistic Competition

Refer to pages 236–239 of your textbook.

A CLOSER LOOK Differentiated Products and Easy Entry and Exit

Monopolistic competition is a market structure in which a large number of firms produce differentiated products. Firms easily enter or exit the industry. Each firm sells a very small portion of the market share and has little market power. Firms act independently, and one firm has little effect on the other firms.

In these ways, the monopolistically competitive firm sounds very similar to the perfectly competitive firm. However, the key difference is **product differentiation.** While products are substantially the same, the firms make slight changes and then heavily advertise those differences in an effort to draw new customers away from competing firms. One gas station may offer a car wash, while another may sell food inside the station. One dry cleaner may offer one-hour service, while another offers alterations. One motel may be located next to a major highway, while another offers small kitchens in the rooms. What you'll notice is that their advertising doesn't focus on the primary product. "We sell gasoline!" "We get your clothes clean!" "We have beds in our motel rooms!" It is what makes them *different* that will be the focus of their advertising. **Nonprice competition** focuses on advertising product differences, rather than lower prices, to attract consumers. Grocery stores, hair salons, and local fast-food restaurants are often considered monopolistically competitive markets.

Monopolistically competitive firms are very competitive, so where does the "monopoly" part of the term come from? Consider how many gas stations are located within a 20-mile radius of your home. Do you tend to use the same station repeatedly? Most people do, because of the location, price (including discounts for using the company's credit or loyalty card), or another feature. The market is quite competitive, but you act almost as though there's a monopoly because you keep returning to that same station. As a result, the monopolistically competitive firm has just a little bit of **market power.** Due to customer brand loyalty, the firm can *slightly* raise the price without losing many customers. However, if the firm significantly raises its price, customers could easily change behavior to buy a substitute.

This brand loyalty also serves as a barrier to entry for new firms. New firms can easily enter a perfectly competitive industry because customers cannot distinguish which firm is producing the identical product. In monopolistic competition, the differences between products matter—and the firms heavily advertise those differences. So a new firm has to not only introduce its own product, but also break customers' brand loyalty to the product they are already purchasing.

Monopolistically competitive firms have a strong incentive to innovate and further differentiate their products in order to draw in more customers. This innovation leads to a wide variety of products for consumers. Because of the changes in the product and advertising expenses, production costs can vary markedly for monopolistically competitive firms. As you will see later, monopolistically competitive firms do not earn long-run economic profit; nor do they achieve productive or allocative efficiency.

Caution

It is very important to make the distinction between monopolistic competition and monopoly. The terms are similar, but the markets are very different. Focus on the word "competition" to remember that monopolistic competition is very similar to perfect competition, except that the products are differentiated rather than identical. The monopoly is distinctly different, as the only firm in the industry.

PRACTICE **Differentiated Products and Easy Entry and Exit**

Complete the table to identify the differences between the market structures.

	Perfect Competition	Monopolistic Competition	Monopoly
1. How many firms are in the industry (many or one)?			
2. Are products identical or differentiated?			
3. Do firms heavily advertise in nonprice competition?			
4. How much market power does the firm have?			
5. Is it difficult for firms to enter the industry?			
6. Can the firm earn long-run economic profit?			
7. Does the firm achieve productive efficiency?			
8. Does the firm achieve allocative efficiency?			

Price and Output in Monopolistic Competition

Refer to pages 239–241 of your textbook.

A CLOSER LOOK The Short Run: Profit or Loss and The Long Run: Only a Normal Profit

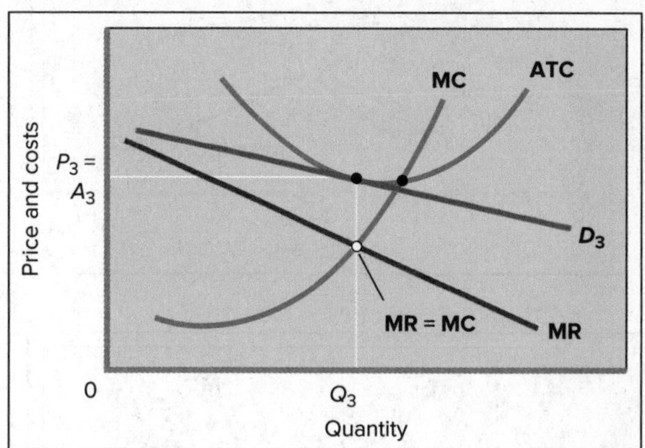

The graph for monopolistic competition, shown here to the right, is very similar to the monopoly. Demand slopes downward because the firm must lower its price to sell more. Marginal revenue is below the demand curve, because when the firm reduces its price, it must reduce the price of all of the units of output. As with the monopoly, a monopolistically competitive firm maximizes profit at the output where MR = MC and sets the price on the demand curve at the point directly above the output where MR = MC.

Important differences also exist between monopolistic competition and monopoly graphs. Demand and marginal revenue are much flatter for monopolistic competitors. Demand is more elastic precisely because there *is* so much competition. It is easy for consumers to buy substitutes, and other firms can easily enter or exit the industry, so consumers are sensitive to price changes. As a result, the monopolistically competitive firm acts more like a perfectly competitive firm. When more competitors enter the industry and products are less differentiated, demand becomes more elastic.

Another difference between the market structures is that in long-run equilibrium, after adjustments are complete, the ATC for the monopolistically competitive firm lies above the demand curve and then only tangentially touches the demand curve where price is set, above where MR = MC. The monopolistically competitive firm may earn short-run economic profit or loss, but in the long run, the firm will earn zero economic profit. The monopoly establishes complete barriers to entry to prevent competitors from entering the industry; therefore, it can sustain long-run profit. The perfectly competitive firm, on the other hand, has no barriers to entry. So other firms are enticed to enter the market when profits occur, and firms leave the industry in periods of loss. The same is true for monopolistic competition; ease of entry and exit extends to the monopolistically competitive market, and long-run economic profit is zero.

As was true for the other market structures, changes in costs affect the output and profit of the firm. If a *per-unit cost* (a variable cost like labor or materials or a per-unit tax) rises, marginal cost and ATC both increase. As marginal cost shifts up, it crosses marginal revenue at a lower output. So the firm reduces its output and sells its product at a higher price. But also notice that the average total cost shifts up, leaving the firm producing at a loss in the short run until the industry adjusts. If a per-unit cost falls (from lower production costs, lower per-unit taxes, or a per-unit subsidy), the firm increases its output and sells at a lower price. The firm will also enjoy a short-run economic profit until the industry adjusts.

If a *lump-sum cost* (a fixed cost such as a property tax or a licensing fee) increases, only the AFC and ATC increase. Marginal cost does not change, so output and price do not change. Because ATC increases, the firm will incur a short-run loss until the industry adjusts. Conversely, if a lump-sum cost falls (from lower production costs, a lump-sum tax cut, or a lump-sum subsidy), the firm still will not change output or price, but the firm will enjoy short-run profit until the industry adjusts.

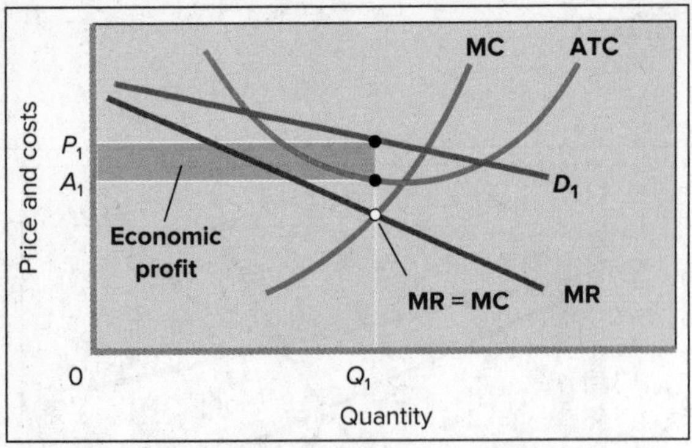

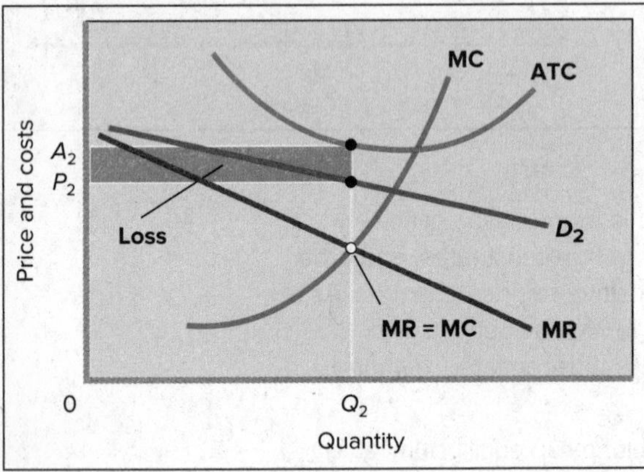

A monopolistically competitive firm earns economic profit, when at profit-maximizing output, ATC is lower than price. Profit per Unit = P – ATC; Total Profit = Profit per Unit × Output. When a monopolistic competitor enjoys a short-run economic profit, new firms are drawn into the industry. As the new firms enter, the demand curve for existing firms shifts to the left and becomes more elastic (flatter). This occurs because the new firms increase the total production of output, and the individual existing firms each provide a smaller portion of the total market output. Demand becomes more elastic because the increased competition allows customers to become even more sensitive to price changes. The price falls, output for the firm falls, and economic profit returns to zero in the long run.

When a monopolistic competitor incurs a short-run loss, some firms will leave the industry. We use the same formula we used for perfect competition and monopoly to determine whether the firm should continue to operate when it incurs a loss. At the loss-minimizing output (MR = MC), if the product price is equal to or higher than AVC, the firm should remain in business in the short run. In that scenario, the firm is receiving enough revenue to cover its variable costs and can put any additional revenue toward the fixed cost. But if price is lower than AVC, the firm should shut down. As firms leave the industry, the demand curves for the remaining firms shift to the right and become less elastic. Consumers have fewer firms to choose from, so the firms will enjoy a greater market share and will have a little market power to raise the price. In the long run, the exit of firms from the industry reduces the loss to zero (which also means zero economic profit). Firms are no longer enticed to either enter or exit the industry, and ATC is again tangential to the demand curve at the point where price is set above the MR = MC output.

Caution

Remember that even though the firm is not earning economic profit, the firm is earning a normal profit to pay the entrepreneur and the opportunity cost of other business resources. Economic profit is just the *excess* profit that causes other firms to enter the industry. When economic profit falls to zero in the long run, current producers are covering all of their explicit and implicit costs and will remain in business, but there is no excess profit to draw new firms into the industry.

Monopolistically competitive firms do not achieve productive or allocative efficiency. **Productive efficiency** occurs at the output where MC = ATC at its minimum point, so the firm is producing at its lowest average cost. As you can see in the graph at the top of the next page, the monopolistic competitor produces at Q_3, where MR = MC, an output lower than Q_4, where MC = ATC. The firm restricts output in order to raise the price, so it produces where ATC is higher than minimum.

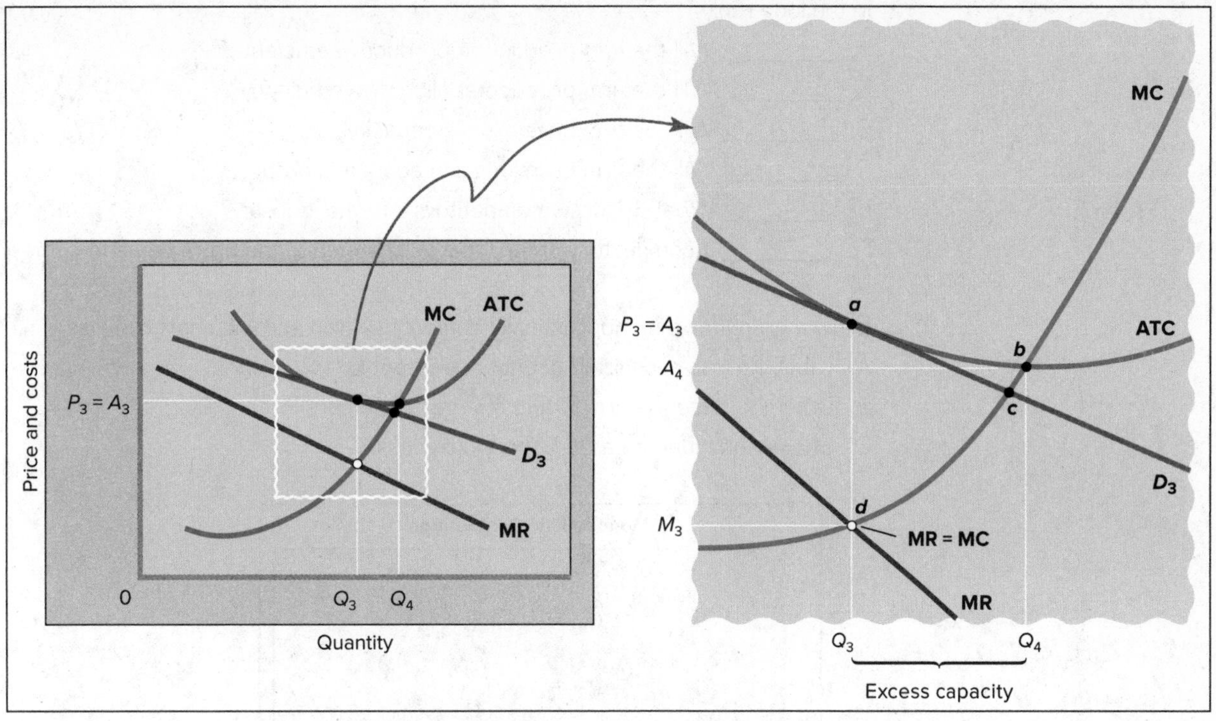

At **allocative efficiency,** scarce resources are used to produce the mix of goods society wants, at P = MC. The graph shows that in monopolistic competition, allocative efficiency is achieved at an output greater than the profit-maximizing output.

The difference in output between productive efficiency and profit maximization is called excess capacity. **Excess capacity** occurs when plant and equipment remain unused because the firm has restricted its output from what would be productively efficient. In the graph above, it is the distance between Q_3 and Q_4. Hotels with consistently unused beds or factories with idle equipment are examples of excess capacity that represent inefficiency.

While the perfectly competitive firm might not achieve productive or allocative efficiency in the short run, long-run adjustments would bring the firm back to efficiency. However, the monopolistically competitive firm fails to achieve productive and allocative efficiency, even in the long run. Because the firm does not produce at minimum ATC, the firm is not productively efficient, leaving the firm with excess capacity in the long run.

PRACTICE The Short Run: Profit or Loss and The Long Run: Only a Normal Profit

1. Draw a graph for a monopolistically competitive firm earning short-run economic profit.
   A. Label the profit-maximizing quantity of output Q.
   B. Label the price the firm would charge consumers P.
   C. Shade and label the area of economic profit.

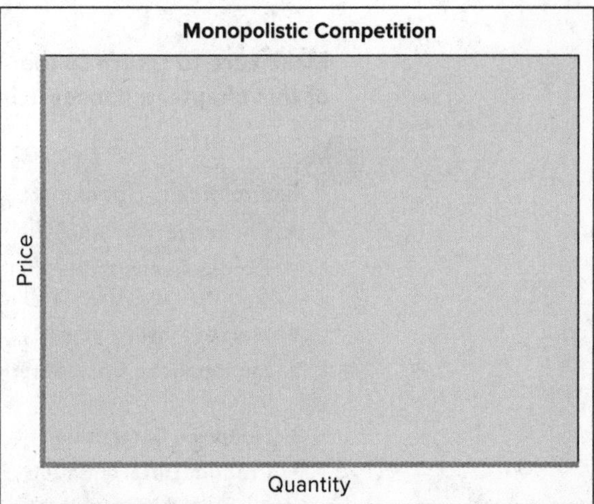

2. In the long run:
   A. __________ Will the firm produce at productive efficiency?
   B. __________ Will the firm produce at allocative efficiency?
   C. __________ Will the firm have excess capacity?
   D. __________ Will the firm earn long-run economic profit?
   E. __________ What will draw competitors into the industry?
   F. __________ If competitors enter, what will happen to the firm's demand curve?

3. Draw a graph for a monopolistically competitive firm earning short-run loss.
   A. Label the loss-minimizing quantity of output Q.
   B. Label the price the firm would charge consumers P.
   C. Shade and label the area of economic loss.

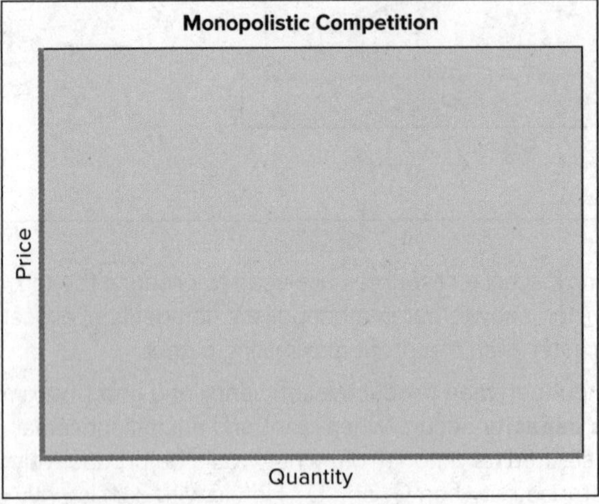

4. Given the current scenario:
   A. __________ In order to stay in operation, the price must be greater than what?
   B. __________ If the firm's price is lower than in 4(A), what should the firm do?
   C. __________ In the long run, what will happen to the firm's economic loss?

Make sure to return to the AP Key Concepts section above to check your understanding of this chapter's concepts important to AP coursework.

Economically Speaking

- **Allocative Efficiency** the market produces the mix of products society values most highly
- **Excess Capacity** the plant and equipment that are underused because the firm is producing an output less than productive efficiency
- **Market Power** the ability of a firm to control the price of its product
- **Monopolistic Competition** a market structure in which a large number of firms produce a differentiated product
- **Nonprice Competition** firms focus on advertising product differences, rather than lower prices
- **Product Differentiation** competing firms focus on making their products different, in order to advertise those differences and attract consumers
- **Productive Efficiency** a product is produced in the least costly way

Chapter 13

Oligopoly and Strategic Behavior

While monopolies hold complete market power and perfectly competitive firms hold none, most American businesses fall between these two extremes. Monopolistic competition, as we learned in Chapter 12, shares most of the characteristics of perfect competition. Chapter 13 introduces the oligopoly, which is very similar to the monopoly, though the firm does have a few competitors and the rivalry among those firms leads to an interdependent relationship.

Material from Chapter 13 is found in a few multiple-choice questions on the AP Microeconomics exam, and game theory questions often appear as complete free-response questions.

Key Concepts

Below is a summary of the chapter's concepts important to AP coursework. Upon completing the lessons that follow, return to these concepts to make sure you understand them and how the practice exercises you completed relate to them.

- An oligopoly is a market dominated by a few large firms.
- Oligopolies rely on mutual interdependence; profit depends not only on the firm's decisions, but also on how its rivals react to those decisions.
- Demand slopes downward because the firm must lower the price to sell more products.
- Marginal revenue falls faster than demand because the firm must lower the price of all units in order to sell more.
- The firm maximizes profit by setting output where MR = MC.
  - The firm sets the price on the demand curve directly above where MR = MC.
  - Profit per Unit = P − ATC; Total Profit = Profit per Unit × Output.
  - Oligopolists can sustain economic profit in the long run due to barriers to entry.
- If the firm incurs a short-run loss, it continues to operate if P > AVC; if the firm cannot cover its variable costs, it should shut down.
- Changes in per-unit costs change the firm's output, price, and profit or loss.
- Changes in lump-sum costs do not change output, only profit or loss.
- The oligopoly does not achieve productive or allocative efficiency.
- Oligopolists may be willing to match rivals' price cuts, but not necessarily price increases.
- Oligopolists focus on product differentiation and advertise with nonprice competition.

- Game theory is the study of an oligopoly's strategic decisions.
  - In a payoff matrix, firms compare their profits based on how rivals will react.
  - Firms attempt to make decisions that will maximize their profit and remain stable.
- If firms form a cartel and collude to set prices, they can increase their profit.
- Firms may cheat on their collusive agreement if they can increase their profit by doing so.
- Cartels and collusion are illegal under United States antitrust laws.
- A dominant strategy in game theory exists when one choice is better for the firm, regardless of the other firm's decision.
- Oligopolists have reached Nash equilibrium if both firms have an optimal strategy that is stable.

Now, let's examine more closely the following concepts from your textbook:

- **Three Oligopoly Models**
- **Oligopoly Behavior: A Game Theory Overview**
- **Game Theory and Strategic Behavior**

These sections were selected because interdependence is unique to oligopoly, and game theory requires practice to understand how firms make their decisions. Understanding game theory can have a significant impact on the AP Microeconomics exam score if it appears as a free-response question.

Three Oligopoly Models

Refer to pages 252–257 of your textbook.

A CLOSER LOOK Kinked-Demand Theory, Cartels and Other Collusion, and Price Leadership Model

An **oligopoly** is a market dominated by a few large firms. Products can be standardized (oil or steel) or differentiated (cars or soft drinks). "A few" firms could range from two to several, but the key is that this small number of firms controls the industry through barriers to entry. Like monopolies, oligopolies use economies of scale, costs of capital, ownership of raw materials, patents, and strong consumer loyalty to repel the entry of new competitors into the industry. Oligopolistic firms can develop by differentiating their product enough to attract great numbers of consumers or by merging with other firms to grow significantly larger. Like monopolistically competitive firms, oligopolies rely heavily on advertising and nonprice competition. Aluminum, tire, cereal, and cigarette industries are oligopolistic.

Mutual interdependence makes the oligopoly unique among the market structures. Each firm's profit depends not only on its own production and pricing decisions, but also on the reaction of other firms in the industry. Few firms compete in the industry, so any decision by one firm may affect the profits of the others. Oligopolists must take their rivals' reactions into account when making strategic decisions.

Caution

Mutual interdependence complicates the oligopoly graph. Because firms cannot be sure how their rivals will react to production decisions, they cannot easily estimate their demand or marginal revenue, so oligopolistic firms cannot easily determine their profit-maximizing output or price. However, we can make the assumption that rivals do not react, in order to develop a theoretical graph such as follows.

The oligopoly graph looks just like the monopoly one. Demand slopes down because the firm must lower its price to sell more products. Marginal revenue falls faster than demand, because when the firm lowers the price to sell more, it must lower the price of all units. The firm maximizes profit at the output where MR = MC and sets its price on the demand curve directly above that point. Profit per unit is determined by the distance between the price (on the demand curve) and average total cost. Due to significant barriers to entry into the industry, firms are able to sustain economic profit in the long run. If the firm incurs a short-run loss, it remains in business as long as price > AVC and shuts down if price < AVC. Like the other market structures, changes in per-unit cost change the firm's output, price, and profit or loss, while changes in lump-sum cost only change the firm's profit or loss. Like the monopoly and monopolistic competition, the oligopoly does not achieve productive or allocative efficiency.

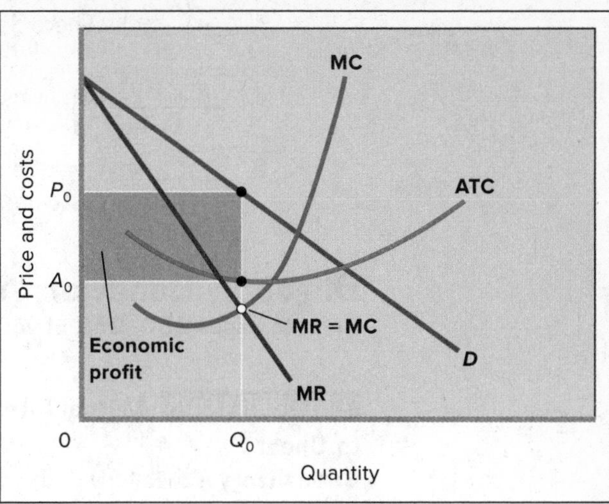

Some oligopolists use price leadership to change prices. If a major firm changes its price, other firms may match it. When fuel prices rose, one airline added a surcharge for suitcases. When other airlines realized consumers were not sensitive to the price increase, they quickly followed suit. The theory of the kinked demand curve is based on the idea that oligopolists respond differently when rivals change prices. When one firm lowers its price, rivals will generally lower their prices as well, to avoid losing customers. But if one firm raises its price, rivals may *not* match the price increase, hoping consumers will leave the high-priced firm and instead buy their product. As a result, demand above the current price is elastic, while demand below the current price is inelastic, creating a "kinked" demand curve.

Keep in Mind

The theory of the kinked demand curve is controversial and has not appeared on an AP Microeconomics exam. It is important to understand that oligopolists respond to the actions of competitors, but no questions requiring graphing of the oligopoly market have appeared on previous exams.

Given the difficulty of predicting how rivals will respond to price changes, oligopolists prefer nonprice competition, focusing on product differentiation and heavily advertising those differences. This brand of cereal contains more vitamins and minerals. That brand of tissue is softer. While advertising may provide consumers with important product information to make informed choices, some advertising is misleading, so consumers must beware of advertising claims.

PRACTICE Kinked-Demand Theory, Cartels and Other Collusion, and Price Leadership Model

1. __________ How do oligopolists limit the number of competitors in the industry?

2. __________ What is the term for the idea that firms base their decisions on rivals' reactions?

3. _________ Where do oligopolists set profit-maximizing output?

4. _________ Can firms in an oligopoly maintain long-run economic profit?

5. _________ What do oligopolists heavily advertise, in order to attract new customers?

Oligopoly Behavior: A Game Theory Overview

Refer to pages 250–252 of your textbook.

A CLOSER LOOK Mutual Interdependence Revisited, Collusion, and Incentive to Cheat

Game theory is the study of the oligopoly's strategic decisions. A **payoff matrix** is a set of cells showing the profit to each firm for each combination of strategies. The payoff matrix here shows the choices available to two firms in an oligopoly. Each firm can choose between two pricing strategies: setting a high price or setting a low price. RareAir's choices are on the top margin, while Uptown's choices are on the side margin. Each lettered cell shows a combination of possible strategies by the firms. Numbers in the upper right corner of each cell show the profit RareAir would earn with that combination of choices, while the numbers in the lower left corner of each cell show the profit Uptown would earn.

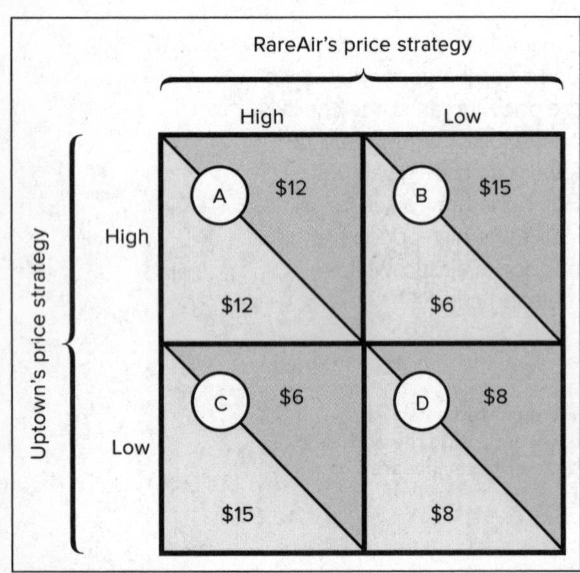

The profit a firm earns depends on the other firm's decision. If both firms set a high price (Box A), each firm earns a $12 million profit. But if Uptown sells its shoes for a high price and RareAir sells its shoes for a low price (Box B), many customers will buy from RareAir instead of Uptown, so RareAir's profit will increase to $15 million while Uptown's profit will fall to $6 million. If Uptown anticipates RareAir's low-price strategy, Uptown could also use a low-price strategy (Box D) so that both firms earn $8 million in profit. Lower prices are better for consumers, but remember that firms seek to maximize profit.

Another solution would allow *both* firms to increase profit. If the firms use **collusion**, working together to set prices, RareAir and Uptown could agree to a high-price strategy so that both firms earn the higher $12 million profit (Box A). Both firms are better off colluding rather than settling for the $8 million profit they would each earn using a low-price strategy (Box D), but each firm is still eyeing that higher $15 million profit for taking the low-price strategy alone. If Uptown cheats on the agreement so that RareAir keeps its high-price strategy and Uptown uses the low-price strategy (Box C), Uptown's profit will increase from $12 million to $15 million, while RareAir's profit will fall from $12 million to $6 million. Once RareAir figures out that Uptown has cheated, it will use the low-price strategy as well, and both will return to $8 million profit (Box D).

Cartels, organizations that engage in collusive agreements, often find it difficult to enforce these agreements. The incentive to cheat on collusive agreements, differences in costs and demand among firms, and the potential entry of new firms all explain why cartels find it so difficult to maintain collusive agreements. The clearest example of a cartel is OPEC, the Organization of Petroleum Exporting Countries. OPEC oil ministers agree to restrict output by each country in order to keep oil prices higher than they would be if the rivals competed. But such agreements often collapse when countries cheat to produce more oil. You may have heard of drug cartels, which attempt to enforce agreements through violence. Cartels and their collusive activities are illegal in the United States under antitrust legislation. But because we import products produced by cartels, an understanding of their operation is important.

PRACTICE Mutual Interdependence Revisited, Collusion, and Incentive to Cheat

The payoff matrix below shows the profit that can be earned by two firms selling memberships to online political discussion forums. The firms must determine whether the forum will be strictly moderated or members will be free to say anything. Robbie and Dak cannot change that decision during the year due to member contracts. The first number in each cell is Dak's profit; the second number is Robbie's profit.

		Robbie's Moderating Strategy	
Dak's		Moderators	No Moderators
Moderating	Moderators	$100, $200	$90, $300
Strategy	No Moderators	$80, $100	$60, $250

1. __________ Is Dak's best strategy to use moderators or no moderators?

2. __________ If Dak chooses to run a forum with moderators, what is Robbie's best strategy?

3. __________ If both firms use their best strategies and do not collude, what is Dak's profit?

4. Assume the government offers Robbie and Dak a $30 subsidy for each forum, but only if the owner agrees *not* to moderate the discussions. Change the profits in the payoff matrix to reflect what the profits would be if each firm accepted the subsidy.

Game Theory and Strategic Behavior

Refer to pages 260–265 of your textbook.

A CLOSER LOOK A One-Time Game: Strategies and Equilibrium

Oligopolists can find long-run equilibrium without collusion. In the payoff matrix, each firm must determine if it has a **dominant strategy** – a choice that is better for the firm, regardless of the other firm's decision.

If Dramco sells its products internationally, it would earn $11 million if Chipco chooses an international strategy and $20 million if Chipco chooses a national strategy. Both positions are better than the profit Dramco would have earned with a national strategy, whether Chipco chose an international strategy ($11 > $5) or a national strategy ($20 > $17).

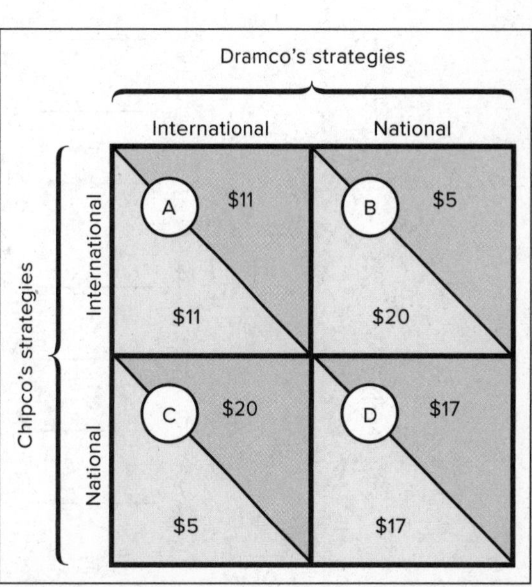

Therefore, Dramco's dominant strategy is to choose an international strategy, as it is better off using that strategy, regardless of what Chipco chooses to do.

Chipco must also determine if it has a dominant strategy. If Chipco chooses an international strategy, it would earn $11 million if Dramco chooses an international strategy and $20 million if Dramco chooses a national strategy. Both positions result in a higher profit for Chipco than if it had chosen a national strategy and Dramco chose an international strategy ($11 > $5) or a national strategy ($20 > $17). As a result, Chipco also has a dominant strategy to choose an international strategy.

Both Dramco and Chipco choose an international strategy, and each firm earns $11 million in profit. Both firms chose the optimal strategy for their firm, so this arrangement, called **Nash equilibrium**, will tend to remain stable and long-lasting. (It is named for John Nash, the Nobel Prize-winning economist whose story is the subject of the film *A Beautiful Mind*.) Not all games will have a dominant strategy, and the lack of a dominant strategy can explain the volatility of some oligopolistic markets.

Keep in Mind

Applications of game theory in payoff matrices have appeared consistently in multiple-choice and free-response questions on AP Microeconomics exams. It is important to understand the matrix mechanics, determine whether a dominant strategy exists for either firm or both, and find the profit for each firm.

PRACTICE A One-Time Game: Strategies and Equilibrium

The payoff matrix below shows profit per week that can be earned by two firms. They must decide whether to set their flower carts on the east side or west side of town. The first number in each cell is Melissa's profit; the second is Robert's profit.

		Robert's Flowers	
		East Side	**West Side**
Melissa's Flowers	**East Side**	$700, $900	$500, $400
	West Side	$600, $600	$700, $300

1. __________ Where will Robert locate, in order to maximize his profits?

2. __________ Does Robert have a dominant strategy?

3. __________ If Robert locates where you indicated in #1, what is Melissa's best location?

4. __________ Does Melissa have a dominant strategy?

5. __________ What will be Robert's weekly profit?

6. __________ What will be Melissa's weekly profit?

7. __________ In this situation, have the firms reached Nash equilibrium?

8. Assume the city offers Robert and Melissa a $200 per week subsidy if they will operate their flower carts on the west side of town. Change the profits in the payoff matrix to reflect what the profits would be if each firm accepted the subsidy.

Robert's Flowers

		East Side	West Side
Melissa's	**East Side**		
Flowers	**West Side**		

9. __________ Given the subsidy, will Robert move his cart to the west side of town?

10. __________ Given the subsidy, will Melissa move her cart to the west side of town?

11. __________ In the cell in which they now operate, what will be Robert's weekly profit?

12. __________ In the cell in which they now operate, what will be Melissa's weekly profit?

13. __________ In this situation, have the firms reached Nash equilibrium?

Make sure to return to the AP Key Concepts section to check your understanding of the chapter's concepts important to AP coursework.

Economically Speaking

- **Cartel** an organization that engages in collusive agreements
- **Collusion** firms agree to work together to set prices or output
- **Dominant Strategy** a choice that is better for the firm, regardless of the other firm's decision
- **Game Theory** the study of how people behave in strategic situations
- **Mutual Interdependence** each firm's profit depends not only on its own price and sales strategies, but also on the reactions of other firms in the industry
- **Nash Equilibrium** both oligopolistic firms have chosen a strategy they find optimal
- **Oligopoly** a market structure of an industry dominated by a few large firms
- **Payoff Matrix** a set of cells showing the profit to each firm for each combination of strategies

14

Chapter

The Demand for Resources

In terms of the circular flow model, we have so far focused on the product market, where households buy products from firms. This chapter begins a three-chapter study of the factor (resource) market, where firms buy the land, labor, capital, and entrepreneurial resources necessary to produce products. Chapter 14 explains the demand for resources, focusing specifically on labor and capital markets.

Material from Chapter 14 consistently appears in a few multiple-choice questions and often appears as a free-response question on the AP Microeconomics exam.

Key Concepts

Below is a summary of the chapter's concepts important to AP coursework. Upon completing the lessons that follow, return to these concepts to make sure you understand them and how the practice exercises you completed relate to them.

- In a perfectly competitive labor market, the individual firm is a wage taker which must accept the wage that is set in the industry.
- Labor is derived demand; demand for labor is based on demand for the product labor produces.
- Total Product is output from all workers together; Marginal Product is the increase in total product resulting from hiring one more worker.
- Diminishing returns occur when specialization wears off and fixed capital is reaching it limits; each additional worker adds to total product, but not as much as the worker before him.
- According to the Law of Diminishing Returns, as more units of labor are added to a fixed amount of capital, marginal product falls.
- Firms hire within the range of diminishing returns, based on the product price and wage.
- Marginal Revenue Product (MRP) is the change in total revenue resulting from hiring one more worker (Change in Total Revenue / Change in the Number of Workers); the demand for labor.
- Marginal Resource Cost (MRC) is the change in total cost resulting from hiring one more worker (Change in Total Cost / Change in the Number of Workers).
- MRP = MRC Rule: firms should continue to hire workers until MRP = MRC. If MRP > MRC, hire more workers; if MRP < MRC, reduce the number of workers.
- If a firm sells products in a perfectly competitive product market, the product price remains the same regardless of output, and MRP falls only because of diminishing returns.

- If a firm sells products in an imperfectly competitive product market, the firm must lower the price to sell more products; MRP falls faster because of diminishing returns *and* price lowering.
- Demand for labor is based on demand for the product, labor productivity, and changes in the prices of substitute and complementary resources.
- Elasticity of resource demand measures the sensitivity of firms to changes in resource costs; demand for labor or capital that cannot be easily replaced tends to be more inelastic.
- The least-cost rule requires firms to decide between hiring labor or capital, hiring until the MP / cost of labor = MP / cost of capital.
- The profit-maximizing rule tells firms how much labor and capital to hire, hiring until the MRP/cost of labor = MRP/cost of capital = 1.
- The profit-maximizing rule includes the least-cost rule within the formula, but a firm achieving least-cost production may not be maximizing profit.
- One theory of income distribution says that workers are paid according to the value of the labor services they contribute to production.
- Critics argue educational opportunities and resource ownership are highly unequal; progressive taxes and a more equitable income distribution are very important to improve the economy.

Now, let's examine more closely the following concepts from your textbook:

- **Marginal Productivity Theory of Resource Demand**
- **Determinants of Resource Demand**
- **Optimal Combination of Resources**

These sections were selected because the formulas and data interpretation to make hiring decisions take some practice to fully understand and apply to questions on the AP Microeconomics exam.

Marginal Productivity Theory of Resource Demand

Refer to pages 274–277 of your textbook.

A CLOSER LOOK Marginal Revenue Product and Rule for Employing Resources: MRP = MRC

An understanding of resource markets is important to understanding incomes, costs of production, the allocation of resources to produce goods, and public policy decisions. We begin our analysis with the assumption that the firm is producing in a perfectly competitive market and hires workers from a perfectly competitive labor market. Like the perfectly competitive product market, the individual firm in the perfectly competitive labor market is a **wage taker** that must accept the wage set in the industry. The firm can hire as many workers as it needs without affecting the wage (the price of workers). We also assume that all workers are equal in terms of ability, motivation, and productivity.

The demand for labor is a **derived demand**, because the demand for labor is based on demand for the product labor produces. If the product gains popularity, the firm hires more workers to produce it; if consumer incomes fall, product demand falls and the firm lays off workers. Due to this derived demand, the demand for labor depends on the productivity of the workers and the market value of the product. Highly productive resources and products with greater value increase the demand for resources.

(1) Units of the Variable Resource (Labor)	(2) Total Product (TP)	(3) Marginal Product (MP), Change in (2)/ Change in (1)		(4) Average Product (AP), (2)/(1)
0	0			—
		10	Increasing marginal returns	
1	10			10.00
		15		
2	25			12.50
		20		
3	45			15.00
		15	Diminishing marginal returns	
4	60			15.00
		10		
5	70			14.00
		5		
6	75			12.50
		0	Negative marginal returns	
7	75			10.71
		–5		
8	70			8.75

As we discussed in detail in Chapter 8, the production function helps to determine how many workers firms will hire. **Total product** is the total output from all of the workers together; **marginal product** is the increase in total product from hiring one more worker. In the table above, the first three workers bring increasing returns. As specialization increases efficiency, each worker adds more to production than the worker before him.

Look at the table again, and you can see, however, that workers four through seven bring **diminishing returns**; as specialization wears off, each worker adds to total product, but not as much as the worker before him. Starting with the eighth worker, the firm enters negative returns, where the workers overwhelm the fixed capital, so production falls with each additional worker. The **Law of Diminishing Returns** explains that as more units of a variable resource (like labor) are added to a fixed resource (like capital), marginal product falls. This concept recognizes the limit on production when a plant and equipment are fixed in the short run.

A firm can use the production function to determine the range of workers where hiring will occur. During increasing returns, every additional worker increases efficiency, so the firm wants to hire all of the workers in this range. During negative returns, every additional worker takes away from production, so the firm would not want to hire anyone in that range. During diminishing returns, each worker adds to output, but not as much as the one before. Firms will hire somewhere in the range of diminishing returns, depending on the price of the product and the cost of the labor. Because a firm will always hire the workers in increasing returns, many tables begin diminishing returns with the first worker.

Keep in Mind

Be very careful when reading questions asking where diminishing returns begin. Some questions will ask "With which worker do diminishing returns begin?" Using the table above, Worker #3 increases marginal product by 20, while Worker #4 increases marginal product by 15. Therefore, diminishing returns begin with Worker #4. But some questions will ask "Diminishing returns begin *after* which worker?" Diminishing returns begin *after* Worker #3. Take care to read such questions carefully.

Marginal Revenue Product (MRP) is the change in total revenue caused by hiring one more unit of a resource (usually labor). Marginal revenue product is the firm's demand for labor.

$$\text{Marginal Revenue Product} = \frac{\text{Change in Total Revenue}}{\text{Change in the Number of Workers}}$$

Marginal Resource Cost (MRC) is the change in total cost caused by hiring one more unit of a resource (usually labor). Marginal resource cost is the firm's supply of labor for the perfectly competitive firm.

$$\text{Marginal Resource Cost} = \frac{\text{Change in Total (Resource) Cost}}{\text{Change in the Number of Workers}}$$

In the same way that firms determine profit-maximizing output by producing where the marginal cost to produce the next product equals the marginal revenue the firm receives from selling it, firms maximize profit by hiring workers where the marginal cost to hire the next worker equals the marginal revenue the firm earns from products produced by that next worker. If the firm will earn more revenue from hiring the next worker than it costs to hire that worker, the firm should hire the worker. But if it costs more to hire the worker than the worker would bring to the firm, the firm should not hire that worker. Similar to the MR = MC profit-maximizing rule for output, the **MRP = MRC rule** says that firms should continue to hire workers until the marginal revenue product equals the marginal resource cost.

Caution

By this point, you should recognize important parallels between the perfectly competitive product market and the perfectly competitive factor market. They are very similar, with most principles transferring between the two markets. The primary difference between them is that the product market is where consumers are buying products from firms, and the factor market is where firms are buying resources from households in order to create those products.

(1) Units of Resource	(2) Total Product (Output)	(3) Marginal Product (MP)	(4) Product Price	(5) Total Revenue, (2) × (4)	(6) Marginal Revenue Product (MRP)
0	0		$2	$ 0	
		7			$ 14
1	7		2	14	
		6			12
2	13		2	26	
		5			10
3	18		2	36	
		4			8
4	22		2	44	
		3			6
5	25		2	50	
		2			4
6	27		2	54	
		1			2
7	28		2	56	

In the table above, we can see total product (output of all workers together) and marginal product (increase in output from hiring one more worker). Marginal product falls because of diminishing returns. The $2 product price does not change because in a perfectly competitive product market, all products are the same price. Total revenue (total product times product price) yields the marginal revenue product (increase in total revenue from hiring one more worker). Worker #2 adds a marginal product of 6, sold for $2 each, so the second worker adds $12 in marginal revenue product to the firm.

If we assume the firm is hiring in a perfectly competitive labor market, all workers are hired at the same wage. Remember, the firm wants to hire where MRP is greater than or equal to MRC. So if the wage is $10, the firm would hire three workers. If the wage is $6, the firm will hire five workers. The quantity of workers demanded increases as the wage falls. What if the wage is $9? No MRP exactly matches. If the firm hires three workers, the MRC (wage) is less than MRP (income to the firm for hiring that worker), so the firm wants that worker. But with the fourth worker, MRC > MRP, so the firm should not hire the worker. What if the wage is $15? The firm cannot cover the variable cost and should shut down.

> **Keep in Mind**
> Given the total product and product price, you must be able to calculate the marginal product, total revenue, and marginal revenue product. Given the wage, you will be expected to calculate the number of workers the firm should hire to maximize profit. Questions requiring this specific skill have appeared consistently in both multiple-choice and free-response questions on the AP Microeconomics exam.

PRACTICE Marginal Revenue Product and Rule for Employing Resources: MRP = MRC

1. __________ What is the profit-maximizing rule for hiring labor?

2. __________ If hiring an additional worker would increase a firm's total cost by more than it would increase its total revenue, should the firm hire the worker?

3. __________ If the MRP is $20 and the wage is $15, should the firm hire the worker?

4. Complete the table below and then use it to answer the questions that follow.

# of Workers	Total Product	Marginal Product	Product Price	Total Revenue	MRP
0	0	-----	$2		-----
1	20		$2		
2	50		$2		
3	70		$2		
4	85		$2		
5	95		$2		
6	100		$2		

A. _______ With which worker is marginal product maximized?

B. _______ With which worker do diminishing returns begin?

C. _______ If the wage rate is $30, how many workers should be hired?

D. _______ What is the highest wage this firm would pay to hire the third worker?

E. _______ If the wage rate is $25, how many workers should be hired?

F. _______ Given the number of workers hired in 4(E), what is the firm's output?

G. _______ If the wage rate is $90, how many workers should be hired?

H. _______ This firm must sell products in a perfectly competitive market because *what* does not change?

5. _________ If labor is the only cost to the firm, wage is $15 per hour, and marginal product is 5 units per hour, what is the marginal cost?

6. _________ A perfectly competitive firm is currently producing at profit-maximizing output. If labor is the only cost, the marginal product of labor is 6 units per hour and the firm pays a wage rate of $24 per hour, what is the price of the product?

7. _________ A firm sells its product in a perfectly competitive market for $10 per unit and pays workers $60 per day. Labor is the only variable cost, and the firm is currently earning profit. If the firm hires one more worker and output increases by 5 units per day, what will happen to the firm's profit?

A CLOSER LOOK Resource Demand under Imperfect Product Market Competition

(1) Units of Resource	(2) Total Product (Output)	(3) Marginal Product (MP)	(4) Product Price	(5) Total Revenue, (2) × (4)	(6) Marginal Revenue Product (MRP)
0	0		$2.80	$ 0	
		7			$18.20
1	7		2.60	18.20	
		6			13.00
2	13		2.40	31.20	
		5			8.40
3	18		2.20	39.60	
		4			4.40
4	22		2.00	44.00	
		3			2.25
5	25		1.85	46.25	
		2			1.00
6	27		1.75	47.25	
		1			−1.05
7	28		1.65	46.20	

Labor hiring in an imperfectly competitive product market is very similar, though you'll notice one major difference. Refer to the table. Comparing this table to the earlier table, you can see that in the perfectly competitive product market, the product price remains the same, regardless of how many products are sold, because the firm is a price taker. In imperfectly competitive product markets (monopolistic competition, oligopoly, or monopoly), price-making firms must lower the price of all of their products in order to sell more. As a result, the price falls, causing the marginal revenue product to fall even more steeply. Therefore, the MRP curve for the firm selling in an imperfectly competitive product market falls for two reasons: diminishing returns and lowering prices in order to sell more products. As a result, labor demand for a firm selling in an imperfectly competitive product market is less elastic than labor demand for a firm selling in a perfectly competitive product market. This can be seen in the firm's decision to restrict output to sell products at a higher price; if the firm produces fewer products, it demands fewer workers to produce those products.

Imperfectly competitive firms also hire where MRP = MRC. Using this table for an imperfectly competitive product market, if the wage is $10, the firm would hire two workers. At a wage of $5, the firm would hire three workers. Note that the imperfectly competitive firm hires fewer workers than the perfectly competitive firm in the previous example.

Caution

The situation of monopoly's marginal revenue separating from demand is replicated here. Remember that MRP falls faster than demand for the monopoly because the firm must lower the price to sell more products. Because it must lower the price for *all* products, not just the last one, marginal revenue falls even faster. For the same reason, MRP falls faster for the imperfect competitor (like a monopolist) than for the firm selling in a perfectly competitive product market. MRP falls not only because of diminishing returns, but also because the firm must lower the price of all products in order to sell more.

PRACTICE Resource Demand under Imperfect Product Market Competition

1. ________ Why does MRP fall faster for imperfect competitors than perfect competitors?

2. Complete the table below and then use it to answer the questions that follow.

# of Workers	Total Product	Marginal Product	Product Price	Total Revenue	MRP
0	0	-----	$4.00		-----
1	20		$3.50		
2	50		$3.00		
3	70		$2.50		
4	85		$2.00		
5	95		$1.50		
6	100		$1.00		

A. ________ If the wage rate is $30, how many workers should be hired?

B. ________ What is the highest wage this firm would pay to hire the third worker?

C. ________ If the wage rate is $25, how many workers should be hired?

D. ________ Given the number of workers hired (in #2C), what is the firm's output?

E. ________ If the wage rate is $90, how many workers should be hired?

F. ________ Fixed cost = $10. Two workers are hired at a $30 wage. What is profit?

3. Compare your answers for the perfectly competitive and imperfectly competitive markets represented in the tables.

A. ________ If the wage is $25, who hires more: the perfect or imperfect competitor?

B. ________ If the wage is $25, who has more output: the perfect or imperfect competitor?

Determinants of Resource Demand

Refer to pages 277–281 of your textbook.

A CLOSER LOOK Changes in Product Demand, Productivity, and Prices of Other Resources

The demand for labor relies on a number of factors. First, with derived demand, an increase in demand for the product increases demand for the labor to produce it. The reverse is true when product demand falls.

Second, if labor becomes more productive, the demand for labor will increase. When workers can produce more at a lower cost per unit, the firm has an incentive to increase production in order to gain more profit. Productivity can be increased through a greater availability of other resources, advances in technology, and increased health, education, and skills of the labor force. High productivity of the workforce helps to explain why American workers' wages are higher than those in many other nations.

Caution

Increased demand for workers who are more productive may seem counter-intuitive. If the workers are faster and produce even more products, wouldn't the firm need *fewer* workers? Remember, the firm is only hiring workers when the MRP earned by the next worker is greater than or equal to the MRC of hiring that worker. If MRP > MRC, the firm actually increases its profit by hiring that worker, and the firm will continue to hire until MRP = MRC.

Changes in the prices of substitute and complementary resources also affect the demand for labor. Substitute capital takes the place of a worker, such as a fast food restaurant machine that automatically dispenses drinks based on a computerized order. If the cost of the machine falls, the firm will increase demand for machines and reduce demand for workers. Complementary resources are capital goods that are used *with* labor. One ultrasound technician is needed for each piece of ultrasound equipment. If the price of capital used as a complementary resource falls, the firm buys more capital and the demand for labor will actually rise, as the firm needs more workers to use the additional equipment.

Keep in Mind

To determine effects of wages on labor hiring, most questions on the AP Microeconomics exam assume labor is the only factor of production, in order to simplify the analysis.

PRACTICE Changes in Product Demand, Productivity, and Prices of Other Resources

Indicate whether each of the following scenarios would cause labor demand to increase or decrease.

1. _______ Demand for the firm's product increases
2. _______ The unemployment rate significantly increases for the firm's customers
3. _______ Improved training makes the workers more productive
4. _______ The cost of a complementary piece of equipment falls
5. _______ The cost of a substitute piece of equipment falls

Optimal Combination of Resources

Refer to pages 282–284 of your textbook.

A CLOSER LOOK The Least-Cost Rule and The Profit-Maximizing Rule

The **least-cost rule** answers the question "Should I hire more labor *or* should I buy more capital to produce at this particular output?" The least-cost rule shows a firm minimizing its costs at a specific output. When the last dollar spent on labor and the last dollar spent on capital both result in the same marginal product, the firm has reached least-cost production.

$$\frac{\text{Marginal Product of Labor}}{\text{Cost of Labor}} = \frac{\text{Marginal Product of Capital}}{\text{Cost of Capital}}$$

If the last worker hired has a marginal product of six at a price of $1, and the last unit of capital hired has a marginal product of four at a price of $1, the marginal products are not equal. The firm would be better off buying less capital and hiring more workers, because it gains more production for the same cost (which is the same as saying the firm produces the same amount at a lower total cost). The firm will continue to choose between labor and capital, shifting between resources to buy more of the resource that provides a higher marginal product and fewer of the resource that provides a lower marginal product, until the marginal products are equal. Then the firm is producing at least cost.

While it is important for the firm to minimize costs, doing so will not necessarily maximize profit. The **profit-maximizing rule** for resources answers a different question: "How *much* labor and how *much* capital should I acquire to maximize profit?" As we know, the firm maximizes profit where MR = MC in the product market and where MRP = MRC in the factor market. In order to maximize profit for the firm in *all* variable resources, we need to extend the MRP = MRC formula to all resources.

$$\frac{\text{MRP of Labor}}{\text{Cost of Labor}} = \frac{\text{MRP of Capital}}{\text{Cost of Capital}} = 1$$

The least-cost rule told us which combination of resources – labor or capital – reduced costs. The profit-maximizing rule tells us how many of *each* resource to buy to maximize profit. The firm should hire labor until the MRP equals the cost of labor. The numerator and denominator of the fraction should be equal. In the same way, the firm should continue to buy capital until the MRP equals the cost of capital. The profit-maximizing rule includes the least-cost rule within the formula, so the firm maximizing profit is achieving least-cost production. A firm achieving least-cost production, though, may not maximize profit. If a firm sells its products for $1 apiece, and the MP for the last unit of labor is nine at a price of $3, and the MP for the last unit of capital is 12 at a price of $4, the firm achieves least-cost production because both labor and capital produce a marginal product of three units per dollar of cost. However, the firm is not maximizing profit, because the MRP is higher than the cost of each resource. The firm should continue to hire labor and buy capital until the MRP of each falls to the cost of each.

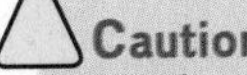

Caution

The least-cost and profit-maximizing formulas look very similar. Be sure to remember that the least-cost rule uses marginal product in the numerator, while the profit-maximizing rule uses marginal *revenue* product in the numerator.

PRACTICE The Least-Cost Rule and The Profit-Maximizing Rule

1. ________ State the least-cost rule to determine how much labor *or* capital to hire.

2. ________ If a firm can produce widgets with one production line using labor and one production line using robots, in order to produce 100 widgets per hour at the lowest cost, it should use each of the production lines at the level where the marginal products per dollar cost for both lines are *what*?

3. ________ A firm sells products for $10 per unit. Labor is the only resource, and the firm is earning a profit. The firm can hire one more worker for $100; he can increase total product by 13 units. Or the firm can buy one piece of capital for $200; it can increase total product by 25 units. Using the least-cost rule, should the firm hire the worker or buy the capital? Why?

4. ________ A firm produces teddy bears by using labor and capital. The cost of labor is $20 per unit, and the cost of capital is $30 per unit. At current output, the marginal product of labor is 40 teddy bears and the marginal product of capital is 90 teddy bears. To reduce the total cost of producing the current output of teddy bears, how should the firm change its spending on labor and capital?

5. ________ State the profit-maximizing rule to decide how much labor *and* capital to hire.

6. ________ A firm sells products for $10 per unit. Labor is the only resource, and the firm is earning a profit. The firm can hire one more worker for $100; he can increase total product by 13 units. The firm can buy one more piece of capital for $200; it can increase total product by 25 units. Using the profit-maximizing rule, should the firm hire the worker, buy the capital, or both? Why?

7. ________ A firm's marginal revenue product for the last unit of labor is $30 and the marginal revenue product for the last unit of capital is $40. What is the highest wage the firm would pay that last worker, and what is the most the firm would pay for the last unit of capital, in order to maximize profit?

Make sure to return to the AP Key Concepts section to check your understanding of the chapter's concepts important to AP coursework.

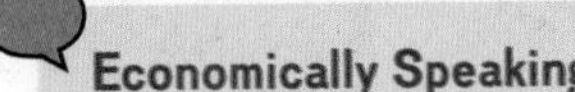

Economically Speaking

- **Derived Demand** the demand for labor is based on demand for the product produced by labor
- **Diminishing Returns** each worker adds to total product, but not as much as the worker before
- **Law of Diminishing Returns** as more units of a variable resource (like labor) are added to a fixed resource (like capital), marginal product falls
- **Least-Cost Rule** firms produce at their lowest cost when MRP of labor per dollar spent = MRP of capital per dollar spent
- **Marginal Product** the increase in total product resulting from hiring one more worker
- **Marginal Resource Cost** (MRC) the change in total cost caused by hiring one more unit of a resource (usually labor)
- **Marginal Revenue Product** the change in total revenue caused by hiring one more unit of a resource (usually labor)
- **MRP = MRC Rule** firms maximize profit when they hire the number of workers where the marginal revenue product equals the marginal resource cost
- **Profit-Maximizing Rule** firms maximize profit when the MRP for labor = the wage and the MRP of capital = the cost of capital
- **Total Product** the total output from all of the workers together
- **Wage Taker** a firm which must accept the wage that is set in the industry

15 Chapter

Wage Determination

The wages earned by workers are important to determining consumers' ability to buy products, the profitability of firms, and economic growth. Chapter 15 identifies the means by which wages are determined in a variety of labor markets, the causes of wage differentials, and market imperfections.

Material from Chapter 15 consistently appears in a few multiple-choice questions and an occasional free-response question on the AP Microeconomics exam. A few multiple-choice questions about real and nominal wages and human capital may also appear on the AP Macroeconomics exam.

Key Concepts

Below is a summary of the chapter's concepts important to AP coursework. Upon completing the lessons that follow, return to these concepts to make sure you understand them and how the practice exercises you completed relate to them.

- Labor includes all work performed by people.
- Wages include direct payment for work, as well as benefits such as insurance and vacation pay.
    - Nominal wage is the pay in current dollars.
    - Real wage is the amount of products that can be bought with the wage.
    - Change in Real Wage = Change in Nominal Wage – Change in Inflation Rate
- US wages are relatively high because of high productivity.
- In a perfectly competitive labor market, many firms hire identical, independent workers.
    - Firms and workers are both wage takers and have no market power to affect wages.
    - Labor supply slopes upward because workers choose between work and leisure.
    - Labor demand slopes downward because of diminishing returns.
    - Equilibrium wage is set by supply and demand in the industry; that wage becomes the wage (MRC) for the individual firm.
    - The individual firm maximizes profit by hiring where MRP = MRC.
    - In the industry, an increase in supply lowers wages; a decrease in supply raises wages.
    - Labor demand increases due to increased productivity or product demand.

    - If industry demand increases, MRC rises and the firm's demand (MRP) also increases.
    - If demand only increases for the firm, only the firm's MRP increases; wage does not.
- A monopsony is a market in which only one firm hires labor; the firm is a wage maker.
    - Supply slopes upward; to hire more workers, the firm must raise the wage.
    - MRC is higher than the wage because when the firm pays a higher wage to hire the next worker, it must also increase the wage of all previous workers.
    - The monopsonist maximizes profit by hiring the quantity where MRP = MRC, but paying the wage on the supply curve.
    - A monopsonist hires fewer workers and pays lower wages than in perfect competition.
- Labor unions use collective bargaining to negotiate better wages, benefits, and work conditions.
    - Exclusive (craft) unions restrict the supply of labor to raise wages.
    - Inclusive (industrial) unions negotiate a wage floor above the equilibrium wage.
- A minimum wage creates a wage floor, and if the wage floor is above the equilibrium wage, it can cause unemployment.
- Bilateral monopoly combines monopsony (one buyer) with an inclusive labor union (one seller).
    - The firm hires the quantity of workers where MRP = MRC.
    - The wage is determined by collective bargaining.
- Wage differences largely result from effects of supply and demand. Wages are higher when:
    - Industries have low labor supply or high labor demand.
    - Workers have high marginal revenue product (professional athletes and entertainers).
    - Workers invest in human capital (education and training to increase productivity).
    - The jobs are difficult, dangerous, or unpleasant.
- Wages also differ due to different abilities, lack of information about jobs and wages elsewhere, geographic immobility, licensing restrictions, discrimination, commission, and bonuses.

Now, let's examine more closely the following concepts from your textbook:

- **Labor, Wages, and Earnings**
- **A Purely Competitive Labor Market**
- **Monopsony Model**
- **Three Union Models**
- **Bilateral Monopoly Model**

These sections were selected because any one of these models could appear on the AP Microeconomics exam, and it is important to be able to draw and interpret each model.

Labor, Wages, and Earnings

Refer to pages 291–293 of your textbook.

A CLOSER LOOK Labor, Wages, and Earnings

Labor refers to any human work, whether performed by factory workers, agricultural workers, service providers, or managers. The **wage** is the firm's payment to workers. Keep in mind that a wage is not only the paycheck the worker receives; it also includes any benefits such as insurance and vacation time.

We must make an important distinction between the nominal wage and the real wage. The **nominal wage** is the pay in current dollars – what the worker sees in the current paycheck. The **real wage** is how many goods and services the worker can afford to buy with that paycheck. This distinction is important because as inflation causes the prices of products rise, the worker's paycheck will not stretch as far.

Change in Real Wage = Change in Nominal Wage – Change in Inflation Rate

If a worker's nominal wage rises 4% this year but prices rise 3% in that same time period, the worker's real wage has only risen 1% (4 – 3 = 1). For the purposes of this analysis, we will use the real wage.

US wages tend to be higher than in many countries because of high productivity. Demand for labor is strong in advanced economies because natural resources, capital, and technology are widely available, and labor quality is high and specialized. In the long run, as productivity increases, real wages rise.

PRACTICE Labor, Wages, and Earnings

1. ________ If nominal wage rises by 10% and prices rise by 8%, what happens to real wage?

2. ________ If nominal wage rises by 5% and prices rise by 2%, what happens to real wage?

3. ________ If nominal wage rises by 3% and prices fall by 2%, what happens to real wage?

4. ________ If nominal wage falls by 4% and prices fall by 1%, what happens to real wage?

5. ________ If nominal wage rises by 2% and prices rise by 2%, what happens to the quantity of goods purchased?

A Purely Competitive Labor Market

Refer to pages 293–295 of your textbook.

A CLOSER LOOK Market Demand and Supply of Labor, and Labor Market Equilibrium

In a **perfectly competitive labor market**, many firms compete to hire labor, and each worker is identical and independent. The market demand for labor consists of all of the demand curves (marginal revenue product curves) for all of the firms in the industry, added horizontally. Thus, the demand for labor in the industry slopes downward. Both the individual firms and the individual workers are wage takers, because neither has the market power to control the wage set in the industry.

Labor supply in the perfectly competitive labor market is represented by an upward-sloping supply curve. Every potential worker has the choice of using time for work or leisure. When wages are low, potential workers see little opportunity cost involved in choosing leisure. But as wages rise, the opportunity cost of remaining idle rises, and more people are enticed to work for a wage. So at a lower wage, the quantity of labor supplied is low, and at a higher wage, the quantity of labor supplied rises. Keep in mind that workers are also free to move between firms and industries, so a higher wage may draw workers from another industry or from serving as a volunteer or homemaker.

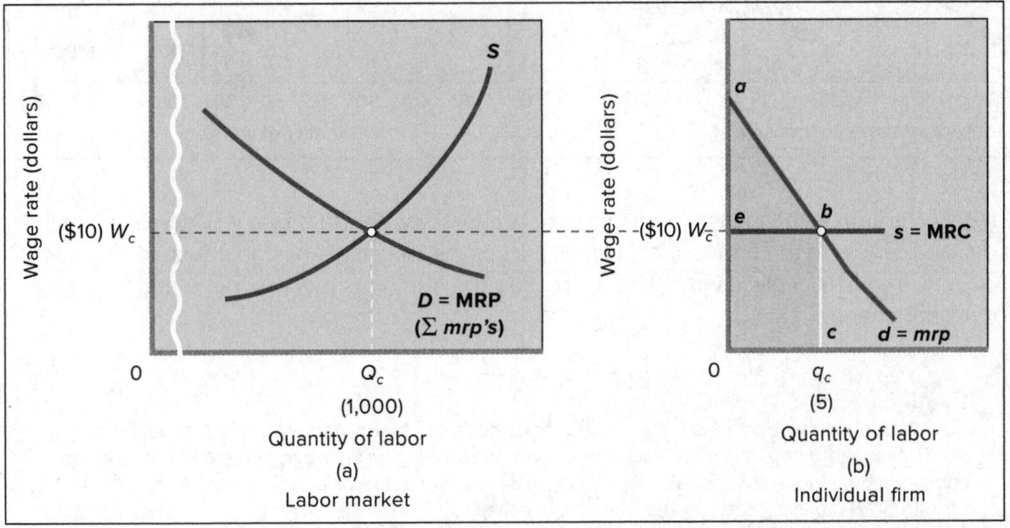

The equilibrium wage and quantity of workers hired are found at the point where supply equals demand for labor. In the graph above, the wage set in the industry translates to a perfectly elastic (horizontal) supply curve, which is the firm's MRC. The firm is a wage taker which must accept the wage set in the industry. The demand curve facing the firm is the downward-sloping portion of the MRP curve. The individual firm maximizes profit at the quantity of labor where MRP (the firm's demand curve) equals MRC (the firm's supply curve). This is the same MRP = MRC rule we saw in Chapter 14 and is very similar to the MR = MC rule the perfectly competitive firm uses to determine profit-maximizing output.

An increase in the supply of workers in the industry lowers the wage, causing MRC to fall for the firm. At a lower wage, the firm is willing and able to hire more workers, hiring where the new MRC = MRP. Conversely, if the supply of workers in the industry decreases, the wage increases, causing MRC to increase for the firm. At a higher wage, the firm hires fewer workers, hiring where the new MRC = MRP.

The demand for labor can shift due to a change in productivity or product price. Productivity can increase due to better training, healthcare, or technology. Product price can increase due to higher consumer income, a change in tastes, expectations for an improving economy, an increase in the price of substitutes, or a decrease in the price of complements.

If the demand for labor increases in the industry, the demand curve shifts to the right. The quantity of workers hired increases and the wage increases. The increased wage transfers to the individual firm, pushing the MRC (wage) for the firm upward. The individual firm's MRP (demand) curve also shifts to the right, and the new equilibrium for the firm occurs where the new MRC equals the new MRP. As illustrated in the graph below, the wage and the quantity of workers hired will increase.

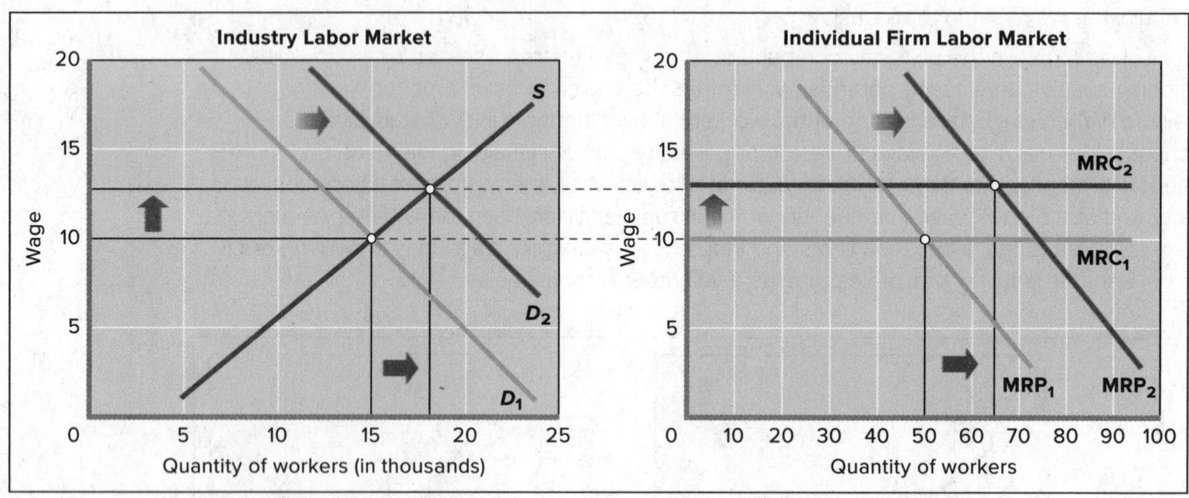

If only one firm in the industry can increase productivity, only that firm will increase its labor demand. Because the firm is such a small part of the industry, it has no effect on the wage. So MRC remains in place while MRP increases; the firm hires more workers and the wage does not change.

Caution

The parallels between perfectly competitive product and labor markets are important. You can see they look flipped. In both cases, the individual firm is a price/wage taker, and a change in supply or demand in the industry translates to a change in the price/wage for the individual firm. In both cases, a change that only affects the individual firm (a change in production cost in the product market or a change in productivity in the labor market) affects only the individual firm, but not the price/wage in the industry.

PRACTICE Market Demand and Supply of Labor, and Labor Market Equilibrium

1. __________ Labor supply is based on a worker's tradeoff between labor and *what*?

2. __________ The firm's demand curve is the downward-sloping portion of *what*?

3. __________ If consumers buy more imports, what happens to demand for US workers?

4. __________ If labor productivity increases, what happens to demand for labor?

5. __________ If the price of substitute capital falls, what happens to demand for labor?

6. In the space below, draw side-by-side graphs of a perfectly competitive labor market. Show the number of workers hired and wage paid in both the industry and the firm. Now assume a large number of workers enter the labor market. Show the effects on the graphs and answer the questions below.

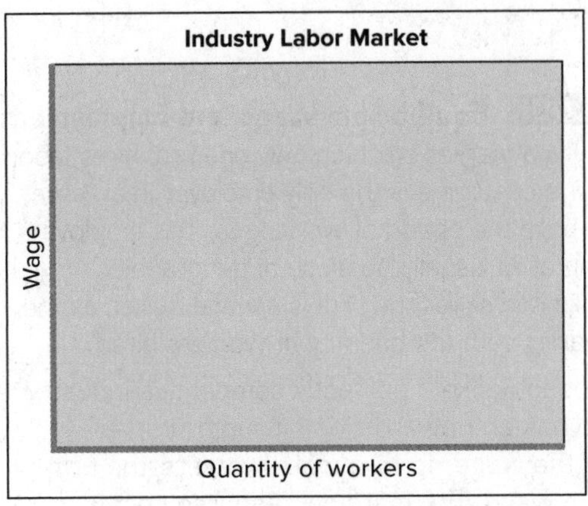

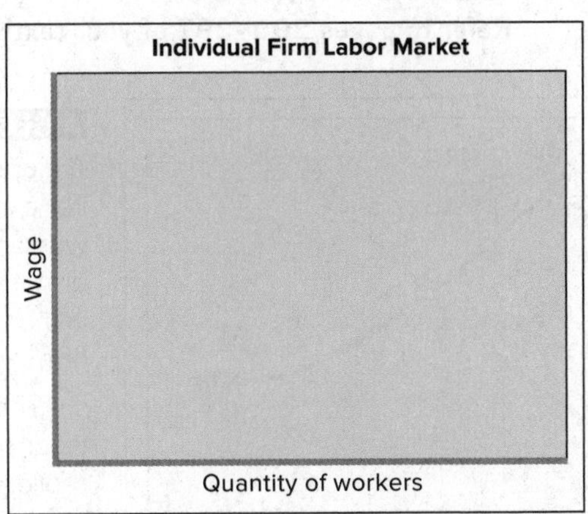

A. __________ Will industry supply increase, decrease, or remain the same?

B. __________ Will the wage increase, decrease, or remain the same?

C. __________ Will the number of workers hired in the industry increase or decrease?

D. __________ Will the number of workers hired by the firm increase or decrease?

7. In the space below, draw side-by-side graphs of a perfectly competitive labor market. Show the number of workers hired and wage paid in both the industry and the firm. Now assume the product becomes very popular and product demand has significantly increased. Show the effects on the graphs and answer the questions below.

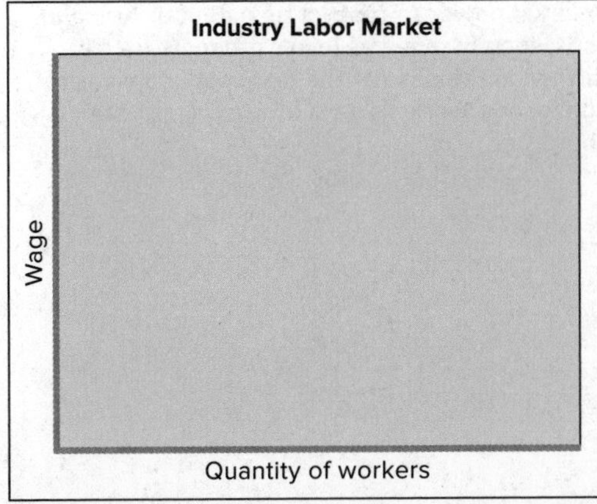

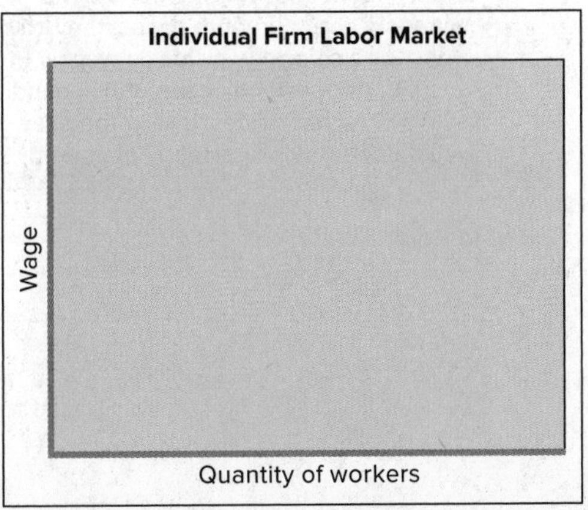

A. __________ Will industry demand increase, decrease, or remain the same?

B. __________ Will the wage increase, decrease, or remain the same?

C. __________ Will the firm's demand for labor increase or decrease?

D. __________ Will the number of workers hired by the firm increase or decrease?

Monopsony Model

Refer to pages 295–297 of your textbook.

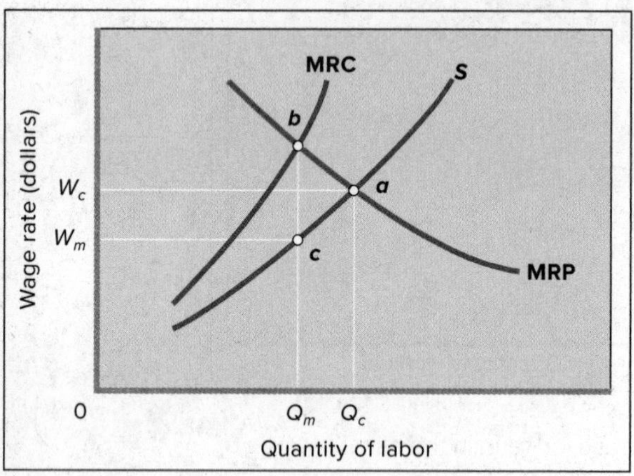

A CLOSER LOOK Equilibrium Wage and Employment

A **monopsony** is a market in which only one firm hires labor. For example, if a coal mine is the only employer in an area, workers only have the option of working for this employer or not working at all, usually because of geographic immobility or limited skills. The firm is a wage maker, as the firm's wage varies with the quantity of workers hired.

The monopsony, like a perfectly competitive industry labor market, has an upward-sloping supply curve, representing the wage. To hire more workers, the firm must raise the wage. The marginal resource cost is higher than the wage, because the firm cannot offer the higher wage only to the next worker hired; it must also raise the wages of all of the other workers in order to prevent unrest. So if the firm hires four workers at a wage of $10, and it must pay a wage of $11 to hire the fifth worker, the marginal resource cost is actually $15, because the firm must also pay the previous four workers the extra $1 in wage.

The monopsonist, like the perfect competitor, maximizes profit at the quantity of workers where MRP = MRC, at Point B on the graph above. However, it will only pay the wage on the supply curve at that quantity (at Point C), because workers are willing to accept that wage. The monopsonist maximizes its profit by hiring fewer workers and paying a lower wage than would occur in the perfectly competitive labor market (at Point A). As a result, fewer products are produced and consumers face higher prices.

Caution

By now, you should recognize parallels between the monopoly selling in the product market and the monopsony hiring in the labor market. The monopsony graph looks like a flipped-over monopoly graph. In both cases, the firm has the market power to restrict its output or hiring in order to raise prices or lower wages. In both cases, society receives fewer products than it would under perfectly competitive conditions. Further, in the case of the monopoly, consumers must pay higher prices, and in the case of the monopsony, workers earn lower wages, than would occur under perfectly competitive conditions.

PRACTICE Equilibrium Wage and Employment

1. __________ Why is MRC higher than the supply curve for the monopsony?

2. In the blank graph on the right, draw a monopsony. Show the number of workers hired and wage paid.

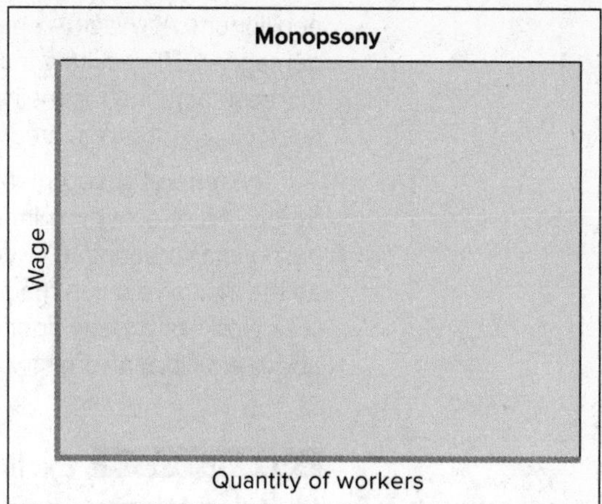

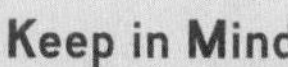

Keep in Mind

Questions on AP Microeconomics exams have overwhelmingly focused on perfectly competitive labor markets and the minimum wage. However, the monopsony model has been tested in both the multiple choice and free-response portions of the exam. The monopsony, union, and bilateral monopoly models are briefly discussed to illustrate the differences among labor markets and explain some differences in wages.

Three Union Models

Refer to pages 297–299 of your textbook.

A CLOSER LOOK Exclusive/Craft Union, Inclusive/Industrial Union, and the Minimum Wage

Labor unions are organizations of workers who sell their labor services collectively. Unions use bargaining power to negotiate for better wages, benefits, and working conditions. Unions recognize that if the wage increases without a corresponding increase in demand, firms will hire fewer workers. So unions work to increase demand for labor by increasing demand for the products they produce, lobbying for government funding and contracts, supporting increases in the minimum wage to reduce substitution of labor, and opposing imported products and immigrant labor.

An **exclusive (craft) union** restricts the supply of labor in order to increase the wage. Doctors, teachers, cosmetologists, electricians, plumbers, and other workers must meet occupational licensing or other requirements that make it difficult to enter the career, so supply is restricted in order to increase wages. Unions also supported legislation to reduce immigration, child labor, and the length of the workweek.

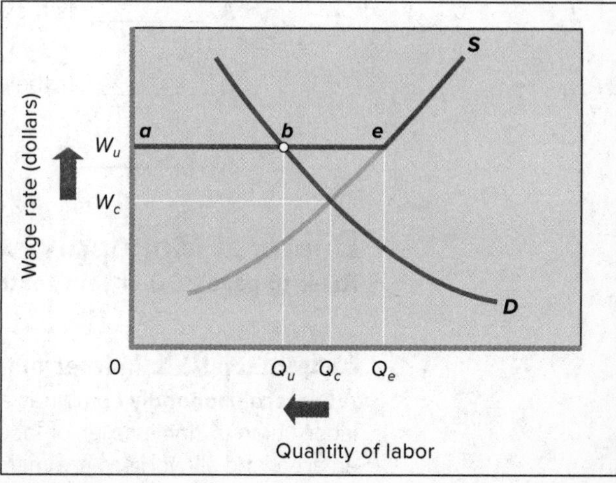

An **inclusive (industrial) union** includes all workers in an industry, such as auto and steel workers. Especially when workers are unskilled or semi-skilled, it is easy for an employer to substitute one worker for another. Rather than trying to exclude others from entering the industry, inclusive unions use the power of numbers to collectively bargain with management for higher wages, creating a wage floor. The higher wage must be paid to all workers, and the firm hires the quantity where supply equals demand. But as illustrated in the graph, the wage floor places the wage above equilibrium. At Wage A, the quantity of workers supplied (E) is greater than the quantity demanded (B), resulting in unemployment. Therefore, union members have an incentive to increase demand for their product, to increase the demand for workers and reduce the unemployment associated with the higher wage.

The federal government and many states set a **minimum wage**, the lowest wage allowed by law. An effective minimum wage creates a wage floor above the equilibrium wage, for the purpose of creating a "living wage" that helps workers avoid poverty. The model is the same as the inclusive union model. If the minimum wage is below or equal to equilibrium, it guarantees workers a wage floor and does not create unemployment. But if the minimum wage is above equilibrium, unemployment could result.

PRACTICE **Exclusive/Craft Union, Inclusive/Industrial Union, and the Minimum Wage**

1. __________ How do exclusive unions raise wages?

2. __________ How do inclusive unions raise wages?

3. In the space below, draw a graph illustrating an effective minimum wage in the labor market. Show the number of workers hired and the wage paid. Then answer the questions below.

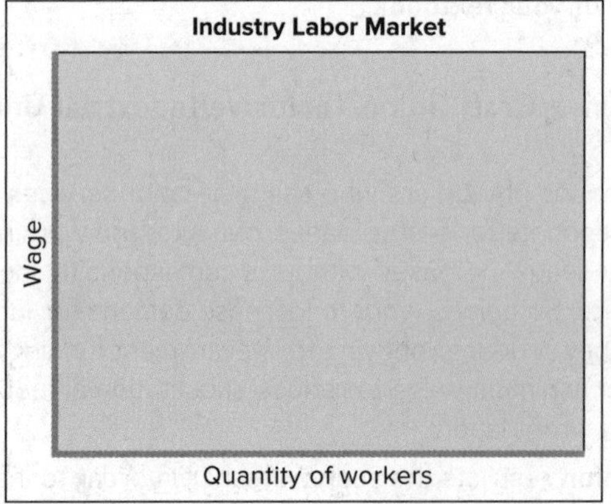

A. __________ Is the wage paid higher or lower than the equilibrium wage?

B. __________ Is the number of workers hired higher or lower than at equilibrium?

C. __________ What will an effective minimum wage cause in the labor market?

Bilateral Monopoly Model

Refer to page 300 of your textbook.

A CLOSER LOOK **Indeterminate Outcome of Bilateral Monopoly**

A **bilateral monopoly** combines a monopsony (a single buyer of labor) with an inclusive labor union (a single seller of labor). An example is a coal mine that is the only employer in an area, and all workers are members of a union. As shown in the graph on the following page, the firm will hire the quantity of workers where MRP = MRC. But where will the wage be set? The firm wants to set the wage down on the supply curve, but the union wants to set the wage up where MRP = MRC. The wage depends on the relative strength of labor and management during negotiations, and will fall somewhere between those two wages.

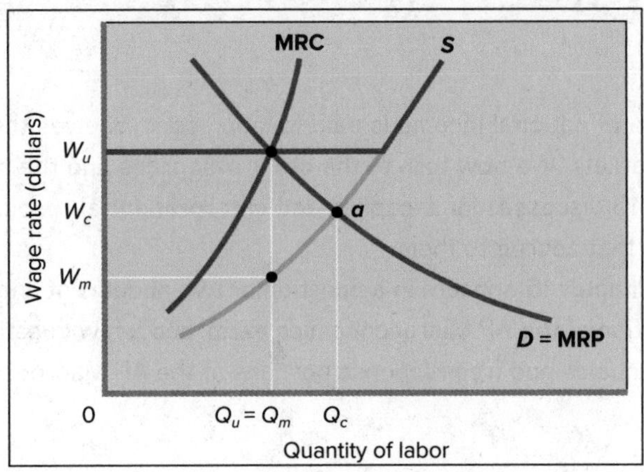

PRACTICE Indeterminate Outcome of Bilateral Monopoly

1. __________ In a bilateral monopoly, will the firm hire more or fewer workers than would be hired at equilibrium in a perfectly competitive labor market?

2. __________ If this market were a monopsony without a union, would wages be higher or lower than equilibrium in a perfectly competitive labor market?

3. __________ If the union is relatively stronger than management, will wages be higher or lower than equilibrium in a perfectly competitive labor market?

Make sure to return to the AP Key Concepts section to check your understanding of the chapter's concepts important to AP coursework.

Economically Speaking

- **Bilateral Monopoly** combines monopsony (one buyer) with an inclusive labor union (one seller)
- **Exclusive (Craft) Union** restricts the supply of labor in order to increase the wage
- **Inclusive (Industrial) Union** includes all workers in an industry
- **Labor** any human work, regardless of what type of work is performed
- **Labor Union** an organization of workers who sell their labor services collectively
- **Minimum Wage** the lowest wage allowed by law
- **Monopsony** a market in which only one firm hires labor
- **Nominal Wage** the wage in current dollars; what a worker sees in a paycheck
- **Perfectly Competitive Labor Market** many firms compete to hire labor, and each worker is identical and independent
- **Real Wage** how much a worker can buy with a paycheck, accounting for inflation
- **Wage** a firm's payment to workers, including any benefits

Chapter 16

Rent, Interest, and Profit

Approximately 70% of national income is paid to labor, so it receives the focus of attention in resource markets. We now turn to the other resources and the returns paid for their use. Chapter 16 discusses land, capital, and entrepreneurial resources and the rent, interest, and profit that accrue to them.

Material from Chapter 16 appears in a question or two about rent and profit on the multiple-choice portion of the AP Microeconomics exam, and a few questions about interest are on the multiple-choice and free-response portions of the AP Macroeconomics exam.

Key Concepts

Below is a summary of the chapter's concepts important to AP coursework. Upon completing the lessons that follow, return to these concepts to make sure you understand them and how the practice exercises you completed relate to them.

- Approximately 70% of national income is paid to labor in wages.
- Land has a perfectly inelastic supply curve; regardless of price, quantity of land does not change.
    - Demand for land slopes downward because of diminishing returns and falling MRP.
    - Economic rent is the payment for land (or another resource) with fixed supply.
    - Changes in the price of land are solely due to changes in the demand for the land.
- In the loanable funds market, interest rates (the price paid to use borrowed money) are set.
    - Supply comes from households who are willing to forego current spending to save.
        - Households save little at low interest rates and more at high interest rates.
        - Supply increases if consumers have an incentive to save more (such as saving for retirement) and decreases if consumers lose jobs or incentive to save.
        - An increase in supply of loanable funds lowers interest rates, and vice versa.
    - Demand for loanable funds comes from consumers, firms, and government.
        - Consumers borrow to buy houses, cars, and college education.
        - Firms borrow to buy capital, expand factories, and start businesses; they will only borrow if expected return on investment is higher than the interest rate.
        - Government borrows to finance federal deficits.
        - An increase in demand for loanable funds raises interest rates, and vice versa.

- An increase in interest rates can reduce investment and the rate of economic growth.
- Time-value of money is the idea that money is more valuable the sooner it is received.
    - If you receive money today, you can put it in a bank to earn compound interest; if you receive the money a year from now, you've lost that foregone interest.
    - Future value is the amount to which a current amount will grow with interest.
    - Present value is the current value of an amount of money you will receive in the future minus the interest you will earn between now and the future date.
- The nominal interest rate is expressed in the current value of dollars.
    - Nominal Interest Rate = Real Interest Rate + Expected Inflation Rate
- The real interest rate is the interest rate adjusted for expected inflation.
    - Real Interest Rate = Nominal Interest Rate – Expected Inflation Rate

- Profit is what motivates entrepreneurs to take the risk to start a business.
    - Explicit costs (accounting costs) are payments the firm makes to outsiders.
    - Implicit costs are the opportunity costs of using resources the firm owns, rather than supplying those resources to others in the market.
    - Accounting profit is the total revenue minus the explicit cost.
    - Normal profit is the payment to the entrepreneur for the opportunity cost of what could have been earned in a different business venture.
    - Economic profit is the total revenue minus the explicit and implicit costs.
    - Monopolies can sustain long-run economic profit due to barriers to entry.

Now, let's examine more closely the following concepts from your textbook:

- **Economic Rent**
- **Loanable Funds Theory of Interest Rates**
- **Role of Interest Rates**

These sections were selected because it can require a little practice to fully understand how to manipulate and interpret the graphs and formulas.

Economic Rent

Refer to pages 319–322 of your textbook.

A CLOSER LOOK Equilibrium Rent and Changes in Demand, and Land Rent: A Surplus Payment

Labor wages constituted 70% of all national income in 2015. Profit and proprietors' income are 16% of national income, while interest is 9% and rent is 5% of national income. The distribution of income has important implications for entrepreneurship, investment in economic growth, and the ability of consumers to buy products and save money for further investment.

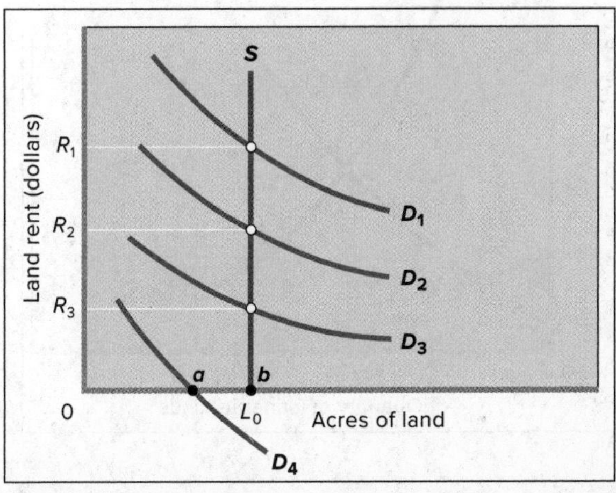

We begin our analysis of land with the assumption that land is fixed in supply, has only one use at a time, is all equal in quality, and is sold in a competitive market with many buyers and sellers who cannot individually affect the price. The distinguishing feature of the land market is that supply is perfectly inelastic. The quantity of land cannot be increased in response to a higher price. Demand (the marginal revenue product) for land slopes downward because of diminishing returns and because as more products produced by the land are sold, the price falls for those products.

Economic rent is the price paid for the use of land (or any other natural resource) that is fixed in supply. The rent is considered a surplus payment, because the same amount of land is available, whether or not anyone is willing to buy it. Because supply is fixed, the economic rent for land is based on the demand for it. The price of goods produced with the land, the productivity of the land, and the costs of other resources (primarily capital) used with the land can all affect the demand for land.

In reality, productivity differs markedly among properties, which explains why farmland in Indiana sells for a much higher price than open land in Wyoming. Strong demand for the land pushes up the price (rent). In addition, land can be used for multiple purposes at once. Farmers can place windmills above the land or drill for oil while still farming the land. Such differences in productivity account for much of the price differential in land. In the United Arab Emirates, off the coast of Dubai, islands have been created in the sea, so even the assumption of a fixed amount of land may no longer hold true.

PRACTICE Equilibrium Rent and Changes in Demand, and Land Rent: A Surplus Payment

1. __________ In the land market, which is perfectly inelastic: supply or demand?

2. __________ As the demand for land increases, does the quantity supplied increase?

3. __________ If desert land is found suitable for the placement of solar panels, what will happen to the price of the desert land?

Loanable Funds Theory of Interest Rates

Refer to pages 323–325 of your textbook.

A CLOSER LOOK Supply of Loanable Funds and Demand for Loanable Funds

Interest is the price paid for the use of borrowed money. Money is not a resource; it is only a means to buy resources (land, labor, capital, and entrepreneurship) to produce goods and services. Interest is an incentive for people to forego current use of money in order to have even more money in the future.

In the **loanable funds market**, the supply of loanable funds comes from households who have saved money and are willing to loan it to others, often through banks. When interest rates are low, people incur little opportunity cost for holding money in cash, so they have little incentive to put savings in a bank. But as interest rates rise, people are more willing to save and loan money to others. Therefore, the supply curve for loanable funds slopes upward. Because many people save for large

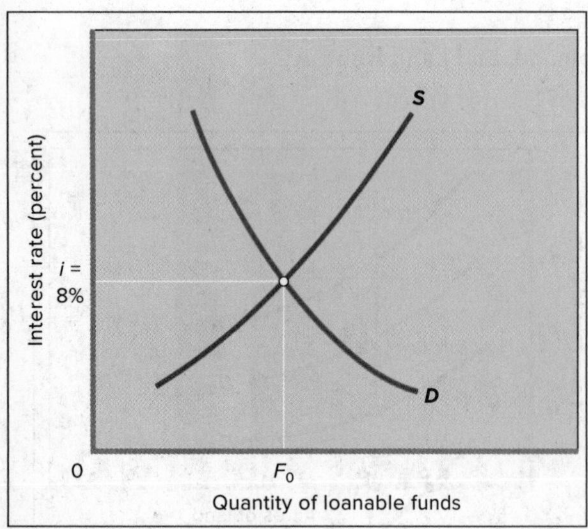

purchases, retirement, or economic security regardless of interest rates, the supply curve may be fairly inelastic.

The demand for loanable funds comes from a number of sources. Consumers borrow to buy houses, cars, and college education. The federal government borrows to finance the national debt. Firms borrow to buy capital, expand factories, and start new businesses. They will only invest if the return on investment is greater than the interest rate charged for the loan. For example, if the firm expects a 6% return on investment, but the interest rate for the loan is 8%, the firm would lose money and should not borrow. As a result, at low interest rates, firms are more willing to borrow, and at higher interest rates, firms are less willing to borrow. Therefore, the demand for loanable funds is a downward-sloping curve.

The supply of loanable funds increases if consumers have an incentive to save more, such as a tax break for interest or parents saving more for their children's future tuition. The supply of loanable funds can decrease if significant numbers of savers lose jobs or income, and households have to dip into their savings for current consumption. In addition to private market actions, the Federal Reserve, the central bank of the United States, can increase or reduce the money supply in the economy through banks as a way of stabilizing the economy. An increase in the supply of loanable funds lowers interest rates; a decrease in the supply of loanable funds increases interest rates.

The demand for loanable funds increases if firms find that new equipment can raise productivity or if product demand pushes up the price, increasing the return on investment. Lower productivity or product prices would lead firms to decrease their demand for loanable funds. An increase in the demand for loanable funds increases interest rates; a decrease in demand lowers interest rates.

Changes in interest rates have implications far beyond the individual firm. High interest rates can deter investment or restrict it to only those projects most likely to see a high return on investment. If firms are less willing to borrow for investment, total spending in the economy can slow, leading to recession. Conversely, lower interest rates make it more profitable for firms to borrow to finance research and development, which can spur innovation and significantly increase long-run economic growth.

PRACTICE Supply of Loanable Funds and Demand for Loanable Funds

1. In the space below, draw a graph of the loanable funds market. Show the interest rate and the quantity of funds loaned. Now assume that the government creates a massive program to build infrastructure across the country and must borrow money to finance it. Show the effects on the graph and answer the questions below.

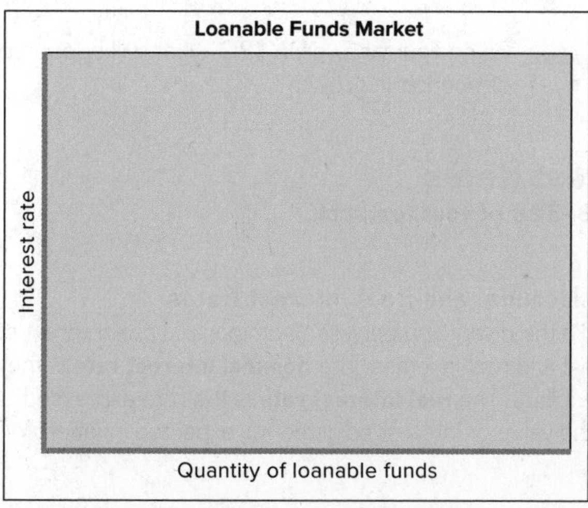

A. _________ What increased for loanable funds: supply or demand?

B. _________ Will the interest rate increase or decrease?

C. _________ Given the change in interest rate (in #1B), what will happen to demand for loans by firms planning capital investment?

D. _________ Given your answer in #1C, what will happen to the national rate of economic growth?

2. In the space below, draw a graph of the loanable funds market. Show the interest rate and the quantity of funds loaned. Now assume that the cost of college tuition increases and parents significantly increase their savings for college funds. Show the effects on the graph and answer the questions below.

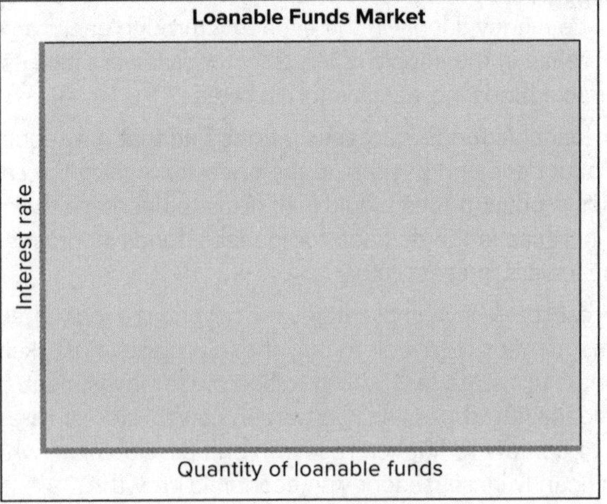

A. _________ What increased for loanable funds: supply or demand?

B. _________ Will the interest rate increase or decrease?

C. _________ Given the change in interest rate (in #2B), what will happen to the quantity of loans demanded by firms planning capital investment?

D. _________ Given your answer in #2C, what will happen to the national rate of economic growth?

Role of Interest Rates

Refer to pages 326–328 of your textbook.

A CLOSER LOOK Nominal and Real Interest Rates

It is important to make the distinction between nominal and real interest rates in the same way we compared nominal and real incomes. The **nominal interest rate** is the rate expressed in the current value of dollars. The **real interest rate** is the rate expressed in the purchasing power of dollars – the value of interest adjusted for expected inflation. When a bank makes a loan, it knows the money repaid by the borrower will be worth less because of inflation. In order to recover the full value of the money loaned, the bank charges the real interest rate plus the expected inflation rate, which equals the nominal interest rate that the borrower sees. So if the bank requires a 4% real interest rate and expects 3% inflation, it charges the customer 7% interest. Because the firm understands it will be repaying the loan with those lower-value dollars, it focuses on the real interest rate in making investment decisions.

Nominal Interest Rate = Real Interest Rate + Expected Inflation Rate
Real Interest Rate = Nominal Interest Rate – Expected Inflation Rate

PRACTICE Nominal and Real Interest Rates

1. __________ If a bank expects inflation to rise, what will it do to the nominal interest rate?

2. __________ If expected return on investment is 10%, the nominal interest rate is 12%, and the real interest rate is 8%, will the firm borrow for capital investment?

3. Complete the table.

Real Interest Rate	Expected Inflation	Nominal Interest Rate
4%	2%	
5%		8%
	7%	9%
12%	–1%	
10%		10%
	–2%	7%

Make sure to return to the AP Key Concepts section to check your understanding of the chapter's concepts important to AP coursework.

Economically Speaking

- **Economic Rent** the price paid for the use of land and other natural resources with a fixed supply
- **Interest** the price paid for the use of borrowed money
- **Loanable Funds Market** where loans are made among households, firms, and government
- **Nominal Interest Rate** the rate expressed in the current value of dollars
- **Real Interest Rate** the rate adjusted for expected inflation

17 Chapter

Public Finance: Expenditures and Taxes

As we have seen, government plays an important role in addressing market failures. But it also plays a significant role in taxation and redistribution of income. Chapter 17 introduces the types, effects, and efficiency losses of taxation.

Material from Chapter 17 consistently appears in one or two multiple-choice questions and infrequently in a free-response question on the AP Microeconomics exam.

Key Concepts

Below is a summary of the chapter's concepts important to AP coursework. Upon completing the lessons that follow, return to these concepts to make sure you understand them and how the practice exercises you completed relate to them.

- Governments attempt to reduce income inequality by collecting taxes from those with higher incomes (especially through progressive income taxes) and transferring the revenue to those with lower incomes.
- Federal, state, and local governments gain and spend the largest portion of revenues differently:
  - Federal revenue from personal income tax; spending on pensions and income security.
  - State revenue from sales, excise, or income tax; spending on education.
  - Local revenue from property tax; spending on education.
- An excise tax is a tax on a specific product, such as cigarettes or airline tickets.
- The benefits-received principle holds that taxpayers that benefit from a specific public good should pay the tax for the use of that public good.
- The ability-to-pay principle holds that taxpayers should be charged according to their income.
- Tax systems affect taxpayers differently:
  - Progressive tax – as income rises, the percentage of income paid in tax rises.
  - Proportional tax – each taxpayer pays the same percentage of income in taxes.
  - Regressive tax – as income rises, the percentage of income paid in tax falls.
- Policymakers must consider tax incidence, or who pays the final burden of a tax.
- To graph the levy of a tax, the supply curve shifts directly up by the amount of the tax.
  - The tax increases the equilibrium price and reduces the equilibrium quantity.
  - The tax creates a deadweight loss, representing loss of consumer and producer surplus.

- If product demand is elastic, the firm must pay most of the tax.
- If product demand is inelastic, consumers must pay most of the tax.
- Governments primarily levy excise taxes on products with inelastic demand because consumers continue to buy the product and government can generate the most revenue.

Now, let's examine more closely the following concepts from your textbook:

- **Apportioning the Tax Burden**
- **Tax Incidence and Efficiency Loss**

These sections were selected because the terms for different taxes can be confusing and it can take some practice to interpret the graph demonstrating the effects of an excise tax.

Apportioning the Tax Burden

Refer to pages 344–347 of your textbook.

A CLOSER LOOK Benefits Received vs. Ability to Pay; Progressive, Proportional, and Regressive Taxes

While private sector firms and households are responsible for most economic activity, government plays many roles in our economy. Government produces public goods, buys products from firms, hires labor from households, regulates businesses, and reduces income inequality by collecting taxes from those with higher incomes and transferring the revenue to those with lower incomes.

While we tend to use the term "government" loosely, federal, state, and local governments have very different roles and responsibilities, so their revenue sources and spending functions are different. The federal government gets the largest part of its revenue from personal income taxes; pensions and income security represent the largest category of spending. States rely on income, sales, and/or **excise tax** (a tax on a specific product), while the largest category of spending is education. Local governments rely on property taxes for most of their revenue and spend the largest portion of it for education.

Once a government determines which goods and services will be provided, it must determine who will pay for those products through taxes. The **benefits-received principle** holds that those who use the public good should pay the taxes to support that public good. Gasoline taxes use this system, with the idea that those who use the roads most will pay the most for their upkeep. However, this principle would be clearly ineffective in the case of imposing higher taxes on those who receive food stamps, housing subsidies, and unemployment checks; the low-income or unemployment status that qualifies them for the benefits also indicates they are the least able to afford a higher tax rate. Further, how can we calculate indirect benefits of public goods in the community? The **ability-to-pay principle** holds that taxpayers should be charged according to their income; those with higher incomes should pay higher tax rates. Federal income taxes are based on this principle, with the idea that those with higher incomes are more financially able to pay taxes than those with lower incomes. One problem with this principle is that it is difficult to determine the relative ability of any particular household to pay a certain tax rate. Critics argue that progressive taxes "punish" financial success and can discourage entrepreneurship. As a result of disagreement over what is a "fair" tax, governments generally levy a variety of taxes.

Under a **progressive tax,** such as a federal income tax, as income rises, the percentage of income paid in tax rises. A person who earns $9,000 might be in a 10% tax bracket, while someone who earns $50,000 might be in a 25% tax bracket. A **proportional tax** requires each taxpayer to pay the same percentage of income in taxes, regardless of income. A 3% state income tax would require each taxpayer to pay 3% of taxable income, whether the person earned $10,000 or $500,000. With a **regressive tax,** those with lower incomes pay a higher percentage of their income in tax than those with higher incomes. Sales taxes are regressive, even though they may seem to be proportional. Those with lower incomes spend a greater proportion of their income on taxable items, while those with higher incomes save and invest part of their income – which is not subject to the sales tax. So the lower-income taxpayer may pay 5% of his income in sales tax, while the higher-income taxpayer pays only 3% of his income in sales tax. Social Security payroll taxes are regressive, in that only the first $118,500 of income is subject to the payroll tax. Workers earning less than that amount pay the payroll tax on their entire income, while those earning higher incomes pay no more payroll tax. Other significant earnings from interest, dividends, and other benefits are not subject to the Social Security payroll tax at all.

PRACTICE **Benefits Received vs Ability to Pay; Progressive, Proportional, and Regressive Taxes**

Identify each of the following taxes as progressive, proportional, or regressive.

1. _________ Every taxpayer must pay 4.5% of income in taxes.

2. _________ Taxpayers must pay 6% sales tax on all products.

3. _________ Each taxpayer must pay $1000.

4. _________ Taxpayers who earn less than $50,000 pay a 10% tax rate; those who earn more than $50,000 pay a 15% tax rate.

If the government wants to reduce income inequality:

5. _________ Should the government levy progressive, proportional, or regressive taxes?

6. _________ What should the government do to taxes for those with higher incomes?

7. _________ What should the government do to taxes for those with lower incomes?

8. _________ What should the government do to spending for poverty programs?

Tax Incidence and Efficiency Loss

Refer to pages 347–350 of your textbook.

A CLOSER LOOK **Elasticity and Tax Incidence, and Efficiency Loss of a Tax**
Policymakers must also consider **tax incidence**, or who pays the final burden of a tax. Sometimes taxes can be shifted to other people. When a property tax increases, a landlord

may simply raise the rent. If a tax is placed on a product, the firm may raise the price for consumers. When graphing an excise tax increase, the supply curve shifts directly upward by the amount of the tax. In the graph below, the $2 tax shifted the supply curve directly upward by $2 (from S to S_t). Market equilibrium shifts to a lower quantity and a higher price. We then need to determine how the burden of the tax is divided; is it paid by the firm, the consumer, or both? In this case, the price to consumers rose from $8 to $9, so consumers paid $1 of the tax. But because the tax is $2, the firm must pay the other $1 of the tax.

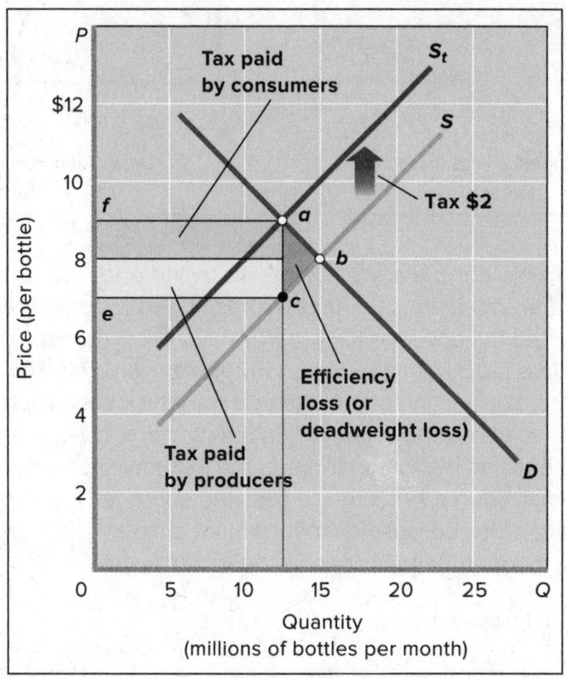

At the new equilibrium quantity of 12.5 million, the firm receives $87.5 million (the $7 revenue to the firm × 12.5 million rectangular area above). The government's revenue from the tax is $25 million (the $2 tax × 12.5 million rectangular area above). A **deadweight loss** appears in triangle *abc*, representing the loss of producer and consumer surplus resulting from the tax. Production and consumption have been reduced from the point where supply equals demand, so we no longer achieve allocative efficiency. It is the same deadweight loss we saw in Chapter 11, although in that case it resulted from the monopoly restricting output to raise the price. In this case, government is raising the price for tax revenue. The triangle of deadweight loss points toward the point of allocative efficiency (Point b).

Elasticity of demand determines how the tax is apportioned. When demand is elastic, consumers are sensitive to price changes. As demonstrated in Graph (a) shown on the next page, an increase in price results in a much lower quantity demanded. If we apply the $2 tax increase with elastic demand, equilibrium quantity falls significantly, from Point b to Point a. The area *abc* indicates the large deadweight loss. But notice that the tax passed on to consumers (the difference between P1 and P2) is quite small, while the tax paid by the firm (the difference between P1 and P3) is relatively large. When demand is elastic, consumers pay little of the tax, while the firm pays more of the tax, and the area of deadweight loss is large. In the extreme, if demand were perfectly elastic (horizontal), any attempt to raise the price of the product through a tax would reduce the quantity demanded to zero. So if the firm wanted to remain in operation, it would be forced to absorb the entire cost of the tax. The more elastic the product demand, the more the firm must absorb the tax responsibility.

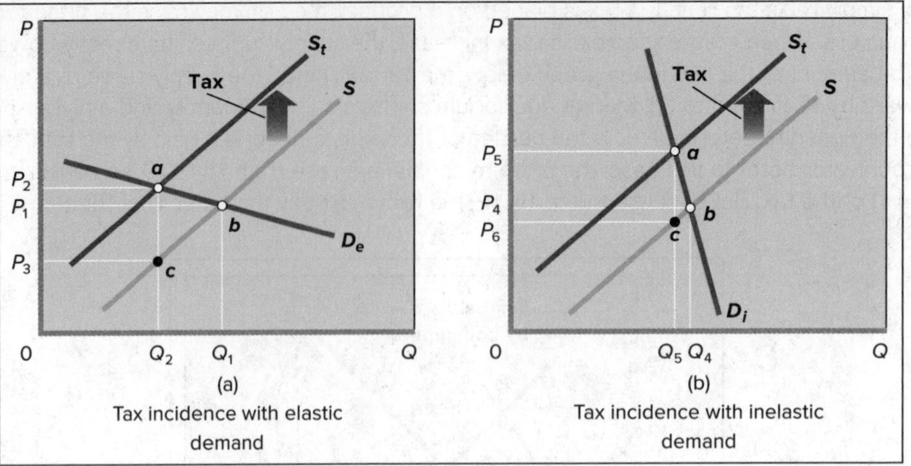

(a)
Tax incidence with elastic demand

(b)
Tax incidence with inelastic demand

When demand is inelastic, consumers are less sensitive to price change, so they only slightly reduce the quantity demanded after the tax. The result, as shown in Graph (b) above, is that most of the tax is shifted to consumers (P4 to P5), while firms pay little of the tax (P4 to P6) and the deadweight loss (*abc*) is small. This is why governments tend to place excise taxes on gasoline, cigarettes, alcohol, and other products for which consumer demand is inelastic; consumers will continue to buy the product, generating more government revenue and leaving little responsibility for the tax on firms. In the extreme situation of a perfectly inelastic (vertical) demand curve, firms would pass the entire tax onto consumers and there would be no deadweight loss because quantity did not change. The more inelastic the product demand, the more of the tax is passed on to consumers.

Keep in Mind
It is important to be able to identify producer and consumer surplus, after-tax deadweight loss, the firm's revenue, the tax revenue, and the relative burdens of the taxes to consumers and the firm, because such questions have appeared on previous AP Microeconomics exams.

PRACTICE Elasticity and Tax Incidence, and Efficiency Loss of a Tax

1. __________ If demand is inelastic, who pays a larger portion of the tax: consumers or firms?

2. __________ Governments are more effective in collecting revenues from excise taxes when demand for the product is: elastic or inelastic?

Use the graph to answer the questions which follow.

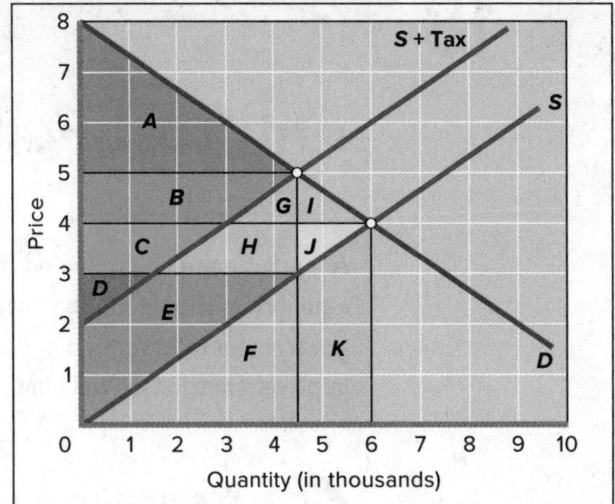

3. At market equilibrium before a $2 tax is imposed:

A. __________ What is the equilibrium price?

B. __________ What is the equilibrium quantity?

C. __________ What letters represent the area of consumer surplus?

D. __________ What letters represent the area of producer surplus?

4. After the $2 tax is imposed:

A. __________ What letters represent the area of tax revenue paid?

B. __________ What letters represent the area of deadweight loss?

C. __________ What letter represents the area of consumer surplus?

D. __________ What letter represents the area of producer surplus?

E. __________ Do the consumers pay the entire $2 tax on each product?

Make sure to return to the AP Key Concepts section to check your understanding of the chapter's concepts important to AP coursework.

Economically Speaking

- **Ability-to-Pay Principle** those who receive higher incomes should pay higher tax rates
- **Benefits-Received Principle** those who use the public good should pay the taxes to support that public good
- **Deadweight Loss** the loss of producer and consumer surplus resulting from a tax
- **Excise Tax** a tax placed on a specific product
- **Progressive Tax** as income rises, the percentage of income paid in tax rises
- **Proportional Tax** each taxpayer pays the same percentage of income in taxes
- **Regressive Tax** those with lower incomes pay a higher percentage of their income in taxes
- **Tax Incidence** who pays the final burden of a tax

Chapter 18

Antitrust Policy and Regulation

A market economy relies on the actions of producers and consumers to determine market equilibrium. But monopoly market power and consumer protection concerns require government intervention in some markets. Chapter 18 describes government intervention in private markets. While important, little from this chapter has appeared on the exams.

Key Concepts

Below is a summary of the chapter's concepts important to AP coursework.

- Antitrust policies restrict monopoly behavior and promote competition.
    - Monopoly price exceeds marginal cost at profit-maximizing output, so monopolies raise prices, reduce output, create barriers to competition, and violate allocative efficiency.
    - Antitrust laws such as the Sherman and Clayton Acts limit monopoly behaviors like price discrimination when they are intended to prevent competition.
- A horizontal merger—a merger of firms making similar products—can create monopoly power.
    - Government regulates mergers that would significantly reduce competition.
    - A vertical merger is a merger between firms at different stages of production.
- Price-fixing and collusion among oligopolists are illegal under US law, and cartels are prosecuted and fined for undertaking such activity.
- A natural monopoly occurs when economies of scale are so strong that it is more efficient to have one producer, rather than several firms in the industry (usually utility companies).
    - Government regulation sets the price equal to where average total cost equals demand.
    - At the "fair return price," the firm still earns a normal profit, but not economic profit.

PRACTICE Antitrust Policy: Issues and Impacts

1. __________ What is the term for laws that restrict monopolies and promote competition?

2. __________ Regulators setting a "fair return" price should set price where demand = *what*?

Economically Speaking

- **Antitrust Policy** government actions to restrict monopoly behavior and promote competition
- **Horizontal Merger** a merger between two firms that make similar products
- **Vertical Merger** a merger between firms at different stages of the production process

Chapter 19

Income Inequality, Poverty, and Discrimination

Differences in household incomes are to be expected in a market economy. But the continuing increase in income inequality has been a source of serious political debate in recent years. Chapter 19 discusses causes of income inequality, a model to measure it, and programs to reduce it.

Material from Chapter 19 may appear in one or two multiple-choice questions on the AP Microeconomics exam.

Key Concepts

Below is a summary of the chapter's concepts important to AP coursework. Upon completing the lesson that follows, return to these concepts to make sure you understand them and how the practice exercise you completed relates to them.

- The Lorenz Curve illustrates the distribution of household incomes in a country.
- The further the Lorenz Curve sags from the line of equality, the more unequal are incomes.
- A higher Gini ratio indicates greater inequality of incomes.
- Income inequality results from differences in ability, education and training, discrimination, preferences and risks, unequal distribution of wealth, market power, luck, and connections.
- Income inequality has increased in the United States in recent decades.
- To reduce income inequality, the government uses progressive income taxes and transfer payments such as Social Security, unemployment checks, welfare benefits, and food stamps.
- Transfer payments account for nearly all of the reduction in income inequality.
- As income inequality is reduced, the Lorenz Curve shifts inward, toward the line of equality.

Now, let's examine more closely the following concepts from your textbook:

- **Facts about Income Inequality**
- **Causes of Income Inequality**

These sections were selected because an understanding of the causes, measurements, and policies to reduce income inequality helps to explain consumer ability to buy products and the effectiveness of policies to stabilize the economy, which will be introduced in later chapters.

Facts about Income Inequality

Refer to pages 376–378 of your textbook.

A CLOSER LOOK The Lorenz Curve and Gini Ratio

In a market economy, incomes vary widely because of differences in opportunities. But just how great is income inequality? The **Lorenz Curve** illustrates the distribution of household incomes in a country.

On the horizontal axis, in the graph below, is the percentage of households in the United States. If each household could be lined up from lowest to highest income, this graph divides them into quintiles, with 1/5 of all of the households in each group. The first 20% are the 1/5 of US households with the lowest incomes. Then 40% represents the 2/5 of US households with the lowest incomes, and so on.

(1) Quintile (2014)	(2) Percentage of Total Income	(3) Upper Income Limit
Lowest 20 percent	3.1	$21,432
Second 20 percent	8.2	41,186
Third 20 percent	14.3	68,212
Fourth 20 percent	23.2	112,262
Highest 20 percent	51.2	No limit
Total	100.0	

Source: Bureau of the Census, **www.census.gov.**

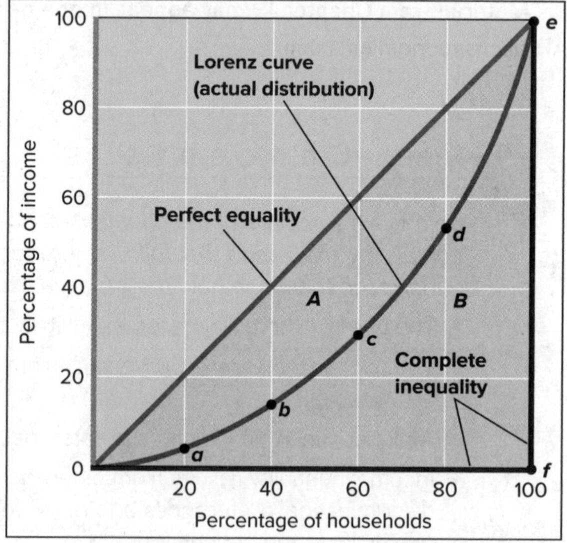

On the vertical axis is the percentage of total household income before taxes and transfer payments that accrues to each quintile. If incomes in the United States were perfectly equal, the first 20% of households would earn 20% of income. The first 40% of households would earn 40% of income, and so on. In the graph above, the straight line demonstrates how perfectly equal income would be distributed in a country.

The Lorenz Curve instead measures the *actual* distribution of incomes to each quintile. The table shows that the 20% of households with the lowest incomes earned just 3.1% of income in 2014. This is represented by Point A on the Lorenz Curve. The second 20% of households received 8.2% of the income. Added together, the lowest 40% of households in the US earned 11.3% of income, represented by Point B. The lowest 60% of households together earn 25.6% of income (Point C), the lowest 80% of households cumulatively earn 48.8% of income (Point D), and the highest-income 20% of households receive 51.2% of income, completing the curve at Point E.

The Lorenz Curve illustrates how far from equality incomes are in a country. The further the Lorenz Curve is from the equality line, the greater the income inequality. Income inequality is also measured by the **Gini ratio**, which calculates the blue area above. A larger Gini ratio indicates a greater degree of income inequality. It is important to recognize that households experience income mobility, moving between quintiles as they receive education or promotions or become unemployed or disabled.

Overall, income inequality has continued to widen in recent years. Between 1975 and 2014, income received by the lowest quintile fell from 4.4% to 3.1% of income, while the income received by the highest quintile increased from 43.2% to 51.2% of income. In fact, the proportion of income earned by the lower 80% of US households has decreased, while only the top quintile has seen an increase in their proportion of income, increasing income inequality. Causes of growing inequality include an increase in demand for highly-skilled workers, the increase in the number of single-parent families due to lack of a second income, the decline of labor unions and their power to negotiate wages, outsourcing high-paying manufacturing jobs, and an increase in the number of immigrant workers.

Governments can choose to reduce income inequality through income redistribution programs. The federal government uses a **progressive tax**, which charges those with higher incomes a higher tax rate. The federal government then redistributes part of that revenue to lower-income households through **transfer payments** such as Social Security, unemployment checks, welfare assistance, food stamps, and housing subsidies. Transfer payments are responsible for nearly all of the reduction in income inequality. The redistribution of income shifts the Lorenz Curve inward, toward income equality.

PRACTICE The Lorenz Curve and Gini Ratio

1. __________ What do the Lorenz Curve and Gini ratio measure?

2. __________ If government chooses to reduce income inequality, should transfer payments be increased or reduced?

3. __________ If government chooses to make income taxes less progressive by lowering the tax rate for those with higher incomes, what will happen to income inequality?

Causes of Income Inequality

Refer to pages 378–380 of your textbook.

A CLOSER LOOK Causes of Income Inequality

Those with higher physical and mental abilities are more likely to earn higher incomes, as are those with more education and training. Workers who choose risky, dangerous, or unpleasant careers are more likely to earn higher incomes, as well. Differences in wealth contribute to income inequality because those who have savings, investments, land, and capital are able to invest that wealth to earn even more income. Those in careers requiring occupational licenses, such as doctors, lawyers, and electricians earn higher incomes because the supply of labor is reduced. Labor market power also plays a role, as members of labor unions are able to collectively bargain to raise wages higher than they would earn in a perfectly competitive market. Product market power also contributes to inequality, as the investors, owners, and executives in monopolies and oligopolies receive excess profits in the form of dividends, bonuses, and higher executive salaries. Discrimination also plays a role, reducing incomes of those who are denied jobs and promotions. More personal situations of networking connections, disability, lengthy periods of unemployment, and even luck can also contribute to income inequality.

We will revisit these concepts later and put the concepts into practice with exercises.

Make sure to return to the AP Key Concepts section to check your understanding of the chapter's concepts important to AP coursework.

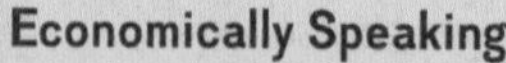

Economically Speaking

- **Gini Ratio** statistic that measures the degree of income inequality
- **Lorenz Curve** illustrates the distribution of household incomes in a country
- **Progressive Tax** a tax which charges those with higher incomes a higher tax rate
- **Transfer Payment** a government payment solely for the purpose of transferring income

An Introduction to Macroeconomics

Up to this point, we have focused on microeconomics, the "little picture" of the economy which explains how consumers and firms, with limited government intervention, make decisions in a market economy. With this chapter, we begin an investigation of macroeconomics, the "big picture" of the economy, the culmination of all of the forces of individual microeconomic decisions. Chapter 20 introduces measures of economic growth and performance that provide the foundation for the study of macroeconomic theory in subsequent chapters.

Material from Chapter 20 may appear in a question or two on the multiple-choice portion of the AP Macroeconomics exam. Concepts introduced in this chapter will be explored more thoroughly in later chapters.

Key Concepts

Below is a summary of the chapter's concepts important to AP coursework. Upon completing the lessons that follow, return to these concepts to make sure you understand them and how the practice exercises you completed relate to them.

- Macroeconomics is the study of the economy as a whole.
- Macroeconomics studies short-run business cycles (recessions) and long-run economic growth.
- Gross domestic product, the value of all final products produced in a country in a year, is the most important statistic economists use to measure economic performance.
  - Nominal GDP is measured using current prices.
  - Real GDP removes the inflation distortion and allows comparison to other years.
- Unemployment occurs when someone does not have a job and is actively looking for a job.
- Inflation is an increase in the overall level of prices.
- The circular flow diagram illustrates the flow of products, resources, and money in the economy.
  - In the factor (resource) market, households sell resources (usually labor) to businesses in return for money. Consumers use that money to buy products in the product market.
  - In the product market, businesses sell households products in return for money. Firms use that money to buy more resources in the factor market to make more products.

- Economic growth depends on saving and investment.
  - Savings are the amount of income which is not consumed.
  - Investment is spending by businesses for capital (plants and equipment) specifically designed to increase future production. (It is not the purchase of stocks or bonds, which is the general meaning of the term "investment" outside of economics.)
  - Savings are borrowed by firms to make investments; therefore, the level of investment in future economic growth is limited by the level of saving.
  - However, increased saving reduces current consumption, which could lead to recession, so policymakers must be careful to balance current and future consumption.
- Demand and supply shocks cause short-run instability in the macroeconomy.
  - Economists believe most economic cycles are caused by demand shocks.
  - Because prices are "sticky," demand shocks usually affect output and employment.
  - A decrease in demand reduces output and employment.
- Macroeconomic theories hold different assumptions about the economy, so they differ in their recommendations about government responses to economic events.

Now, let's examine more closely the following concepts from your textbook:

- **Performance and Policy**
- **Uncertainty, Expectations, and Shocks**

These sections were selected because they include explanations that separate microeconomics from macroeconomics, define terms that will be used in the following chapters, and introduce chains of linkage from one economic event to others.

Performance and Policy

Refer to pages 400–402 of your textbook.

A CLOSER LOOK Performance and Policy

Macroeconomics, the study of the entire economy, is composed of two separate areas of study. The first is long-run economic growth, which brings increased production and higher standards of living throughout the economy. The second is the **business cycle,** which explains short-run rapid increases and declines in production, inflation, and unemployment. A **recession,** an extended, serious downturn in the economy, causes output and employment to fall.

Economists analyze economic data to evaluate the current performance of the economy and to predict short-run future performance. The primary statistic economists use is **gross domestic product,** the value of all final goods and services produced in a country in one year. Changes in GDP affect employment and can signal government officials to use policies to stabilize the economy. **Nominal GDP** measures the output of the economy in current dollars. Because inflation contributes to increases in nominal GDP, it can distort apparent increases in production over time. In order to remove the inflation distortion, **real GDP** uses constant dollars to measure the actual change in production. Real GDP is our primary measure of economic growth, which is important to us because it allows increased production possibilities for products throughout the economy.

Changes in the macroeconomy also affect the rates of unemployment and inflation. **Unemployment** is the condition of not having a job, but actively seeking one. A decline in real GDP reduces output, and because fewer workers are needed to produce that output, they are laid off and the unemployment rate increases. **Inflation** is an increase in the overall level of prices. It is important to keep inflation rates low, because if the rate of inflation rises more quickly than wages, standards of living fall, reducing the potential for even greater economic growth. The role of economic policymakers is to promote long-run economic growth while minimizing business cycles and the effects of unemployment and inflation.

PRACTICE Performance and Policy

Indicate whether each of the following subjects is a part of microeconomics or macroeconomics.

1. _________ Determining the equilibrium wage for computer security analysts.

2. _________ Explaining why unemployment is increasing in the economy.

3. _________ Exploring how consumers decide between buying apples and oranges.

4. _________ Determining what output to produce to maximize profit.

5. _________ Examining the reasons why national output is decreasing.

6. _________ Exploring why product prices across the nation are increasing.

Uncertainty, Expectations, and Shocks

Refer to pages 404–408 of your textbook.

A CLOSER LOOK The Importance of Expectations and Shocks

Expectations are important in understanding short-run fluctuations in the macroeconomy. If consumers fear a recession and the possibility of losing their jobs, they reduce their demand for products, which slows GDP growth. If firms expect lower returns on their investment, they are less likely to engage in investment spending. A **demand shock** causes short-run economic changes when positive shocks (like a surge in consumer confidence) or negative shocks (like a significant drop in incomes) occur. A **supply shock,** such as a natural disaster or a significant innovation in technology, can also cause short-run economic volatility. Economists believe that most economic cycles are caused by demand shocks.

Because prices tend to be "sticky" for many products, changing slowly in response to economic forces, most demand shocks instead result in changes in output and employment. Manufacturing firms often create inventories to cushion sudden increases and decreases in demand and smooth the sales process. But if decreases in demand are sustained, the firm decreases output and, due to derived demand, lays off workers because fewer workers are needed to produce the product. If demand instead increases, output and employment both increase.

Prices of other products such as gasoline, airline tickets, and stocks are very flexible. Such prices often change daily or even within minutes in response to changes in supply and demand. However, most products have relatively stable prices because consumers want predictable prices and because firms must be concerned about the reactions of rivals. If the firm reduces its price, it will only gain additional customers from another firm if that firm does not lower its price as well. But if the other firm matches the price cut, the first firm is left worse off because it not only gained no new customers, it is now selling its normal output at a lower price. This risk leaves most firms hesitant to change their prices.

Prices that are sticky in the short run tend to be much more flexible in the long run. As a result, macroeconomic theories differ in their assumptions about the flexibility of prices. These models allow us to see how the economy behaves at different points in the business cycle and how government policies affect GDP, employment, and prices.

PRACTICE The Importance of Expectations and Shocks

1. _________ If consumers fear a recession is coming and they may lose their jobs, what would happen to their demand for products in the economy?

2. _________ Given your answer in #1, what will happen to output by firms?

3. _________ Given your answer in #2, what will happen to employment?

4. _________ Given your answer in #2, what will happen to real GDP?

Make sure to return to the AP Key Concepts section to check your understanding of the chapter's concepts important to AP coursework.

Economically Speaking

- **Business Cycle** fluctuation in real GDP, output, and employment
- **Demand Shock** unexpected change in demand for goods and services
- **Gross Domestic Product** the value of all final goods and services produced in a country in a year
- **Inflation** an increase in the overall level of prices
- **Investment** spending by firms for capital specifically designed to increase future production
- **Macroeconomics** the study of the economy as a whole
- **Nominal GDP** the GDP calculated using current prices
- **Real GDP** the GDP calculated by removing the inflation distortion
- **Recession** a downturn in the economy during which output and employment fall
- **Savings** the amount of income which is not consumed
- **Supply Shock** unexpected change in supply of goods and services
- **Unemployment** condition of having no job and actively looking for a job

Chapter 21

Measuring Domestic Output and National Income

Gross domestic product (GDP) is the primary measure of a nation's macroeconomic performance. So it is important to understand how GDP is calculated and to address cautions in its use. Chapter 21 explains the details of the GDP calculation and nominal and real GDP. These measures underlie the discussions of economic performance and economic theories throughout the macroeconomics course.

Material from Chapter 21 is very likely to appear in a few multiple-choice questions and occasionally is a free-response question on the AP Macroeconomics exam.

Key Concepts

Below is a summary of the chapter's concepts important to AP coursework. Upon completing the lessons that follow, return to these concepts to make sure you understand them and how the practice exercises you completed relate to them.

- National income accounting measures how well the economy is performing.
- Gross domestic product (GDP) is the dollar value of all final goods and services produced in an economy in one year; GDP = quantity produced × price for every product in the economy.
- To more accurately measure GDP, many economic activities are not counted:
    - Intermediate goods, used in making other goods, are left out to avoid double counting.
    - Purely financial transactions, like government transfer payments, gifts, and stock market transactions, are left out because no output was produced as a result of the activity.
    - Secondhand sales (used goods) are left out because no new output was produced.
- GDP can be measured from an expenditure or income approach, because one person's spending is another person's income.
    - The income approach adds all incomes earned in the economy.
        - GDP = Wages + Rent + Interest + Proprietors' Income + Corporate Profits + Taxes
        - Disposable income (personal income – taxes) measures the income households actually have available to spend.
    - The expenditure approach adds all spending in the economy.
        - GDP = Consumer + Investment + Government + Net Exports
        - The consumer sector is the largest, representing 68% of GDP.
        - The investment sector includes inventories, products produced but not yet sold.

- The government sector does not include transfer payments.
- Net Exports = Export Spending – Import Spending; the US imports more than it exports, so this is a negative number for the US.

- The circular flow model on a national level includes many inflows and outflows.
  - Households have an inflow of disposable income and outflow of spending and savings.
  - Businesses have inflows of funds for investment and an outflow of investment spending.
  - Government has an inflow of tax revenues and an outflow of purchases and transfers.
  - Net exports affect the circular flow, as foreign spending on US exports adds to US GDP, while US spending for imports takes away from US GDP.
- Nominal GDP is calculated using current prices; real GDP uses constant price to remove inflation.
- A price index measures the prices of a market basket of goods and services.
  - Price Index = (Price of This Year's Market Basket/Price of Base Year's Market Basket) × 100
  - Real GDP = Nominal GDP / Price Index
  - % Change in Nominal GDP = % Change in Real GDP + % Change in Prices
- GDP faces shortcomings as a measure of economic activity, as it does not include nonmarket activities, leisure, the underground economy, externalities, product distribution, or well-being.

Now, let's examine more closely the following concepts from your textbook:

- **Assessing the Economy's Performance**
- **The Expenditures Approach**
- **Nominal GDP versus Real GDP**
- **Shortcomings of GDP**

These sections were selected because a clear understanding of GDP is important to understanding how a number of factors can impact economic performance in each sector of GDP.

Assessing the Economy's Performance

Refer to pages 414–417 of your textbook.

A CLOSER LOOK Avoiding Multiple Counting and GDP Excludes Nonproduction Transactions

National income accounting measures how well the economy is performing. A variety of statistics are used to evaluate production, income, and economic growth or decline. The statistics are then used to determine appropriate policies to stabilize the economy and promote long-run economic growth.

Gross domestic product (GDP) is the dollar value of all final goods and services produced in a country in one year. US GDP in 2015 was nearly $18 trillion. This statistic includes all final products produced in the US, regardless of the home nation of the company. Until 1992, gross national product (GNP) was the primary measure of economic performance, measuring production based on the home country of the firm. Coca Cola's output in Japan counted in US GNP; Honda's production in Indiana, using US workers and resources, was counted in

Japan's GNP. The change to GDP, based on where products are actually produced, gives us a better picture of what is actually produced within the boundaries of a country.

GDP is calculated by multiplying the quantity of each product produced by the price of each product in the market. Then the total values are added together to find the GDP. Let's assume we have a little island. Residents of the island produce coconuts, bananas, and wood. How do we calculate GDP?

Product	Quantity Produced	Price	Total
Coconuts	200	$2.00	$400
Bananas	500	$0.50	$250
Cords of Wood	50	$1.00	$50

Summing the total value of output, the GDP of this little island economy is $700. In modern economies, it is impossible to determine precise quantities of products produced, and prices vary. So the official GDP for any particular country is the best estimate the nation's economists can make.

In order to more accurately measure production, certain economic activities are not included in GDP. **Intermediate goods** are goods that are used in the production of other goods, such as tires sold to an auto producer, or buns sold to a fast food restaurant. Intermediate goods are not counted, because if the tires were counted when sold to the auto manufacturer, and then the value of the completed car was counted, the value of the tires would have been counted twice. So while sales of final products to consumers, firms, and government are counted in GDP, sales of intermediate products are not.

Purely financial transactions are also not counted as part of GDP. Government **transfer payments** such as Social Security or unemployment benefits are not counted because households create no production in return for the checks. If transfer payments were counted in GDP, and then households used that income to purchase consumer goods which were counted in GDP, the value of those transfer payments would be counted twice. Private transfer payments such as monetary gifts or stock market transactions are also not counted as part of GDP because no output was created as a part of the transaction.

Secondhand sales, or used goods, are also not counted in current GDP. The sale of used goods creates no new output. Further, the products were counted when they were originally produced. By not counting intermediate goods, purely financial transactions, and secondhand sales, economists attempt to increase the accuracy of GDP as a measure of production that can be compared from year to year.

GDP can be measured by expenditure or income approaches. The **expenditure approach** adds all of the spending for final goods and services in the economy. The **income approach** adds all of the incomes earned in the economy: wages, rent, interest, proprietors' income, corporate profits, and taxes on production and imports. One common measure of income is **disposable income,** a household's personal income minus taxes; it is what people have available to spend. If we could obtain completely accurate numbers, GDP calculated by the two approaches would be equal, because spending by one person is income to another. If you bought $20 of gasoline, it would contribute $20 toward GDP, whether we counted it from your perspective of spending or from the gas station's perspective as income.

PRACTICE **Avoiding Multiple Counting and GDP Excludes Nonproduction Transactions**

1. State whether each of the following activities would *count* or *not count* in the official US GDP.

   A. __________ An investor purchases stock on the New York Stock Exchange

   B. __________ A retail store sells a coat to a customer

   C __________ An American firm produces goods in Bolivia

   D. __________ A farmer sells her corn at a roadside stand

   E. __________ A jewelry store sells a necklace from last year's inventory

   F. __________ The government makes Social Security transfer payments

   G. __________ A Japanese firm produces computers in California

   H. __________ A father buys a used car from a neighbor

   I. __________ Two friends charge clients for day care center services

   J. __________ A bakery purchases flour to make its cakes

2. What are the two methods for calculating GDP?

   A. ____________________ B. ____________________

3. __________ What is the GDP for the country whose output is in the below table?

Output	Price
500 pounds of beef	$4 per pound
100 gallons of milk	$2 per gallon
300 pounds of cheese	$3 per pound

The Expenditures Approach

Refer to pages 417–420 of your textbook.

A CLOSER LOOK **Consumption + Investment + Government + Net Exports**

The expenditure approach to GDP calls for adding the spending by the four sectors of the economy:

- C is personal consumption expenditures
- I is gross private domestic investment

- G is government purchases
- X is net exports

$$GDP = C + I + G + X$$

Personal consumption expenditures (the consumer sector) consist of household spending for durable goods that last for years (such as cars and furniture), nondurable goods (such as food and medicine), and services. Personal consumption is the majority of the US economy, constituting about 68% of GDP.

Gross private domestic investment (the investment sector) measures firms' spending for equipment, home and business construction, changes in inventories, and research and development. **Inventories** are products produced but not yet sold. Because we are measuring total output and not just product sales, we must include inventories. Another way to measure investment sector spending is **net private domestic investment** – gross private domestic investment minus **depreciation**, the amount by which the value of capital falls in a year. Firms must replace equipment that wears out, and the replacements do not actually add to capital stock. So net investment only counts investment beyond depreciation. Gross investment is generally greater than depreciation, so the amount of capital increases each year. But when the economy is in strong decline, firms may significantly reduce investment in capital, resulting in negative investment. *Gross* investment is used to calculate GDP, accounting for about 17% of GDP.

Government purchases (the government sector) constitute the third area of GDP. Government spends revenue for goods and services (including labor) needed to produce public goods, publicly-owned capital such as highways, and research and development. Remember that transfer payments are not counted in the government sector. Government purchases are responsible for approximately 18% of GDP.

Net exports (the foreign sector) are spending for **exports** (products produced in the US and sold in other countries) minus spending for **imports** (products produced in other countries and sold in the US). Because we want to measure production within the US, we must include products that were produced in the US and then exported, while subtracting US spending for products that are imported. The US imports significantly more than it exports, so the foreign sector actually produces a negative number, reducing the GDP from what it would have been if trade were balanced, by approximately 3% of GDP.

Keep in Mind

The relationships between the various types of income and spending can be mind-boggling, especially when viewing a flow chart like the one in the textbook. Questions about the calculation of GDP on the AP Macroeconomics exam have been much more straightforward. Questions have focused primarily on the expenditure model, such as identifying the sectors or specific types of spending that would be included in the calculation. A multiple-choice question about the income approach is likely to focus on identifying incomes: wages, rent, interest, proprietors' income, corporate profit, and taxes.

PRACTICE Consumption + Investment + Government + Net Exports

1. State how each of the following types of spending would be counted in the official US GDP: Consumer, Investment, Government, or Net Exports.

   A. __________ A US firm produces a shirt in the US and sells it in Egypt

   B. __________ A construction company builds and sells a new home

C. __________ People rush to buy the new version of cell phones

D. __________ A firm purchases new equipment for the factory

E. __________ Businesses add to their inventories

F. __________ Military spending increases for new weapons

G. __________ A student rents an apartment in a complex built five years ago

2. __________ If net investment is negative, what will happen to potential future GDP growth?

3. __________ If spending of the consumer, investment, and government sectors equals 109% of a nation's GDP, what percentage of GDP must net exports be?

4. __________ Why are net exports a negative number for the United States?

Nominal GDP versus Real GDP

Refer to pages 424–428 of your textbook.

A CLOSER LOOK Adjustment Process in a One-Product Economy

Nominal GDP is calculated using the current prices of products. But what happens if our economy produces exactly the same number of products as last year, but prices have increased by 5%? Nominal GDP will indicate that we have actually increased production by 5%. At any point in time, part of the change in nominal GDP is due to changes in output, while the rest is due to changes in prices. To compare production over time without the inflation distortion, we must calculate **real GDP.** In order to do that, we must construct a **price index** to measure the prices of a market basket of goods and services. The price index used to convert nominal GDP to real GDP is called the **GDP price deflator.**

$$\text{Price Index} = \frac{\text{Price of Market Basket This Year}}{\text{Price of Market Basket in Base Year}} \times 100$$

If the price of a market basket last year was $1,000, and this year that same market basket costs $1,200, the calculation would be $1,200 / $1,000 = 1.2 × 100 = 120. This number tells us that the price of the market basket this year is 120% of the price of the market basket last year. Just subtract 100 from the price index to find the rate of inflation as compared to the base, expressed as a percentage – in this case, a 20% increase in prices.

In order to convert nominal GDP to real GDP, we divide inflation out of the equation.

$$\text{Real GDP} = \frac{\text{Nominal GDP}}{\text{Price Index (as a Decimal)}}$$

If nominal GDP for this year is $1,200 and you want to compare this year's GDP to last year's GDP, you must remove the inflation for that time period. Thus, $1,200 / 1.2 = $1,000 for this year's real GDP.

When calculating the percentage change in nominal GDP, it is important to remember that the statistic includes changes in both output and prices.

% Change in Nominal GDP = % Change in Real GDP + % Change in Prices

If real GDP rose by 3% and prices rose by 2%, nominal GDP would increase by 5%. By converting the formula, we can also see that if nominal GDP rose by 5% and prices rose by 2%, real GDP rose by 3%.

Caution

Sometimes it can be confusing to remember how to remove inflation from nominal GDP. A quick trick is to look at whether you're converting a raw number (in dollars) or a percentage change. When working with the dollar amount of GDP, *divide* inflation out of the GDP using the price index. When working with a percentage change in GDP, *subtract* the inflation percentage from GDP.

Keep in Mind

You may need to calculate a price index or real GDP from data on either the multiple-choice or free-response sections of the AP Macroeconomics exam. These basic formulas will repeat throughout the rest of the Macroeconomics course in a variety of measures.

PRACTICE Adjustment Process in a One-Product Economy

1. If nominal GDP this year is $1,500 and the price index increased from a base of 100 to 120:

   A. ________ What is the inflation rate, expressed as a percentage?

   B. ________ What is the Real GDP this year?

2. If nominal GDP this year is $1,000 and the price index increased from a base of 100 to 125:

   A. ________ What is the inflation rate, expressed as a percentage?

   B. ________ What is the Real GDP this year?

3. ________ If total spending increased but real GDP did not change, what increased?

4. ________ If real GDP grew 5% and prices grew 3%, how much did nominal GDP grow?

5. ________ If real GDP grew 3% and nominal GDP grew 4%, how much did prices grow?

6. ________ If nominal GDP fell 4% and prices grew 1%, how much did real GDP fall?

7. ________ If nominal GDP grew 6% and prices grew 6%, how much did real GDP grow?

Shortcomings of GDP

Refer to pages 428–429 of your textbook.

A CLOSER LOOK Shortcomings of GDP

A measure as broad as GDP, while providing important information about our economy, still has its shortcomings. Nonmarket activities (or home production), such as cooking your own dinner or painting your own house, are also excluded from GDP calculation. It is difficult to get an accurate measure of such production, and money was not exchanged for this economic activity, so official GDP misses a great deal of economic activity.

GDP also cannot measure the value of leisure people have gained as the result of shorter workweeks and labor-saving appliances and services. Further, GDP cannot adequately measure improvements in the quality of life due to higher quality products.

The underground economy is specifically left out of GDP calculations. Illegal activity is significant, but it is very difficult to find reliable figures to quantify the level of activity, so it is left out. In addition, people who work for cash "under the table" or who under-report tips or business incomes in order to avoid taxes also contribute to a lower level of official GDP than the actual level of economic activity.

Further, the GDP cannot measure negative externalities such as pollution and other negative effects of production on the quality of life. GDP says nothing about the mix of goods, making no judgment about whether most of the spending in the country is for government goods or consumer goods. GDP also does not note the distribution of incomes; if 90% of national income went to the top 1% of citizens, the standard of living for most citizens would be low. And while GDP gives us an idea about the economic well-being of a nation's citizens, it cannot measure their feelings of safety and peace, the quality of education, the limitations on government power, or the protection of the nation's natural resources.

GDP is the most important statistic economists use to measure the state of the economy. But it is important to recognize the limitations on GDP so that you can interpret the data with the understanding that the well-being of a nation's people is based on far more than simply the officially reported GDP.

PRACTICE Shortcomings of GDP

State whether each of the following activities would *count* or *not count* in the official US GDP.

1. __________ A firm dumps pollution in a major river
2. __________ The government buys environmental cleanup supplies
3. __________ A parent cooks dinner for his family
4. __________ A family enjoys dinner at a restaurant
5. __________ Someone is selling a secretly recorded CD of a rock music concert
6. __________ A Boy Scout sells popcorn to a neighbor

Make sure to return to the AP Key Concepts section to check your understanding of the chapter's concepts important to AP coursework.

Economically Speaking

- **Depreciation** the amount by which the value of capital falls during a year
- **Disposable Income** personal income minus taxes
- **Expenditure Approach** calculating GDP as the sum of all spending in the economy
- **Exports** products produced in the US and sold in other countries
- **GDP Price Deflator** the price index used to convert nominal GDP to real GDP
- **Gross Domestic Product** the dollar value of all final goods and services produced in a country in one year
- **Gross Private Domestic Investment** firms' spending for equipment, construction, and inventory
- **Imports** products produced in other countries and sold in the US
- **Income Approach** calculating GDP as the sum of all incomes in the economy
- **Intermediate Goods** the goods that are used in the production of other goods
- **Inventories** products that have been produced, but have not yet been sold
- **National Income Accounting** measures how well the economy is performing
- **Net Exports** the foreign sector of GDP; spending for exports minus spending for imports
- **Net Private Domestic Investment** gross private domestic investment minus depreciation
- **Nominal GDP** the GDP calculated using current prices
- **Personal Consumption Expenditures** spending for consumer products by households
- **Price Index** measures the prices of a market basket of goods and services
- **Real GDP** the GDP adjusted for changes in the price level
- **Transfer Payments** government payments to households strictly to transfer income

Chapter 22

Economic Growth

With a thorough understanding of how real GDP is calculated, we can explore how it is used to determine economic growth and the importance of economic growth for society. Chapter 22 examines the causes of economic growth, government policies that can promote growth, and benefits of growth.

Material from Chapter 22 is likely to appear in one or two multiple-choice questions and occasionally in a free-response question on the AP Microeconomics and AP Macroeconomics exams, specifically with reference to the production possibilities curve and the causes of economic growth.

Key Concepts

Below is a summary of the chapter's concepts important to AP coursework. Upon completing the lessons that follow, return to these concepts to make sure you understand them and how the practice exercises you completed relate to them.

- Economic growth is an increase in real GDP or real GDP per capita over time.
    - Real GDP measures the value of final goods produced in a country in one year.
    - Real GDP per capita measures Real GDP per person (Real GDP / Population).
- The percentage rate of economic growth is generally positive, but it falls during recessions.
    - % of Economic Growth = [(Current Real GDP – Base Real GDP) / Base Real GDP] × 100
- Economic growth is one of our most important goals because it reduces the burden of scarcity.
- Economic growth focuses on increasing supply.
- The most important factors directly increasing the rate of economic growth are the quality and quantity of land, labor, and capital, and improvements in technology.
- Firms increase investment when interest rates are low (due to greater household saving) or when government uses subsidies or tax credits to reduce the cost of purchasing capital.
- Structural supports for economic growth include strong property rights, efficient financial institutions, widespread education, free trade, and a competitive market system.
- The production possibilities curve illustrates economic growth by shifting outward.
- An increase in the labor force participation rate (those over 16 working or seeking work) can increase the rate of economic growth.
- Increases in labor productivity have accounted for nearly all economic growth since the 1950s.

- Labor productivity rises with technological advance, the amount of capital, investment in human capital (knowledge and skills of workers), economies of scale, and improved resource allocation.

Now, let's examine more closely the following concepts from your textbook:

- **Economic Growth**
- **Determinants of Growth**
- **Accounting for Growth**

These sections were selected because if you understand what causes economic growth, you can better understand business and government decisions that promote that long-run economic growth.

Economic Growth

Refer to pages 436–437 of your textbook.

A CLOSER LOOK Economic Growth

Economic growth is an increase in real GDP or real GDP per capita over time. While **real GDP** measures the value of the total output of a country, **real GDP per capita** measures the output per person, taking population differences into account to allow for a more accurate comparison of standards of living.

$$\text{Real GDP Per Capita} = \frac{\text{Real GDP}}{\text{Population}}$$

The rate of economic growth uses the same formula for real GDP or real GDP per capita, simply using per capita numbers for the per capita calculation. While growth rates are generally positive, real GDP falls during a **recession,** leaving economic growth as a negative number.

$$\text{\% of Economic Growth} = \frac{\text{This Year's Real GDP} - \text{Base Year's Real GDP}}{\text{Base Year's Real GDP}} \times 100$$

Economic growth is one of our most important goals. Scarcity is the fundamental economic problem, and economic growth helps to reduce the burden of scarcity. Higher real incomes raise standards of living, reduce poverty, increase investment and the provision of public goods, and allow us to produce more consumer and capital goods at the same time, promoting even more future growth.

The real GDP of the United States has increased by an average of 3% per year since 1950, while real GDP per capita has grown by an average of 2% during that same period. It is important to note that this only represents average growth, because short-term fluctuations have brought about faster growth or even declines during recessions. The caveats that we noted in the last chapter for using GDP as a measure of well-being also extend to using GDP as a measure of *growth* in well-being. GDP cannot account for improvements in product quality, additional leisure time, externalities, or quality of life.

Differences in GDP growth and standards of living among countries can result from differences in the amount of technology and innovation, the length of time the nation has engaged in modern economic growth, the labor supply, labor productivity, and government policies that promote economic growth.

PRACTICE **Economic Growth**

Indicate the percentage rate of economic growth for each of the following countries.

1. _________ Real GDP last year was $50,000. Real GDP this year is $60,000.

2. _________ Real GDP last year was $100,000. Real GDP this year is $108,000.

3. _________ Real GDP last year was $30 million. Real GDP this year is $33 million.

4. _________ Real GDP last year was $200 billion. Real GDP this year is $192 billion.

Determinants of Growth

Refer to pages 442–444 of your textbook.

A CLOSER LOOK Supply, Demand, and Efficiency Factors and Production Possibilities Analysis

Economists identify a number of factors that promote economic growth. Strong property rights encourage entrepreneurs to invest in opening businesses with the knowledge that government cannot take over the business. Patents and copyrights promote invention and innovation by protecting the ownership rights of inventors and allowing them to financially gain from their creations. Efficient financial institutions funnel the savings of households to firms in order to promote investment in capital and economic growth. Literacy and widespread education increase worker productivity and promote further invention and implementation of new technologies. Free trade promotes growth because countries specialize in what they produce most efficiently, promoting efficient use of resources and allowing growth to spread among countries. A competitive market system allows firms to follow market signals in setting output and prices. Stable political systems, enforcement of contracts, and cultural values with a positive attitude toward work and risk-taking also help to promote economic growth.

The factors directly increasing the rate of economic growth include the quantity and quality of the factors of production – land, labor, and capital – and improvements in technology. Demand must keep pace with the increasing supply of products, or firms will respond to increasing inventories by cutting production. Efficiency and full employment are also important, as productive efficiency (producing at lowest cost) and allocative efficiency (producing the mix of goods consumers want) ensure that resources are used in ways that maximize well-being.

Another important factor in economic growth is the cost of investment for firms. Firms generally borrow in order to buy capital. When the interest rate is low, it is more likely that the expected return on investment will exceed that interest rate, so firms are more likely to make that investment. When households increase their saving, the supply of loanable funds increases, causing interest rates to fall. The government can also reduce the cost of investment by making grants or giving firms subsidies or tax credits for purchasing capital. When the cost of investment falls, firms increase investment.

One of the first models we examined was the **production possibilities curve,** which illustrates maximum possible production, given current resources and technology. In order to produce more of one product, we must produce less of another. Our short-run goal is to reduce unemployment and produce at efficiency on the curve at Point (a). Our long-run goal is economic growth, shifting out the production possibilities curve, allowing us to produce more of *both* goods at Point (b). When the economy falls into recession, at Point (c), the economy produces fewer goods than potential and resources are unemployed.

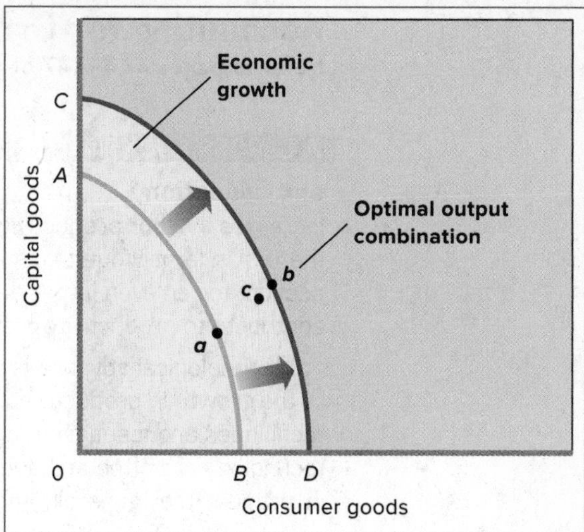

Economic growth focuses on increasing supply. The primary factors are increases in the number and productivity of resources, particularly labor. The equation below uses another model to calculate GDP.

Real GDP = Hours of Work × Labor Productivity

The **labor force participation rate** is the percentage of people over age 16 who are working or seeking work. If a nation can increase the labor force participation rate or the length of the average workday or workweek, real GDP rises. Labor productivity can be increased through improvements in technology, the quality of labor and capital, health and education of workers, management, and worker morale. Improvements in these factors are important for increasing the economic growth of a country.

PRACTICE Supply, Demand, and Efficiency Factors and Production Possibilities Analysis

Indicate whether each of the following factors will increase or decrease the rate of economic growth.

1. __________ A reduction in the number of immigrants allowed into the country

2. __________ An increase in the labor force participation rate

3. __________ An increase in the interest rate for bank loans

4. __________ High protective tariffs to limit imports of capital equipment

5. __________ A new tax credit for firms buying capital

6. __________ An increase in the amount of household saving in banks

7. __________ A reduction in the amount of capital equipment used by firms

Accounting for Growth

Refer to pages 444–447 of your textbook.

A CLOSER LOOK Labor Inputs, Technological Advance, Quantity of Capital, and Education

Increases in labor productivity have accounted for nearly all of the economic growth since the 1950s, largely due to computer and information technology. Economists project it will account for an even larger percentage of economic growth in the future. Five factors contribute to productivity growth.

Technological advance is the most important factor, responsible for approximately 40% of the growth in productivity. Technological advance comes in the form of new production techniques and management methods, capital investment, and innovation. Advances in technology are often embedded within new capital, so when firms increase their capital investment, they generally implement new technology.

The second major factor in the growth of labor productivity is the amount of capital available to workers. More and better factories and equipment account for about 30% of the productivity increase. Government investments in public infrastructure, such as highways, also improve labor productivity.

A third important factor in improving the productivity of labor is investment in **human capital** – the knowledge and skills of workers. Education and training, whether formal or on-the-job, account for approximately 15% of the increase in labor productivity.

A fourth factor increasing labor productivity is **economies of scale,** as larger firms become more efficient. As output increases, the firm can buy more efficient equipment, increase the specialization of labor, and spread research and development costs over more output, increasing productivity. The final factor is improved resource allocation. The movement of workers into higher-productivity jobs, elimination of discrimination that prevents qualified workers from moving into such jobs, and wider international trade have all helped to reallocate workers and other resources into their most productive areas, improving efficiency. These two factors together represent the other 15% of growth.

While economic growth can cause negative externalities, higher stress for workers, and environmental issues, it is essential for increasing standards of living. Government can implement policies to correct externalities and address resource issues. Because improvements in education and technology can lead to the more efficient use of resources, economic growth can result in benefits across societies and economic systems.

PRACTICE Labor Inputs, Technological Advance, Quantity of Capital, and Education

Indicate whether each of the following factors will increase or decrease the rate of economic growth.

1. __________ An increase in state government spending for public education

2. __________ An increase in the interest rate for college student loans

3. __________ An increase in corporate investment in new technology

4. __________ An increase in labor productivity

5. __________ An increase in the rate of technological change

6. __________ Legislation restricting the size of growth of corporations

7. __________ An increase in government spending for technical schools

Make sure to return to the AP Key Concepts section to check your understanding of the chapter's concepts important to AP coursework.

Economically Speaking

- **Economic Growth** an increase in output over time
- **Economies of Scale** as a firm becomes larger, it becomes more efficient
- **Human Capital** the knowledge and skills of workers
- **Labor Force Participation Rate** the percentage of people over age 16 who are working or seeking work
- **Production Possibilities Curve** model which illustrates the maximum possible production in a country, given current resources and technology
- **Real GDP** the GDP measured in constant prices to remove the inflation distortion
- **Real GDP Per Capita** Real GDP per person in an economy
- **Recession** a period of decrease in real GDP

23 Chapter

Business Cycles, Unemployment, and Inflation

While long-run economic growth is sustained, short-run economic performance is much more variable. Business cycles commonly result in changes in output, unemployment, and inflation. Chapter 23 explores macroeconomic instability, explaining the causes and phases of business cycles. Discussion continues with the measurement, types, causes, and effects of unemployment and inflation. An understanding of business cycles and their effects lays the foundation to understand macroeconomic models, competing theories, and government policies to address macroeconomic instability.

Material from Chapter 23 is very likely to appear in several multiple-choice questions on the AP Macroeconomics exam and occasionally as a free-response question.

Key Concepts

Below is a summary of the chapter's concepts important to AP coursework. Upon completing the lessons that follow, return to these concepts to make sure you understand them and how the practice exercises you completed relate to them.

- A business cycle includes a peak, recession, trough, and expansion.
  - In a recession, real GDP (output) and employment fall, and prices are sticky but may fall.
  - In expansion, real GDP (output), employment, and prices rise.
- Shocks are the primary cause of business cycles, resulting from changes in consumer confidence, investment spending, inventions and innovations, productivity, the money supply, political events, or instability in financial markets.
- Producers of capital and durable goods are more deeply affected by business cycles than are producers of services and non-durable goods.
- Unemployed people are those who are not working, but are actively seeking work.
  - The labor force consists of those who are employed and those who are unemployed.
  - Those who cannot or choose not to work (retirees, students) are outside the labor force.
  - Unemployment Rate = (Unemployed / Labor Force) × 100
  - Underemployed (working part-time) and discouraged (dropped out of the labor force) workers are not counted as unemployed, so the official rate underestimates the total.
  - Types of unemployment:
    - Frictional — temporarily between jobs.
    - Seasonal — at the same time every year.

        - Structural — a worker's skills do not match available jobs.
        - Cyclical — layoffs as the result of a recession.
- Full employment (natural rate of unemployment) is the absence of cyclical unemployment.
    - At full employment, the economy is producing at potential and real GDP is at capacity.
    - The GDP gap is the difference between potential and actual GDP.
    - GDP Gap = Actual GDP – Potential GDP
    - Okun's Law — for every 1% the unemployment rate is higher than the natural rate of unemployment (5%), the GDP gap increases by 2%.
- Inflation, a general increase in price level, is primarily measured by the Consumer Price Index.
    - CPI = (Total Market Basket Price This Year / Total Market Basket Price Base Year) × 100
    - Rate of Inflation = [(This Year's CPI – Base Year's CPI) / Base Year's CPI] × 100
    - Types of inflation:
        - Demand-pull inflation is caused by excessive demand, often due to a significant increase in the money supply.
        - Cost-push inflation is caused by an increase in the cost of production.
        - A wage-price spiral occurs when firms raise prices, so workers demand higher wages, so firms raise prices in a continuing spiral.
    - Nominal income is the income earned in the current value of dollars.
    - Real income is the measure of what a consumer's income will actually buy.
    - Real Income = Nominal Income / Price Index (as a Decimal)
    - % Change in Real Income = % Change in Nominal Income – % Change in Price Level
    - If nominal income rises more quickly than the price level, real income increases.
    - Unanticipated inflation hurts those on fixed incomes, savers, and lenders.
    - Unanticipated inflation helps borrowers, as they repay with dollars that are worth less.
    - Cost-of-living adjustments require wages to increase at the same rate as inflation.
    - Lenders try to anticipate inflation by adding an inflation premium to real interest rates.
        - Nominal Interest Rate = Real Interest Rate + Expected Inflation Rate

Now, let's examine more closely the following concepts from your textbook:

- **The Business Cycle**
- **Unemployment**
- **Inflation**
- **Redistribution Effects of Inflation**

These sections were selected because a thorough understanding of the causes of business cycles and the effects on output, employment, and prices will help you to understand why economists and government officials propose specific policies to address economic instability and why they disagree.

The Business Cycle

Refer to pages 456–459 of your textbook.

A CLOSER LOOK Phases of the Business Cycle and Causation: A First Glance

Business cycles, the increases and decreases in real GDP over time, are composed of four phases. The **peak** is the highest point of real GDP in the cycle, where the economy

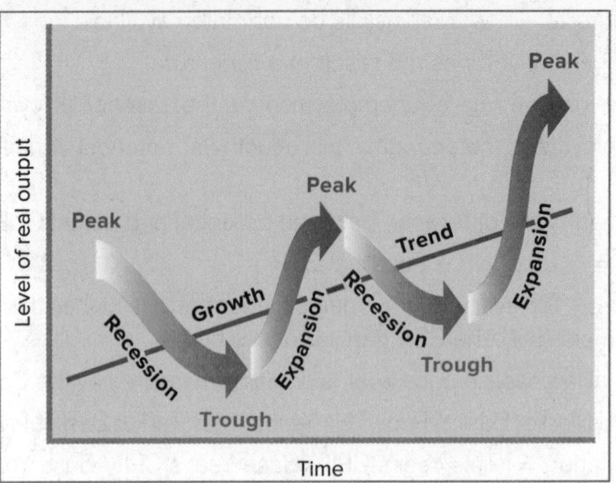

experiences full employment, output at or near capacity, and generally rising prices. A **recession** is a period of decrease in real GDP, generally six months or longer, during which employment falls and sometimes prices may fall. The **trough** is the lowest point of real GDP in the cycle, where output and employment reach their lowest levels. A **depression** is depicted as a very deep, extended trough. **Expansion,** or recovery, is the fourth phase of the business cycle. Real GDP begins to rise, and employment and prices rise along with it. Business cycles vary in depth and duration, but the long-term growth trend is positive.

Keep in Mind

Watch very carefully to see if questions on the AP Macroeconomics exam refer to *employment* or *unemployment*. Unless the question is specifically addressing unemployment, AP questions generally ask about employment for reasons related to the specific definition of unemployment. It is critical to read the word correctly because *employment* will fall at the same time *unemployment* is rising!

Caution

It is important to remember how real GDP, prices, and employment change in each phase of the business cycle. If you keep in mind that all three generally move in the same direction, it will help you to keep the effects straight. Some students expect prices to rise during an economic downturn, thinking that firms must raise prices to make up for lost sales. Remember, if demand and production fall, firms must *lower* prices to attract customers back; consumers respond to *higher* prices by buying even less!

Shocks – unexpected changes in the economy – are the primary cause of business cycles. The vast majority of these shocks result in an unexpected change in the amount of total spending in the economy. Prices tend to be downwardly sticky, because in order to reduce costs, producers would have to cut wages. Contracts prevent wage cuts in many cases, and disgruntled employees cause enough concern that other firms that *could* make wage cuts won't do so. So instead, changes in supply and demand in the macroeconomy generally affect output and employment. The root causes of these shocks can be changes in consumer confidence, investment spending, inventions and innovations, productivity, the money supply, political events such as war, or instability in financial markets.

A positive demand shock raises output, and employment increases as workers are hired to produce that output. The increased demand pushes up the price level, so real GDP, employment, and prices increase together. A negative demand shock causes firms to reduce output. Fewer workers are needed to produce the output, so employment falls. Prices tend to be sticky downward in the short run, but fall if the downturn is sustained. Again, real GDP, employment, and prices move in the same direction.

While business cycles impact all sectors of the economy, the relative strength of impact differs among industries. Producers of capital goods (such as construction and equipment) and consumer durable goods (such as cars and appliances) tend to be more deeply affected by changes in the business cycle. When product demand falls, firms expect a lower return on investment in capital, so they reduce capital spending and instead produce with existing resources. During economic downturns, consumers also reduce purchases of homes, cars, and appliances, making repairs rather than buying new items. When the economy is strong, consumption of such items tends to rise significantly. Thus, producers of these capital and durable goods are subject to strong cyclical swings in economic activity.

Producers of services and non-durable goods do not face strong cyclical changes. During recessions, consumers still purchase food, gasoline, medical care, and haircuts, and demand does not significantly rise in expansions. As a result, output and employment in capital goods and durable goods industries tend to be more strongly affected by economic cycles than in non-durable goods and service industries.

PRACTICE **Phases of the Business Cycle and Causation: A First Glance**

Indicate whether each of the following events is more likely to lead to a *recession* or an *expansion*.

1. __________ Consumers lose confidence in the economy and fear losing their jobs
2. __________ An important new technology improves efficiency for producers
3. __________ Firms experience an unplanned increase in inventories
4. __________ Worker productivity increases due to better education
5. __________ Firms reduce investment in capital due to rising interest rates
6. __________ An economic shock occurs when the costs of oil and gasoline double
7. __________ The government increases the money supply

Unemployment

Refer to pages 459–464 of your textbook.

A CLOSER LOOK **Measurement and Types of Unemployment**

To calculate the unemployment rate, the Bureau of Labor Statistics conducts a random sample of US households, calling approximately 60,000 households per month. People who are younger than 16, or institutionalized, or not working by choice (for example, retired, students, or homemakers) are outside of the labor force. They are not included in the unemployment statistics because they are unavailable or unwilling to join the workforce. Within the **labor force** are two groups: the employed and the unemployed. Those who are not working but are actively seeking work are counted as **unemployed.** The **unemployment rate** is the percentage of people in the labor force who are actively seeking work.

$$\text{Unemployment Rate} = \frac{\text{Unemployed}}{\text{Labor Force}} \times 100$$

It is important to note that while the BLS uses scientific methodology, the official unemployment rate underestimates unemployment. Because samples are used, many unemployed people may be missed in the sample, such as people without phones or living with others. **Underemployed workers** work part-time because they cannot find full-time jobs, or work in jobs for which they are overqualified because they cannot find appropriate jobs. They are counted as fully employed, though the designation isn't fully accurate. Discouraged workers are also entirely left out of the statistics. **Discouraged workers** are those who have been unemployed for so long that they have stopped looking for work. They would accept a job if offered, but under the definition of unemployment, they have left the labor force and are not included. Because of the method of gathering data, underemployment, and discouraged workers, the official unemployment rate underestimates the actual level of unemployment in the economy.

People are unemployed for a variety of reasons. **Frictional unemployment** refers to people who are temporarily between jobs. People who have been fired, have quit, are looking for first jobs, or are returning to the labor force briefly experience frictional unemployment while they search for new jobs. Frictional unemployment always exists, because there are always people moving between jobs.

Seasonal unemployment occurs at the same time each year. Lifeguards at outdoor pools in the north, field workers harvesting crops, ski instructors, and commercial fishermen experience unemployment due to seasonal conditions and often seek other jobs during the off-season.

Structural unemployment occurs when a worker's skills do not match the available jobs. This occurs when the structure of the economy has changed. Structural unemployment can result from a change in product demand, as when autos replaced horses, reducing demand for blacksmiths to make horseshoes. It also results from industry migration; when steel production grew overseas and mills closed in the US, American steelworkers lost careers. **Automation** can also cause structural unemployment when machines replace workers. Structural unemployment is generally long-term, requiring workers to relocate to where jobs still exist or to retrain for new careers where demand is higher.

Cyclical unemployment results from layoffs due to a recession in the business cycle. You can see the word "cycle" right in the word "cyclical." When total spending in the economy falls and firms reduce output during a recession, they lay off workers. During expansion, cyclical unemployment falls. Cyclical unemployment is generally the target of government policy to stabilize the economy.

PRACTICE Measurement and Types of Unemployment

1. Indicate whether each of the following people would be *counted* or *not counted* as unemployed.

   A. _________ Andrew chooses to stay home to raise his children

   B. _________ Brett was fired and is looking for a new job

   C. _________ Cameron has been out of work so long he is no longer looking for a job

D. _________ DeShawn was replaced by a machine and is seeking a different career

E. _________ Elena works part-time at a store because no teaching jobs are available

2. Identify whether each worker faces *frictional, seasonal, cyclical,* or *structural* unemployment.

A. _________ Abdul lost his job because a recession lowered product demand

B. _________ Becky lost her job when she was replaced by a robot

C. _________ Cheryl quit her last job and is looking for a new one

D. _________ Duy lost his job as a snow ski instructor because it is summer

3. _________ If labor force participation increases, does it become *more* or *less* difficult to reduce the unemployment rate?

4. Use the data for Country X in the table below to answer the questions that follow.

Population	600 million
Employed	380 million
Unemployed	20 million

A. _________ What is the size of this nation's labor force?

B. _________ What is this nation's unemployment rate?

A CLOSER LOOK Definition of Full Employment and Economic Cost of Unemployment

It is impossible for an economy to reach zero percent unemployment, because frictional, seasonal, and structural unemployment always exist in a dynamic economy. **Full employment** is defined as the absence of cyclical unemployment. Full employment is also known as the natural rate of unemployment. At the **natural rate of unemployment** (NAIRU), the economy is producing at its full potential output; real GDP is at capacity.

The natural rate of unemployment can change over time as demographics and policies change. The natural rate of unemployment rose as women and teenagers joined the labor force in large numbers and as unemployment benefits allowed people to extend their job searches longer. It fell as birth rates fell and fewer people entered the labor force, as the Internet made job searches easier, and as changes in government policy required work for welfare recipients. An unemployment rate of 5–6% is now considered full employment.

As we learned in Chapter 1, unemployment is illustrated by a point inside the production possibilities curve. So the cost of unemployment is the forgone output that could have been produced by society. The **GDP gap** is the difference between potential and actual GDP.

GDP Gap = Actual GDP – Potential GDP

Potential GDP increases each year at the expected rate of long-run growth, around a 2–3% increase. If unemployment is higher than the natural rate, it reduces actual output, resulting in the GDP gap. The higher the unemployment rate, the higher the GDP gap. If unemployment is less than the natural rate of unemployment, actual GDP can exceed the expected potential GDP, resulting in a negative gap – more output than expected. But because rapid expansion causes inflation, it cannot be sustained long-term.

Okun's Law defines the relationship between unemployment and the GDP gap. Under Okun's Law, for every percentage point the unemployment rate is above the natural rate of unemployment, the GDP gap increases by two percentage points. So if the natural rate of unemployment is 5% and current unemployment is 7%, the GDP gap would be 4%.

The effects of unemployment are distributed unequally. The workers who are more likely to be unemployed – and unemployed longer than other workers – include those in lower-skill occupations, teenagers, African-Americans, Hispanics, men during recessions, and those with less education. Deep, sustained unemployment can also lead to poverty, crime, divorce, and political unrest, if severe enough.

PRACTICE Definition of Full Employment and Economic Cost of Unemployment

1. __________ Does full employment mean the unemployment rate is 0%?

2. __________ Full employment is defined as the absence of what kind of unemployment?

3. __________ What is the term for the difference between potential and actual GDP?

4. __________ According to Okun's Law, if the natural rate of unemployment is 5% and the current unemployment rate is 9%, what is the GDP gap?

Inflation

Refer to pages 465–467 of your textbook.

A CLOSER LOOK Meaning, Measurement, and Types of Inflation

Inflation is an increase in the general price level. During a period of inflation, the value or purchasing power of the dollar decreases, and people cannot buy as much as they once did with the same income.

Inflation is primarily measured by the **Consumer Price Index** (CPI). The Bureau of Labor Statistics creates a "market basket" of hundreds of goods and services that a typical urban household would buy in a year. The quantity of each item in the market basket is multiplied by the price of that item, and these totals are added. CPI then compares the price of a current market basket to that in a base year or another year.

$$\text{CPI} = \frac{\text{Total Price of the Market Basket This Year}}{\text{Total Price of the Market Basket in the Base Year}} \times 100$$

To find the rate of inflation for the year, use the same basic formula as for the rate of economic growth.

$$\text{Rate of Inflation} = \frac{\text{This Year's CPI} - \text{Base Year's CPI}}{\text{Base Year's CPI}} \times 100$$

Demand-pull inflation, the most common kind of inflation in the United States, is an increase in the price level resulting from demand that is greater than the ability of the economy to produce the output. A significant increase in the money supply can cause such an increase in demand. Because firms are producing at capacity, they cannot increase output, so demand pulls the price up, resulting in inflation.

Cost-push inflation occurs when the cost of production rises, and firms pass the increased cost onto consumers. A supply shock such as a rise in material costs can cause cost-push inflation. Increased costs reduce the firm's profit, so the firm reduces output and pushes the price upward. As supply falls, output and employment fall while prices rise.

A **wage-price spiral** can pose a serious problem for economic policymakers. It can begin with either demand-pull or cost-push inflation. Let's say costs of production have significantly increased. Workers, facing higher prices, negotiate higher wages to keep up with inflation. Now firms face even higher labor costs, so they must increase product prices, causing workers to demand higher wages, causing firms to raise prices, in a dramatic spiral. How do we stop the spiral? Do we put price controls in place, so firms face higher labor costs but cannot recoup those costs with higher product prices? Or do we put wage controls in place, so workers face higher product prices but cannot increase their wages to afford them?

PRACTICE Meaning, Measurement, and Types of Inflation

1. Use the data for Country Y in the table below to answer the questions that follow.

	Quantity	2016 Price per Unit	2017 Price per Unit
Housing	12 units	$80	$100
Food	50 units	$20	$30
Clothing	4 units	$10	$25

A. __________ What is the price index for housing between 2016 and 2017?

B. __________ What is the price index for food between 2016 and 2017?

C. __________ What is the price index for clothing between 2016 and 2017?

D. __________ What is the inflation rate for the entire market basket in 2017?

2. __________ If the Consumer Price Index rises from 60 to 72, what is the inflation rate?

3. __________ If the Consumer Price Index rises from 300 to 306, what is the inflation rate?

4. __________ What kind of inflation results from a significant increase in the cost of materials?

5. __________ What kind of inflation results from a significant increase in the money supply?

Redistribution Effects of Inflation

Refer to pages 468–471 of your textbook.

A CLOSER LOOK Nominal and Real Income, and Who is Hurt, Unaffected, or Helped by Inflation?

As we saw with GDP, inflation can distort the value of production. In the same way, inflation can distort the value of income. **Nominal income** is the income earned in the current value of dollars. **Real income** is the measure of what a consumer's income will actually buy, or in other words, the purchasing power of a dollar. Note that this is the same basic formula used to convert nominal GDP to real GDP.

$$\text{Real Income} = \frac{\text{Nominal Income}}{\text{Price Index (as a Decimal)}}$$

If you earn $10,000 this year and the price index in decimal form is 1.05 (an inflation rate of 5% since last year), your real wage for this year is $9,523.81. In other words, it will cost your entire $10,000 income in its current value to buy what $9,523.81 of income would have bought at its value last year.

This is important when we compare the inflation rate to the change in nominal income, to see if nominal income kept up with inflation, rose above inflation, or fell behind. Note that this is the same basic formula we used to find the percentage change in real GDP.

$$\text{\% Change in Real Income} = \text{\% Change in Nominal Income} - \text{\% Change in Price Level}$$

If you received a 3% raise at work this year and the inflation rate was 3%, you would experience no change in real income. Although you would be paid more in current dollars, the value of those dollars fell enough that you could not purchase any more than you did last year. If your nominal income rises more quickly than the price level, your real income increases; if your nominal income rises less quickly than the price level, your real income actually declines. In the latter case, even though the amount on your paycheck has increased, it won't stretch to buy as much as last year's income at its value did.

Unanticipated inflation hurts some people and helps others, while others are unaffected. People living on a fixed income, such as retirees on a fixed pension or workers earning the minimum wage, are hurt by inflation. They receive the same dollar amount of income, but it will not buy as much as it once did. Savers are also hurt by inflation, because the interest rate on the savings account or CD does not increase with the inflation rate, so the interest payment will not stretch as far as it once did.

Lenders are also hurt, but borrowers are helped by unanticipated inflation. Inflation erodes the value of money over time, so the money repaid is not worth as much as the money that was originally borrowed. The lender receives the full dollar amount of the loan back, but that money will not buy as much as it would have when the loan was originated. So the lender loses real income.

People who have flexible incomes are less likely to feel the impact of unanticipated inflation. Workers who can negotiate their wages may keep pace or even exceed the inflation rate. If firms are able to raise prices higher than the increase in production costs, profits can increase as well.

If people are able to anticipate inflation, they can mitigate or eliminate the effects on their real incomes. Some workers have **cost-of-living adjustments** (COLAs) built into their contracts, requiring that wages increase at the same rate as inflation. Social Security benefits also automatically adjust with inflation. Lenders also try to recoup the diminishing value of the dollar over time by building the expected inflation rate into the interest rate they charge customers. So the **nominal interest rate** banks charge is the **real interest rate** plus a premium for expected inflation.

Nominal Interest Rate = Real Interest Rate + Expected Inflation Rate

If a bank would charge a 4% interest rate for a one-year loan in the absence of inflation, and the bank expects a 3% increase in the price level next year, it would charge 7% interest on the loan. That way, the repaid dollars (with a 3% inflation premium) hold the overall same value as the dollars originally loaned.

At the extremes of the inflation picture are deflation and hyperinflation. **Deflation,** a general decrease in prices, can occur as the result of a deep, sustained recession. **Hyperinflation,** an extremely high rate of inflation, is usually due to a huge increase in the money supply and can lead to an economic collapse.

PRACTICE Nominal and Real Income, and Who is Hurt, Unaffected, or Helped by Inflation?

1. __________ What does inflation do to the value and purchasing power of the dollar?

2. __________ If nominal wage rises 5% and inflation is 1%, what is the change in real wage?

3. __________ If nominal wage rises 3% and inflation is 5%, what is the change in real wage?

4. __________ If the real interest rate is 5.3% and expected inflation is 8.5%, what is the nominal interest rate?

5. __________ If the nominal interest rate is 8.2% and the real interest rate is 5.7%, what is the expected inflation rate?

6. Indicate whether each of the following is *hurt, helped,* or *unaffected* by unanticipated inflation.

   A. __________ People on fixed incomes

   B. __________ People who have savings accounts with a fixed interest rate

   C. __________ Workers who have COLAs built into their wage contracts

D. __________ Firms that sell products on which government has set a price ceiling

E. __________ Banks that have loaned out money at a fixed interest rate

F. __________ People who have borrowed money at a fixed interest rate

Make sure to return to the AP Key Concepts section to check your understanding of the chapter's concepts important to AP coursework.

Economically Speaking

- **Automation** a worker is replaced by a machine
- **Business Cycle** an increase and decrease in real GDP over time
- **Consumer Price Index** a measure of inflation using a market basket of goods bought by urban consumers
- **Cost-of-Living Adjustment** wages increase at the same rate as inflation
- **Cost-Push Inflation** price level increase caused by an increase in the cost of production
- **Cyclical Unemployment** occurs due to layoffs during a recession
- **Deflation** a general decrease in prices
- **Demand-Pull Inflation** price level increase caused by an increase in demand beyond available supply
- **Depression** an extended, very deep trough in a business cycle
- **Discouraged Worker** one who has been unemployed for so long that he has stopped looking for work
- **Expansion** a period of increase in real GDP
- **Frictional Unemployment** occurs when a worker is temporarily between jobs
- **Full Employment** the absence of cyclical unemployment
- **GDP Gap** the difference between potential and actual GDP
- **Hyperinflation** an extremely high rate of inflation
- **Inflation** an increase in the general price level
- **Labor Force** people over age 16 who are either working or actively seeking work
- **Natural Rate of Unemployment** the unemployment rate when the economy is producing at full potential output
- **Nominal Income** the income earned in the current value of dollars
- **Nominal Interest Rate** the interest rate charged by lenders, including anticipated inflation
- **Okun's Law** for every percentage point the unemployment rate is above the natural rate of unemployment, the GDP gap increases two percentage points
- **Peak** the highest point of real GDP in a business cycle
- **Real Income** the measure of what a consumer's income will actually buy
- **Real Interest Rate** the interest rate with expected inflation removed
- **Recession** a period of decrease in real GDP
- **Seasonal Unemployment** occurs at the same time each year
- **Structural Unemployment** occurs when a worker's skills do not match the available jobs
- **Trough** the lowest point of real GDP in a business cycle
- **Underemployed Workers** those who work part-time because they cannot find full-time jobs
- **Unemployed** people who are not working but are actively seeking work
- **Unemployment Rate** the percentage of people in the labor force who are actively seeking work
- **Wage-Price Spiral** an increase in prices causes workers to demand higher wages, which increases firms' production costs, so they raise prices; a continuous spiral to higher prices

Chapter 24

Basic Macroeconomic Relationships

An understanding of gross domestic product, economic growth, and business cycles lays the foundation for understanding the aggregate expenditure model of macroeconomic analysis. Changes in aggregate (total) spending cause short-run economic instability, and government policies address this instability. Chapter 24 introduces the marginal propensities to consume and save, the relationship between interest rates and investment, and the multiplier effect of spending throughout the economy. These principles provide the basis for understanding the aggregate demand – aggregate supply model in subsequent chapters.

Material from Chapter 24 may appear in a few multiple-choice questions on the AP Macroeconomics exam.

Key Concepts

Below is a summary of the chapter's concepts important to AP coursework. Upon completing the lessons that follow, return to these concepts to make sure you understand them and how the practice exercises you completed relate to them.

- Disposable income is the most important factor in determining a country's level of consumption.
  - Disposable Income = Consumption + Saving
- The consumption function shows that as income rises, consumption rises.
- Households with higher incomes save a higher proportion of their income.
- Average propensity to consume is the percentage of total income spent.
  - APC = Consumption / Income
- Average propensity to save is the percentage of total income saved.
  - APS = Saving / Income
- All income must be spent or saved, so APC + APS = 1.
- Marginal propensity to consume is the percentage of a change in income that is consumed.
  - MPC = Change in Consumption / Change in Income
- Marginal propensity to save is the percentage of a change in income that is saved.
  - MPS = Change in Saving / Change in Income
- All changes in income must be spent or saved, so MPC + MPS = 1.
- The level of a household's consumption is also determined by wealth, borrowing, expectations about future prices and income, changes in real interest rates, and taxes.

- Firms invest in plant and equipment if the expected rate of return is greater than the interest rate to pay for borrowed funds.
- Firms increase investment if the costs of capital fall, taxes fall, excess capacity is reduced, unplanned inventories are low, new technologies are introduced, and firms are optimistic.
- Investment spending is the most volatile sector of the economy.
- The multiplier effect shows that an initial change in spending causes a larger change in GDP.
    - Multiplier = Change in Real GDP / Initial Change in Spending
    - Change in GDP = Multiplier × Initial Change in Spending
    - Multiplier = (1 / MPS) or [1 / (1 – MPC)]
- The smaller the percentage of income consumed, the smaller the spending multiplier.
- A larger MPC causes a larger multiplier, creating a larger effect on GDP.

Now, let's examine more closely the following concepts from your textbook:

- **The Income-Consumption and Income-Saving Relationships**
- **Nonincome Determinants of Consumption and Saving**
- **The Interest Rate – Investment Relationship**
- **The Multiplier Effect**

These sections were selected because they provide practice identifying causes of changes in consumer spending and investment, calculating multipliers, and determining the effects of multipliers on real GDP.

The Income-Consumption and Income-Saving Relationships

Refer to pages 478–483 of your textbook.

A CLOSER LOOK Average and Marginal Propensities

The most important factor in determining a country's levels of consumption is **disposable income,** household income after personal taxes are paid. It is the income consumers have available to do one of two things: consume or save.

Disposable Income = Consumption + Saving

Americans consume nearly all of their income. The **consumption function** measures the relationship between income and consumption. It is a direct relationship; as income rises, consumption rises. Those with lower incomes consume a larger percentage of their incomes (save less) than those with higher incomes. In fact, those with low incomes may **dis-save,** spending more than their current income by spending previous savings, borrowing, or selling assets.

Caution

You may notice a subtle difference between "saving" and "savings." This difference is important. Saving is an action, a choice to not spend a stream of income. Savings is a quantity of past income that has been set aside and not spent. Pay careful attention to which word is used to discern whether we're talking about a person's current saving decision or the amount of savings previously set aside.

Average propensities to consume and save measure what consumers do with their entire incomes. **Average propensity to consume** (APC) is the percentage of total income that is spent.

$$APC = \frac{\text{Consumption}}{\text{Income}}$$

The **average propensity to save** (APS) is the percentage of total income that is saved.

$$APS = \frac{\text{Saving}}{\text{Income}}$$

If you earn $10,000 of total income this year and spend $9,000, APC is 0.90 (90%) and APS is 0.10 (10%). Because income can only be consumed or saved, the percentage consumed plus the percentage saved must equal 100% of income.

$$APC + APS = 1$$

With these relationships, we can determine either consumption or saving by knowing the other. If the APC is 0.75, the APS must be 0.25. If APS is 0.01, APC must be 0.99.

Marginal propensities to consume and save measure what consumers do with *changes* in income. If a household normally saves 5% of its income but then gains an additional $1,000 of income from overtime work, a tax cut, a gift, or a winning lottery ticket, what will the household do with the additional income? Some households will spend all of the additional income as a bonus to themselves, while others will save all of it for future spending, and other households will choose combinations between those extremes. The formulas for marginal propensities to save and consume look like the formulas for average propensities to save and consume, but the marginal formulas only deal with the *change* in income, rather than the *total* income.

Marginal propensity to consume (MPC) is the percentage of the change in income that is consumed.

$$MPC = \frac{\text{Change in Consumption}}{\text{Change in Income}}$$

The **marginal propensity to save** (MPS) is the percentage of the change in income that is saved.

$$MPS = \frac{\text{Change in Saving}}{\text{Change in Income}}$$

If you earn $1,000 of additional income and spend $600, MPC is 0.60 (60%) and MPS is 0.40 (40%). Just as with average propensities, the additional income can only be consumed or saved, so the percentage consumed plus the percentage saved must equal 100% of income.

$$MPC + MPS = 1$$

Given these formulas and data, consider the following scenario. Assume Deb's income is $20,000 and her APC is 0.75. She works overtime hours and earns an additional $2,000.

Her MPC is 0.60. How much of Deb's overall income will she spend? How much will she save? Deb spends 75% of her original $20,000 ($15,000) plus 60% of her additional $2,000 ($1,200), so she spends a total of $16,200. Remember that what wasn't spent must be saved. So Deb must have saved 25% of her original $20,000 ($5,000) plus 40% of her additional $2,000 ($800), so she saves a total of $5,800.

Keep in Mind
Once you have found the total consumption of income, it may be tempting to take a shortcut to just subtract the consumption from total income to determine the total saving. But it is in your best interest to take the extra time to separately calculate the saving, because you can then compare that answer to the shortcut answer to make sure your math is correct. Don't lose points for a silly math error!

PRACTICE Average and Marginal Propensities

1. ________ If Irene earns an additional $1,000 in income, her spending will probably increase by less than $1,000. What will she do with the rest of the income?

2. If Kaitlin's average propensity to consume is 0.60 and her income is $1,000:

 A. ________ How many dollars will she spend?

 B. ________ How many dollars will she save?

3. If Samantha's marginal propensity to consume is 0.75 and her income rises by $2,000:

 A. ________ How many dollars will she spend?

 B. ________ How many dollars will she save?

4. If Alejandro's disposable income is $10,000, his average propensity to consume is 0.8, his marginal propensity to consume is 0.7, and his income rises by $500:

 A. ________ How many dollars did he spend of his original $10,000 income?

 B. ________ How many dollars did he save of his original $10,000 income?

 C. ________ How many dollars will he spend of his $500 increase in income?

 D. ________ How many dollars will he save of his $500 increase in income?

 E. ________ How much of the total $10,500 was consumed?

 F. ________ How much of the total $10,500 was saved?

Nonincome Determinants of Consumption and Saving

Refer to pages 483–485 of your textbook.

A CLOSER LOOK Nonincome Determinants of Consumption and Saving

While a household's disposable income is the primary factor in determining the relative amounts the household will choose to consume or save, other factors also help to make that determination.

Wealth is the value of assets owned by the household (from prior saving) minus the debts owed. According to the **wealth effect,** when wealth increases, households tend to increase consumption and reduce saving; reductions in wealth lead to reductions in consumption and increases in saving.

Borrowing also affects consumption, because if households can borrow money to spend beyond their disposable incomes, consumption increases. It is important to keep in mind that although consumption increases in the short-term, consumption must decrease later for the household to repay the debt.

Expectations about future prices and income also affect consumption decisions. If consumers expect prices to rise in the near future, they may increase consumption now, in order to buy before the price rises. The reverse is also true. If consumers are concerned about the possibility of losing their jobs during a recession, they are likely to reduce spending and increase saving to prepare for that possibility.

Changes in real interest rates can also affect consumption and saving. If interest rates fall, consumers tend to consume more because of the lower cost of borrowing. At the same time, they tend to save less because the interest they earn on savings is lower. This effect tends to be weaker than the wealth, borrowing, and expectation effects, because interest rates only affect products bought with credit, and the interest rate is not the primary determinant of whether consumers save. Saving as a long-term investment for retirement, education, or emergencies seems to be a more powerful consideration.

Taxes can also affect consumption. If taxes rise, less disposable income is available for both consumption and saving. If taxes fall, both consumption and saving tend to increase.

PRACTICE Nonincome Determinants of Consumption and Saving

Indicate whether each of these events is more likely to increase *consumption*, *saving*, or *both*.

1. __________ A worker is concerned about the increasing number of layoffs across the nation

2. __________ An investor is happy to see that the value of her stocks has increased by 10%

3. __________ A couple decides to take out a mortgage to buy a new home

4. __________ The government decreases the income tax rate

5. __________ The real interest rate for auto loans increases

The Interest Rate – Investment Relationship

Refer to pages 485–487 of your textbook.

A CLOSER LOOK Expected Rate of Return and Investment Demand Curve

Remember that economists define **investment** as firms' spending for plants, capital equipment, and other materials to increase future production. If the marginal benefit (the expected rate of return, which is the expected additional profit divided by the cost of the investment) is greater than the marginal cost (the interest rate to pay for borrowed funds), the firm will make the investment. But if the interest rate the firm must pay is greater than the expected return on the investment, the firm will not invest. These same conditions are met if the firm is using savings to invest, because in that situation, the interest rate represents forgone interest the firm could have earned on the savings. At lower real interest rates, firms are more willing to invest; at higher interest rates, firms are less willing to invest.

It is important to note that the firm is using the real interest rate, rather than the nominal interest rate, in its investment decisions. The nominal interest rate includes an extra factor to compensate for the expected rate of inflation. But because the firm would repay the loan with those inflated dollars, the inflation premium in the nominal interest rate is not a concern.

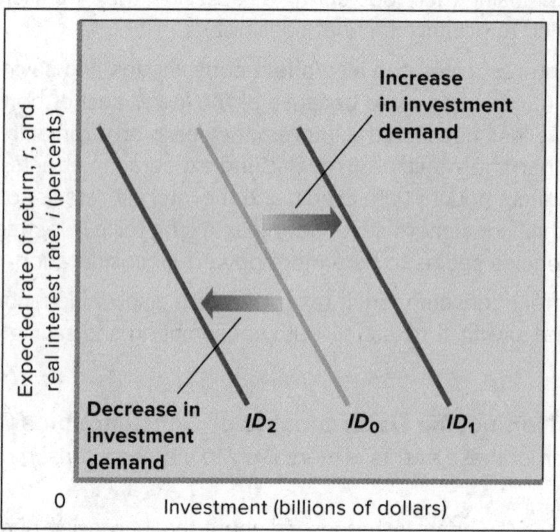

If firms expect a larger return on investment, their investment demand increases, shifting to the right. If firms expect lower returns on investment, their investment demand decreases and shifts to the left.

The costs of capital, operation, and maintenance are central to the investment decision. If these costs rise, firms' expected return on investment will fall and firms will be less willing to invest. Increased taxes on firms also reduce expected return on investment, lowering investment demand. If firms have excess capacity (unused plant and equipment) or large unplanned inventories, firms expect little return on investment and are less willing to invest in even more plant and equipment. On the other hand, firms increase investment if they expect to make additional returns from planned inventories. Technological progress increases investment, as firms must adopt new technology to increase profit or at least keep up with competitors. Expectations also affect investment. Optimism about the economy and expected return on investment increase investment demand; pessimism reduces investment demand.

Investment spending is the most volatile sector of the economy, and most of the business cycle effects on output and employment can be traced to changes in investment. Part of the instability is due to the durability of capital goods. They are built for longer-term use, and firms can make repairs to keep older capital functioning instead of purchasing new capital. Innovation also occurs irregularly, and investment tends to increase significantly when it is released. Changes in actual profits also affect investment in terms of providing funds to finance the investment and changing expectations about future profit. Quickly changing expectations about future sales, consumer confidence, the stock market, political events, international trade, and economic shocks can also increase the variability of investment.

PRACTICE **Expected Rate of Return and Investment Demand Curve**

1. __________ A firm will invest if the expected return on investment is greater than *what*?

2. __________ If a new piece of equipment costs $50,000, the firm expects profit to increase by $60,000 as a result of the investment, and the real interest rate to borrow money to buy the equipment is 6%, should the firm invest in the equipment?

Indicate whether each of the following events is more likely to *increase* or *decrease* investment.

3. __________ The cost to build a new factory increases

4. __________ The government increases corporate income taxes

5. __________ New technology has been developed which significantly increases productivity

6. __________ Corporate profits significantly increase

7. __________ The real interest rate increases

The Multiplier Effect

Refer to pages 490–494 of your textbook.

A CLOSER LOOK **The Multiplier and the Marginal Propensities**

Increased spending causes an increase in real GDP, but the effects reach beyond the initial change in spending. With the **multiplier effect,** an initial change in spending leads to an even larger change in real GDP. To determine how large the effect will be, we must calculate the spending multiplier.

$$\text{Multiplier} = \frac{\text{Change in Real GDP}}{\text{Initial Change in Spending}}$$

If investment spending rises by $5 billion, causing real GDP to increase by $20 billion, the multiplier is 4. We can convert the formula to calculate how an initial change in spending causes real GDP to change.

$$\text{Change in GDP} = \text{Multiplier} \times \text{Initial Change in Spending}$$

If investment spending rises by $2 million and the multiplier is 3, real GDP will increase by $6 million.

While initial changes in spending are often attributed to the investment sector because spending in that sector is so volatile, it is important to remember that changes in spending can also originate in the consumer, government, and net export sectors. It is also important to note that decreases in spending also result in multiplied effects on GDP.

The spending multiplier results from the fact that one person's spending is another's income. When spending increases, the recipient saves part of that income and spends the rest. Those who receive that second round of spending again spend part of that income and save the rest. The initial spending is multiplied as it goes through round after round of spending in the economy, until there is no more income left to spend. We can also calculate the specific changes in GDP resulting from the initial change in spending by using the marginal propensities to consume and save.

$$\text{Multiplier} = \frac{1}{\text{MPS}} \quad \text{or} \quad \text{Multiplier} = \frac{1}{1 - \text{MPC}}$$

If the marginal propensity to save is 0.2, the spending multiplier is 5, whether you divide directly by MPS or subtract the MPC (which must be 0.8) from 1 (the 100% of income).

The smaller the percentage of income consumed, the smaller the spending multiplier. If a smaller percentage of income is actually spent in each round of spending, even less money is available for the next round of spending, and this continues round after round.

For example, if the initial change in spending is $1,000 and MPC is 0.9, people spend 90% of the change in income. In the first round of spending, $900 of additional spending occurs ($1,000 × 0.9). In the second round, $810 of additional spending occurs ($900 × 0.9). The multiplier for this change in spending is 10 (1 / 0.1). Therefore, the change in GDP resulting from this $1,000 initial change in spending is $10,000 ($1,000 × 10).

If, instead, the MPC were 0.5, people would only spend 50% of the change in income. In the first round of spending, $500 of additional spending occurs ($1,000 × 0.5), and round two brings only $250 of additional spending ($500 × 0.5). The spending multiplier for this lower MPC is only 2 (1 / 0.5), so the change in GDP resulting from this $1,000 initial change in spending is only $2,000 ($1,000 × 2). A larger MPC causes a larger multiplier, creating a larger effect on GDP from an initial change in spending.

How large is the US multiplier? Actual estimates are complicated by purchases of imports, taxes, and inflation. Economists estimate the actual US spending multiplier is somewhere between zero and 2.5.

Keep in Mind

It is important to know how to use both the MPS and MPC formulas to calculate the multiplier, because AP Macroeconomics exam questions may only provide you the MPC or MPS, and you must be able to convert information from one measure to the other.

PRACTICE The Multiplier and the Marginal Propensities

1. If a firm increases capital investment by $1 million in an economy where MPC is 0.75:

   A. __________ What is the multiplier?

   B. __________ As a result of the multiplier, by how much would real GDP increase?

2. If a firm increases capital investment by $2 million in an economy where MPC is 0.9:

   A. __________ What is the multiplier?

   B. __________ As a result of the multiplier, by how much would real GDP increase?

3. If investment increases by $10 million and real GDP increases by $40 million:

   A. __________ What is the MPS?

   B. __________ What is the MPC?

Make sure to return to the AP Key Concepts section to check your understanding of the chapter's concepts important to AP coursework.

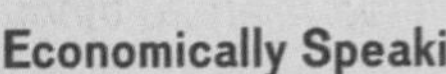

Economically Speaking

- **Average Propensity to Consume** the percentage of total income that is spent
- **Average Propensity to Save** the percentage of total income that is saved
- **Consumption Function** measures the direct relationship between income and consumption
- **Disposable Income** household income available after personal taxes have been paid
- **Dissave** spend more than current income by using previous savings, borrowing, or selling assets
- **Investment** firms' spending for plant, capital, and materials to increase future production
- **Marginal Propensity to Consume** the percentage of the change in income that is consumed
- **Marginal Propensity to Save** the percentage of the change in income that is saved
- **Multiplier Effect** an initial change in spending leads to an even larger change in real GDP
- **Wealth** the value of assets owned by the household minus the debts owed
- **Wealth Effect** when wealth increases, households increase consumption and reduce saving

Chapter 25

The Aggregate Expenditures Model

Now that you have a basic understanding of how changes in investment and disposable income (including decisions about consumption and saving) affect real GDP, we will bring the aspects of the Keynesian aggregate expenditures model together. Chapter 25 begins with a closed private sector economy and then adds international trade and the government sector into the model. This model explains the effects of changes in spending in each sector on real GDP, the causes of recessionary and inflationary gaps, and the role of government in reducing such gaps.

Material from Chapter 25 may appear in several multiple-choice questions on the AP Macroeconomics exam, and free-response questions frequently focus on the appropriate fiscal policy measures taken to address recessionary and inflationary gaps.

Key Concepts

Below is a summary of the chapter's concepts important to AP coursework. Upon completing the lessons that follow, return to these concepts to make sure you understand them and how the practice exercises you completed relate to them.

- Classical theory holds that the economy naturally operates at full employment unless there is a shock; then the economy will automatically adjust with flexible wages and prices, so no government intervention is necessary.
- Keynesian theory holds that the economy often operates at less than full employment due to economic fluctuations, especially in the investment sector.
    - Output and employment are flexible, but prices and wages are not.
    - Government must intervene to correct economic instability.
- Equilibrium GDP occurs where the quantity produced (GDP) equals the quantity purchased (aggregate spending).
- If saving exceeds planned investment, real GDP falls; if planned investment exceeds saving, real GDP rises.
- At equilibrium GDP, firms have no unplanned inventories; if unplanned inventories begin to rise, firms reduce output and employment.
- An initial change in spending, multiplied by the multiplier, changes the real GDP.
    - Multiplier = Change in Real GDP / Initial Change in Spending
- Net Exports = Exports − Imports
    - If exports exceed imports, net exports are positive.
    - Because US imports exceed exports, net exports have been negative since the 1980s.
- Net exports and real GDP increase if incomes abroad increase, the international value of the dollar depreciates, or the US imposes a tariff or other trade barrier (in the short run).

- Increases in government spending and decreases in taxes raise real GDP.
- Changes in government spending have a greater effect than changes in taxes on GDP, because households will save part of a tax cut and pay part of a tax increase from savings.
- Savings, imports, and taxes are leakages from the circular flow; they are income not spent.
- Investments, exports, and government spending are injections into the circular flow; they are spending beyond current income to purchase output in the domestic economy.
- A recessionary gap is the amount by which current aggregate spending is less than full-employment GDP. It causes cyclical unemployment.
- An inflationary gap is the amount by which current aggregate spending is greater than full-employment GDP. It causes demand-pull inflation.
- Keynes advocated the use of fiscal policy, with government changing taxes and spending to correct GDP gaps and restore full-employment GDP.
- To close a gap, government only needs to change its spending by the amount of the initial change in spending, because the multiplier affects both government and investment spending.
- To close a gap, government must change taxes by more than it would change spending, because households save part of tax cuts and pay part of tax increases from savings.
    - Spending Multiplier = 1 / MPS
    - Change in Real GDP = Spending Multiplier × Change in Government Spending
    - Tax Multiplier = MPC × (1 / MPS)
    - Change in Real GDP = Tax Multiplier × Change in Taxes
    - Amount By Which Tax Must Be Changed = (1 / MPC) × Recessionary Gap

Now, let's examine more closely the following concepts from your textbook:

- **Assumptions and Simplifications**
- **Equilibrium GDP**
- **Changes in Equilibrium GDP and the Multiplier**
- **Adding International Trade**
- **Adding the Public Sector**
- **Equilibrium versus Full-Employment GDP**

These sections were selected because the aggregate expenditure model, which describes activity within each of the four sectors of the macroeconomy, can explain details of changes in GDP which will be illustrated in the aggregate supply – aggregate demand model in subsequent chapters.

Assumptions and Simplifications

Refer to page 499 of your textbook.

A CLOSER LOOK Assumptions and Simplifications

Classical theory was the first modern economic theory. It was developed by economists such as Adam Smith, David Ricardo, John Stuart Mill, Thomas Malthus, and Jean Baptiste Say. Classical theorists believed that a market economy would maintain full-employment output in the long run. According to classical theorists, wages and prices were flexible, but output and employment were not. They theorized that even if an economy experienced a short-run shock like a crop failure, a war, or a discovery of new resources, market forces would automatically adjust. If **aggregate spending** fell in the economy, prices, wages, and interest rates would fall in response, enticing consumers to increase their spending again and restoring the economy to full-employment output. Classical economists were also convinced that supply would create its own demand, because the spending for resources to produce the output would create income for resource owners, who would in turn buy that output. Because they believed that a laissez-faire economy experiencing instability would self-correct, they argued that no government intervention was necessary.

Classical theory was the dominant theory for well over a century – until the Great Depression. The Depression dragged on for years, with an extreme drop in GDP and a dramatic rise in unemployment. The economy did not self-adjust. Because the classical model failed to explain the Depression, British economist John Maynard Keynes brought about a whole new way of thinking about the economy.

Keynes, who built his model on Depression-era economic conditions, argued that aggregate spending in the economy constantly fluctuated, especially in the investment sector. Output and employment were flexible, but prices and wages were not. As a result, it was possible for aggregate spending to remain below full-employment output for an extended period of time. Prices were so sticky downward that they would not change in response to changes in demand. Firms were left with large unplanned inventories, so they reduced production and laid off workers – or closed entirely. If demand were to increase, a reduction in those inventories would signal to firms to increase production. Because millions of workers were unemployed, firms wouldn't have to raise wages to attract workers, so prices need not rise. The economy just needed a stimulus to bring aggregate demand back up. **Keynesian theory** called for the government to take an instrumental role in correcting economic instability.

To begin this analysis of the Keynesian model, we make several simplifying assumptions. We begin with only households and firms – no government or international sectors. We also assume that because there are no taxes, real GDP equals disposable income. Remember, GDP can be calculated using either the expenditure or income approaches, because one person's spending is another person's income. We also assume the excess plant capacity and high unemployment conditions of the Great Depression, so that increases in output and employment will not put upward pressure on the price level.

PRACTICE **Assumptions and Simplifications**

Indicate whether each of the following statements reflects *Classical* or *Keynesian* theory.

1A. _________ In the short run, prices and wages are fixed; output and employment change.

B. _________ In the short run, output and employment are fixed; prices and wages change.

2A. _________ Aggregate spending constantly fluctuates, particularly in the investment sector.

B. _________ Aggregate spending is generally stable unless there is some kind of shock.

3A. _________ The economy naturally operates at full-employment output.

B. _________ The economy frequently operates at less than full-employment output.

4A. _________ Government should intervene to solve economic problems.

B. _________ Government should not intervene in the economy; it will automatically adjust.

Equilibrium GDP: $C + I_g = GDP$

Refer to pages 500–503 of your textbook.

A CLOSER LOOK Equilibrium GDP: $C + I_g = GDP$

In a closed (no international trade) private sector (no government) economy, consumption spending by households plus planned investment spending by firms equals the aggregate (total) spending in the economy. Remember that **investment** consists of planned spending for plant and equipment plus inventories. Firms sometimes plan to build inventory before an expected increase in product demand – candy companies before Halloween, florists before Valentine's Day, and toymakers before Christmas. **Equilibrium GDP** is the quantity of output at which the quantity produced (GDP) equals the quantity bought (aggregate spending), and there are no unplanned inventories.

At equilibrium GDP, saving equals planned investment. In the circular flow model, saving is considered a **leakage** from the flow of income, because that income is not immediately spent for goods or services. However, firms also do not sell their entire output to households, because capital equipment sold to other firms is investment. This investment is considered an **injection** of spending back into the circular flow model. Household savings are borrowed by firms to buy capital equipment, so when the economy is in equilibrium, the amount households save is borrowed by firms and spent for investment. If saving is greater than planned investment, the leakage is greater than the injection and real GDP falls. Conversely, if planned investment is greater than saving, the injection is greater than the leakage and real GDP increases.

At equilibrium GDP, firms have no unplanned inventories. If current spending is less than production, unplanned inventories begin to rise; therefore, firms reduce production until the market returns to equilibrium. If current spending is greater than production, inventories begin to decline and firms increase output until the market returns to equilibrium.

PRACTICE Equilibrium GDP: $C + I_g = GDP$

1. _________ If an economy is operating at equilibrium GDP, saving is equal to *what*?

2. _________ If an economy operates at equilibrium GDP, how much is unplanned inventory?

3. _________ If unplanned inventories increase, should firms increase or reduce production?

4. _________ If unplanned inventories increase, should firms increase or reduce employment?

5. _________ If a leakage is greater than an injection, what will happen to real GDP?

Changes in Equilibrium GDP and the Multiplier

Refer to pages 504–505 of your textbook.

A CLOSER LOOK Changes in Equilibrium GDP and the Multiplier

Equilibrium GDP is affected by changes in consumer or investment spending, but investment is the more volatile sector. If the real interest rate increases and firms expect their rate of return on investment to be lower than the new interest rate, they reduce their investment spending. This results in a reduction in GDP, causing firms to reduce output and employment. But the reduction in GDP doesn't just end with the initial decrease in investment. Remember, the decrease in spending ripples through the economy over and over, and the multiplier is needed to calculate the total effect on GDP.

$$\text{Multiplier} = \frac{\text{Change in Real GDP}}{\text{Initial Change in Spending}}$$

If the initial reduction in investment is $1 million and the multiplier is 5, the reduction in investment will create a $5 million reduction in real GDP.

PRACTICE Changes in Equilibrium GDP and the Multiplier

1. __________ Which sector of the economy has the most volatile changes in spending?

2. __________ If a $12 billion decrease in investment causes a $48 billion reduction in real GDP, what is the multiplier?

3. __________ If consumer spending increases by $15 billion and the multiplier is 2, by how much will real GDP increase?

Adding International Trade

Refer to pages 505–508 of your textbook.

A CLOSER LOOK Net Exports and Equilibrium GDP

Releasing one of our beginning assumptions, we now open the economy and include **net exports** (exports minus imports). Foreign demand for domestically-produced products increases output and employment. But US demand for imports reduces demand for domestically produced products, so US spending for imports must be subtracted from foreign purchases of US exports.

If exports exceed imports, net exports are positive. They increase aggregate spending, real GDP, and employment to a level higher than they would have been in a closed economy. But if imports exceed exports, the negative net exports reduce aggregate spending, real GDP, and employment from what they would have been in a closed economy. The US has had negative net exports since the 1980s.

A number of factors affect imports and exports. The first factor is the relative difference in incomes. If real incomes abroad increase, consumers in those countries are better able to afford US exports, so our exports rise, increasing net exports. If US incomes rise more quickly than incomes in other countries, US imports will rise more quickly than our exports, causing net exports to fall.

A second factor affecting net exports is the **exchange rate,** which is the value of one currency in terms of another. If the international value of the dollar were to **depreciate,** becoming less valuable, the foreign currency would **appreciate,** increasing in value. Because the foreign currency is more expensive, the price of imports appears to rise, so imports decrease. At the same time, the relative price of American goods seems to have decreased to foreign consumers, so they buy more, increasing our exports. Because exports rise and imports fall, net exports rise and real GDP increases.

A third factor affecting international trade is the use of **trade barriers,** which are policies designed to limit trade. If the US imposes a **tariff** (tax on imports), US consumers will buy fewer imports because of the higher price. At the same time, US consumers will buy more domestic products as substitutes. These effects reinforce each other to increase real GDP and employment in the short run. However, if we buy fewer imports from other countries, the decrease in demand for their products reduces employment and incomes abroad, reducing their demand for US exports. Further, other countries may retaliate with trade barriers of their own, further reducing demand for US exports. In the long run, US tariffs may actually reduce net exports, rather than increasing them.

PRACTICE Net Exports and Equilibrium GDP

Indicate whether each of these factors would cause an *increase* or *decrease* in net exports and real GDP.

1. ____________ Consumers in Canada increase their purchases of American-produced tomatoes.

2. ____________ US incomes are rising more quickly than incomes in China.

3. ____________ The international value of the dollar appreciates, making imports less expensive.

4. ____________ The US imposes a tariff on imports from Germany (short-run effect).

Adding the Public Sector

Refer to pages 508–511 of your textbook.

A CLOSER LOOK Government Purchases, Taxation, and Equilibrium GDP

Releasing another beginning assumption, we now add government revenues and spending to the economy in order to see the full picture of our mixed-market economy. Remember the GDP formula C + I + G + (X – M); the government sector completes the formula. In this analysis, we assume that government spending does not affect the other sectors and that government collects the same amount of tax revenue, no matter what happens to GDP.

Increases in government spending increase aggregate spending and the real GDP. Just as with consumption and investment spending, government spending is affected by the multiplier. If government spending increases by $10 million and the multiplier is 5, the real GDP would increase by $50 million. If government spending decreased, the real GDP would decrease, as well.

Taxes also affect real GDP. A **lump-sum tax** is a tax that brings in the same amount of revenue to the government, regardless of the level of GDP. When a tax is levied, consumers pay part of the tax from savings and the other part from reduced consumption. We know the percentages from the marginal propensities to consume and save. If the MPC is 0.8, a $10 million tax will reduce consumption by $8 million; the other $2 million of tax revenue will come from reduced saving. Therefore, the increase in tax lowers the real GDP by the amount that consumption falls – by $8 million, not the entire $10 million.

It is very important to note that changes in government spending and changes in taxes have different effects on real GDP. Changes in government spending have a full impact on real GDP, because the total spending goes right out into the economy. However, when taxes are changed, this action has less than a full impact on the economy, because due to the MPC and MPS, part of the impact is on consumption and part is on saving. For example, if the government increases spending by $50 million, the real GDP initially increases by the full $50 million. But if taxes decrease by $50 million and the MPC is 0.8, the real GDP initially only increases by $40 million because the other $10 million is an increase in saving.

Keep in Mind
It is important to remember the differences between the effects of taxes and spending; spending has a fuller effect on GDP than taxes because consumers save some of tax cuts and use savings to pay part of tax increases. Questions about this concept commonly appear on the AP Macroeconomics exam.

PRACTICE Government Purchases, Taxation, and Equilibrium GDP

1. ________ Will an increase in government spending raise or lower real GDP?

2. ________ Will an increase in taxes raise or lower real GDP?

3. ________ If MPC is 0.9 and government spending increases by $10 billion, by how much will real GDP increase in the first round of spending?

4. ________ If MPC is 0.9 and taxes decrease by $10 billion, by how much will real GDP increase in the first round of spending?

5. ________ The effects of government spending are greater than the effects of tax changes, because households do *what* with part of their tax cuts?

Equilibrium versus Full-Employment GDP

Refer to pages 511–515 of your textbook.

A CLOSER LOOK Recessionary Expenditure Gap and Inflationary Expenditure Gap

Now that we have included all four sectors of spending into the circular market flow, we must address the leakages and injections in the model, recognizing that leakages from the flow must equal the injections into the flow. Savings, imports, and taxes are all leakages from the circular flow, because they represent income that was not spent to purchase output in the domestic economy. Investments, exports, and government spending are all injections into the circular flow, because they represent additional spending beyond current income to purchase output in the domestic economy. At equilibrium GDP, the sum of the leakages must equal the sum of the injections. If the leakages and injections differ, GDP is not at equilibrium.

In the Keynesian model, current spending and full-employment GDP need not be equal. In fact, Keynesian analysis illustrated current GDP to be well below full-employment GDP during the Depression. A **recessionary expenditure gap** is the amount by which current aggregate spending is less than full-employment GDP, causing an increase in **cyclical unemployment.** An initial decrease in spending is subject to the multiplier, so a $3 billion initial decrease in spending with a multiplier of 5 will eventually create a recessionary expenditure gap of $15 billion.

Keynes advocated **fiscal policy,** the use of taxes or government spending, to correct a GDP gap. Government can increase spending or reduce taxes to increase aggregate spending. Then the same multiplier that affects the initial decrease in spending also works to multiply the increase in government spending and return the economy to full employment. In the case of the $3 billion initial decrease in spending discussed above, government need only increase its spending by that same amount to fill the entire $15 billion recessionary expenditure gap between current GDP and full-employment output.

$$\text{Spending Multiplier} = \frac{1}{\text{MPS}}$$

$$\text{Change in Real GDP} = \text{Spending Multiplier} \times \text{Change in Government Spending}$$

The second tool of fiscal policy is to change taxes. In the case of the $3 billion recessionary expenditure gap with a multiplier of 5, government must reduce taxes by enough to eventually fill the $15 billion difference between current GDP and full-employment GDP. But remember that taxes are not as effective as government spending in changing GDP, because with tax changes, only a fraction of consumption will be affected; consumers will save the rest of the tax cut. So if government reduced taxes by $3 billion, it would not create the full $15 billion in spending to fill the gap. A multiplier of 5 indicates the marginal propensity to save is 0.2, so consumers would actually save 20% of their tax cut ($0.6 billion) and spend the other $2.4 billion. Therefore, tax changes must be larger than government spending changes to achieve the same result.

$$\text{Tax Multiplier} = \text{MPC} \times \frac{1}{\text{MPS}}$$

$$\text{Change in Real GDP} = \text{Tax Multiplier} \times \text{Change in Taxes}$$

How large must a tax reduction be to make up for the recessionary expenditure gap?

$$\text{Amount by Which Tax Must Be Reduced} = \frac{1}{\text{MPC}} \times \text{Recessionary Gap}$$

If the initial change in spending is $3 billion and the MPC is 0.8, government must reduce taxes by $3 billion multiplied by 1 / MPC (1 / 0.8 = 1.25), or $3.75 billion, in order to completely fill the gap. If the government reduces taxes by $3.75 billion, the MPS of 0.2 indicates that consumers will save $0.75 billion and spend the other $3 billion, returning the GDP to full-employment GDP over time.

An **inflationary expenditure gap** is the amount by which current aggregate spending is greater than full-employment GDP. While an economy may be able to temporarily produce an output greater than full-employment level via employees working overtime and the heavier use of other resources, such an output cannot be sustained in the long term. Therefore, any increased spending beyond full employment can only cause **demand-pull inflation,** raising prices. An inflationary expenditure gap can be reduced by using fiscal policy to increase taxes or reduce government spending. Government spending is more powerful because it receives the full effect of the multiplier, while changes in taxes are less effective because consumers will use savings to pay some part of the tax. Therefore, taxes must be increased by a larger amount than the spending would be reduced in order to obtain the same effect.

Bringing reality to the theory, the use of fiscal policy is not as easy as the model suggests. It is very difficult to determine the amount of an initial change in spending, so it is difficult to project the appropriate amount of change in taxes or government spending to correct a gap. This theory also presumes that marginal propensities to consume and save are fixed. But in reality, during a recession, many consumers significantly increase the percentage of income saved to prepare for a possible job loss, while others stop saving entirely because they have lost their jobs and must use their savings for purchases. In addition, firms significantly reduce investment in capital because unplanned inventories have increased and it makes little sense to expand when consumer demand has decreased. One other concern is that fiscal policy is conducted by the President and Congress; changes in taxes or government spending must be approved by them, which is a time-consuming and difficult political process.

PRACTICE Recessionary Expenditure Gap and Inflationary Expenditure Gap

1. ________ Will a recessionary gap result in inflation or cyclical unemployment?

2. ________ What kind of policy did Keynes support, using taxes and government spending?

3. ________ To correct a recessionary gap, should government spending rise or fall?

4. ________ To correct a recessionary gap, should government increase or decrease taxes?

5. ________ Assume consumer spending falls by $2 billion, causing an $8 billion recessionary gap. By how much should government spending increase to fill the gap?

6. ________ Assume consumer spending falls by $2 billion, causing an $8 billion recessionary gap. By how much should government lower taxes to fill the gap?

7. ________ Will an inflationary gap result in demand-pull or cost-push inflation?

8. ________ To correct a $5 million inflationary gap, would a $1 million reduction in government spending or a $1 million increase in taxes be more effective?

Make sure to return to the AP Key Concepts section to check your understanding of the chapter's concepts important to AP coursework.

Economically Speaking

- **Aggregate Spending** the total spending in the economy
- **Appreciate** the value of a currency increases in international exchange markets
- **Classical Theory** assumes the economy generally operates at full-employment output and will automatically adjust after economic shocks
- **Cyclical Unemployment** layoffs due to recession
- **Demand-Pull Inflation** an increase in the general price level caused by an increase in demand
- **Depreciate** the value of a currency decreases in international exchange markets
- **Equilibrium GDP** the quantity produced (GDP) equals the quantity bought (aggregate spending)
- **Exchange Rate** the value of one currency in terms of another
- **Fiscal Policy** the government's use of taxes or government spending to correct a GDP gap
- **Inflationary Expenditure Gap** the amount by which current aggregate spending is greater than full-employment GDP
- **Injection** spending beyond current income to purchase output in the domestic economy
- **Investment** spending by firms for plant and equipment plus inventories
- **Keynesian Theory** assumes the economy is volatile and often produces at less than full-employment output; calls for government intervention to stabilize the economy
- **Leakage** income that is not spent to purchase output in the domestic economy
- **Lump-Sum Tax** a tax that brings in the same amount of revenue, regardless of the GDP level
- **Net Exports** a country's exports minus imports
- **Recessionary Expenditure Gap** the amount by which current aggregate spending is less than full-employment GDP
- **Tariff** a tax on imports
- **Trade Barriers** policies which are designed to limit trade

Chapter 26

Aggregate Demand and Aggregate Supply

The aggregate demand – aggregate supply (AD-AS) model provides the key graph depicting changes in the macroeconomy. Shifts in aggregate supply and aggregate demand explain changes in real output, employment, and price levels in the economy. Chapter 26 introduces the AD-AS model, bringing together the concepts of GDP, inflation, unemployment, and recessionary and inflationary gaps that have been introduced throughout the macroeconomics chapters.

Material from Chapter 26 is very likely to appear in a large number of multiple-choice questions and as part of a free-response question on nearly every AP Macroeconomics exam.

Key Concepts

Below is a summary of the chapter's concepts important to AP coursework. Upon completing the lessons that follow, return to these concepts to make sure you understand them and how the practice exercises you completed relate to them.

- Aggregate demand illustrates the total amount of output demanded at each price level.
    - The real balances effect shows that at a higher price level, real wealth falls, so consumers buy less.
    - The interest rate effect shows that at a higher price level, interest rates rise, so consumers buy less.
    - The foreign purchases effect shows that at a higher US price level, US consumers buy more imports and foreigners buy fewer US exports.
- Changes in aggregate demand are caused by changes in each of the four sectors of GDP:
    - Consumer demand shifts due to changes in wealth, borrowing, expectations, and taxes.
    - Investment demand shifts due to changes in interest rates and expected return on investment. It is the most volatile of the four sectors.
    - Government demand shifts due to changes in priorities for government spending.
    - Net exports demand shifts due to changes in foreign incomes and exchange rates.
- Initial changes in spending are subject to the multiplier, which causes a greater total change in aggregate demand in the economy.

- Aggregate supply illustrates the total amount of goods produced at each price level.
  - In the immediate period, both resources costs and prices charged to consumers are fixed; aggregate supply is horizontal, so output and employment can change, but price level cannot change.
  - In the short run, resource costs are fixed or very sticky, but prices charged to consumers are flexible; aggregate supply is upward-sloping, so output, employment, and price level can all change.
  - In the long run, resource costs and prices charged to consumers are flexible; aggregate supply is vertical, so price level can change, but output and employment cannot change.
- Changes in aggregate supply are caused by changes in costs of production, productivity, and government policies such as taxes, subsidies, and regulation.
- Investment in capital increases aggregate demand in the short run and aggregate supply in the long run.
- Equilibrium GDP, where aggregate supply equals aggregate demand, sets price level and GDP.
- An increase in aggregate demand causes demand-pull inflation and an inflationary gap.
- A decrease in aggregate demand causes cyclical unemployment and a recessionary gap.
- A decrease in aggregate supply causes cost-push inflation and, if sustained, stagflation.
- It is possible for aggregate supply and aggregate demand to move simultaneously, though the effects on price level or real GDP may not be clear.

Now, let's examine more closely the following concepts from your textbook:

- **Aggregate Demand**
- **Changes in Aggregate Demand**
- **Aggregate Supply**
- **Changes in Aggregate Supply**
- **Changes in Equilibrium**

These sections were selected because the aggregate demand – aggregate supply model is essential to understanding changes in the economy and how tools to stabilize the economy, which will be introduced in subsequent chapters, can be effective.

Aggregate Demand

Refer to pages 521–522 of your textbook.

A CLOSER LOOK Aggregate Demand Curve

Aggregate demand is a curve showing the total amount of output demanded (by consumers, firms, governments, and foreign buyers) at each price level. When the price level rises, fewer products are demanded; when the price level falls, more products are demanded. Therefore, aggregate demand slopes downward, with the negative slope resulting from three effects: the real balances effect, the interest rate effect, and the foreign purchases effect.

The **real balances effect** focuses on the value of consumers' wealth. At a higher price level, the real value of a consumer's assets (a home, stocks, and savings) falls. With less real wealth, consumers are less likely to buy products. Lower prices increase real wealth, increasing quantity demanded.

The second reason for the downward slope of aggregate demand is the **interest rate effect.** When prices rise, consumers and firms must borrow more money to make the same purchases. That increased demand for money pushes up the **interest rate** (the price of borrowing money), which discourages consumer borrowing to buy products. It also causes firms to reduce spending for capital, because the higher interest rate can exceed the expected return on investment.

The third cause of the downward slope in aggregate demand is the **foreign purchases effect.** When the US price level increases (if exchange rates do not change), US consumers buy more imports and foreigners buy fewer US exports. As a result, the quantity of US goods demanded falls at higher prices and rises at lower prices.

Graphing Guidance

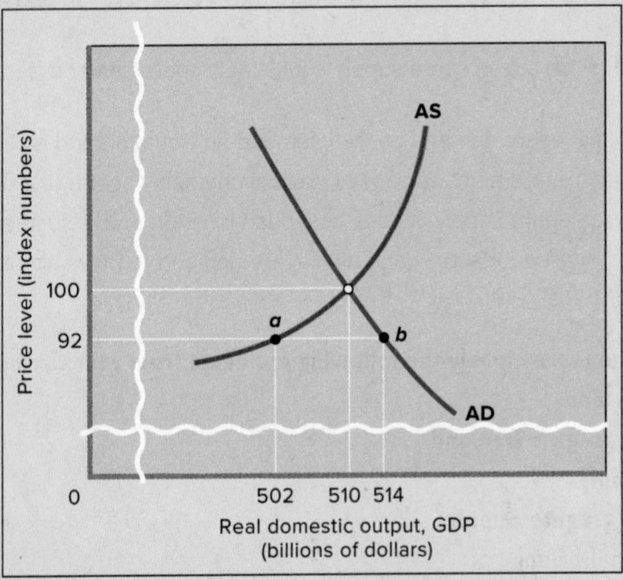

The aggregate demand – aggregate supply model is part of a free-response question on almost every AP Macroeconomics exam. As part of the question, you may be asked to draw a correctly labeled graph. Although the curves look similar, it is important to recognize the differences between the demand curve for a specific product and the aggregate demand curve for the macroeconomy. It is very important that you use the correct labeling to distinguish macroeconomic graphs from microeconomic graphs.

Notice the differences in the axis labels. For individual product demand, the label for the vertical axis is "price;" for aggregate demand, the label is "price level." This is because, when we're dealing with the demand for all of the products in the economy, there is no one "price" for everything – and "average" price makes little sense if we're talking about the average price of a home and a toothpick. So instead we talk about a price level, which can show us changes in prices, but not precise prices for products.

The horizontal axis, which is labeled "quantity" for the individual product, is labeled "real GDP" or "real output" for macroeconomic analysis, because we're looking at the total spending in the economy. So while the demand curve for specific products could help us to identify the specific price of the product and the specific quantity sold, the aggregate demand curve shows much more general information about the performance of the entire economy.

Finally, the curves themselves have different labels. "Supply" and "demand" curve labels are not enough; they must be "aggregate supply" and "aggregate demand" because they show totals in the economy. Careful labeling will help you earn the points you deserve.

PRACTICE **Aggregate Demand Curve**

For each scenario, indicate whether the quantity of aggregate demand would *increase* or *decrease*.

1. __________ A decrease in the price level causes the real value of households' assets to rise.

2. __________ An increase in the price level causes interest rates to increase.

3. __________ An increase in the US price level causes Americans to buy more imports.

4. __________ A decrease in the US price level causes foreigners to buy more US exports.

Changes in Aggregate Demand

Refer to pages 522–524 of your textbook.

A CLOSER LOOK **Consumer, Investment, Government, and Net Export Spending**

While the real balances, interest rate, and foreign purchases effects can cause movement *along* the aggregate demand curve, a number of factors can actually cause the aggregate demand curve to *shift*. As was true for the individual product demand curve, increases in aggregate demand shift the curve to the right, while decreases shift it to the left. It is important to remember that because of the multiplier effect, an initial change in aggregate demand, depicted by the dashed lines below, actually results in a much larger total effect on GDP. Changes in aggregate demand can result from changes in all four sectors of the macroeconomy.

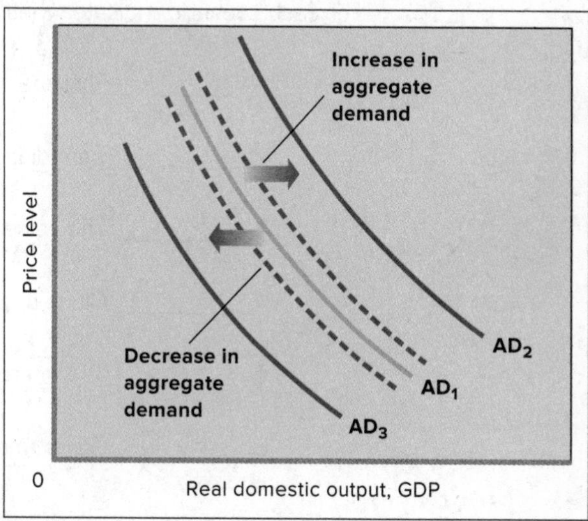

Consumer sector demand can shift due to changes in wealth, borrowing, expectations, and taxes. According to the **wealth effect,** if consumer wealth significantly rises (such as an inheritance or an increase in stock value), consumers gain confidence and increase their demand for products at all prices. The same effect occurs when consumers reduce their debt by paying off mortgages and credit cards. If consumers borrow money, their demand for products increases. If consumers expect their real incomes to increase, or if they fear inflation in the near future, they increase demand for products ahead of the price increase. If personal taxes decline, consumers have more disposable income to spend, so aggregate demand increases. But if consumers experience a reduction in wealth, reduce borrowing, fear a decrease in real income, or experience a tax increase, then household saving increases and consumption falls, so aggregate demand shifts to the left.

The investment sector's spending for capital goods depends on the interest rate and expected return on investment. If real interest rates fall, aggregate demand increases because costs are now lower than expected return on investment. Firms also increase investment if they expect returns on investment to increase due to optimism about future business conditions, improvements in technology, a reduction in excess capacity, or a reduction in business taxes. But higher interest rates and lower expected returns on investment reduce aggregate demand through investment. Because interest rates and expectations can change so quickly and often, the investment sector is the most volatile of the four sectors.

The third sector, government spending, is straightforward. If government spending increases (and taxes and interest rates do not change), aggregate demand increases. Decreases in government spending reduce aggregate demand.

Finally, changes in net exports can also change aggregate demand. If exports increase due to higher foreign incomes, US aggregate demand increases. If the **exchange rate** of the US dollar **depreciates** in foreign exchange markets, foreign currency gets stronger. Because it costs foreigners less to buy US dollars, it looks like US products are cheaper. In this case, demand for US exports increases. At the same time, because the US dollar is weaker, it costs Americans more dollars to buy foreign currency. As a result, imports look more expensive, so US imports decrease. Because US exports increase while US imports decrease, net exports increase, increasing aggregate demand. But if foreign incomes decline or the US dollar **appreciates** in international currency markets, US aggregate demand falls.

Caution

Causes of the downward slope of aggregate demand may seem very similar to the causes of shifts in the aggregate demand curve. The real balances effect looks like the wealth effect, and the interest rate and foreign purchases effects look very similar to other causes of change in aggregate demand. A way to keep them straight is to look at the cause of each effect. For the three factors that explain the downward slope, a higher *price level* is the root cause of each effect. The rise in price level *causes* a decline in the value of wealth, a higher interest rate for borrowing, and a shift toward buying relatively lower-priced imports. At higher prices, people buy fewer products. But for the causes of change in aggregate demand, shifts in the curve result from causes *other* than a change in the prices of products in the economy. Changes in expectations for economic performance, tax rates, incomes, and currency values are among the reasons the entire curve would shift.

PRACTICE Consumer, Investment, Government, and Net Export Spending

For each scenario, indicate whether aggregate demand would *increase* or *decrease*.

1. ________ Personal income taxes increase.
2. ________ Canadian purchases of US exports decrease.
3. ________ The value of stocks held by households increases.
4. ________ Cities buy more fire and police equipment.
5. ________ The international value of the US dollar increases.
6. ________ Government increases FEMA disaster spending.
7. ________ Consumers expect a recession.
8. ________ Interest rates for corporate loans decrease.
9. ________ Consumer saving increases.
10. ________ Incomes of Japanese consumers fall.

Aggregate Supply

Refer to pages 525–528 of your textbook.

A CLOSER LOOK Aggregate Supply in the Immediate Short Run, Short Run, and Long Run

Aggregate supply is the quantity of goods produced in an economy at all price levels. The shape of the aggregate supply curve varies depending on the time period discussed. The costs of inputs (resources) and prices of outputs to consumers tend to be sticky or unchangeable in the short run, but more flexible in the long run. Output prices usually adjust more rapidly than the costs of resources.

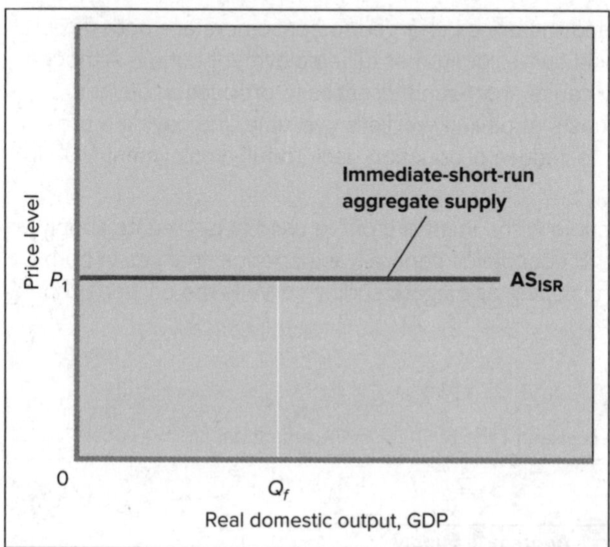

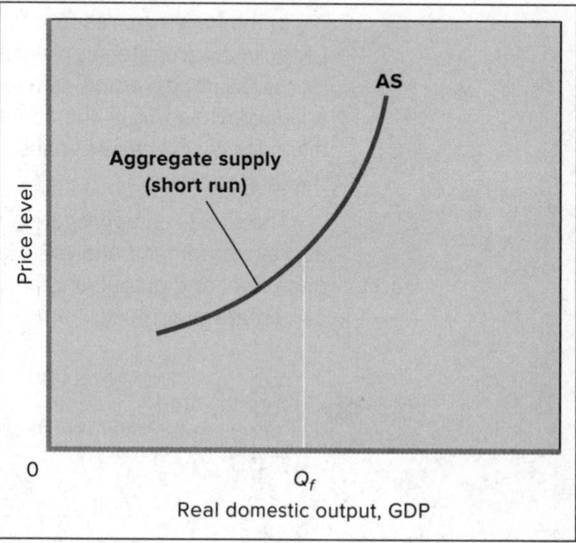

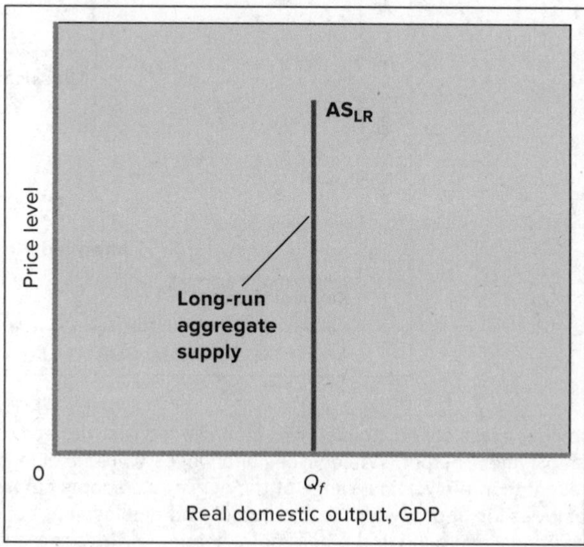

In the **immediate period** (or immediate short run), both resource costs and the prices charged to consumers are fixed. The cost stickiness is primarily due to wages, because so many workers are paid via a contract whose terms cannot be changed quickly. The price stickiness results from contracts producers have made to sell products at a particular price to retail stores or through catalogs, websites, and ads. As a result, the aggregate supply curve is horizontal in the immediate period. If aggregate demand increases in this time period, output increases (meaning employment also increases), but the price level does not change.

In the **short run,** resource costs are either fixed or very sticky, but the prices charged to consumers are flexible. As a result, the short-run aggregate supply curve is slopes upward. Producers provide more products as the price level rises and fewer products as the price level falls. When current output is significantly lower than the firm's capacity, firms can increase output with little increase in production cost. But as production approaches or even passes full-employment output, the per-unit cost of production increases much more quickly. As a result, the short-run aggregate supply curve slopes upward, becoming steeper as output increases.

In the **long run,** resource costs and the prices charged to consumers are both flexible. Long-run aggregate supply is a vertical curve, located at full-employment output. Although increases in aggregate demand may cause short-run increases in production beyond full-employment GDP, the additional costs of paying workers overtime and paying a premium for resources will cause firms to reduce production back to full-employment GDP in the long run.

The short-run aggregate supply curve is the standard curve used in aggregate supply – aggregate demand analysis. Real-world economies generally experience changes in both price level and output, and an upward-sloping aggregate supply curve is the only one that can create that result.

Keep in Mind

The aggregate supply curve can also represent the Keynesian, intermediate, and classical ranges.

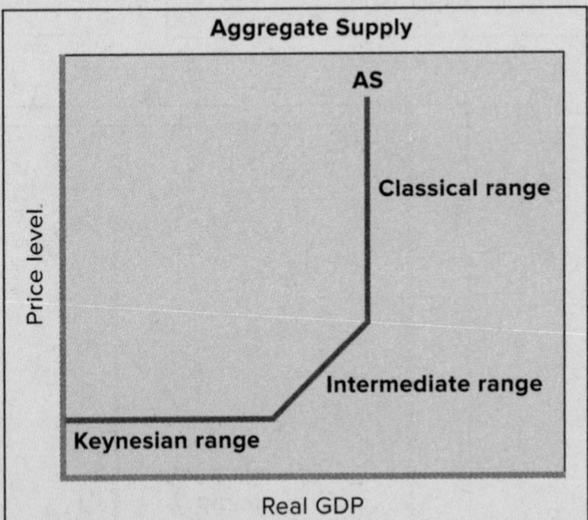

Remember, classical economists were convinced that the economy naturally produced at full-employment output. While prices and wages were flexible, output was not. This theory is represented in the vertical range of the aggregate supply curve. Keynesian theory held the opposite assumptions, with flexible output and employment but fixed prices and wages. These assumptions are found in the horizontal section of the aggregate supply curve. The intermediate range of the aggregate supply curve corresponds with the short-run aggregate supply curve discussed in the text. AP Macroeconomics exam questions about short-run aggregate supply generally refer to this upward-sloping aggregate supply curve unless they specifically note they are discussing a vertical or horizontal aggregate supply curve. If you see a question referring to the intermediate range of the aggregate supply curve, it is referring to the upward-sloping section.

PRACTICE **Aggregate Supply in the Immediate Short Run, Short Run, and Long Run**

For each range of the aggregate supply curve, identify whether each of the following is flexible.

	Prices	Wages	Output	Employment
1. Keynesian				
2. Intermediate				
3. Classical				

Changes in Aggregate Supply

Refer to pages 528–530 of your textbook.

A CLOSER LOOK **Input Prices, Productivity, and Legal-Institutional Environment**

Changes in aggregate supply are directly connected to changes in the per-unit costs of production faced by firms. If costs of production fall, aggregate supply increases, shifting the curve to the right, so that more output is produced at every price level. Increases in the cost of production reduce aggregate supply, shifting the curve leftward.

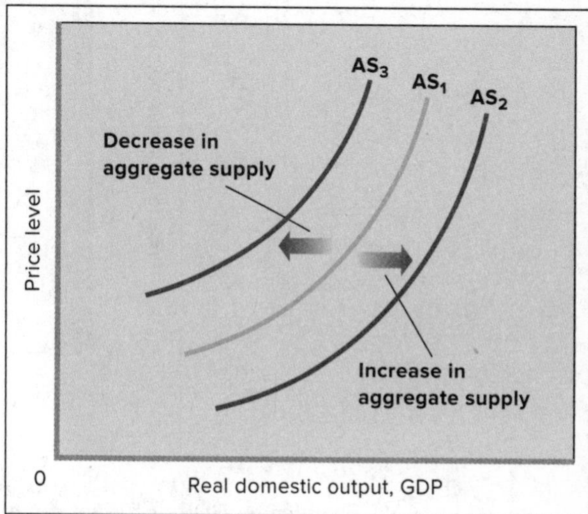

Changes in the costs of land, labor, and capital resources are a major determinant in changing aggregate supply. As domestic or foreign resource costs fall, firms raise supply, raising output and employment, and lowering prices. Productivity is another important determinant of aggregate supply. If productivity increases as a result of better worker education or technology, aggregate supply increases, so firms increase output and employment while lowering prices. Changes in government policy can also affect aggregate supply. If the government reduces business taxes, offers firms subsidies, or removes regulations, the reduced costs of production increase aggregate supply. But if costs of production increase, productivity falls, or government raises business taxes, reduces subsidies, or increases regulation, the higher per-unit costs of production lead firms to reduce production, and aggregate supply falls.

Caution

Capital investment poses a special case in the aggregate demand – aggregate supply model because it affects both curves at different points in time. When firms invest in capital, in the short run, the investment increases aggregate demand because the investment sector is increasing its purchases. But in the long run, when the firms have received the capital and bring it on line, they are able to increase their productive capacity – increasing aggregate supply. So when considering the purchase of capital, it is important to make clear whether you are considering the short-run (aggregate demand) or long-run (aggregate supply) effect of that investment.

PRACTICE **Input Prices, Productivity, and Legal-Institutional Environment**

For each scenario, indicate whether aggregate supply would *increase* or *decrease*.

1. __________ The costs of raw materials for firms increase.

2. __________ Worker productivity increases.

3. __________ The costs of oil for manufacturing firms significantly increase.

4. __________ Worker training improves.

5. __________ Government increases corporate income taxes.

6. __________ The state implements new worker safety regulations.

Changes in Equilibrium

Refer to pages 530–536 of your textbook.

A CLOSER LOOK Increases and Decreases in AD, Decreases and Increases in AS

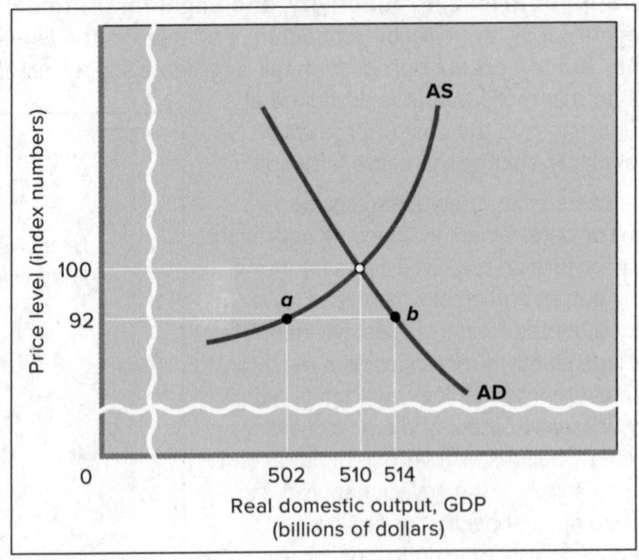

Equilibrium GDP occurs at the output where aggregate demand equals aggregate supply. Equilibrium establishes the price level and real GDP for the economy. In the figure above, equilibrium occurs at a real GDP of $510 billion in output and a price level of 100. At price level 92, firms would only produce $502 billion of output, while aggregate demand at that price level is $514 billion in output. Given the shortage of goods at that price, consumers would bid up the price. The higher price level leads firms to increase production and consumers to reduce quantity demanded until equilibrium is again reached.

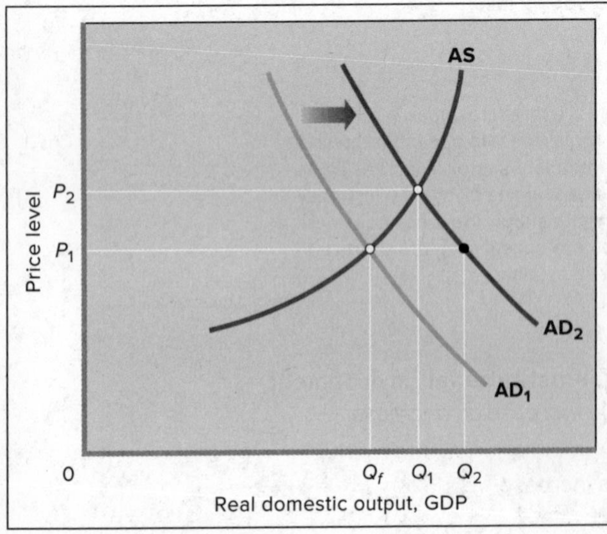

If the economy is in equilibrium at full-employment output, an increase in aggregate demand causes **demand-pull inflation** and an **inflationary gap,** as actual GDP exceeds full-employment GDP. Prices increase as well as real GDP. It is important to note that because the price increased, the full multiplier effect did not occur. The full multiplier effect requires a horizontal aggregate supply curve so that the full amount of the multiplier goes to output, rather than being partially absorbed by a price increase.

If the economy is in equilibrium at full-employment output, a decrease in aggregate demand causes a decrease in production – a **recessionary gap**, as actual GDP is less than full-employment GDP. Employment falls and **cyclical unemployment** rises as a result, because firms do not need as many workers to produce fewer products. The effect on prices can be harder to determine. With the lower demand, **disinflation** (a reduction in the rate of inflation) tends to occur. But do prices actually fall – **deflation**? Wages and prices are sticky downward, so in many recessions, the decrease in aggregate demand fully impacts output but does not cause a change in price level. This is sometimes called the "**ratchet effect**" – prices tend to go up, but don't come back down. As illustrated in the figure below, when the price does not change, the full effect of the multiplier occurs in the changing real GDP. If prices do actually fall, part of the multiplier effect is absorbed by the falling price, and real GDP does not fall by the full amount of the change in aggregate demand.

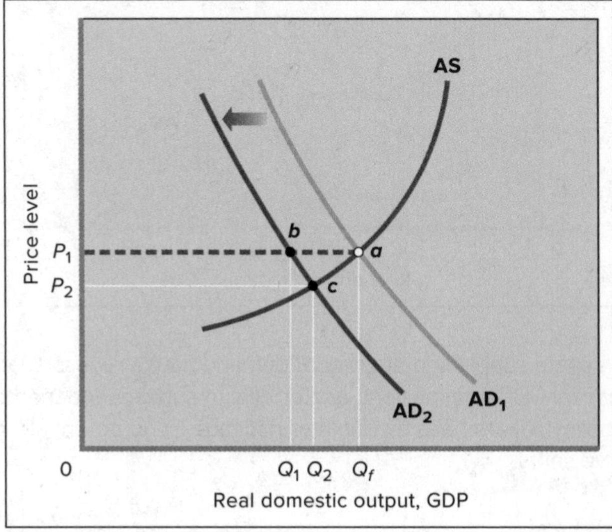

A reduction in aggregate supply causes **cost-push inflation**. As the cost of production increases, firms reduce output and raise prices. A sustained decrease in aggregate supply is known as **stagflation** – a stagnant economy, high inflation (thus the name "stagflation"), and high unemployment all at the same time. High oil prices in the 1970s sent the US economy into its most significant period of stagflation in history. The opposite effects can occur when an increase in aggregate supply, resulting from increased productivity and technology, shifts the aggregate supply curve to the right. Real GDP and employment increase, and prices can fall as a result of the lower per-unit costs of production.

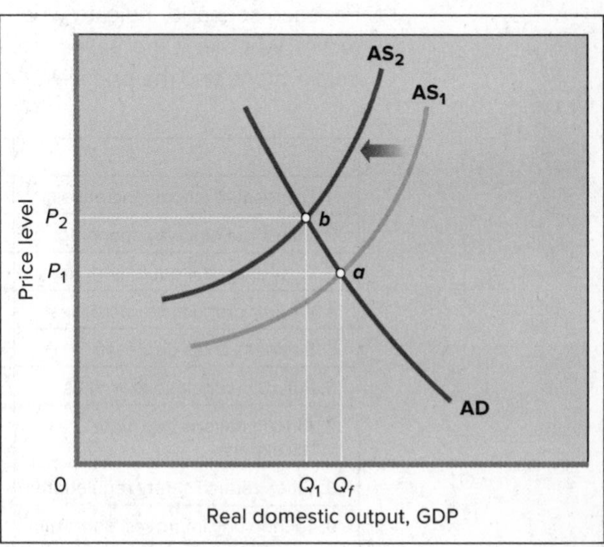

It is possible for both aggregate demand and aggregate supply to shift at the same time, as multiple factors affect the economy. In the 1990s, full employment, higher incomes, and higher consumer confidence led to higher aggregate demand. At the same time, increases in technology and productivity via computers increased aggregate supply. Increases in both curves significantly increased real GDP, while the price level only moderately increased because the curve shifts had contradictory effects on prices. The price, rather than moving from Point (a) to Point (b) in the graph below, moved to Point (c).

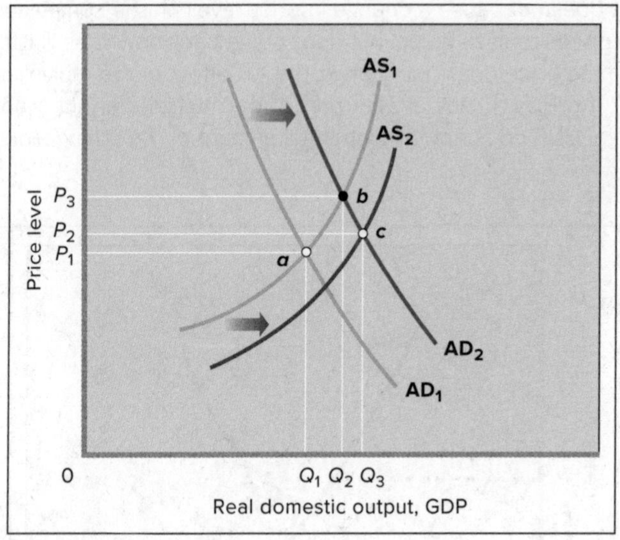

Changes in aggregate supply and aggregate demand cause recessionary and inflationary gaps and affect real GDP, employment, and prices. In subsequent chapters, we will examine the tools policymakers have available to mitigate – and potentially reverse – the effects of such curve shifts.

PRACTICE Increases and Decreases in AD, Decreases and Increases in AS

For each scenario, indicate whether the *aggregate demand* or *aggregate supply* curve moves, whether it *increases* or *decreases,* and the effect of the curve shift on output, employment, and the price level.

	Curve	Incr/Decr	Output	Employment	Price Level
1. Disposable income increases					
2. States cut highway spending					
3. Cost of capital equipment rises					
4. Worker productivity increases					
5. Business taxes decrease					
6. Pollution regulations increase					
7. African nations buy more US exports					
8. Cities reduce safety regulations					
9. Technology improves (short run)					
10. Technology improves (long run)					

Make sure to return to the AP Key Concepts section to check your understanding of the chapter's concepts important to AP coursework.

Economically Speaking

- **Aggregate Demand** a curve showing the amount of output demanded at each price level
- **Aggregate Supply** a curve showing the quantity of goods produced at all price levels
- **Appreciate** the value of a currency increases in the foreign exchange market
- **Cost-Push Inflation** an increase in prices caused by an increase in the cost of production
- **Cyclical Unemployment** layoffs due to recession
- **Deflation** a general decrease in prices
- **Demand-Pull Inflation** an increase in prices caused by an increase in aggregate demand
- **Depreciate** the value of a currency decreases in the foreign exchange market
- **Disinflation** a reduction in the rate of inflation
- **Equilibrium GDP** output where aggregate supply equals aggregate demand
- **Exchange Rate** the value of one currency in terms of another
- **Foreign Purchases Effect** when US prices rise, US consumers buy more imports and foreigners buy fewer US exports, reducing the quantity demanded
- **Immediate Period** both resource costs and the prices charged to consumers are fixed; aggregate supply is horizontal
- **Inflationary Gap** amount by which actual GDP exceeds full-employment GDP
- **Interest Rate** the price to borrow money
- **Interest Rate Effect** higher prices cause an increase in demand for money, raising interest rates and reducing quantity demanded
- **Long Run** resource costs and the prices charged to consumers are both flexible; aggregate supply is vertical
- **Ratchet Effect** prices tend to increase, but tend not to decrease again
- **Real Balances Effect** when prices rise, the real value of wealth falls, so quantity demanded falls
- **Recessionary Gap** amount by which actual GDP is less than full-employment GDP
- **Short Run** resource costs are either fixed or very sticky, but the prices charged to consumers are flexible; aggregate supply slopes upward
- **Stagflation** a stagnant economy, high inflation, and high unemployment occur simultaneously
- **Wealth Effect** when consumer wealth increases, aggregate demand increases

Chapter 27

Fiscal Policy, Deficits, and Debt

Changes in aggregate demand and aggregate supply affect output, employment, and price level in the economy. But Keynesian theory calls for government to use fiscal policy tools to close inflationary and recessionary gaps, all with the goal of returning the economy to full-employment output. Chapter 27 details the use of these tools and provides cautions about how their use can cause budget surpluses or deficits and affect the national debt.

Material from Chapter 27 is included in several multiple-choice questions and is commonly part of a free-response question on the AP Macroeconomics exam.

Key Concepts

Below is a summary of the chapter's concepts important to AP coursework. Upon completing the lessons that follow, return to these concepts to make sure you understand them and how the practice exercises you completed relate to them.

- Fiscal policy is the use of government spending or taxes to stabilize the economy.
- Expansionary fiscal policy increases aggregate demand to correct a recessionary gap.
    - Government can increase spending to raise aggregate demand.
        - Spending must only be raised by the amount of the initial reduction in spending.
        - The multiplier will completely fill the rest of the recessionary gap.
    - Government can reduce taxes to increase disposable income, raising aggregate demand.
        - Taxes must be reduced by more than the initial reduction in spending.
        - Consumers will save part of a reduction in taxes; the smaller the MPC, the larger tax cut necessary to achieve the same result.
        - Once the tax cut goes into effect, the multiplier will fill the rest of the gap.
    - Expansionary fiscal policy creates a budget deficit, which increases the national debt.
- Contractionary fiscal policy reduces aggregate demand to correct an inflationary gap.
    - Government can reduce spending to reduce aggregate demand.
        - An increase in aggregate spending beyond full-employment GDP raises both output and prices.
        - Due to the ratchet effect, fiscal policy cannot reduce prices to original levels.
        - Government spending must be reduced by less than the initial change in consumer or investment spending to get back to full-employment GDP.
        - The multiplier will then reduce aggregate demand by the rest of the gap.

    - Government can raise taxes to reduce disposable income, lowering aggregate demand.
        - Because households will use savings to pay part of a tax increase, government must increase taxes by more than it would reduce spending to fill the gap.
        - The multiplier will then continue to fill the rest of the gap.
    - If the budget is balanced at the start of the process, contractionary fiscal policy creates a budget surplus, which can be used to reduce the national debt. If a budget is in deficit, contractionary fiscal policy reduces the size of the deficit and its impact on the national debt.
- Automatic stabilizers are government programs that automatically change spending or taxes during economic instability.
    - Spending for safety net programs such as unemployment benefits and food stamps rises during a recession because more people become eligible when incomes fall.
    - Progressive taxes take a higher percentage of income as income rises. In a period of inflation, households will rise into higher tax brackets, reducing disposable incomes.
- Drawbacks of fiscal policy include time lags to recognize the problem and pass and implement policy; political considerations; taxpayers saving tax cuts; pro-cyclical effects of balanced-budget requirements in state and local governments; and crowding out.
- Crowding out occurs when government uses expansionary fiscal policy, causing a budget deficit. Government must borrow money to finance the deficit, increasing demand in the loanable funds market. The higher interest rates crowd firms out of the market, reducing investment.
- Budget deficits increase the national debt. Borrowing through the sale of government securities raises income inequality. Foreign-owned debt causes interest payments to leave the country.

Now, let's examine more closely the following concepts from your textbook:

- **Fiscal Policy and the AD-AS Model**
- **Built-In Stability**
- **Problems, Criticisms, and Complications of Implementing Fiscal Policy**
- **The US Public Debt**

These sections were selected because they introduce the tools of fiscal policy and explain complications that can make these tools difficult to use effectively.

Fiscal Policy and the AD-AS Model

Refer to pages 543–547 of your textbook.

A CLOSER LOOK Expansionary Fiscal Policy

Fiscal policy is the use of discretionary government spending or taxes in order to stabilize the economy. If aggregate demand falls, output falls and cyclical unemployment rises. If prices are downwardly sticky, the full effect of the decrease in aggregate demand accrues in lower output. Government can use **expansionary fiscal policy** to correct a **recessionary gap,** shifting aggregate demand to the right by increasing government spending, reducing taxes, or both.

Precisely how much taxes or spending must change depends on the marginal propensity to consume and the related multiplier. In the graph, aggregate demand decreased from AD_1 to AD_2, reducing real GDP from $510 billion to $490 billion and creating a $20 billion recessionary gap. Say government officials decide to close the recessionary gap by increasing government spending. If the MPC is 0.75, the MPS is 0.25 and the multiplier is 4 (1/0.25). To close a $20 billion gap, government spending would only have to increase by $5 billion, because the multiplier (4) would continue to fill the rest of the $20 billion gap to return to full-employment output.

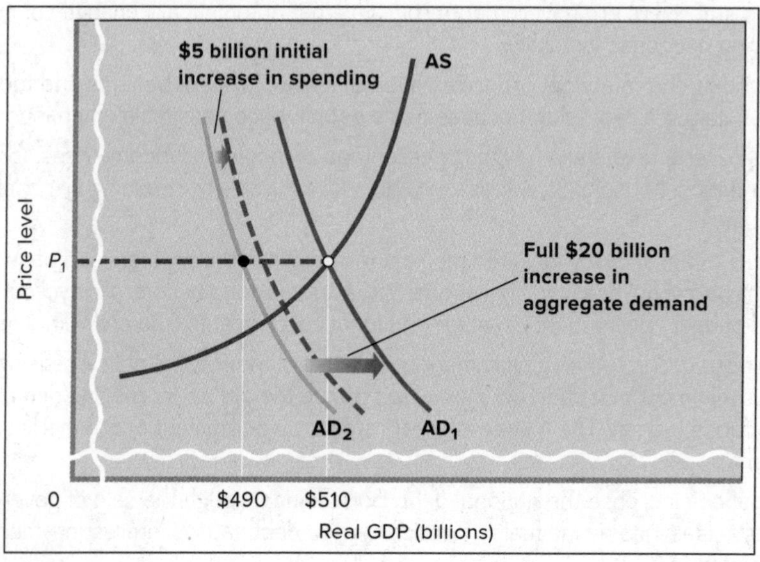

Policymakers could choose instead to correct a recessionary gap by lowering taxes. However, we know that a tax cut is not as effective as an increase in government spending, because consumers will save some of the tax cut. In this case, with an MPC of 0.75, consumers would only spend 75% of a tax cut. So taxes would have to be reduced by $6.67 billion (0.75 × $6.67 billion = $5 billion) to achieve the same $20 billion increase in aggregate demand that was achieved by a $5 billion increase in government spending. The smaller the MPC, the larger the tax cut necessary to achieve the same result.

Expansionary fiscal policy also has ramifications for the federal budget. Assume the US begins with a balanced budget. If the government lowers taxes or increases spending as part of expansionary fiscal policy, it will create a **budget deficit** – spending more than its revenues in a year. Government must borrow through the sale of **government securities** (bonds, bills, and notes) to finance that deficit. A deficit also adds to the **national debt,** the total amount the government has borrowed over the years.

Caution

Remember the GDP formula? GDP = C + I + G + (X – M). Fiscal policy uses G to correct changes in C and I. So if consumer or investment spending falls, government spending rises to replace it. Or if consumer or investment spending rise too quickly, government spending falls to bring GDP back into balance.

PRACTICE **Expansionary Fiscal Policy**

1. __________ To correct a recessionary gap, should government *raise* or *lower* its spending?

2. __________ To correct a recessionary gap, should government *raise* or *lower* taxes?

3. __________ Will the fiscal policy actions in #1 and #2 *raise* or *lower* aggregate demand, output, and employment?

4. __________ Will the fiscal policy actions in #1 and #2 create a budget *surplus* or *deficit*?

5. __________ Will the budget change in #4 *increase* or *reduce* the national debt?

6. __________ How does the federal government finance budget deficits?

A CLOSER LOOK **Contractionary Fiscal Policy and Policy Options: G or T?**

If aggregate demand rises, part of the **inflationary gap** increases output, while the other part increases prices with demand-pull inflation. **Contractionary fiscal policy** is the use of a tax increase, a reduction in government spending, or both to reduce an inflationary gap. A reduction in spending directly affects aggregate demand. But in determining how far to lower spending, it is important to keep the **ratchet effect** in mind. Once the price level ratchets up, it tends not to come back down, due to the sticky wages and prices we discussed earlier. So when the government decides how much to reduce spending, it must take this ratchet effect into account. In the graph below, assume the economy begins at Point a, with full-employment output of $510 billion. Then assume that a $5 billion initial increase in spending, times the multiplier of 4, increases aggregate demand from AD_3 to AD_4. Although total spending in the economy has increased by $20 billion, real GDP has only risen to $522 billion, creating a $12 billion inflationary gap. The other $8 billion of the increase in spending is due to an increase in the price level. You can see that both output and the price level have increased to a new equilibrium at Point (b).

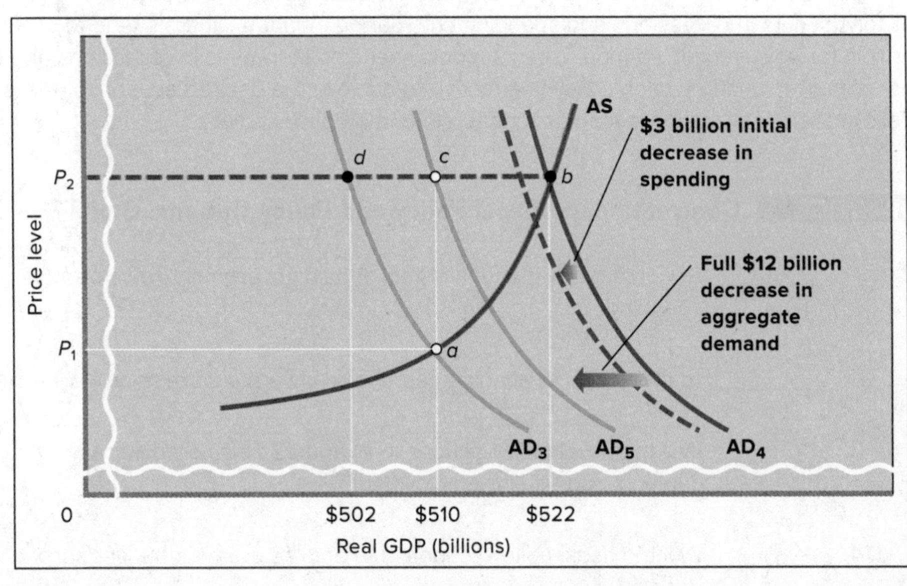

How can the government use a change in spending to close this inflationary gap? If the increase in real output is $12 billion, and the multiplier is 4, the government should reduce spending by $3 billion. Aggregate demand will be reduced to full employment GDP of $510 billion at Point c. Notice, however, that the price remains at the higher level. The contractionary fiscal policy is able to stop the escalation of the inflation rate, but generally is not effective in reducing prices to their former levels.

Caution

It is very important to note that when government is trying to resolve an inflationary gap, because of the ratchet effect, it cannot simply reduce spending in the same amount as the initial increase in consumer or investment spending. Remember that in the scenario above, an initial $5 billion increase in spending, with a multiplier of 4, created only a $12 billion inflationary gap, with the other $8 billion accounted for in higher prices. If government were to reduce its spending by that same initial change of $5 billion, with a multiplier of 4, total spending in the economy would drop by $20 billion – *more* than the $12 billion inflationary gap – and open up a recessionary gap at Point d. Government officials certainly do not want to cause a recession! So it is very important to properly calculate the size of the inflationary gap, take the higher price level into account, and only reduce spending by the amount necessary to return to full-employment GDP.

The government also has the option of closing an inflationary gap by increasing taxes. As we have noted, changes in taxes are not as effective as spending changes, because part of the tax increase will be paid from savings, rather than reducing consumption by the full amount of the tax. If the MPC is 0.75, consumers will use savings to pay 1/4 of their tax increase. So in order to fill the gap, government must increase taxes by $4 billion in order to reduce consumption by $3 billion. The multiplier of 4 will then continue to reduce consumption by the entire $12 billion GDP gap.

Contractionary fiscal policy also has ramifications for the national budget. If government begins with a balanced budget, the increase in taxes or reduction in government spending to address the inflationary gap will create a **budget surplus** – tax revenues greater than government spending for a year. This surplus can reduce the amount of the national debt. Even if government begins with a budget deficit, the increase in taxes or reduction in spending can at least reduce the size of the deficit.

While we know that changes in taxes and government spending can be effective in closing recessionary and inflationary gaps, which policy is best? It depends on your view of government. Conservatives tend to prefer a smaller role for government, so are more likely to call for tax cuts in recessions and spending cuts during inflation. Liberals tend to prefer a larger role for government, so more often support spending increases in recessions and tax increases during inflation. Each policy is effective to achieve the desired economic result, but policymakers' political philosophies tend to guide the policy choices.

PRACTICE Contractionary Fiscal Policy and Policy Options: G or T?

1. ________ To correct an inflationary gap, should government *raise* or *lower* its spending?

2. ________ To correct an inflationary gap, should government *raise* or *lower* taxes?

3. ________ Will the fiscal policy actions in #1 and #2 *raise* or *lower* aggregate demand, output, and employment?

4. ________ Will the fiscal policy actions in #1 and #2 create a budget *surplus* or *deficit*?

5. ________ Will the budget change in #4 *increase* or *reduce* the national debt?

6. ________ If government cuts spending by too much as it tries to correct an inflationary gap, what economic problem could the government create?

Built-In Stability

Refer to pages 547–548 of your textbook.

A CLOSER LOOK Automatic or Built-In Stabilizers

Automatic stabilizers are government programs that automatically change spending and taxes during economic instability, without requiring government to pass a new policy. The two primary automatic stabilizers are transfer payments from safety net programs and progressive income taxes. During a recession, as workers lose jobs and incomes fall, more households become eligible for government programs such as unemployment benefits, food stamps, and rent subsidies. Government spending automatically rises to mitigate the amount by which aggregate demand declines, helping to stabilize the economy. Nations with stronger safety net programs have more effective automatic stabilizers.

Progressive income taxes base the tax rate on household income level. Those with lower incomes pay a lower percentage of their income in taxes, while those with higher incomes pay a larger percentage of their income in taxes. During periods of inflation, as incomes increase, taxpayers can ascend into higher tax brackets. As a result, they pay a higher percentage of their income in taxes, leaving less income available for consumption spending. The higher tax rate helps to reduce inflation by reining in consumer spending. Economies with more strongly progressive tax structures have more effective tax stabilizers.

In general, when GDP increases, tax revenues increase from all sources – individual income taxes, business taxes, excise taxes, and payroll taxes – because as more jobs are created, incomes rise and consumers are able to buy more products. During periods of recession, tax revenues from all of these sources decline. Transfer payments work in reverse, with government spending for these programs increasing during periods of recession and declining as the economy grows. As a result, the federal budget is affected by economic instability even before fiscal policy is considered. During recessions, a balanced budget tends to go into deficit because tax revenues fall as government spending increases. During economic growth or even inflation, a balanced budget tends to go into surplus because tax revenues rise as government spending declines. But automatic stabilizers alone are usually not powerful enough to deal with significant swings in aggregate demand, so government action is required.

PRACTICE Automatic or Built-In Stabilizers

1. ________ When consumer spending falls during a recession, spending automatically increases in which sector?

2. ________ Are automatic stabilizers more effective when programs are *strong* or *weak*?

3. ________ During inflation, when household incomes rise into higher tax brackets, what happens to disposable income?

4. ________ Are tax stabilizers more effective when taxes are *progressive* or *regressive*?

Problems, Criticisms, and Complications of Implementing Fiscal Policy

Refer to pages 552–555 of your textbook.

A CLOSER LOOK Crowding-Out Effect

A number of problems face policymakers in enacting and implementing fiscal policy. A **recognition lag** refers to the time – often months – between the beginning of a recession or inflation and when it is recognized. In December 2008, the National Bureau of Economic Research announced that the US economy had already been in recession for a full year before it was recognized. An **administrative lag** follows, as Congress takes time – often months – to pass legislation to change taxes or spending to address the identified gap. Finally, an **operational lag** requires time – six months to a year – for the policy to actually take effect, as changes ripple through the system and the multiplier takes effect. These combined lags illustrate how long a recession or inflation can be underway before a fiscal policy solution can take effect. They also point out the importance of automatic stabilizers in helping to reduce the impacts of economic instability.

Another problem with fiscal policy is the political considerations involved in making policy. Voters don't want to hear about tax increases or cuts in their favorite programs, so public officials may hesitate to use contractionary policy when it is warranted. And in order to gain votes at election time, public officials have an incentive to reduce taxes and increase spending for popular programs, even if such actions are contrary to the fiscal policy appropriate for the economic situation. In addition, the government may need to significantly increase spending to deal with a crisis – a natural disaster or a war – even during a time of inflation, exacerbating an inflationary gap.

Another complication occurs when households view tax cuts as temporary. If taxpayers are sent a "tax rebate" check, but then must repay that check when filing taxes – or if taxpayers expect taxes in general to increase again – they tend to simply save the tax cut, rather than spend it. In such cases, the fiscal policy is ineffective.

A more significant problem is that most state and local governments face constitutional or legal requirements to balance their budgets annually. Such requirements are "pro-cyclical," meaning that they only make recessions or inflation worse. During a recession, state and local revenues fall. Under balanced-budget requirements, these governments must *reduce* their spending – at the very moment that it is critical for them to *increase* their spending. So the recession deepens, putting even more people out of work, reducing product sales even more, forcing state and local governments to cut spending even more deeply – and the recession spirals out of control. Even as the federal government increases spending and reduces taxes because it faces no such mandate, state and local governments are counteracting the federal government's fiscal policy measures. During the Great Recession, the $787 billion stimulus package directed a great deal of the aid to states, in order to reduce this problem.

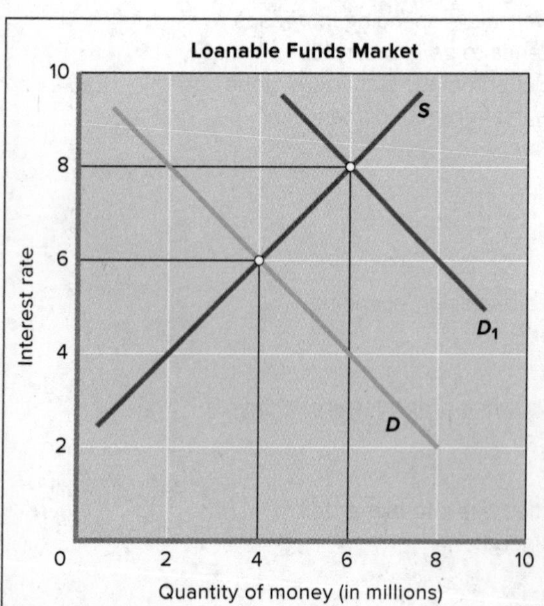

Crowding out is another problem with fiscal policy. When the government uses expansionary fiscal policy to increase spending and reduce taxes, a budget deficit develops. Government must borrow money to finance the deficit. As government demand for money in the loanable funds market increases, interest rates rise. We already know that investment spending is the most volatile of the four sectors, because firms will only invest if the expected return on investment is higher than (or equal to) the interest rate. As interest rates rise, firms may significantly reduce investment spending, so government borrowing "crowds out" firms in the loanable funds market. So while government is borrowing money to increase aggregate demand, "crowding out" offsets that increase by reducing aggregate demand from the investment sector, reducing the effectiveness of the fiscal policy. The higher interest rate can also reduce interest-sensitive consumer spending for homes, cars, and durable goods, further reducing aggregate demand. The crowding out effect, if it occurs at all, is less likely to occur during a recession, because consumer and investment demand for loans has likely decreased already. Consumers are less likely to make large purchases when they fear job losses, and firms won't expand when demand is already down. But if the government increases deficit spending when the economy is at or near full-employment output, crowding out is likely to have a more substantial effect on aggregate demand.

These complications leave economists with an understanding that while fiscal policy can be effective in reducing the effects of significant, long-lasting recessionary and inflationary gaps, it is not nearly as precise as the multiplier suggests. Because of significant lags in recognizing the problem, and passing and implementing policy, economists suggest that fiscal policy should be used to support long-run economic growth. For example, implementing tax cuts to encourage firms to invest in capital, or using government spending to improve infrastructure, would not only increase aggregate demand in the short run, but it could promote an increase in long-run aggregate supply.

PRACTICE **Crowding-Out Effect**

In the space below, draw the loanable funds market in equilibrium. Then show the effects of crowding out due to a government budget deficit. Then answer the questions below.

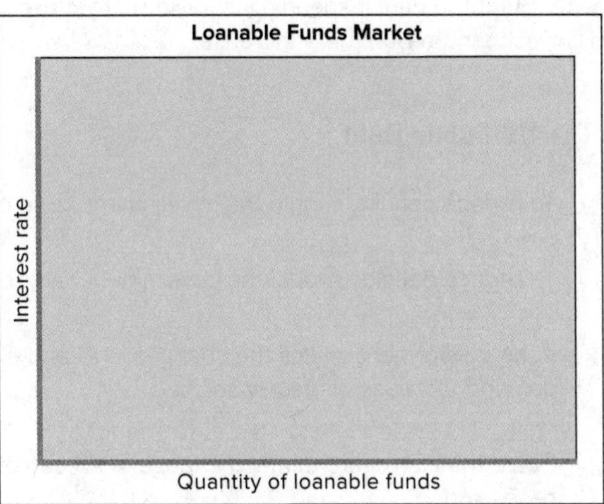

1. __________ Does a budget deficit *increase* or *decrease* interest rates?

2. __________ Will the change in interest rates in #1 *increase* or *reduce* capital investment?

3. __________ Will the change in capital investment in #2 *increase* or *reduce* long-run growth?

The US Public Debt

Refer to pages 555–560 of your textbook.

A CLOSER LOOK The US Public Debt

Each year the federal government incurs a budget deficit, it adds to the national debt. Deficits over the years have primarily resulted from wars, recessions, and fiscal policy. In 2016, the national debt reached $19 trillion. Policymakers undertook unprecedented debt in 2008 and 2009 with the stimulus and bailout packages as the economy dramatically deteriorated, so interest payments on the debt will only increase. And those payments do not pay off the debt; they only service the interest on the debt. This significant increase in interest payments leaves policymakers with the difficult decision of raising taxes or cutting spending to make these interest payments – or borrowing even more to pay current interest.

Some people are concerned that the national debt will bankrupt the federal government, but it will not do so. The debt can be refinanced by selling new bonds, and the federal government always has the option to raise taxes for additional funding.

A more serious concern is the redistribution of income from those with lower incomes to those with higher incomes. Government securities and the interest they earn are disproportionately held by those with higher incomes because of their ability to save. Because the federal income tax system is only slightly progressive, those with lower and middle incomes largely pay the taxes that will return interest to the bondholders with higher incomes. Because this results in increasing income inequality, it contradicts a societal goal.

Many people are concerned about the level of foreign-owned public debt. More than 1/3 of the national debt is owned by foreign citizens and countries, and so interest payments on that debt flow out of the US economy. Finally, concerns about the level of crowding out due to extensive borrowing in a full-employment economy may have serious implications for future economic growth. But if the deficit spending is for infrastructure or other capital improvements, overall investment may actually increase.

PRACTICE The US Public Debt

1. ________ To reduce deficits, should the government *raise* or *lower* taxes?

2. ________ To reduce deficits, should the government *raise* or *lower* spending?

3. ________ If the government makes the changes in #1 and #2, will aggregate demand *increase* or *decrease*?

4. ________ Could the aggregate demand change in #3 cause *inflation* or *recession*?

Make sure to return to the AP Key Concepts section to check your understanding of the chapter's concepts important to AP coursework.

Economically Speaking

- **Administrative Lag** the time required for policymakers to pass fiscal policy legislation
- **Automatic Stabilizers** government programs that automatically change spending and taxes during economic instability
- **Budget Deficit** government spending is greater than revenue in one year
- **Budget Surplus** government revenue is greater than spending in one year
- **Contractionary Fiscal Policy** raising taxes and lowering government spending to fix an inflationary gap
- **Crowding Out** an increase in demand in the loanable funds market to finance government deficits drives up the interest rate, reducing available funds for private borrowing
- **Expansionary Fiscal Policy** lowering taxes and raising government spending to fix a recessionary gap
- **Fiscal Policy** the use of taxes and government spending to stabilize the economy
- **Government Securities** bonds, bills, and notes sold by federal government to finance the debt
- **Inflationary Gap** amount by which current spending is greater than full-employment GDP
- **National Debt** total amount of money the government has borrowed
- **Operational Lag** the time required for fiscal policy to actually take effect
- **Progressive Income Tax** a tax whose rate increases with income
- **Ratchet Effect** once prices have increased, it is unlikely they will decrease again
- **Recessionary Gap** amount by which current spending is less than full-employment GDP
- **Recognition Lag** the time between the initial development of a gap and when it is recognized

Chapter 28

Money, Banking, and Financial Institutions

While fiscal policy is central to economic stabilization, government officials have a second set of stabilization tools in monetary policy. Money is essential for a modern economy, facilitating the movement of goods and services through the circular flow and serving as the incentive for entrepreneurs and workers. Chapter 28 begins a three-chapter exploration of the role of money in the economy, describing the functions and definitions of money and the structure of the Federal Reserve System. An understanding of these functions and structures paves the way for exploration of how the Federal Reserve uses money to stabilize the economy.

Material from Chapter 28 may appear in a multiple-choice question or two on the AP Macroeconomics exam.

Key Concepts

Below is a summary of the chapter's concepts important to AP coursework. Upon completing the lessons that follow, return to these concepts to make sure you understand them and how the practice exercises you completed relate to them.

- Money is anything widely accepted by buyers and sellers as a medium of exchange.
    - Money serves as a medium of exchange, a unit of account, and a store of value.
    - Commodity money has intrinsic value; fiat money has value because it is accepted.
    - M1 is perfectly liquid money, consisting of currency and demand deposits.
    - M2 is M1 plus savings accounts, CDs, and money market mutual funds which must be converted to cash.
    - US dollars are fiat money and are not backed by gold or any other precious metal.
    - Purchasing power is the amount of products money will buy; inflation erodes it.
- The Federal Reserve System is the central banking system for the US.
    - The Board of Governors, appointed by the President and Senate, runs the Fed.
    - The Regional Banks hold deposits and make loans to member banks.
    - The Federal Open Market Committee conducts open market operations, buying and selling government securities to change the money supply and interest rates.
    - Member banks are the financial institutions the public uses.

- Roles of the Fed include:
    - Setting the reserve requirement, the percentage of deposits banks cannot loan.
    - Setting the discount rate, the interest rate the Fed charges member banks for loans.
    - Conducting monetary policy, changing the money supply to stabilize the economy.
- The Federal Deposit Insurance Corporation (FDIC) protects depositors' bank accounts.
- The Great Recession began with failures in the financial services industry.
- The federal government and Federal Reserve bailed out the banking and auto industries.
- Legislation is intended to prevent another crisis, but many are concerned that the continued consolidation of the financial services industry will eventually create another economic crisis.

Now, let's examine more closely the following concepts from your textbook:

- **Functions of Money**
- **The Federal Reserve and the Banking System**
- **Fed Functions, Responsibilities, and Independence**

These sections were selected because monetary policy is our most frequently used method to stabilize the economy, and an understanding of money and the powers of the Federal Reserve set the stage for understanding monetary policy.

The Functions of Money

Refer to page 571 of your textbook.

A CLOSER LOOK Functions of Money

In general, **money** is anything that is widely accepted by buyers and sellers as a medium of exchange. Money serves three purposes. First, it is a **medium of exchange,** which means it is used for buying goods and services. It is very difficult, if not impossible, for **barter** (trading goods and services without the use of money) to work in an economy as large as that of the United States. Money facilitates exchange, making the process more efficient. Second, money is a **unit of account,** making it easier to determine the relative values of goods. Rather than having to remember that four tomatoes equal one gallon of gas and ten gallons of gas equal one sweater, monetary amounts make comparison easier. Finally, money serves as a **store of value.** You can save money over time and use it for future purchases.

Money has perfect **liquidity,** meaning it can be spent instantly. Other investments, such as stocks or baseball cards or homes, are less liquid, because it takes time to sell the asset and convert it to cash. Stocks can be sold fairly quickly to get spendable money, while it may take weeks or months to sell a home. Liquidity is important, because aggregate demand depends on the ability to purchase products.

Money can take a variety of forms, including bills, coins, animal teeth, precious metals, or crops – anything buyers and sellers accept. **Commodity money** has intrinsic value, such as gold coins, corn, or tobacco; it can be used for another purpose and has value for that purpose. **Fiat money** only has value because society accepts that it has value. US dollars state "This note is legal tender for all debts, public and private." Fiat money is the common form of currency used in the US and the world today.

M1, perfectly liquid money that can be instantly spent, is the most commonly used measure of the money supply. M1 consists of currency (paper money and coins) and **demand deposits** (checking accounts, including travelers' checks and debit cards which directly draw from your bank account to make purchases). **M2** is a broader definition of money, including M1 plus the "near money" of savings deposits, certificates of deposit (CDs) of less than $100,000, and money market mutual funds. "Near money" is fairly liquid but requires a withdrawal to convert it to cash or a demand deposit.

Caution

You may have noticed that credit cards, another method of apparently instant payment for goods and services, are not included in the money supply. This is because credit cards are not money; they allow short-term loans from the institution that issued the credit card. The bank makes the payment at the time of purchase, and at the end of the month, you must pay the bill with currency or a check.

Because US currency is fiat money, it has no intrinsic value. As late as the early 20th century, US dollars were "backed" by gold, meaning dollars could be traded in at a bank for a specific amount of gold per dollar. This backing was designed to inspire consumer confidence in the value of currency. However, tying the money supply to a precious metal left the money supply susceptible to wild swings in the gold supply. Economists today agree that it is better to be able to change the money supply to meet the needs of the economy. Therefore, the money supply today is not backed, and the money supply is controlled by the Federal Reserve System.

Three things help money to maintain its value today: acceptability, designation as legal tender, and relative scarcity. As long as buyers and sellers accept that a dollar is worth a dollar, that money has value. The government's declaration that money has value, as noted on dollar bills, gives people confidence in that value. The Federal Reserve controls the supply of money in the economy, limiting its availability in order to keep it relatively scarce, to ensure that it keeps its value.

Purchasing power is the amount of goods and services a specific amount of money will buy. Inflation causes the value of the dollar to fall; the same dollars don't have the same purchasing power and cannot stretch to buy as much as they could before the inflation. In order to keep inflation in check, Congress and the president can use fiscal policy to change government spending and taxes, while the Federal Reserve can use **monetary policy** to control the money supply and interest rates on credit.

PRACTICE Functions of Money

1. __________ Three functions of money are: a unit of account, a store of value, and *what*?

2. __________ Are US dollars *commodity money* or *fiat money*?

3. __________ M1 consists of currency (paper money and coins) and *what*?

4. __________ What, if anything, "backs" US dollars today?

5. __________ During inflation, does the purchasing power of money *increase* or *decrease*?

The Federal Reserve and the Banking System

Refer to pages 576–579 of your textbook.

A CLOSER LOOK Board of Governors, the 12 Federal Reserve Banks, FOMC, and Commercial Banks

The **Federal Reserve System,** also known as the Fed, is the central banking system for the US. Its primary role is to control the country's money supply and determine monetary policy. The Fed was created in 1913 to address problems with privately-printed money, banking crises, runs on banks, and the lack of confidence in the banking system that seriously affected economic performance.

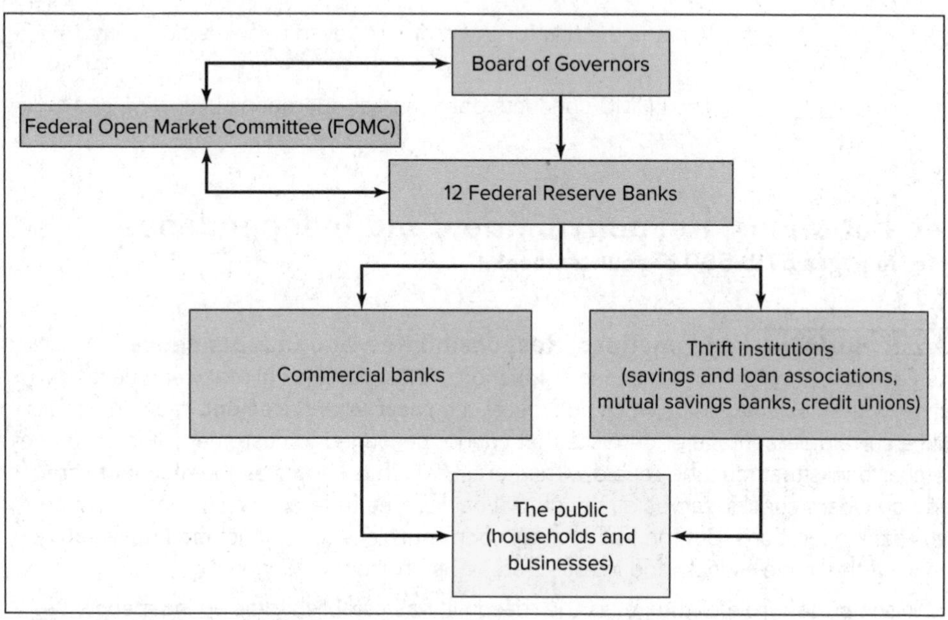

The **Board of Governors** consists of seven members who are appointed by the president and confirmed by the Senate. Members cannot be fired by the president and serve non-renewable, 14-year staggered terms, in order to insulate the Fed from political pressure. There is significant political pressure to keep interest rates low, so consumers can afford to buy homes and cars, and so firms can invest in capital. However, too great an increase in the money supply can result in inflation. For this reason, the Fed was developed as an independent agency of government. The primary role of the Board of Governors is to control the money supply and run the Federal Reserve System.

The 12 regional **Federal Reserve Banks** throughout the US serve as "bankers' banks," performing the same functions for banks that your local bank performs for you as a customer. Regional banks allow member banks to deposit cash on account and provide loans to member banks. These regional banks implement monetary policy as determined by the Board of Governors. Regional banks are a unique hybrid of private ownership and public control, because the regional banks are actually owned by the member banks of each district, but public officials control the banking system and its policies.

The **Federal Open Market Committee (FOMC)** consists of the seven members of the Board of Governors, the President of the New York Federal Reserve Bank, and four other regional bank presidents who serve on a rotating basis. The role of the FOMC is to conduct **open market operations** – buying and selling government securities (Treasury bonds, bills, and notes) in the market to change the money supply and interest rates. Because these open market operations are performed through the New York Federal Reserve, that bank's president is a permanent member of the committee.

Member banks consist of the many kinds of financial institutions customers use. While credit unions and savings and loans are regulated by agencies outside of the Fed, they are still subject to the same monetary controls of the Fed.

PRACTICE Board of Governors, the 12 Federal Reserve Banks, FOMC, and Commercial Banks

1. ________ The primary role of the Federal Reserve System is to control *what*?

2. ________ What is the title for the group of seven people who control the Fed?

3. ________ The FOMC conducts open market operations by buying and selling *what*?

Fed Functions, Responsibilities, and Independence

Refer to pages 579–580 of your textbook.

A CLOSER LOOK Fed Functions, Responsibilities, and Independence

The Fed is responsible for a number of functions. It issues new currency and destroys currency that is damaged or worn out. It sets the **reserve requirement,** requiring banks to hold a certain percentage of deposits that cannot be loaned to customers. It loans money to member banks that must be repaid with interest, which is known as the **discount rate.** The Fed also clears checks, serves as the official bank of the federal government, and supervises bank operations. But the Fed's most important role is to conduct **monetary policy,** changing the money supply and interest rates to stabilize the economy.

This important role of the Fed is the reason it was established as an independent agency. Members of Congress can sometimes be pressured to reduce taxes and increase spending for popular government programs in order to be reelected. But such uses of fiscal policy can cause inflation. Federal Reserve Governors who are appointed rather than elected, who cannot be fired by the president, and whose terms cannot be renewed (so they have no reelection pressures) can make painful but necessary choices, such as raising interest rates, which will keep inflation under control.

Even with a number of controls in place, the Great Recession began with failures in the financial industry. One problem was the repeal of the Glass-Steagall Act, which had required commercial banks to remain separate from riskier investment institutions. The removal of this wall allowed commercial banks to take more risk (therefore placing customer accounts at greater risk). One way was that many banks began to issue subprime loans—high-interest home loans for people with poor credit. Banks began to "bundle" thousands of these risky mortgages into bonds backed by the mortgage payments, and sold the bonds to investors. Banks then gave investors loans to buy the bonds. Investors thought these "mortgage-backed securities" were safe, because if homeowners failed to pay their mortgages, the homes could simply be foreclosed and resold to another buyer. Because banks thought they had removed themselves from any risk, many of them stopped running credit checks, made loans to more and more unqualified buyers, and even allowed buyers to lie about their incomes – putting these new homeowners in positions where they could not possibly pay their mortgages.

When the Great Recession began in 2007, unemployment rose and these homeowners could not make their mortgage payments. As a result, so many homes were foreclosed upon and put up for sale, that home values plunged. Many borrowers who had made low or no down payments on their homes realized they owed more on their home than it was worth, and they simply walked away without making any more payments. Investors, including individuals and pension funds, now held mortgage-backed securities that had lost nearly all of their value. Banks and other financial institutions couldn't recover the loans they had made to purchasers of these securities, and they began to collapse. Large banks went out of business; others were taken over by competitors. Many were rescued by the government, arguably because they were "too big to fail;" failure of those institutions would create a domino effect, potentially causing a crash of the entire US economy and spreading to other economies around the world.

The federal government used several methods to save the financial industry. In 2008, Congress created the Troubled Asset Relief Program (TARP) to make $700 billion in loans to financial institutions, and, later, to GM and Chrysler to save the auto industry. The Federal Reserve purchased approximately $1 trillion in government bonds, mortgage-backed securities, and other bonds held by member banks so that the member banks could use the cash to make other loans to keep money flowing through the economy. The Fed also reduced its interest rates to near zero to promote lending and to encourage spending to get the economy back on its feet. The **Federal Deposit Insurance Corporation (FDIC),** which protects depositors' bank accounts, increased protection from $100,000 to $250,000 on each account. It closed more than 200 banks and reopened them as branches of other banks.

By the end of 2016, not all of the TARP loans had been repaid, but including interest and fees, the federal government had been repaid more than it originally loaned to bail out the financial and auto industries. In 2010, Congress passed the Wall Street Reform and Consumer Protection Act (commonly referred to as Dodd-Frank), which gave the Fed more power to regulate financial institutions, created more oversight of the financial industry, required banks to keep more of the risk associated with mortgage loans, and created the Bureau of Consumer Financial Protection. While the law might prevent some of the actions that led to the 2007 financial crisis, many are concerned that the continued consolidation of financial institutions has allowed even more firms to become "too big to fail," requiring bailouts in the next financial crisis. Still others, including Congressional Republicans following the 2016 elections, prefer to repeal or dismantle key provisions of Dodd-Frank, arguing that the regulations unnecessarily stifle growth. They argue for simply increasing capital requirements on the financial institutions.

PRACTICE Fed Functions, Responsibilities, and Independence

1. _________ The reserve requirement is a percentage of deposits banks cannot use for *what*?

2. _________ What is the term for the interest rate the Fed charges member banks for loans?

3. _________ What is the term for the Fed's policy of controlling the money supply?

4. _________ What is the name of the economic crisis that began in 2007?

5. _________ What government agency protects depositors' bank accounts?

Make sure to return to the AP Key Concepts section to check your understanding of the chapter's concepts important to AP coursework.

Economically Speaking

- **Barter** trading goods and services without the use of money
- **Board of Governors** runs the Federal Reserve System
- **Commodity Money** a form of money that has intrinsic value, such as gold
- **Demand Deposit** a checking account
- **Discount Rate** the interest rate the Fed charges member banks for loans
- **Federal Deposit Insurance Corporation (FDIC)** government agency that protects bank deposits
- **Federal Open Market Committee (FOMC)** conducts open market operations to control the money supply
- **Federal Reserve Banks** "bankers' banks" that hold deposits and make loans to member banks
- **Federal Reserve System (Fed)** the central banking system for the United States
- **Fiat Money** a form of money that only has value because people accept that it has value
- **Liquidity** how easily an asset can be converted into cash
- **M1** perfectly liquid money; currency and demand deposits
- **M2** money held in another form which must be converted to cash, like a savings account
- **Medium of Exchange** the use of money to purchase goods and services
- **Member Banks** financial institutions used by the public
- **Monetary Policy** changing the money supply and interest rates to stabilize the economy
- **Money** anything widely accepted by buyers and sellers as a medium of exchange
- **Open Market Operations** the Fed buying and selling government securities to change the money supply
- **Purchasing Power** the amount of goods and services money will buy
- **Reserve Requirement** requires banks to hold a percentage of deposits that cannot be loaned
- **Store of Value** money can be saved to be used later for purchases
- **Unit of Account** money is used as a measure, to determine the relative values of products

Money Creation

The Federal Reserve System plays a crucial role in the US economy, controlling the money supply and using monetary policy to stabilize the economy. As part of this process, banks create money through the fractional reserve system. Chapter 29 explains the process by which banks increase the money supply and the role of the money multiplier in determining the total increase in the money supply. This knowledge lays the foundation for understanding how monetary policy works.

Material from Chapter 29 usually appears in a few multiple-choice questions on the AP Macroeconomics exam, as well as occasionally occurring as a complete free-response question on money creation.

Key Concepts

Below is a summary of the chapter's concepts important to AP coursework. Upon completing the lessons that follow, return to these concepts to make sure you understand them and how the practice exercises you completed relate to them.

- The US uses a fractional reserve banking system, which requires banks to keep a portion of all deposits in reserve at the bank or Fed.
- Banks create money by issuing loans.
- The Fed can increase or decrease the money supply by changing the reserve requirement.
- The FDIC insures bank deposits to instill confidence among depositors and reduce bank runs.
- The two purposes of a bank are to provide a safe place for savings and to issue loans.
- On a bank's balance sheet, assets (what the bank owns, reserves, and loans owed to the bank) equal liabilities (the bank's expenses and debt) and net worth (owners' assets).
- Actual reserves are the total amount of reserves the bank holds.
    - Required reserves are the percent of deposits the Fed requires the bank to hold.
    - Excess reserves are the reserves the bank holds beyond required, which can be loaned.
- The purpose of the reserve requirement is to limit the growth of the money supply.
- If a customer deposits cash into a demand deposit account, the money supply doesn't change.
- If a bank issues a loan or buys a government security (from a securities dealer), the money supply increases.
- Money Multiplier = 1 / Reserve Requirement

- Potential Money Creation = Excess Reserves × Money Multiplier
- The money supply may not grow to its potential because customers do not completely redeposit cash in the bank, because banks don't want to loan out all available excess reserves, or because customers choose not to borrow all available excess reserves.

Now, let's examine more closely the following concepts from your textbook:

- **The Fractional Reserve System**
- **A Single Commercial Bank**
- **Money-Creating Transactions of a Commercial Bank**
- **The Banking System: Multiple-Deposit Expansion**
- **The Money Multiplier**

These sections were selected because an understanding of money creation is necessary for understanding how the Fed uses the tools of monetary policy to stabilize the economy.

The Fractional Reserve System

Refer to pages 589–590 of your textbook.

A CLOSER LOOK Significant Characteristics of Fractional Reserve Banking

The US banking system is known as a **fractional reserve system,** meaning that banks are required to keep a fraction of all money in **demand deposits** (checking accounts) in reserve at the bank or Fed. The remaining deposits can be loaned out to other customers. As a result, bank reserves are only a fraction of the total money supply.

The banking system creates money by issuing loans. Because the money is loaned and reloaned, it can create a money supply that is significantly larger than the original deposit. If the bank retains a large proportion of its deposits, few dollars are available to be loaned, so the growth of the money supply will be low. But if the fraction of deposits held by the bank is low and the bank keeps loaning large proportions of the subsequent deposits, the money supply can grow rapidly. The ability to change these fractional reserves gives the Federal Reserve considerable flexibility in changing the money supply.

But a fractional reserve system carries significant risks for panics and bank runs. If the bank has loaned a significant amount of the original deposits, and those deposit-holders return to withdraw those funds, the bank will not have the money available to repay those funds on demand. The money hasn't disappeared; it will be repaid with interest. But depositors who don't get their money back right away can start a panic, causing other customers to rush to retrieve their funds. The FDIC was created to prevent such bank runs by insuring deposits, now up to $250,000. When depositors know their accounts are insured by the FDIC, they have confidence their money is safe, and runs are unlikely.

PRACTICE Significant Characteristics of Fractional Reserve Banking

1. __________ How does the banking system increase the money supply?

2. __________ Does the money supply grow more quickly if the fraction of deposits held by the bank is *high* or *low*?

3. __________ Bank runs are unlikely today because of the protection of what agency?

A Single Commercial Bank

Refer to pages 590–594 of your textbook.

A CLOSER LOOK Depositing Reserves

Banks perform two primary functions for customers: they provide a safe place for savings, and they loan out money. A bank's **balance sheet** lists the **assets** (what the bank owns, the cash on hand, and the money owed to the bank), **liabilities** (the bank's expenses and debts), and **net worth** (claims of the owners). The balance sheet must remain balanced.

Assets = Liabilities + Net Worth

Say a new bank is created with $250,000 of stock bought by shareholders, which is a liability for the bank because it is owned by the stockholders. From the stock proceeds, $240,000 is spent on property and capital, and $10,000 remains in cash, which are assets of the bank. The balance sheet is balanced.

If customers make $100,000 in deposits into checking accounts, those deposits show up on both sides of the balance sheet – the bank holds cash as an asset and checking accounts as a liability it owes the depositors. However, the economy's money supply has not changed. Remember, M1 consists of currency held by the public and demand deposits at the bank. When the deposits were made, the form of the money changed from currency to checkable deposits, but the quantity of money did not change.

Accepting Deposits
Balance Sheet 3: Wahoo Bank

Assets		Liabilities and net worth	
Cash	$110,000	Checkable deposits	$100,000
Property	240,000	Stock shares	250,000

The **reserve requirement** is the percentage of checkable deposits the Fed requires banks to hold in reserve that they cannot loan out. The bank can hold the reserve in the bank vault or keep it at a regional Federal Reserve Bank. If customers deposit $100,000 and the reserve requirement is 10%, the bank must hold $10,000, and it can loan out the other $90,000 to customers.

Actual reserves are the total amount of reserves the bank holds. **Excess reserves** are the amount of reserves the bank holds beyond the required reserves; these are the funds that can be loaned out to other customers.

Excess Reserves = Actual Reserves – Required Reserves

While it may appear that the purpose of a reserve requirement is to ensure liquidity so that funds will be available when depositors attempt to withdraw their funds, this is not the real purpose of a reserve requirement. The purpose of the reserve requirement is to control the money supply. When a bank makes loans to customers, it increases the money supply; when the loan is repaid, it decreases the money supply. The Federal Reserve can change the reserve requirement, which changes the money supply, to address recession or inflation. The reserve requirement limits how far the money supply can grow in order to prevent significant inflation in the economy.

PRACTICE Depositing Reserves

1. __________ The two primary roles of banks are to provide a safe place for savings and *what*?

2. __________ What term describes the total amount of reserves a bank currently holds?

3. __________ What term describes the amount of reserves the bank can currently loan?

4. __________ What term describes the amount of reserves the Fed demands that banks keep?

5. __________ If a bank holds $100,000 in actual reserves and $40,000 in required reserves, how much does the bank hold in excess reserves?

6. __________ What is the reserve requirement actually designed to control?

Money-Creating Transactions of a Commercial Bank

Refer to pages 594–596 of your textbook.

A CLOSER LOOK Granting a Loan and Buying Government Securities

Consider the balance sheet (eliminating the stock shares and property holdings) for another bank:

Assets		Liabilities	
Reserves	$100,000	Demand Deposits	$100,000

If the reserve requirement is 10%, the bank must hold 10% of its demand deposits ($10,000) in required reserves. That means the bank can loan out as much as $90,000. So assume Vanessa takes out a $70,000 loan to buy a home. The balance sheet changes:

Assets		Liabilities	
Reserves	$100,000	Demand Deposits	$170,000
Loans	$ 70,000		

The bank actually *creates* money by putting $70,000 into demand deposits and listing it as a loan in its assets. When the home seller deposits Vanessa's check to buy the home in *his* bank, the money is removed from Vanessa's bank and the balance sheet changes again:

Assets		Liabilities	
Reserves	$30,000	Demand Deposits	$100,000
Loans	$70,000		

The $70,000 check is subtracted from the bank's demand deposits, and the same $70,000 is removed from the bank's actual reserves. Where did the $70,000 go? Into the home seller's demand deposit account at a bank somewhere else, increasing *that* bank's demand deposits and reserves.

So now where does *our* bank stand? It still faces a 10% reserve requirement, so the bank must hold $10,000 in required reserves. That leaves $20,000 in excess reserves that the bank can loan out to someone else, if it chooses to do so.

Let's assume that this bank, rather than making more loans, decides to buy $20,000 in government bonds (securities) from a securities dealer. The bank adds $20,000 in securities to its assets and puts $20,000 into checking to pay for the bonds. The balance sheet then changes:

Assets		Liabilities	
Reserves	$30,000	Demand Deposits	$120,000
Loans	$70,000		
Securities	$20,000		

When the securities dealer cashes the $20,000 check from the bank, the demand deposits fall by the $20,000, and actual reserves fall by the same $20,000, so the balance sheet changes:

Assets		Liabilities	
Reserves	$10,000	Demand Deposits	$100,000
Loans	$70,000		
Securities	$20,000		

Now where does the bank stand? The 10% reserve requirement requires the bank to hold 10% of its demand deposits in cash – which is the $10,000 in actual reserves the bank is currently holding. There are no excess reserves left, so the bank cannot make any more loans or buy any more securities until someone deposits more money into the bank.

Keep in Mind

It is important to note the difference between a change in money supply resulting from a new deposit of cash versus the bank buying securities. A customer deposit causes no change in the money supply, because the money is only changing form from currency to a demand deposit, both of which are forms of M1. However, if the bank buys a bond from a securities dealer, the money supply does increase. The bank puts money into the economy to buy the bond, while absorbing a non-money asset into its accounts. In answering AP exam questions, it is important to pay careful attention to the initial action in order to determine whether money is created in that initial action or created later in the process through loans.

Banks are like any other business – they seek profit. Banks make profit by paying a low interest rate on deposits and using those deposits to make loans for which they charge a higher interest rate. Banks can also use those deposits to buy securities which earn a higher interest rate. Banks have an incentive to loan out as much of their excess reserves as possible. The bank has another objective, though. It has to maintain liquidity for depositors who want to make withdrawals. So it can't loan out so much of the excess reserves that if depositors unexpectedly write a large number of checks at the end of the day, the bank would be left with less than the required reserves.

PRACTICE Granting a Loan and Buying Government Securities

Assume ABC Bank has the balance sheet below, and the reserve requirement is 20%. Then answer the questions that follow.

Assets		Liabilities	
Reserves	$10,000	Demand Deposits	$30,000
Loans	$20,000		

1. ________ How much money must ABC Bank hold in required reserves?

2. ________ How much money does ABC Bank hold in excess reserves?

3. ________ If a customer applies for a $5,000 car loan, can ABC Bank make that loan?

4. ________ If a customer deposits $4,000, how much will the total demand deposits be?

   A. ________ How much will the actual reserves be?

   B. ________ How much will the required reserves be?

   C. ________ How much will the excess reserves be?

5. ________ Given your answer in #4(C), could ABC Bank make the loan to the customer from #3?

The Banking System: Multiple-Deposit Expansion

Refer to pages 597–598 of your textbook.

A CLOSER LOOK The Banking System's Lending Potential

We have seen how a single bank can increase the money supply by making loans. But by looking at the entire banking system, we can see how the increase in the money supply can multiply. Let's start with a few assumptions. All of the banks must meet the reserve requirement (10% in our example), and the banks start with no excess reserves. Further, we will assume that every time a bank makes a loan, the recipient writes a check for the entire amount, which is fully redeposited in another bank. Finally, we assume that banks will loan out all excess reserves.

	Deposits	Required Reserves	Excess Reserves	Loans	Total Increase in Money Supply
Customer A	$1,000				$ 0
		$100	$900		
Customer B				$900	$ 900
Customer C	$ 900				
		$ 90	$810		
Customer D				$810	$1,710
Customer E	$ 810				
		$ 81	$729		

Let's assume Customer A takes $1,000 from under his mattress and deposits it into his checking account at the bank. Did the money supply change? No. The money only changed form, from currency to a demand deposit. If the bank must hold 10% in cash to meet the reserve requirement, it must hold $100 and, therefore, has $900 available in new excess reserves that it can loan to customers.

Customer B takes out a $900 loan to buy a computer from Customer C. At this point, the banking system creates $900 in new money. How? Customer A still has his $1,000 in a demand deposit at his bank, but now Customer B has a $900 check, a loan from the bank to buy the computer – the same $900 has been used twice.

Customer B buys the computer from Customer C, who deposits the $900 in his checking account at a *different* bank. Did this action create more money? No, the money just changed location, from a customer check based on the loan from Customer B's bank to a new deposit in Customer C's checking account at a *different* bank. Of the new $900 deposit, Customer C's bank is required to reserve $90 (so banks now hold a total of $190 in required reserves), leaving $810 in excess reserves available for loans.

Customer D comes to the bank to borrow $810, to pay Customer E for car repairs. In creating the loan from the excess reserves, the bank has created another $810 in new money, for a total of $1,710 of new money created by the banking system from the original $1,000 deposit. When Customer E deposits the $810 payment from Customer D into *another* bank, *that* bank must again keep the 10% required reserve ($81) and can again loan the $729 in new excess reserves. This process continues with deposit after deposit, loan after loan.

But an important question arises from this multiple-bank expansion of the money supply. Once the excess reserves have been loaned and reloaned, what if Customer A comes back to the bank and wants to withdraw his $1,000 deposit? It isn't there. Nearly all of it has been loaned out to Customer B. If Customer A can't get his money and makes panicked calls to his friends, Customers C and E, they may rush to their banks to try to get their deposits as well – a classic run on the banks. In modern banking, Customer A is only one of the thousands of people who have deposits at each bank, and it is extremely unlikely that everyone would show up at once to withdraw their deposits. Even if they did, the FDIC provides government protection of deposits, up to a limit, in case the bank actually collapses. The understanding of that protection keeps customers from panicking and making runs on banks.

PRACTICE **The Banking System's Lending Potential**

1. ________ If Jorge deposits $1,000 of cash into his checking account, by how much does the money supply increase?

2. ________ If the bank holds $1,000 in demand deposits and the reserve requirement is 25%, how much must the bank hold in required reserves?

3. ________ If the bank holds $1,000 in demand deposits and the reserve requirement is 25%, how much does the bank have available in excess reserves?

4. ________ If the bank chooses to loan out $300 to a customer, by how much does the money supply immediately increase?

The Monetary Multiplier

Refer to pages 599–601 of your textbook.

A CLOSER LOOK **The Money Multiplier**

An important implication is that with every loan, the money supply keeps growing. How large will it grow? To find out, we need to calculate the **money multiplier,** which shows the relationship between excess reserves and the maximum amount of money that can be created from those reserves.

$$\text{Money Multiplier} = \frac{1}{\text{Reserve Requirement}}$$

If the reserve requirement is 10%, the money multiplier is 1 / 0.1, or 10. If the reserve requirement is 20%, the money multiplier is 1 / 0.2, or 5. The larger the reserve requirement of deposits that the bank must hold, the smaller the multiplier becomes. At this point, you can begin to understand the significance of the reserve requirement in limiting the money supply. In economics, anything divided by zero is infinity. So if there were no reserve requirement, the money multiplier would be infinity!

Keep in Mind

You cannot use a calculator on AP Economics exams, and you can count on questions that require you to calculate the money multiplier. An easy trick of the trade to calculate the multiplier is to think about the denominator (the reserve requirement) as a fraction of a dollar. For example, if the reserve requirement is 10%, the denominator is 0.10 – which looks like 10 cents. What must you multiply your dime by to get to a dollar? Ten. Your multiplier is 10. If the reserve requirement is 25%, your denominator is 0.25 – a quarter. You multiply a quarter by 4 to get to a dollar, so your multiplier is 4.

Now that we know the multiplier, we can calculate the maximum potential growth of the money supply resulting from an initial deposit.

$$\text{Potential Money Creation} = \text{Excess Reserves} \times \text{Money Multiplier}$$

In our earlier example, the initial $1,000 deposit with a 10% reserve requirement left $900 in excess reserves. With a money multiplier of 10, the banking system created $9,000 through loans ($900 × 10). Added to the $1,000 initial deposit, the total money supply is $10,000. Now we can begin to see the full impact of changes in the multiplier. If the reserve requirement had been 20% with a multiplier of 5, the money supply could have grown only by $4,000 ($800 × 5) for a total money supply of $5,000, because banks were more limited. If the reserve requirement were 50% with a multiplier of 2, the money supply could have grown only by $1,000 ($500 × 2) for a total money supply of $2,000.

Keep in Mind

It is very, very important to carefully look at what the question is asking on the AP exam. One question may ask how much money can be created by the banking system. Another may ask what the maximum size of the money supply may be, once the money is completely loaned. Using the $1,000 deposit with the 10% reserve requirement, the money supply could *grow* by $9,000, for a *total* money supply of $10,000. Look at the question carefully, because the other response is likely to be one of your options!

The money multiplier is a concept very similar to the spending multiplier and marginal propensity to consume. With the MPC, one person's spending is another person's income, so an initial change in spending eventually leads to a much larger change in real GDP as the money is spent and re-spent. In the same way, an initial deposit into the banking system is loaned and re-loaned, spent and re-spent, so that an initial deposit into the banking system results in a much larger effect on the money supply.

Another implication of this multiple-deposit expansion system is the importance of the reserve requirement in controlling the growth of the money supply. Assume for a moment that no reserve requirement existed. If banks were free to loan out all deposits made to the bank, how large would the money supply grow? It would grow *infinitely*. There would be no means to limit the perpetual re-loaning of funds, causing massive inflation. Therefore, a reserve requirement is essential for limiting the growth of the money supply and the rate of inflation.

Will the money supply always grow to its potential? Generally not. Remember our opening assumptions – that banks loan out all of their excess reserves and customers redeposit all of their funds at their banks. In reality, consumers hold cash in their wallets and in their homes for purchases, and money not deposited at the bank cannot be used to further expand the money supply. Further, banks may not fully loan funds if they are concerned about meeting their reserve requirements. Customers simply may choose not to take out as many loans during an economic downturn. So while we know the maximum *potential* growth of the money supply, the *actual* change in the money supply may be less.

It is important to note that this process also works in reverse. As loans are paid off, checkable deposits and loans decrease, and money is "destroyed." In our sophisticated banking system, the creation of money at some banks is accompanied by the "destruction" of money at others, making it highly unlikely that all banks will ever be "loaned out" or that runs on the banks will be a serious threat again.

PRACTICE The Money Multiplier

1. If $1,000 is deposited in the bank and the reserve requirement is 20%:

   A. __________ How much is the bank required to hold in cash?

   B. __________ What is the value of loans that can be made from the deposit?

C. ________ What is the multiplier?

D. ________ What is the maximum amount created by the banking system?

E. ________ What will be the total money supply, if the money is fully loaned?

2. If $1,000 is deposited in the bank and the Fed reduces the reserve requirement to 5%:

   A. ________ How much is the bank required to hold in cash?

   B. ________ What is the value of loans that can be made from the deposit?

   C. ________ What is the multiplier?

   D. ________ What is the maximum amount created by the banking system?

   E. ________ What will be the total money supply, if the money is fully loaned?

3. ________ Given your answers in #1(E) and #2(E), does a smaller reserve requirement result in a *smaller* or *larger* money supply?

4. The actual change in money supply will be less than the maximum potential growth if one or more of these three things happen. For each item, indicate which choice given in italics is correct for this statement.

   A. ________ Customers *hold money in cash* or *deposit all money in the bank.*

   B. ________ Banks choose to loan out *all* or *less than all* excess reserves.

   C. ________ Customers choose to borrow *all* or *less than all* excess reserves.

Make sure to return to the AP Key Concepts section to check your understanding of the chapter's concepts important to AP coursework.

Economically Speaking

- **Actual Reserves** total amount of reserves held in the bank
- **Assets** the value of things owned by the bank or owed to the bank
- **Balance Sheet** statement of a bank's assets and liabilities
- **Demand Deposit** checking account
- **Excess Reserves** the reserves a bank holds beyond the required reserves, which can be loaned
- **Fractional Reserve System** only a fraction of bank deposits are held by banks or the Fed
- **Liabilities** the bank's expenses and debts owed to others
- **Money Multiplier** shows the relationship between excess reserves and the maximum amount of money that can be created from those reserves
- **Net Worth** the claims of the bank owners against the bank's assets
- **Reserve Requirement** percentage of checkable deposits a bank must hold in reserve

Chapter 30

Interest Rates and Monetary Policy

Changes in the money supply have an important impact on interest rates, aggregate demand, price levels, and employment. The Federal Reserve uses a number of tools to play a central role in determining interest rates and stabilizing the economy. Chapter 30 focuses on the supply and demand for money, the tools of monetary policy and how they are used, and the effects of monetary policy on GDP and economic stabilization. These principles complete the discussion of the role of money in the macroeconomy.

Material from Chapter 30 consistently appears in a significant number of multiple-choice questions on the AP Macroeconomics exam, and is part of a free-response question on nearly every exam.

Key Concepts

Below is a summary of the chapter's concepts important to AP coursework. Upon completing the lessons that follow, return to these concepts to make sure you understand them and how the practice exercises you completed relate to them.

- The interest rate is the price paid for the use of borrowed money, set by supply and demand.
  - Transactions demand is the money people hold to make purchases.
  - Asset demand is the money people hold to put into savings or investments as a store of value.
  - The total demand for money is Transactions + Asset Demand and is downsloping.
  - The Federal Reserve determines the money supply, a vertical curve.
  - An increase in demand or decrease in supply raises the interest rate, and vice versa.
- When interest rates rise, the prices of bonds fall because demand for existing bonds falls.
- Open market operations are the Fed's activity of buying and selling government securities.
  - The Fed buys bonds to increase the money supply and sells them to reduce it.
  - This is the most frequently used tool of the Fed because it is quick and can "fine tune."
- The reserve requirement is the percent of deposits banks must hold in reserve and cannot loan.
  - The Fed lowers the reserve requirement to increase the money supply; raises to cut it.
  - This is the most powerful tool of the Fed because it affects reserves and the multiplier.

- The discount rate is the interest rate the Fed charges on loans to commercial banks.
    - The Fed lowers the discount rate to increase the money supply; raises to cut it.
    - These rates serve as incentives for commercial banks to borrow from the Fed.
- The Fed can reduce interest rates on reserves kept at the Fed to encourage banks to loan more.
- The federal funds rate is the interest rate banks charge each other for overnight loans.
- Expansionary "easy money" monetary policy raises the money supply to close recessionary gaps.
    - Interest rate falls, investment rises, aggregate demand rises, and real GDP rises.
- Contractionary "tight money" monetary policy lowers money supply to close inflationary gaps.
    - Interest rate rises, investment falls, aggregate demand falls, and real GDP falls.
- Advantages of monetary policy include speed of decision-making, flexibility to "fine tune" the economy, insulation of the Fed from political pressure, and a singular agenda for the Fed.
- Limitations of monetary policy include recognition and operational lags.
    - Monetary policy is more effective in addressing inflationary gaps than recessionary gaps, because people may choose not to borrow money, because banks may choose not to grant loans, or because customers may not redeposit money in the banks.
- During the Great Recession, the US economy entered a liquidity trap, rendering monetary policy less effective because lowering interest rates further had no stimulative effect.
- The Fed used quantitative easing, buying $4 trillion in bonds to increase the money supply.
- The Fed and Congress do not coordinate their policies, which can create a variety of effects.
    - Expansionary fiscal policy and expansionary monetary policy will both stimulate aggregate demand. But while fiscal policy increases interest rates (causing crowding out), monetary policy reduces interest rates, so the combined effect is unknown.
    - If contractionary monetary policy and expansionary fiscal policy are used together, the combined effect on aggregate demand is unknown, but both raise interest rates.
- Lower interest rates promote long-run economic growth through investment.
- Be sure to carefully study the flow charts to review the details of policy implementation.

Now, let's examine more closely the following concepts from your textbook:

- **Interest Rates**
- **Tools of Monetary Policy**
- **Targeting the Federal Funds Rate**
- **Monetary Policy, Real GDP, and the Price Level**
- **Monetary Policy: Evaluation and Issues**

These sections were selected because a full understanding of monetary policy is critical for success on the AP Macroeconomics exam. Additional practice using the tools of monetary policy and its combination with fiscal policy should make causes and effects more clear.

Interest Rates

Refer to pages 604–607 of your textbook.

A CLOSER LOOK The Demand for Money and the Equilibrium Interest Rate

The **interest rate** is the price paid for the use of borrowed money. There are several different interest rates: mortgage interest, auto loan interest, student loan interest, savings account interest, and the interest paid on bonds, among many others. Discussion of "the interest rate" in this context only refers to a general concept, rather than a specific interest rate for a particular purpose.

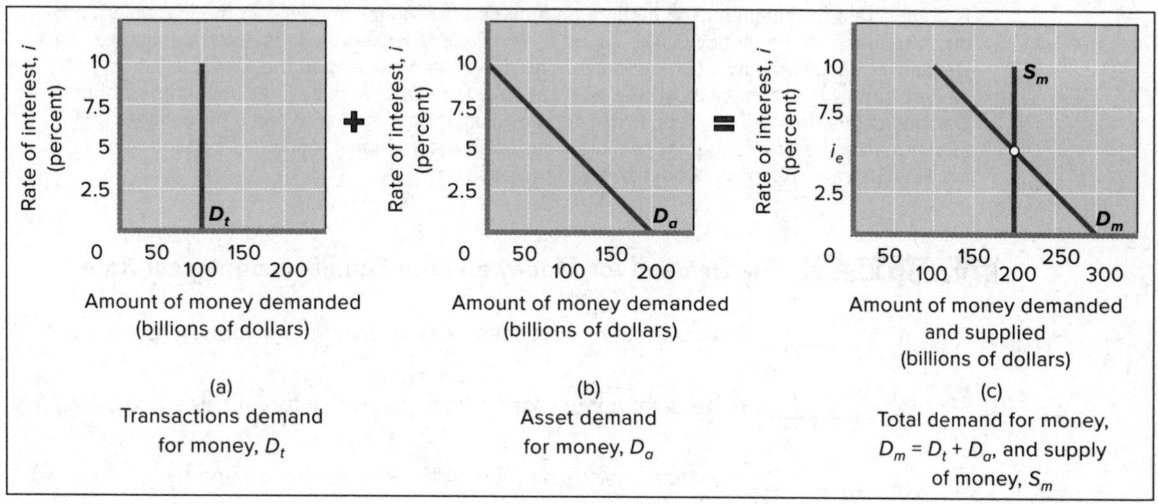

(a) Transactions demand for money, D_t

(b) Asset demand for money, D_a

(c) Total demand for money, $D_m = D_t + D_a$, and supply of money, S_m

The money market illustrates the supply and demand for money and the equilibrium interest rate. The demand for money is determined by the two reasons people hold money: purchases and savings. **Transactions demand** refers to the amount of money people hold as a medium of exchange in order to make purchases. People keep some of their income in cash to pay for gas, groceries, entertainment, and other purchases. Transactions demand changes with nominal GDP, because as output or prices increase, consumers need more money to be able to pay for products. Transactions demand is a vertical curve (Graph (a) above) because it is not related to the interest rate.

Asset demand is the amount of money people hold as a store of value, as an asset they can keep to use for future purchases. People can put their savings into stocks, bonds, or savings accounts, or they can hold it in cash. Holding cash gives a person immediate liquidity and protects the asset against a potential loss that could occur with stocks or other investments. However, cash earns no return on investment, so people must determine the tradeoffs in deciding what to do with their savings. Asset demand is inversely related to the interest rate, because at a high interest rate, people suffer a higher opportunity cost for holding their savings in cash rather than putting it in a bank; at a lower interest rate, the opportunity cost is lower, so people are more willing to hold a greater quantity of their money in cash. As a result, asset demand slopes downward (Graph (b) above).

The total demand for money is the transactions demand plus the asset demand for money – added horizontally. Since the Federal Reserve determines the money supply, it is a vertical curve. In Graph (c) above, the equilibrium interest rate is determined by the intersection of the demand and supply of money. When the nominal GDP increases, consumers want to buy more, so the demand for money increases; a lower nominal GDP reduces demand for money. An increase in demand or a decrease in supply of money will cause interest rates to increase. A decrease in demand or an increase in supply of money causes the interest rate to fall. This is the nominal interest rate, incorporating the real interest rate and the expected rate of inflation.

Changes in interest rates also affect bond prices. The prices of bonds are determined by supply and demand in bond markets. When interest rates rise, the demand for existing bonds falls because buyers can get a higher return on the new bonds. So the price of existing bonds must fall so the percentage return on investment matches that of new bonds. When interest rates rise, bond prices fall.

Caution

It is important to remember the distinction between the money market and the loanable funds market. Supply in the money market is set by the Federal Reserve and is a vertical curve. Demand is based on how much consumers hold in cash or assets. In the loanable funds market, supply is determined by how much people want to save in savings accounts or bonds. Demand comes from consumers, firms, and government borrowing to make purchases. The money market describes the entire money supply in the economy, while the loanable funds market illustrates changes in borrowing in the economy.

PRACTICE The Demand for Money and the Equilibrium Interest Rate

1. __________ If nominal GDP increases, will the demand for money *rise* or *fall*?

2. __________ If the demand for money increases, will interest rates *rise* or *fall*?

3. __________ Is a consumer using *transactions* or *asset* demand by holding cash in a wallet?

4. __________ If the Fed increases the money supply, will interest rates *rise* or *fall*?

5. __________ If interest rates rise, will the price of bonds *rise* or *fall*?

Tools of Monetary Policy

Refer to pages 608–614 of your textbook.

A CLOSER LOOK Open Market Operations, Reserve Ratio, Discount Rate, Interest on Reserves

The Federal Reserve has four primary tools by which it can change the money supply: open market operations, the reserve requirement (or ratio), the discount rate, and interest on reserves.

Open market operations are the Fed's activities in buying and selling government bonds to commercial banks and the public. When the Fed buys a bond, it creates money in order to pay for the bond. If the Fed buys a bond from a commercial bank, the Fed takes the bond, and the bank is given more excess reserves. The banks can loan out those reserves, so the money supply can increase. Similarly, if the Fed buys a bond from an individual, the Fed writes a check, which the person deposits in the bank, increasing the bank's excess reserves. The only (and important) difference is that when the Fed increases the bank's reserves by the price of the bond, the entire amount deposited is excess reserves. But when an individual deposits the Fed's check, the bank must withhold the reserve requirement, leaving fewer excess reserves than from the direct Fed purchase. Either way, the result is the same: when the Fed buys bonds, the money supply increases. Conversely, when the Fed sells bonds, the money supply decreases because the commercial bank reserves that could have been used for loans have been used instead to buy the bonds from the Fed.

Caution

Open market operations can be confusing, in determining whether the Fed should buy or sell bonds. A simple way to remember this is to put yourself in the role of the Fed. During a recession, is the public spending too much or too little? Should you put more money *into* their hands or take money *out* of their hands? During a recession, households are buying too little, so the Fed wants to put money *into* their hands. If you are the Fed, to put more money into their hands, would you *buy* a bond *from* a household (you get the bond, and they get the money) or *sell* a bond *to* a household (you get the money and they get the bond)? To give them the money to spend, the Fed would buy a bond from them. So to correct a recessionary gap, we want the Fed to buy bonds. (And the reverse during an inflationary gap.)

The **reserve requirement** (or reserve ratio) is the percentage of deposits that banks must hold in reserve and cannot loan out. In order to increase the money supply, the Fed reduces the reserve requirement, which increases excess reserves and allows banks to make more loans. Using the money multiplier (1 / Reserve Requirement), if the reserve requirement is 10%, the multiplier is 10. A $1,000 initial deposit in the bank will result in an increase in the money supply to $10,000 ($1,000 from the initial deposit and $9,000 from the banking system). But if the reserve requirement is reduced to 5%, the multiplier becomes 20, and the same $1,000 deposit results in a $20,000 money supply ($1,000 from the initial deposit and $19,000 from the banking system). To instead reduce the money supply, the Fed increases the reserve requirement, requiring the bank to hold onto a higher percentage of checkable deposits and reduce the amount of loans. Changes in the reserve requirement are extremely powerful because they change both the amount of excess reserves and the multiplier.

The **discount rate** is the interest rate the Fed charges on loans to commercial banks. In order to increase the money supply, the Fed lowers the discount rate. The lower discount rate encourages commercial banks to borrow from the Fed, which increases the excess reserves available for loans. As more is loaned out, the money supply in the economy increases. In contrast, an increase in the discount rate makes it more expensive for commercial banks to borrow from the Fed, so they borrow less. As a consequence, banks loan out less, reducing the money supply.

Caution

Don't get confused by the word "discount," thinking of it as a coupon. Often, students think that if the discount rate is larger, a bank can borrow for a lower interest rate. Just the opposite is true. Remember that it is an interest rate, the cost of borrowing money. Also keep in mind that if the Fed is using each of its tools of monetary policy, the reserve requirement and the discount rate would move in the same direction to have the same effect. To increase the money supply, lower the reserve requirement and discount rate; to lower the money supply, raise the reserve requirement and discount rate.

As a direct result of the financial crisis, in 2008, the Fed was given a fourth tool of monetary policy – interest on excess reserves. Before that time, any excess reserves banks chose to keep at the Fed earned no interest, so banks kept little money there. Now, if the Fed wants to reduce the money supply, it can raise the interest rate paid on excess reserves stored there, so banks will move their excess reserves to the Fed rather than loaning them out. To instead increase the money supply, the Fed just lowers the interest rate it pays on these excess reserves, so banks reduce those reserves from the Fed and instead use them to make loans to households and firms.

Open market operations are the most commonly used tool of the Fed. This tool is the most flexible with the most immediate effects, allowing the Fed to make minor changes in the money supply quickly and easily. The reserve requirement is the most powerful Fed tool, because changes in the multiplier have a very powerful effect on the money supply. As a result, the Fed uses this tool very rarely – it has not been changed since 1992! The discount rate is an intermediary tool used during more serious economic downturns, while interest on excess reserves is a new tool that has hardly changed.

PRACTICE **Open-Market Operations, Reserve Ratio, Discount Rate, Interest on Reserves**

1. Assume the US is experiencing an inflationary gap and the Fed takes action to eliminate the gap.

   A. ________ Should the Fed *increase* or *decrease* the money supply?

   B. ________ Should the Fed *raise* or *lower* the reserve requirement?

   C. ________ Should the Fed *raise* or *lower* the discount rate?

   D. ________ Should the Fed *buy* or *sell* securities on the open market?

   E. ________ Should the Fed *raise* or *lower* the interest rate paid on excess reserves?

   F. ________ If the Fed undertakes steps A-E, will interest rates *rise* or *fall*?

2. ________ Which tool of the Fed is the most powerful?

3. ________ Which tool of the Fed is most frequently used?

Targeting the Federal Funds Rate

Refer to pages 614–619 of your textbook.

A CLOSER LOOK **Expansionary Monetary Policy and Restrictive Monetary Policy**

The Fed also controls the **federal funds rate,** the interest rate banks charge each other for overnight loans. At the end of each business day, banks that are holding too few reserves to meet their reserve requirement can borrow the excess reserves of other banks overnight, and repay with the federal funds rate of interest. The Fed can use open market operations to target the levels of excess reserves in banks, in order to set the desired federal funds rate. The federal funds rate is closely related to the **prime rate,** which is the lowest interest rate banks charge their best customers for loans. So the Fed's actions in changing the federal funds rate result in changes in the interest rates faced by consumers and firms across the nation. During the 2008 financial crisis, the Fed bought so many bonds that banks held massive excessive reserves, causing the federal funds rate to plunge to near zero. As long as these banks continue to hold such significant excess reserves, they need not seek overnight loans.

To resolve a recession, the Fed uses **expansionary monetary policy,** or "**easy money policy,**" to raise the money supply. Expansionary policy is achieved when the Fed lowers the reserve requirement, lowers the discount rate, buys bonds, or lowers the interest rate paid on excess reserves. When the Fed increases the money supply, interest rates fall. The lower interest rates encourage consumers to borrow to buy products and entice firms to borrow for capital investment in plant and equipment. The increase in aggregate demand causes real output and employment to increase.

If inflation is the problem, the Fed uses **contractionary monetary policy,** or "**tight money policy,**" to reduce the money supply. The Fed can increase the reserve requirement, increase the discount rate, sell bonds, or raise the interest rate paid on excess reserves to achieve contractionary policy. By reducing the money supply, the Fed allows interest rates to rise, discouraging firms and consumers from borrowing. The reduction in borrowing leaves firms and consumers with fewer funds to buy products in the economy, reducing aggregate demand, real output, and employment.

PRACTICE Expansionary Monetary Policy and Restrictive Monetary Policy

1. __________ If the Fed uses easy money policy, is it trying to correct *inflation* or *recession*?

2. __________ To conduct easy money policy, will the Fed *raise* or *lower* the money supply?

   A. __________ To achieve the objective in #2, should the Fed *raise* or *lower* the reserve requirement?

   B. __________ To achieve the objective in #2, should the Fed *raise* or *lower* the discount rate?

   C. __________ To achieve the objective in #2, should the Fed *buy* or *sell* securities in the open market?

   D. __________ To achieve the objective in #2, should interest rates paid on excess reserves *rise* or *fall*?

3. __________ If the money supply changes as indicated in #2, will interest rates *rise* or *fall*?

4. __________ If interest rates change as indicated in #3, will capital investment *rise* or *fall*?

5. __________ If investment changes as indicated in #4, will aggregate demand *rise* or *fall*?

6. __________ If aggregate demand changes as indicated in #5, will real GDP *rise* or *fall*?

7. __________ If real GDP changes as indicated in #6, will employment *rise* or *fall*?

8. __________ If all of the changes in #'s 1-7 occur, will the problem identified in #1 be resolved?

Monetary Policy, Real GDP, and the Price Level

Refer to pages 619–623 of your textbook.

A CLOSER LOOK Cause-Effect Chain, Effects of Expansionary and Contractionary Monetary Policy

The series of graphs below illustrates how monetary policy works through the linkages among the money, investment, and aggregate demand – aggregate supply markets.

Graph (a) represents the money market, with money demand representing both transactions and asset demand and the money supply set by the Fed. The equilibrium real interest rate is determined by the supply and demand for money. When the Fed increases the money supply from S_{m2} to S_{m3}, the real interest rate falls from 8% to 6%. When the Fed reduces the money supply from S_{m2} to S_{m1}, the real interest rate rises from 8% to 10%.

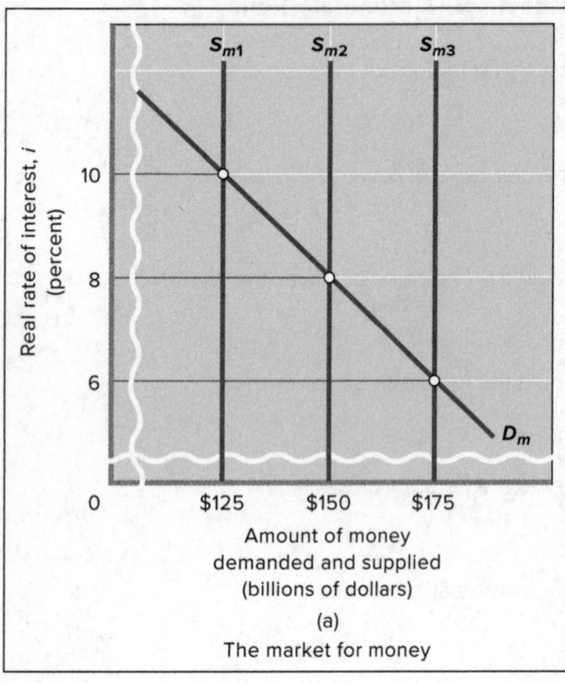

(a)
The market for money

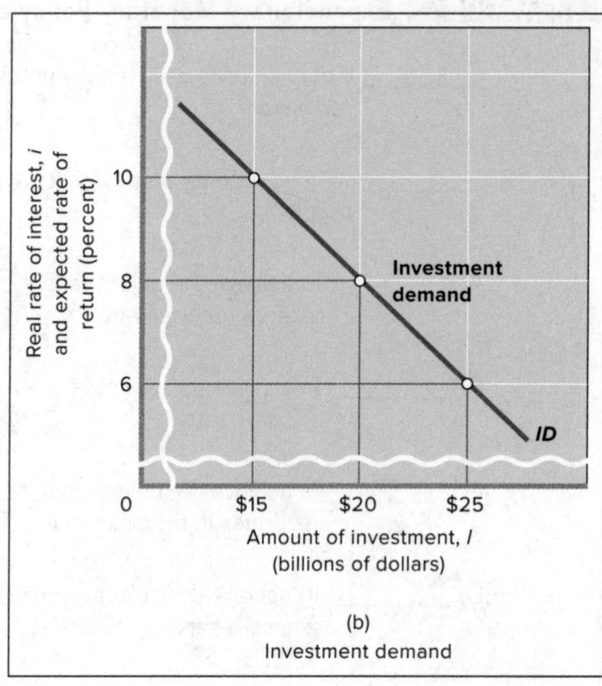

(b)
Investment demand

Graph (b) represents the investment market, where firms borrow money for equipment, expansions, and other long-term purchases. Remember, firms borrow for capital investment *only* if they expect the return on investment to be greater than the real interest rate they must pay to borrow for the purchase. When the interest rate rises, firms borrow less for capital investment. In this example, when the Fed reduces the money supply from S_{m2} to S_{m1}, raising the interest rate from 8% to 10%, investment falls from $20 billion to $15 billion. But if the interest rate falls, the quantity of money demanded for investment increases. In this example, when the Fed increases the money supply from S_{m2} to S_{m3}, the interest rate falls from 8% to 6%, causing investment to increase from $20 billion to $25 billion. Interest rate changes also affect interest-sensitive consumer borrowing for large purchases like homes and cars.

Graph (c) illustrates the effects of a recession. Assume the economy begins at full-employment equilibrium at AS and AD_2, with a real GDP of $900 billion and a price level of P_2. Then a $5 billion decrease in investment causes aggregate demand to decrease. If MPC is 0.75, with a multiplier of 4, aggregate demand falls to AD_1, resulting in a $20 billion decrease in GDP ($900 billion – $880 billion). Remember, because of the ratchet effect, prices are downwardly sticky, so the entire decrease in aggregate demand accrues to lower output.

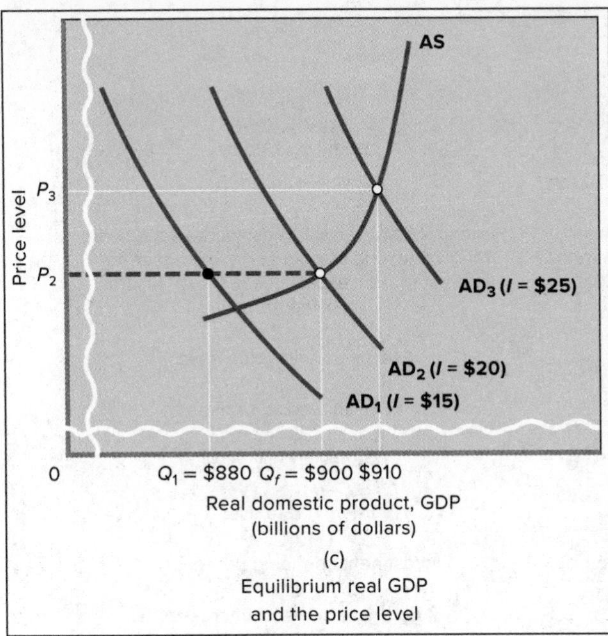

(c)
Equilibrium real GDP
and the price level

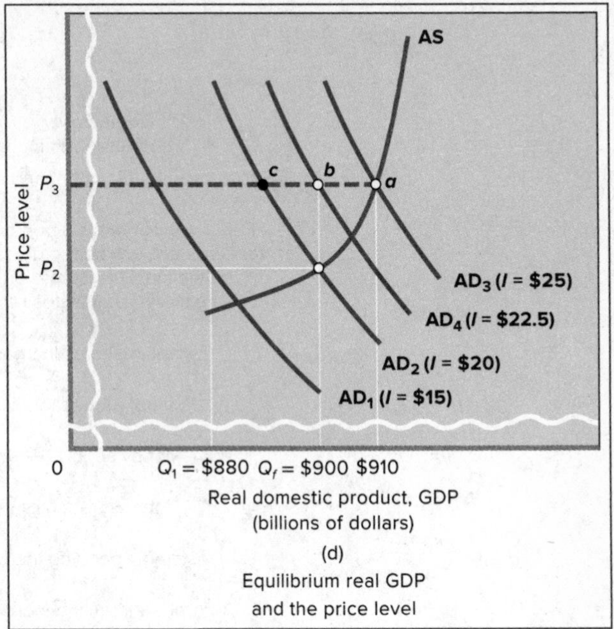

(d)
Equilibrium real GDP
and the price level

So how can the Fed increase aggregate demand to its former level? It can increase the money supply by reducing the reserve requirement or discount rate, buying bonds, reducing interest paid on excess reserves, or any combination. Using Graph (a), if the Fed increases the money supply by \$25 billion, interest rates fall by 2%. In Graph (b), the reduction in interest rates increases investment by \$5 billion. With the multiplier of 4, in Graph (c), aggregate demand expands to AD_2 again, increasing the GDP by \$20 billion and closing the recessionary gap.

Graph (d) illustrates the effects of an inflationary gap. We begin at full-employment equilibrium with AS and AD_2, with a real GDP of \$900 billion and a price level of P_2. Then assume that investment spending increases from \$20 billion to \$25 billion, shifting the aggregate demand curve from AD_2 to AD_3. Notice that with a multiplier of 4, the \$5 billion in increased investment spending would cause spending in the economy to increase by \$20 billion. But the real GDP only increased by \$10 billion, from \$900 billion to \$910 billion. Where did the other \$10 billion go? The new equilibrium at Point (a) is at price level P_3. The additional spending went into higher prices. We now have an inflationary gap of \$10 billion. The Fed can reduce the money supply by increasing the reserve requirement or discount rate, selling bonds, increasing the interest rate paid on excess reserves, or any combination. But by how much should the Fed reduce the money supply? Remember, the ratchet effect prevents the price level from falling, so any reduction in aggregate demand will accrue to output. The Fed cannot simply reduce investment by the same \$5 billion it originally increased, or aggregate demand would fall back down to AD_2, reaching equilibrium at Point c, reducing real GDP to \$890 billion, and creating a recessionary gap! The Fed only needs to reduce real GDP by \$10 billion to return to full-employment GDP at Point (b). Working with the same multiplier of 4, the Fed only needs to reduce investment by \$2.5 billion (\$10 billion / 4). So in Graph (a), the Fed would reduce the money supply by \$12.5 billion, raising the real interest rate by 1%. In Graph (b), that higher interest rate reduces investment by \$2.5 billion. Then, in Graph (d), AD_3 falls to AD_4; the \$2.5 billion initial reduction in investment, with a multiplier of 4, reduces real GDP by \$10 billion, eliminating the inflationary gap and returning the economy to equilibrium at Point (b).

Keep in Mind

(1) Expansionary Monetary Policy	(2) Restrictive Monetary Policy
Problem: unemployment and recession	*Problem:* inflation
↓	↓
Federal Reserve buys bonds, lowers reserve ratio, lowers the discount rate, reduces the interest rate on excess reserves, or initiates repos	Federal Reserve sells bonds, increases reserve ratio, raises the discount rate, increases the interest rate on excess reserves, or initiates reverse repos
↓	↓
Excess reserves increase	Excess reserves decrease
↓	↓
Federal funds rate falls	Federal funds rate rises
↓	↓
Money supply rises	Money supply falls
↓	↓
Interest rate falls	Interest rate rises
↓	↓
Investment spending increases	Investment spending decreases
↓	↓
Aggregate demand increases	Aggregate demand decreases
↓	↓
Real GDP rises	Inflation declines

Several AP Macroeconomics exam questions will depend on your ability to explain how the Fed should use its tools to address specific economic problems. You must be able to explain the changes in each step of the cause-and-effect chain. Memorize these cause-and-effect chains!

PRACTICE Cause-Effect Chain, Effects of Expansionary and Contractionary Monetary Policy

Assume the economy is in a recessionary gap. Draw a graph of the money market, labeling the equilibrium quantity of money Q_1 and the equilibrium real interest rate IR_1. Then illustrate what the Fed would change in the money market to address the recessionary gap. Label the new equilibrium quantity of money Q_2 and the new equilibrium real interest rate IR_2. Then answer the questions below.

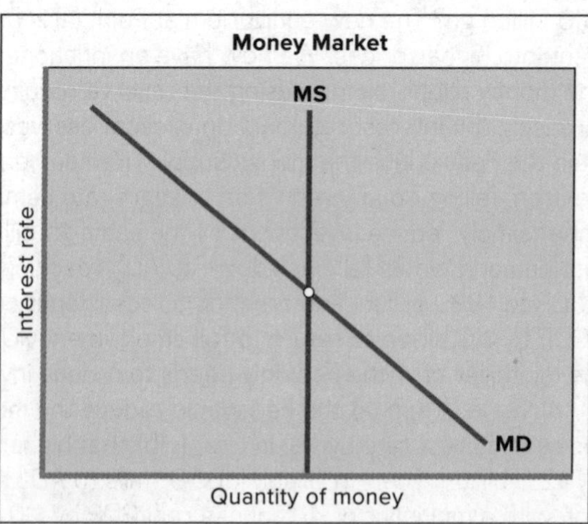

1. __________ If the Fed wants to raise spending, what open market operation should it use?

2. __________ If the Fed does as indicated in #1, what will happen to the money supply?

3. __________ If money supply changes as indicated in #2, what will happen to interest rates?

4. __________ If the interest rate changes as indicated in #3, what will happen to investment?

5. __________ If investment changes as indicated in #4, what happens to aggregate demand?

6. __________ If aggregate demand changes as indicated in #5, what will happen to real GDP?

7. __________ If real GDP changes as indicated in #6, what will happen to employment?

Monetary Policy: Evaluation and Issues

Refer to pages 623–625 of your textbook.

A CLOSER LOOK Problems and Limitations

One primary advantage of monetary policy is that it can be made very quickly in a meeting of the Board of Governors, while Congress may take months to pass fiscal policy. A second advantage is the flexibility of monetary policy. The Fed can buy or sell bonds on a daily basis in an attempt to "fine tune" the economy, while fiscal tax and spending measures have much broader effects across the economy. A third important advantage is that members of the Fed are insulated from political pressure, making it easier for them to reduce the money supply and raise interest rates to fight inflation. Members of Congress who must be reelected find it much more difficult to raise taxes or cut government spending on popular programs during periods of inflation. Another important difference is that Congress has a wide variety of items on its agenda, and if taxes or spending must be changed to address a more important concern – for example, a decision to go to war – the economic impact is only a secondary concern. The Fed's *only* concern is the economy, so its policies are determined from that focus.

Monetary policy also faces limitations. Remember that fiscal policy faces recognition, administrative, and operational lags before fully taking effect. Monetary policy also encounters problems with the time required to recognize that an economic problem has surfaced, as well as a three- to six-month lag for the interest rate changes to affect investment, aggregate demand, and real GDP. The Fed, however, avoids the administrative lag of actually making the policy; it can do so within days. But even monetary policy implementation requires time to address economic instability.

A more serious problem of monetary policy is that it is much more effective in reducing inflation than it is in stimulating aggregate demand during a recession. During inflation, the Fed can effectively reduce the money supply and raise interest rates to levels that reduce investment and aggregate demand. However, when it comes to expansionary monetary policy, the Fed faces challenges. While it makes reserves available for banks to lend, it can't do anything more than make those reserves available. It cannot force anyone to borrow the money. During recessions, many people lose jobs or fear losing their jobs, so they are less likely to seek loans to buy homes or cars. Firms are also hesitant to borrow during recessions, because as they reduce production, revenues fall and they gain excess capacity. Due to the lack of confidence in the economy, even the lower interest rate may not entice firms and households to borrow. The banks may also choose not to grant as many loans at the lower interest rates, hoping the recession will be short and they can begin lending at higher interest rates again. Another limitation is that customers may not deposit their money back into banks. If loans and deposits are not made, the money multiplier cannot take effect to increase the money supply. This has been referred to as the Fed "pushing a rope." While the Fed can effectively use the money supply as a rope to pull down aggregate demand, it cannot as effectively push the rope to increase aggregate demand.

In October 2008, as the financial crisis deepened, Congress passed TARP to purchase assets and equity from banks, to encourage them to make loans. In December 2008, the Fed reduced the federal funds rate to 0-1/4% and the discount rate to 1/2%. By February 2009, banks were not increasing loans, and firms needing loans to survive the recession faced a credit crisis. The Fed's attempts to "push the rope" weren't effective enough. By that point, the US economy had entered a **liquidity trap,** a condition where interest rates have already fallen so low that reducing them further would have no stimulative effect on the economy. So the Fed instead engaged in **quantitative easing,** buying nearly $4 trillion in bonds, not for the purpose of reducing interest rates (because they were already at or near zero), but solely for the purpose of increasing the amount of reserves in the banking system.

The Federal Reserve and Congress each make policy independent of the other, though members of Congress often invite the Chairman of the Federal Reserve Board of Governors to testify about economic conditions and the effects of fiscal and monetary policy in certain conditions. Because the policies are made independently and affect the economy in different ways, it is important to consider how such policies work in combination.

If the Fed identifies a recessionary gap and increases the money supply, interest rates fall. Investment increases, so aggregate demand rises, increasing real GDP and employment. If Congress identifies the same recessionary gap and uses fiscal policy to directly stimulate aggregate demand, then real GDP and employment will increase. The monetary and fiscal policies have the same effect in the aggregate demand – aggregate supply model. But because Congress must borrow money to finance the deficit created by the expansionary policy, the government's increased demand for money in the loanable funds market pushes the interest rate up, which can crowd out private investment. While expansionary monetary policy reduces interest rates, expansionary fiscal policy increases interest rates, and the effects of monetary policy can be diluted by the **crowding out.** The final effect on interest rates depends on the relative strength of the policies.

If, instead, Congress and the Fed decide to address different economic problems, their policies could have contradictory effects. In the case of **stagflation,** where high inflation and high unemployment occur simultaneously, the Fed may choose to address the inflation problem because its tools are most effective in addressing inflation. So if the Fed reduces the money supply to increase interest rates, then aggregate demand and employment fall. The Fed has addressed the problem of inflation, but it has caused an increase in unemployment. At the same time, Congress may choose to address the problem of unemployment, because constituents will oppose fiscal anti-inflation measures. If Congress reduces taxes and raises spending to increase aggregate demand, it will reduce unemployment, but it will probably increase the inflation rate. In addition, to conduct this fiscal policy, government must borrow funds, and the increased demand in the loanable funds market will again raise interest rates. In this case, both the fiscal and monetary policies are consistent in increasing interest rates, but the monetary policy works to reduce aggregate demand while the fiscal policy works to increase it.

One last consideration is how these policies affect long-run economic growth. Long-run economic growth results from investment in plant and equipment and increased productivity of workers. Keeping interest rates low is essential to investment. When interest rates are low, firms are more likely to invest in plant and equipment, so the aggregate demand increases in the short run as firms make those purchases. But low interest rates also increase long-run aggregate supply after the firms have finished expansions and installation of equipment, because production increases at a lower cost per unit. Expansionary monetary policies reduce interest rates in the money market to promote investment, while contractionary fiscal policies reduce government borrowing in the loanable funds market, and the combination holds interest rates down to promote long-run economic growth.

Disagreements about the use of fiscal and monetary policy abound. Some members of Congress don't want "unelected" members of the Fed using monetary policy, while some in the Fed would prefer that Congress leave economic policy decisions to the professional economists at the Fed. Others argue that attempts by Congress and the Fed to stabilize the economy only make the economy more unstable! Even among those who agree to use fiscal and monetary policy, disputes arise as to whether an inflationary or recessionary gap is large enough to merit intervention – and further arguments ensue about which tools to use and how powerfully to employ them. Remember, the multiplier is in play, and policymakers are attempting to make decisions in real time. How much of a gap is initial, and how much is as a result of the multiplier, as the gap continues to widen? And what are the policy side-effects for employment, exchange rates, international trade, and investment? Now you can see how what seemed like such an easy remedy is in fact very complicated and has serious ramifications for the economy.

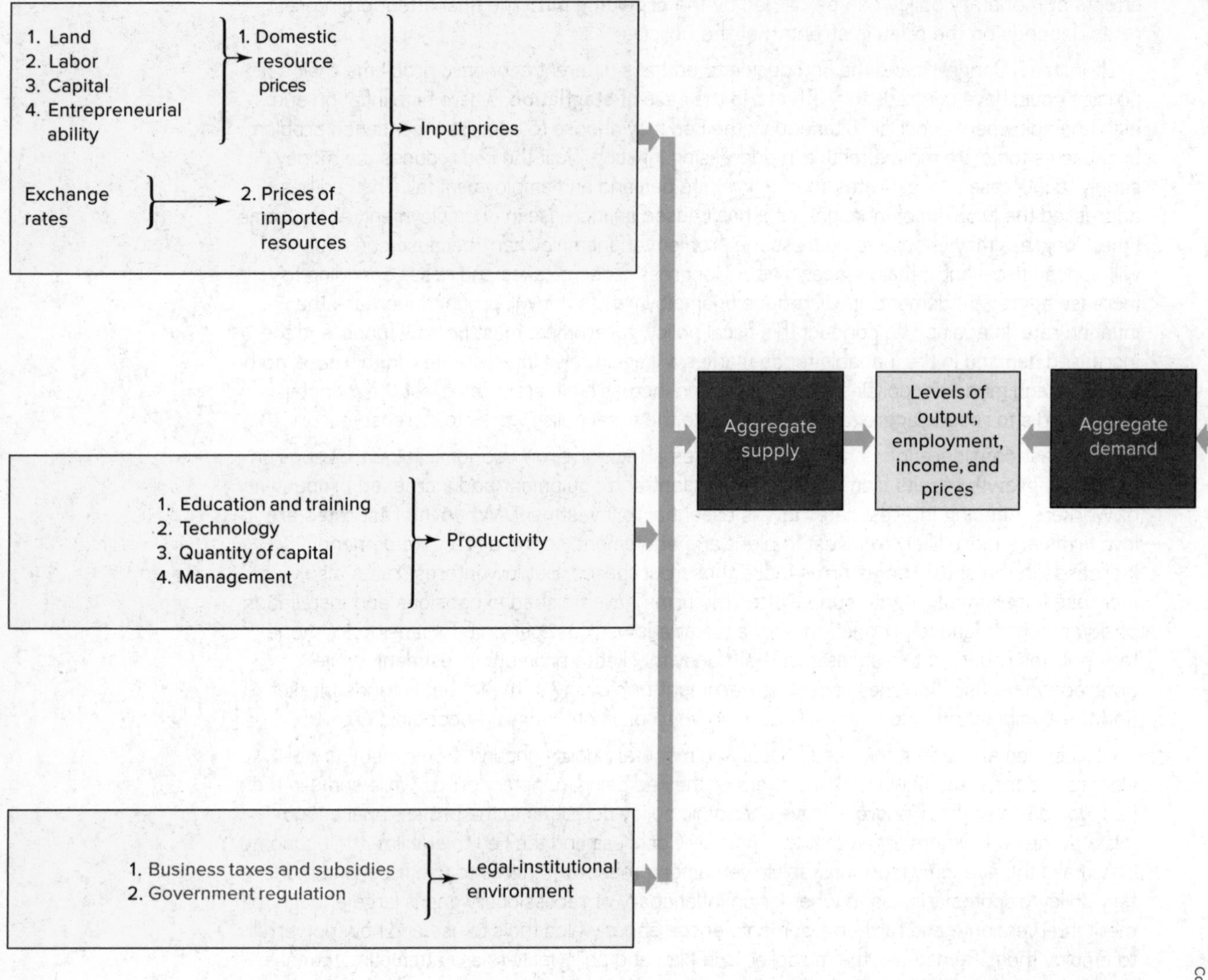

Caution

"The Big Picture" brings together aggregate supply and aggregate demand in a way that shows the cause-and-effect linkages of monetary and fiscal policy. This figure explains the process in a way that will help you to achieve stronger scores on free-response questions of the AP Macroeconomics exam.

PRACTICE Problems and Limitations

1. Monetary policy tends to be less effective if:

   A. __________ People choose to apply for *more* or *fewer* loans.

   B. __________ Banks choose to grant *more* or *fewer* loans.

   C. __________ People choose to hold their money *at the bank* or *at home.*

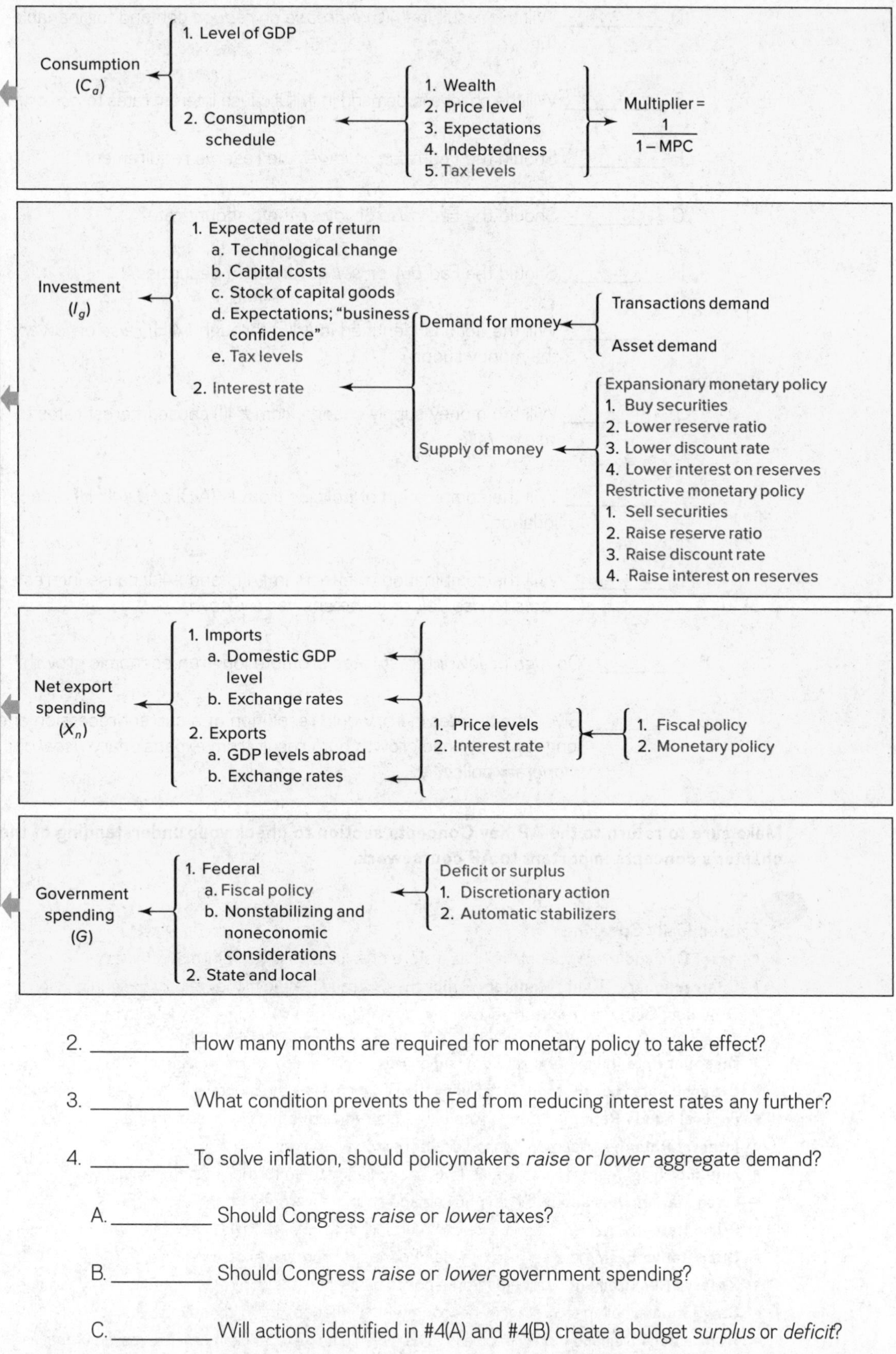

2. __________ How many months are required for monetary policy to take effect?

3. __________ What condition prevents the Fed from reducing interest rates any further?

4. __________ To solve inflation, should policymakers *raise* or *lower* aggregate demand?

   A. __________ Should Congress *raise* or *lower* taxes?

   B. __________ Should Congress *raise* or *lower* government spending?

   C. __________ Will actions identified in #4(A) and #4(B) create a budget *surplus* or *deficit*?

D. _________ Will the result in #4(C) *increase* or *reduce* demand for loanable funds?

E. _________ Will the change in demand in #4(D) cause interest rates to *rise* or *fall*?

F. _________ Should the Fed *raise* or *lower* the reserve requirement?

G. _________ Should the Fed *raise* or *lower* the discount rate?

H. _________ Should the Fed *buy* or *sell* government securities?

I. _________ Will the actions identified in #4(F) through #4(H) *raise* or *lower* the money supply?

J. _________ Will the money supply change from #4(I) cause interest rates to *rise* or *fall*?

K. _________ Will the combination of policies from #4(A-B) and #4(F-H) reduce inflation?

L. _________ Will the combination of effects in #4(E) and #4(J) cause interest rates to *rise, fall*, or is the answer *unknown*?

5. _________ Do *high* or *low* interest rates promote long-run economic growth?

6. _________ Given the answer in #5, would resolution of a current recession and long-run economic growth both result from expansionary *fiscal* or *monetary* policy?

Make sure to return to the AP Key Concepts section to check your understanding of the chapter's concepts important to AP coursework.

Economically Speaking

- **Asset Demand** money people hold as a store of value, to use for future purchases
- **Contractionary "Tight" Monetary Policy** the Fed reduces the money supply to fight inflation
- **Crowding Out** an increase in government demand for money to finance deficits raises the interest rate in the loanable funds market, reducing private investment
- **Discount Rate** the interest rate the Fed charges on loans to commercial banks
- **Expansionary "Loose" Monetary Policy** the Fed increases the money supply to fight recession
- **Federal Funds Rate** the interest rate banks charge each other for overnight loans
- **Interest Rate** the price paid for the use of borrowed money
- **Liquidity Trap** interest rates are so low that reducing them further has no stimulative effect
- **Open Market Operations** the Fed buying and selling government bonds
- **Prime Rate** the lowest interest rate commercial banks charge their best customers for loans
- **Quantitative Easing** the Fed's purchase of bonds to increase excess reserves
- **Reserve Requirement** percentage of deposits banks must hold in reserve and cannot loan out
- **Stagflation** simultaneous stagnant economy, high inflation, and high unemployment
- **Transactions Demand** money people hold as a medium of exchange in order to make purchases

Financial Economics

While firms engage in economic investment to buy plant and equipment, financial investment is the term most people use to refer to the purchase of assets for future income. Chapter 31 describes financial instruments in which people invest.

Little material from Chapter 31 is likely to appear on an AP Economics exam, although the concept of present value is important to understand.

Key Concepts

Below is a summary of the chapter's concepts important to AP coursework.

- Economic investment is firms' addition to capital stock – new factories or equipment or new replacements for depreciated capital equipment.
- Financial investment, as the term is commonly used, refers to individuals buying an asset with the expectation of making a financial gain on the investment (buying stock, commodities, real estate, baseball cards, or famous paintings).
- Present value calculates the current value of money that one expects to receive in the future from an investment.
- A specific amount of money is more valuable the sooner it is received, because it can be invested with compound interest. This is why you will often see lottery winners take smaller payoffs now rather than waiting for annual payments over many years; they can invest the smaller amounts now and make even better returns than the original lottery winnings.
- Stocks are shares of ownership in corporations; profits are paid to shareholders as dividends.
- Bonds are loans to corporations or the government that are repaid with interest.
- Diversification, spreading money among many different investments, helps to reduce risk.
- A mutual fund combines the funds of hundreds or thousands of investors. A professional manager diversifies the investment over a variety of stocks and bonds. Professional management and diversity provide the investor some protection from risk in the market.
- Investments with higher risk tend to have a higher expected rate of return, to compensate those who are willing to take the higher risk.
- Changes in the value of stock and bonds create a wealth effect, which can affect aggregate demand in the economy. If investment values rise, consumers increase their demand for products; when investment values fall, aggregate demand falls.

- Changes in Federal Reserve policies that affect interest rates also change aggregate demand. If interest rates rise, firms tend to reduce investment and consumers buy fewer interest-sensitive goods, such as houses and cars. Lower interest rates tend to increase aggregate demand in the short run, as firms buy capital and consumers buy goods. Lower interest rates also increase long-run economic growth, and increase aggregate supply, as a result of capital investment.

PRACTICE Financial Economics

1. __________ Are higher rates of return usually paid on investments with *higher* or *lower* risk?

2. __________ As the values of stocks rise and households have more wealth, will aggregate demand *rise* or *fall*?

3. __________ Given the difference between the present value and future value of money, would a contractor prefer to be paid $50,000 in two installments each (ex: one payment now and one, six months from now) or the entire sum of $100,000 now?

Economically Speaking

- **Bond** a loan to a corporation or government, which is repaid with interest
- **Compound Interest** the effect of paying interest on an investment, and then paying interest again on the original investment plus all previous interest payments
- **Diversification** spreading money among many different investments
- **Dividends** profit payments to stockholders
- **Economic Investment** a firm's capital purchase of plant and equipment
- **Financial Investment** buying an asset with the expectation of making a financial gain
- **Mutual Fund** a professional combines the funds of many investors to buy stocks and bonds and manages the fund
- **Present Value** the present-day value of returns that are expected to arrive in the future
- **Stock** a share of ownership in a corporation, which earns dividends

Chapter 32

Extending the Analysis of Aggregate Supply

Our exploration of macroeconomics to this point has focused on measuring economic performance and the policies used to achieve short-run economic stabilization. We now turn to long-run economic growth and differing views on policies affecting aggregate supply. Chapter 32 focuses on aggregate supply, the relationship between inflation and unemployment in the short run and long run, and differences among economic theories about aggregate supply. These differences explain much of the debate between schools of economic thought, which will be explored in Chapter 33.

Material from Chapter 32 frequently appears in several multiple-choice questions and as a free-response question on the AP Macroeconomics exam.

Key Concepts

Below is a summary of the chapter's concepts important to AP coursework. Upon completing the lessons that follow, return to these concepts to make sure you understand them and how the practice exercises you completed relate to them.

- In the short run, input prices are fixed; in the long run, input prices are flexible.
- Long-run aggregate supply is a vertical curve placed at full-employment output.
- Long-run equilibrium is when aggregate supply and demand meet at long-run aggregate supply.
    - A recessionary gap shows short-run equilibrium to the left of long-run aggregate supply.
    - An inflationary gap shows short-run equilibrium to the right of long-run aggregate supply.
- In the short run, an increase in aggregate demand increases output, employment, and prices, because when costs of production don't rise, firms make higher profit.
    - In the long run, resource demand pushes up production costs, so aggregate supply falls; firms reduce output and employment and return to full-employment output at a higher price level.
- In the short run, a decrease in short-run aggregate supply reduces output and employment and increases prices, because an increase in the cost of production reduces profit.
    - In the long run, only after a long period of unemployment, workers will accept lower wages, so aggregate supply will increase again; policymakers may instead use expansionary fiscal or monetary policy to increase aggregate demand to return to full-employment output.

- In the short run, a decrease in aggregate demand reduces output, employment, and prices, because when prices fall, firms can't cover the costs of production.
    - In the long run, after some period of unemployment, workers may accept lower wages, so aggregate supply rises; policymakers may instead use fiscal or monetary policy to increase aggregate demand.
- Ongoing inflation occurs because aggregate demand grows slightly more than aggregate supply.
- Long-run economic growth occurs due to improvements in technology, increases in the amount and efficient use of resources, and low interest rates that make investment possible.
- The Phillips curve illustrates the short-run tradeoff between inflation and unemployment rates.
    - In the short run, a rise in aggregate demand lowers unemployment and raises inflation.
    - Policymakers use fiscal and monetary policy to correct inflation and unemployment.
    - A decrease in aggregate supply causes stagflation, causing the Phillips curve to shift outward, so both the unemployment rate and the inflation rate rise together.
- The long-run Phillips curve is vertical at the natural rate of unemployment; it can shift due to changes in the number of workers or policies that change the length of unemployment.
- In the long run, there is no tradeoff between inflation and unemployment.
- Supply-side economists advocate lower taxes to increase aggregate supply for economic growth.
- The Laffer curve shows the relationship between the tax rate and tax revenue.
    - Starting at 0% tax rate, as the tax rate increases, government revenue increases.
    - At some point, a high tax rate creates a work disincentive and revenue falls.
- Attempts to use supply-side theory show that tax cuts increase aggregate demand, not supply.

Now, let's examine more closely the following concepts from your textbook:

- **From Short Run to Long Run**
- **Applying the Extended AD-AS Model**
- **The Inflation-Unemployment Relationship**
- **The Long-Run Phillips Curve**
- **Taxation and Aggregate Supply**

These sections were selected because the transition from short-run to long-run changes in macroeconomic equilibrium can be confusing, and a step-by-step approach to practicing can help.

From Short Run to Long Run

Refer to pages 658–660 of your textbook.

A CLOSER LOOK Short-Run and Long-Run Aggregate Supply and Long-Run Equilibrium

After the Great Depression, economists focused on using the tools of fiscal and monetary policy to stabilize the economy in the short run. Most economists had believed that the economy would correct itself in the long run. John Maynard Keynes said, "In the long run, we are all dead!" Economic performance in both the short run and long run is important to policymakers, firms, and consumers.

The difference between the short run and the long run is the flexibility of input prices, especially wages. In the **short run,** input prices are fixed; in the **long run,** input prices are flexible.

The **short-run aggregate supply curve** is upward-sloping, as shown in Graph (a) below. Point a_1 represents the price level (P_1) at **full-employment output** (Q_f). This output also represents the natural rate of unemployment. If the price level increases to P_2, firms are enticed to increase output, because if production costs do not change, firms can increase their profits. In the short run, the firm increases output beyond full-employment output by hiring workers and offering overtime to current workers. So in the short run, real GDP, the price level, and employment all increase as the unemployment rate falls.

Conversely, if the price level falls to P_3 but costs of production do not fall, revenues no longer cover the firms' costs. As firms lose money, they reduce output and lay off workers. The real GDP falls, prices fall, and employment falls as the unemployment rate increases.

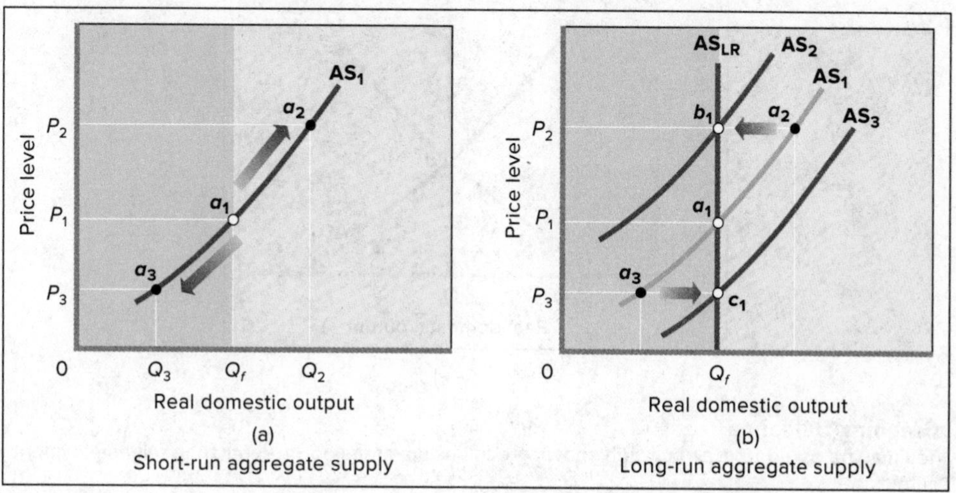

The **long-run aggregate supply curve** is vertical at full-employment output. This long-run aggregate supply curve develops as a result of long-run adjustments to short-run changes in production, as shown in Graph (b). In the short run, an increase in price level to P_2 resulted in a movement from a_1 to a_2 on the aggregate supply curve, with firms increasing output because of increased profit. But this was based on the assumption that the costs of production (notably wages) would not increase. However, in the long run, the increased demand for labor and other materials pushes up the cost of those inputs. As a result of the higher costs of production, the aggregate supply curve shifts back to the left (from AS_1 to AS_2) until output returns to full-employment output on the long-run aggregate supply curve (at Point b_1).

In the same way, a decrease in the price level leads firms to reduce output and employment along AS_1, from a_1 to a_3, because their lower revenues cannot cover their costs. However, in the long run, workers are willing to accept lower wages during a period of high, lengthy unemployment. If wages are downwardly flexible, the lower demand for resources leads to lower resource costs. The lower cost of production causes the short-run aggregate supply curve to increase from AS_1 to AS_3, until output returns to full-employment output on the long-run aggregate supply curve at Point c_1.

Now that we can see the difference between the short-run and long-run aggregate supply curves, we can put them together with aggregate demand on the graph. Long-run equilibrium occurs at full-employment output where short-run aggregate supply and aggregate demand meet long-run aggregate supply at Point a. The economy produces at full-employment output and the natural rate of unemployment is achieved. Short-run equilibrium occurs at the output where short-run aggregate supply equals aggregate demand, but their intersection may not meet at long-run aggregate supply. In the short run, this equilibrium can occur at an output greater than full-employment output (a point to the right of Point a), illustrating an inflationary gap. A short-run recessionary gap can also occur if equilibrium occurs at a lower output, to the left of Point a.

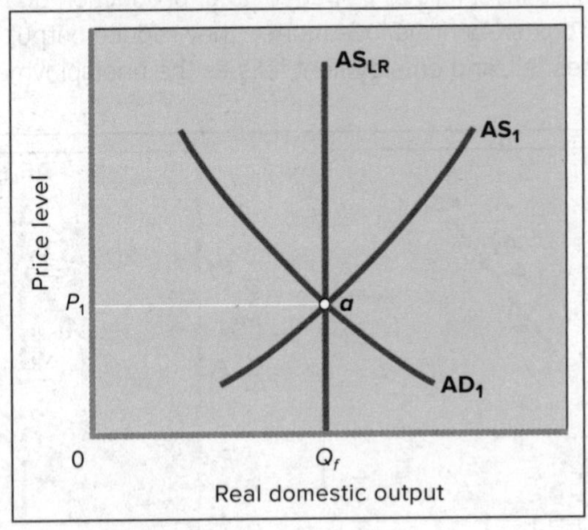

Graphing Guidance

You may be asked to draw a graph showing equilibrium at less or greater than full-employment output.

An economy producing at less than full-employment GDP must show the vertical long-run aggregate supply (LRAS) curve, with short-run aggregate supply (SRAS) and aggregate demand (AD) crossing to the *left* of full-employment output. It is important to draw your equilibrium lines illustrating the current output (real GDP) and price level at that point. An economy producing at greater than full-employment output would have the vertical LRAS, with SRAS and AD crossing to the *right* of full-employment output.

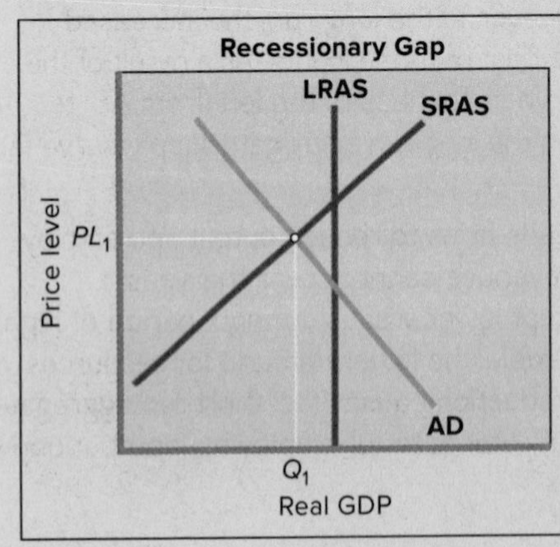

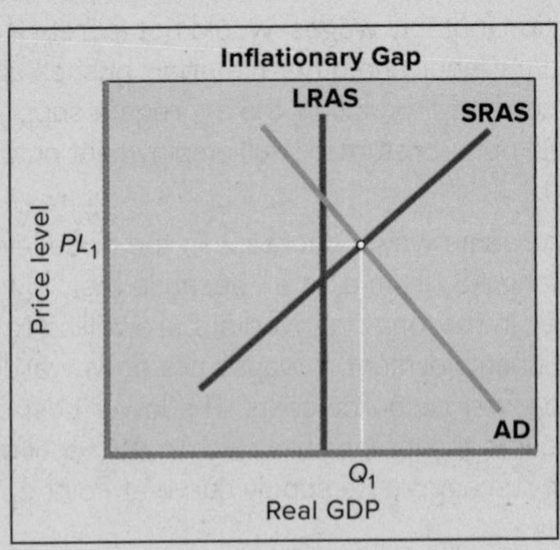

PRACTICE Short-Run and Long-Run Aggregate Supply and Long-Run Equilibrium

Assume the economy is initially in long-run equilibrium, and then aggregate demand increases.

1. ________ Will output *increase, decrease,* or *remain the same* in the short run?

2. ________ Will the price level *increase, decrease,* or *remain the same* in the short run?

3. ________ Will wages *increase, decrease,* or *remain the same* in the short run?

4. ________ Will profit *increase, decrease,* or *remain the same* in the short run?

5. ________ Will wages *increase, decrease,* or *remain the same* in the long run?

6. ________ Will profit *increase, decrease,* or *remain the same* in the long run?

7. ________ Will output *increase, decrease,* or *remain the same* in the long run?

8. ________ Will the price level *increase, decrease,* or *remain the same* in the long run?

Applying the Extended AD-AS Model

Refer to pages 660–664 of your textbook.

A CLOSER LOOK Demand-Pull Inflation in the Extended AD-AS Model

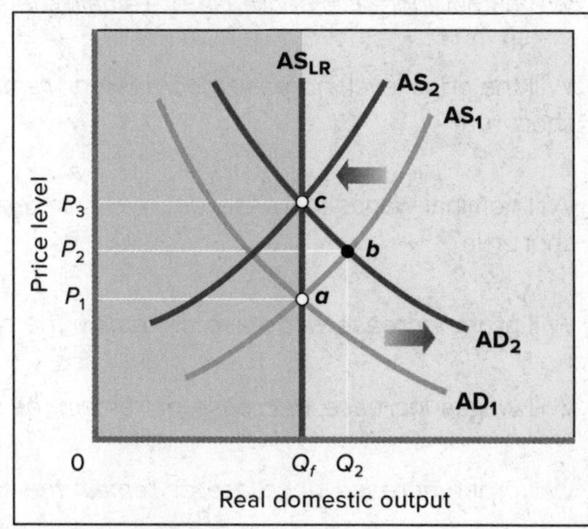

Demand-pull inflation occurs when aggregate demand increases, pushing current spending to greater than full-employment output. An increase from AD_1 to AD_2 increases equilibrium from Point a to Point b and results in a positive GDP gap. In the short run, input prices like wages do not change, so profit rises and output increases beyond full-employment output to Q_2, while the price level increases to P_2.

But in the long run, increased demand for resources like labor causes nominal wages to rise. This raises the firms' costs of production and results in a leftward shift in the short-run aggregate supply curve from AS_1 to AS_2, until equilibrium comes to rest at Point c, with full-employment output at a higher price level (P_3). In the short run, an increase in aggregate demand causes both output and price level to increase; in the long run, only the price level will increase along the vertical long-run aggregate supply curve.

PRACTICE **Demand-Pull Inflation in the Extended AD-AS Model**

Draw an aggregate demand – aggregate supply graph in long-run equilibrium. Label full-employment output Q_e and full-employment price level P_e. Then assume the government significantly increases defense spending. Draw the resulting change in aggregate supply *or* aggregate demand on the graph. Label the new equilibrium output Q_1 and equilibrium price level P_1. Then answer the questions below.

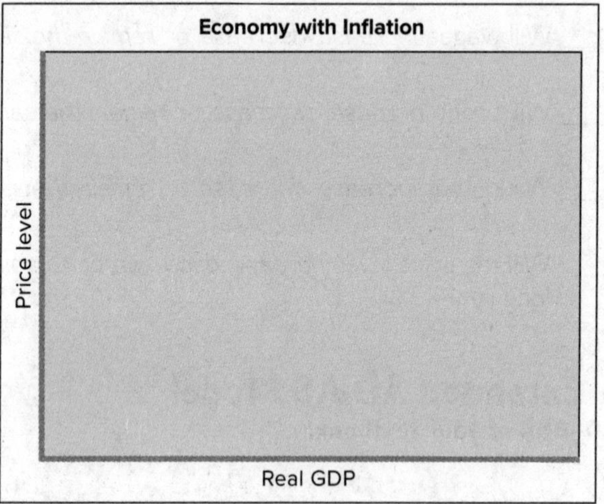

1. __________ Will output *increase, decrease,* or *remain the same* in the short run?

2. __________ Will the price level *increase, decrease,* or *remain the same* in the short run?

3. __________ Will nominal wages *increase, decrease,* or *remain the same* in the short run?

4. __________ Will profit *increase, decrease,* or *remain the same* in the short run?

5. __________ Will wages *increase, decrease,* or *remain the same* in the long run?

6. __________ Will profit *increase, decrease,* or *remain the same* in the long run?

7. __________ Will output *increase, decrease,* or *remain the same* in the long run?

8. __________ Will the price level *increase, decrease,* or *remain the same* in the long run?

A CLOSER LOOK Cost-Push Inflation in the Extended AD-AS Model

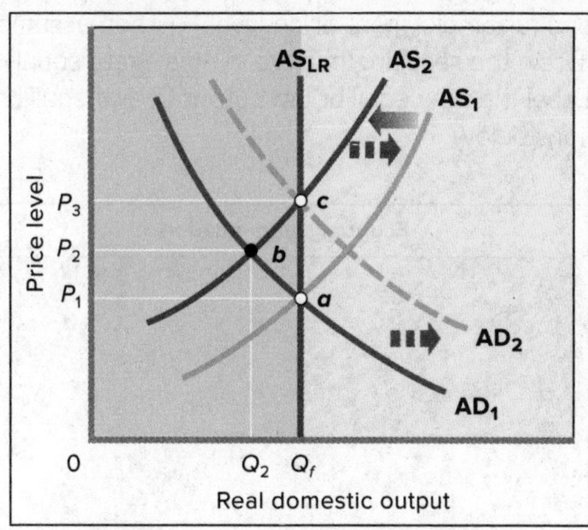

Cost-push inflation results from an increase in costs of production. Short-run aggregate supply falls from AS_1 to AS_2, changing equilibrium from Point a to Point b, causing a negative GDP gap. So the price level rises from P_1 to P_2 and output falls to Q_2. But unlike demand-pull inflation, a leftward shift in aggregate supply will not soon return the economy to full-employment output, because this situation *began* with a decrease in aggregate supply. The economy will not self-adjust with *another* decrease in aggregate supply. If policymakers use fiscal or monetary policy to increase aggregate demand and restore the economy to full-employment output, it does so at the expense of a higher price level of P_3 at Point c.

Policymakers could instead decide to adopt a hands-off approach, allowing the economy to linger in recession until deep unemployment and significant business failures create serious downward pressure on wages. As the costs of production fall, aggregate supply again increases from AS_2 to AS_1, until the economy returns from Point b to Point a at full-employment output with the lower price level.

Stagflation, with high inflation and unemployment, was the dilemma policymakers faced in the 1970s. If policymakers focused on reducing unemployment by increasing aggregate demand, the inflation rate would rise even more steeply. If they instead focused on reducing inflation, they would further increase unemployment. Decreases in aggregate supply create very painful choices for policymakers.

Keep in Mind

AP Macroeconomics exam questions will ask to you assume that wages and prices are flexible or downwardly rigid, or that short-run aggregate supply is horizontal or upward-sloping. Watch for assumptions in the questions, as they provide valuable clues that are essential to your analysis.

PRACTICE Cost-Push Inflation in the Extended AD-AS Model

Draw an aggregate demand – aggregate supply graph in long-run equilibrium. Label full-employment output Q_e and full-employment price level P_e. Then assume the cost of oil significantly increases. Draw the resulting change in aggregate supply *or* aggregate demand on the graph. Label the new equilibrium output Q_1 and equilibrium price level P_1. Then answer the questions below.

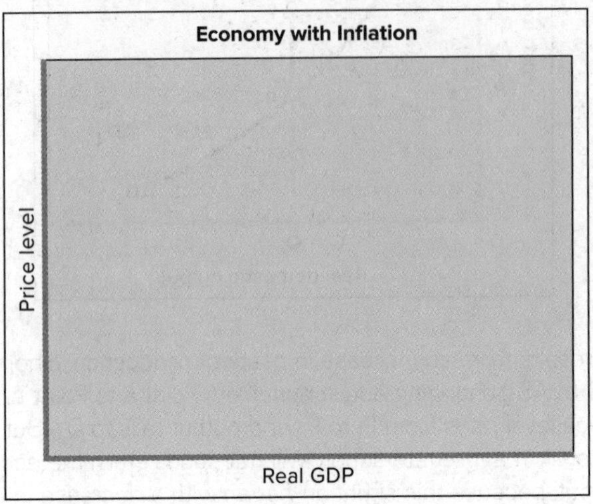

1. _________ Will output *increase, decrease,* or *remain the same* in the short run?

2. _________ Will the price level *increase, decrease,* or *remain the same* in the short run?

3. _________ Will nominal wages *increase, decrease,* or *remain the same* in the short run?

4. _________ Will profit *increase, decrease,* or *remain the same* in the short run?

Now assume policymakers use expansionary fiscal and monetary policy. Answer the question below.

5. _________ Will aggregate demand *increase, decrease,* or *remain the same* in the long run?

6. _________ Will short-run aggregate supply *increase, decrease,* or *remain the same?*

7. _________ Will output *increase, decrease,* or *remain the same* in the long run?

8. _________ Will the price level *increase, decrease,* or *remain the same* in the long run?

A CLOSER LOOK Recession and the Extended AD-AS Model

Recessions result from a decrease in aggregate demand. Assume the economy begins in long-run equilibrium at Point a. Then aggregate demand shifts to the left, from AD_1 to AD_2. If prices are downwardly flexible, the price level falls from P_1 to P_2, while output falls to Q_1, causing an increase in unemployment. If the recession is long and deep enough, workers may finally accept lower wages in order to have any job at all. The lower cost of production for firms would increase aggregate supply from AS_1 to AS_2, eventually restoring the economy to full employment at Point c, at a lower price level.

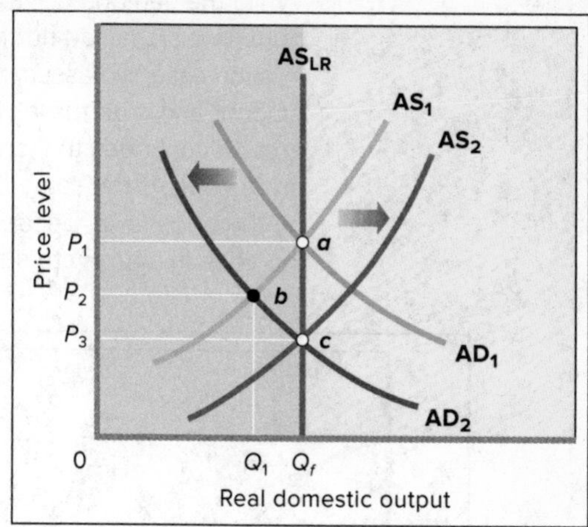

Economists disagree whether adopting a hands-off approach is effective or even reasonable during a recession. It assumes that wages and other costs are downwardly flexible. It also requires a willingness to allow workers to remain unemployed for months or even years, just waiting for costs of production to fall. Economists recognize that this approach is not acceptable, and they promote the use of monetary and fiscal policy to address recessionary gaps. This issue will be explored more deeply in Chapter 33.

PRACTICE Recession and the Extended AD-AS Model

1. Draw an aggregate demand – aggregate supply graph to illustrate an economy in recession. Label full-employment output Q_e and label the short-run equilibrium output Q_1 and equilibrium price level P_1. Then answer the questions below.

Economy in Recession

Price level

Real GDP

A. __________ What open market policy should the Fed use to stimulate the economy?

B. __________ What should Congress do to spending to stimulate the economy?

C. __________ Will fiscal and monetary policy increase aggregate *demand* or *supply*?

D. __________ As a result of #1(A) and #1(B), will output and employment *rise* or *fall*?

E. __________ As a result of #1(A) and #1(B), will the price level *rise* or *fall*?

2. Assume policymakers choose not to act to address the recession.

A. __________ In the long run, will *aggregate demand* or *aggregate supply* increase?

B. __________ As a result of #2(A), will output and employment *rise* or *fall*?

C. __________ As a result of #2(A), will the price level *rise* or *fall*?

A CLOSER LOOK Economic Growth with Ongoing Inflation

While the demand-pull and cost-push models show the effects of a temporary increase in price levels, they do not fully explain the ongoing inflation that occurs in modern economies. In each case, we assumed that the aggregate demand or supply had shifted by a fixed amount and then there was a response. In reality, the curves remain in motion. Economic growth continues to increase aggregate supply, putting a slight downward pressure on the price level. At the same time, increases in aggregate demand put a slight upward pressure on the price level. Because the increase in aggregate demand is slightly stronger than the increase in aggregate supply, a small but persistent inflation rate results.

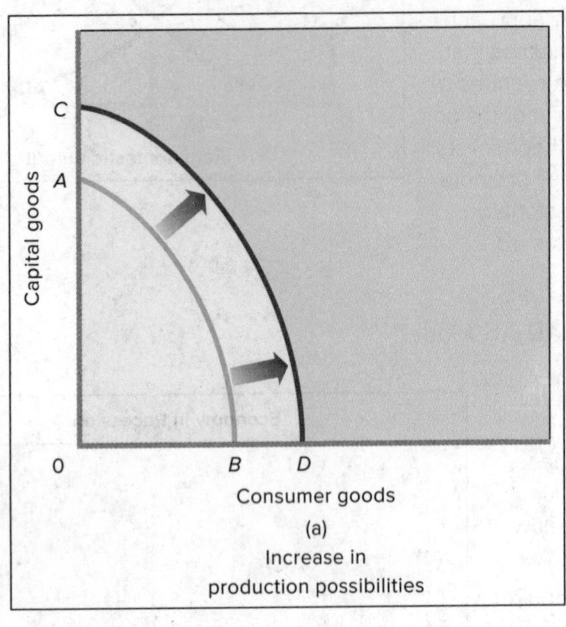

(a)
Increase in production possibilities

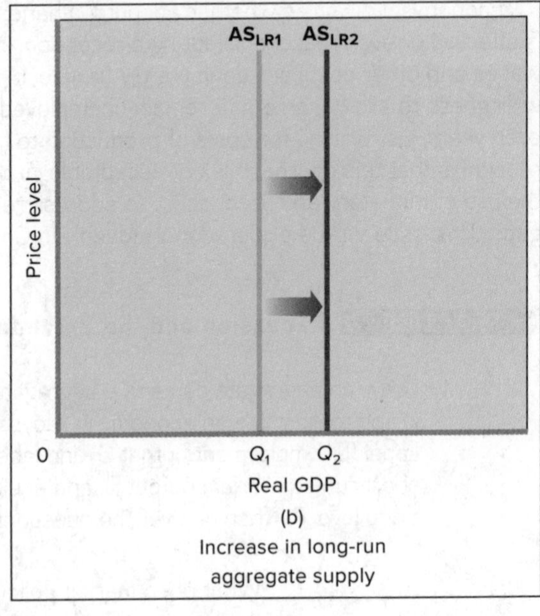

(b)
Increase in long-run aggregate supply

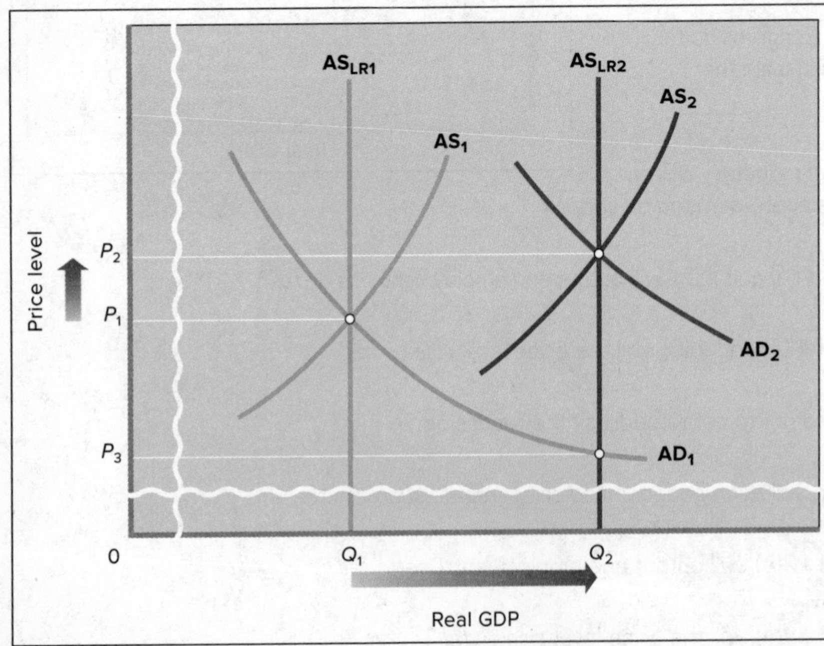

Long-run economic growth results from improvements in technology, an increase in the amount of land, labor, and capital resources, or more efficient use of resources. An outward shift in the production possibilities curve allows us to produce more of all products. In the same way, a rightward shift of the long-run aggregate supply curve demonstrates the economy is capable of producing more products.

Low interest rates, which allow for increased investment in plant and equipment, are important for promoting long-run economic growth. While such purchases of plant and equipment initially increase short-run aggregate demand, bringing such improvements into operation increases the long-run aggregate supply, shifting it to the right. As firms actually increase output at the lower cost of production, short-run aggregate supply increases. And in the long run, short-run aggregate supply and aggregate demand reach equilibrium at the new, increased long-run aggregate supply, with an increased real GDP and a higher price level than was achieved at the previous equilibrium.

Keep in Mind

It is essential to remember the importance of low interest rates in fueling long-run economic growth. While some economic stabilization policies will help to promote both short-run and long-run economic growth, others will not. Expansionary monetary policy increases the money supply, reducing interest rates. This increases aggregate demand in the short run, while increasing aggregate supply in the long run by promoting investment at the lower interest rate. But expansionary fiscal policy, while increasing aggregate demand in the short run, requires government to borrow money to finance deficit spending. Increased demand in the loanable funds market pushes up interest rates, crowding private investment out of the market. Reduced investment slows long-run economic growth. Targeted tax cuts or subsidies for the purchase of equipment, expansion, or more rapid depreciation of capital may promote economic growth by promoting investment. But when questions ask about broader economic policies designed to address a recession or inflation, look for the effect on interest rates to determine the effects on long-run economic growth. Previous multiple-choice and free-response questions have explored this concept, so it is important to clearly understand the implications of such policies in both the short and long run.

PRACTICE **Economic Growth with Ongoing Inflation**

Indicate whether each of these factors would cause the production possibilities curve and long-run aggregate supply to *increase* or *decrease*.

1. __________ A toxic spill renders 2,000 acres of farmland unusable for ten years
2. __________ A new technology improves the speed of production
3. __________ An increase in interest rates reduces the rate of capital investment
4. __________ The cost of capital equipment significantly increases
5. __________ On-the-job training increases the productivity of workers

The Inflation-Unemployment Relationship

Refer to pages 664–667 of your textbook.

A CLOSER LOOK **The Phillips Curve, and Aggregate Supply Shocks and the Phillips Curve**

The **Phillips curve,** named for British economist A.W. Phillips, illustrates the short-run tradeoff between the inflation rate and the unemployment rate. When the inflation rate is high, the unemployment rate is low; at low rates of unemployment, the inflation rate is high. This short-run relationship results from changes in aggregate demand, assuming aggregate supply is stable. When aggregate demand increases, output increases, so more workers are hired, lowering the unemployment rate. At the same time, the increased demand raises the price level.

Thus, when aggregate demand increases, the unemployment rate decreases and the inflation rate increases, causing a leftward movement along the Phillips curve. In the same way, if aggregate demand falls, output and employment fall, increasing the unemployment rate. At the same time, the rate of inflation falls because of the reduction of upward pressure on prices. This causes a rightward movement along the Phillips curve.

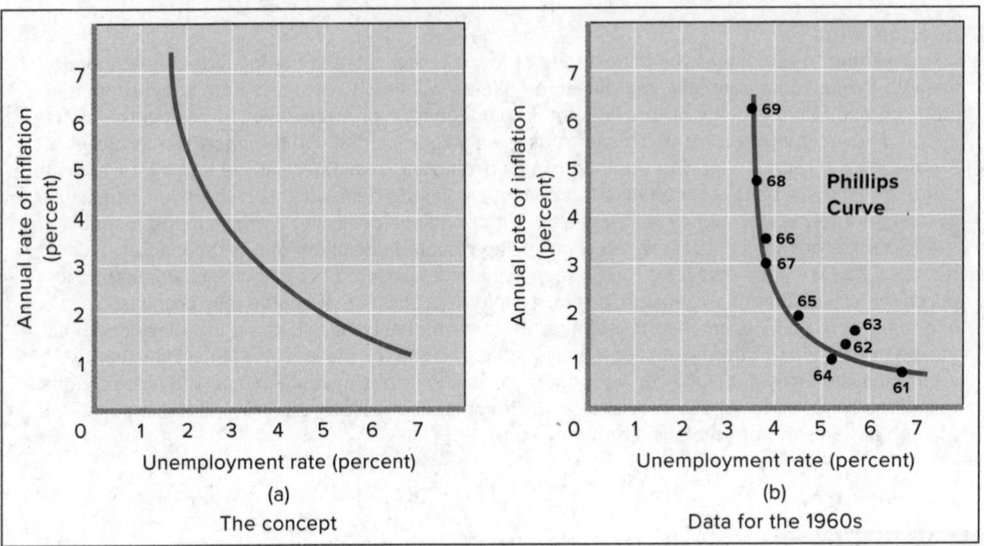

This stable relationship was the basis for our understanding of the effects of fiscal and monetary policy through the 1960s, as demonstrated in Graph (b) above. When the economy fell into recession, policymakers used expansionary fiscal and monetary policy to reduce the unemployment rate, understanding that the inflation rate would increase as a result of the increase in aggregate demand. During periods of inflation, policymakers used contractionary policies to reduce the inflation rate, with the understanding that the tradeoff would be a higher unemployment rate.

Events of the 1970s caused a serious revision of the theory after a series of **aggregate supply shocks** struck the US economy. The primary blow was a quadrupling of oil prices by OPEC, significantly increasing the cost of production and shipping for US manufacturers. Major crop shortfalls, a weak dollar, slow productivity growth, and significant wage increases following release of wage and price controls combined to significantly reduce the aggregate supply. As a result, both the inflation rate and the unemployment rate skyrocketed, violating the assumed tradeoff relationship of the Phillips curve. This new situation, dubbed "**stagflation,**" demonstrated a "hat trick" of bad economic news – a stagnant economy, high inflation, and high unemployment, all at the same time.

In fact, economists discovered that the Phillips curve *could* move in response to changes in aggregate supply. When aggregate supply was stable, changes in aggregate demand caused movement *along* a stationary Phillips curve, as demonstrated on the lowest Phillips curve shown on the following graph. But as aggregate supply fell in the 1970s and 1980s, *both* the inflation and unemployment rates increased, showing that decreases in aggregate supply cause an outward *shift* in the Phillips curve.

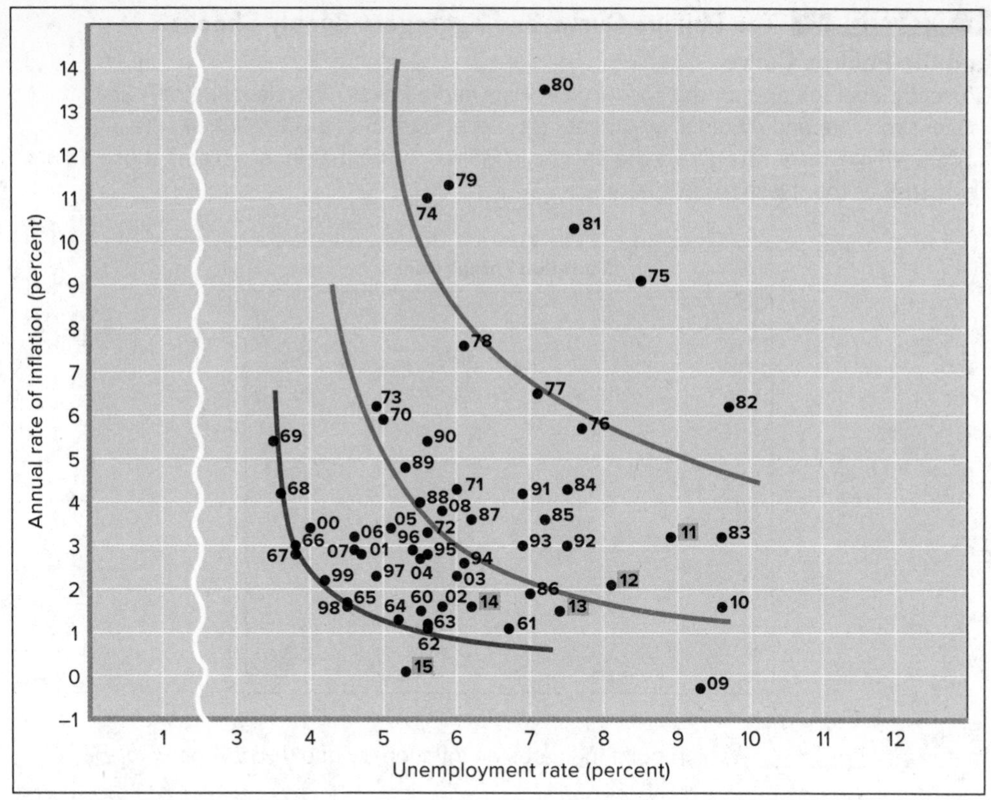

Source: Bureau of Labor Statistics, **www.bls.gov.**

Stagflation created a unique dilemma for policymakers. Given the tradeoff between inflation and unemployment, with both at very high levels, any attempt to reduce one would cause the other to become worse. The Fed significantly reduced the money supply, which reduced inflation but plunged the economy into a severe recession. Eventually, wage and oil price reductions, with improvements in crop yields and worker productivity, combined to shift aggregate supply back to the right. This caused the Phillips curve to shift inward, lowering both the unemployment and inflation rates, as you can see from the data points since the 1990s. After the Great Recession, from 2012 through 2015, inflation and unemployment rates fell, indicating the Phillips curve continued to shift inward. By the Fall of 2016, the Bureau of Labor Statistics reported an unemployment rate of 4.9% and an inflation rate of 1.5%.

Graphing Guidance

Previous free-response questions have asked students to graph points on a Phillips curve and then illustrate how changes in the economy or fiscal and monetary policy would affect movement along the curve. It is very important to remember that the axes for the Phillips curve are very different from most graphs, in that they aren't about prices or output. A trick to remembering that unemployment is on the horizontal axis is that the <u>un</u>employment axis label goes <u>un</u>der the graph, keeping the "un"s together.

PRACTICE The Phillips Curve, and Aggregate Supply Shocks and the Phillips Curve

Correctly label the axes of the short-run Phillips curve below. Then label Point A at 7% inflation rate and 4% unemployment rate. Label Point B at a 3% inflation rate and a 5% unemployment rate. Draw the short-run Phillips curve that incorporates those points. Then answer the questions below.

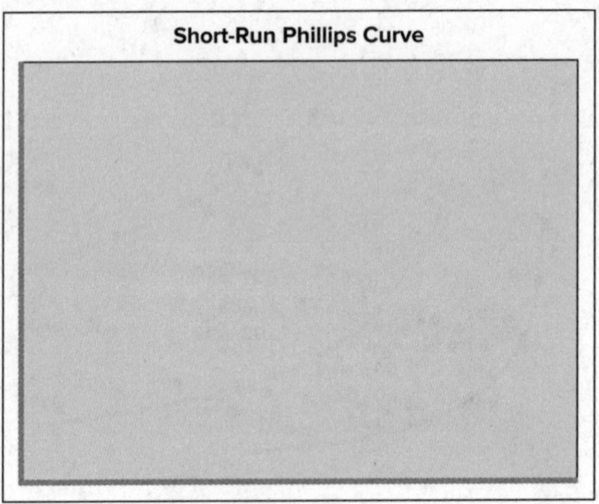

1. _________ Which point indicates an inflationary gap: *Point A* or *Point B*?

2. _________ To move from the point indicated in #1 to the other point, should the Fed *increase* or *decrease* the discount rate?

3. _________ To achieve the effect indicated in #2, should Congress *raise* or *lower* taxes?

4. _________ If policies in #2 and #3 are undertaken, will aggregate demand *rise* or *fall*?

5. _________ Now assume that the latest data indicate a 9% unemployment rate and a 10% inflation rate. Has the Phillips curve shifted *inward* or *outward*?

6. _________ Given the information in #5, has aggregate supply *increased* or *decreased*?

The Long-Run Phillips Curve

Refer to pages 668–669 of your textbook.

A CLOSER LOOK Short-Run Phillips Curve and Long-Run Vertical Phillips Curve

The long-run Phillips curve is a vertical curve set at the natural rate of unemployment where there is no cyclical unemployment. This point is often called the **natural rate of unemployment** or the non-accelerating inflation rate of unemployment (NAIRU). In the long run, there is no tradeoff between inflation and unemployment.

It is, of course, possible for inflation and unemployment rates to change from year to year. In the example on the next page, if the natural rate of unemployment is 5%, the economy is stable at a 3% inflation rate (Point a_1). At the expected 3% inflation rate, workers negotiate 3% increases in their nominal wages to keep their real wages even with inflation, and banks add the 3% expected inflation into nominal interest rates on loans in order to receive dollars in repayment equal to the value of those loaned. But if aggregate demand rose and the inflation rate rose to 6%, firms could raise prices without seeing an increase in their resource costs in the short run. The higher resulting profit would lead firms to increase output and hire workers, reducing the unemployment rate from Point a_1 to Point b_1. Higher-than-expected inflation temporarily increases output and reduces unemployment.

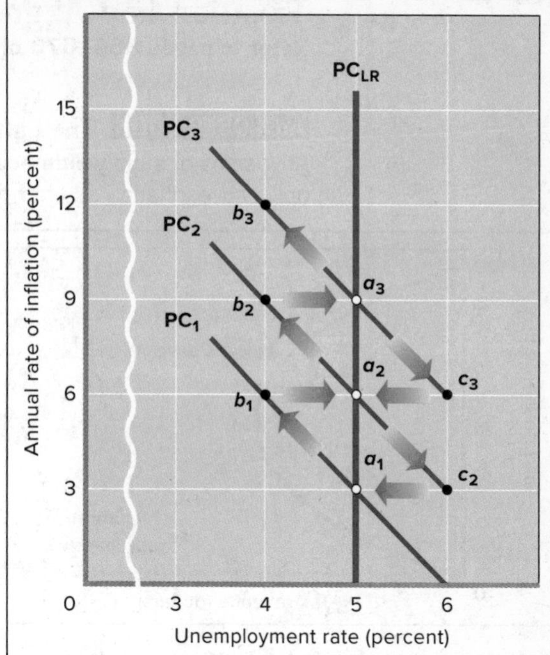

However, this point will not remain stable in the long run. Given time, employees will realize their real wages are falling as inflation climbs, and they will renegotiate their contracts to include 6% wage increases to retain their purchasing power. As resource costs increase, firms' profits fall and they reduce production, laying off workers until unemployment returns to its natural rate of 5% – but inflation remains higher (PC_2 on the new Phillips curve) than the initial 3% inflation rate. This can become a significant problem because of the role of expectations. Workers now *expect* higher inflation rates, so they *expect* higher wage increases to keep up with that inflation. Those higher wage costs for firms fuel the very inflation increases workers expected.

The same thing happens in reverse during periods of recession. If the aggregate demand falls, profits decrease, firms cut back production and lay off workers, and unemployment temporarily increases. As a result of the layoffs and lower inflationary expectations, workers accept lower wages (or at least lower increases in the wage rates), firms increase production at the lower cost, more workers are hired, and the unemployment rate returns to the natural rate of unemployment.

It is important to note that the natural rate of unemployment can shift in response to changes in the labor force, technology, and economic policy. For example, child labor laws removing children under the age of 16 from the labor force decreased the natural rate of unemployment. The influx of women into the labor force in the 1970s increased the natural rate of unemployment. Unemployment benefits increased the natural rate of unemployment because workers could lengthen job searches. Improvements in technology and job search websites have contributed to another decrease in the NAIRU because unemployed workers can find information about positions more quickly and easily.

PRACTICE Short-Run Phillips Curve and Long-Run Vertical Phillips Curve

1. Indicate whether each factor would cause the long-run Phillips curve to *increase* or *decrease*.

   A. __________ Unemployment benefits are extended from 26 weeks to 52 weeks

   B. __________ Baby boomers are retiring, reducing workers in the labor force

   C. __________ Computerized job-search websites make job searches easier

2. __________ If policymakers use expansionary policy to increase aggregate demand, will the long-run Phillips curve *increase*, *decrease*, or be *unaffected*?

Taxation and Aggregate Supply

Refer to pages 669–673 of your textbook.

A CLOSER LOOK The Laffer Curve

Advocates of **supply-side economics** argue that fiscal and monetary (demand-side) policies only cause inflation and harm incentives to work, save, and invest. Supply-siders argue that policymakers should focus on increasing aggregate supply. They promote lower tax rates, arguing that if workers are allowed to keep more of their disposable income, they will work overtime, postpone retirement, and even more workers will be drawn into the labor force. Further, supply-siders argue that lowering the tax rate on interest from savings encourages households to increase saving, which increases the funds available for investment. Supply-siders also call for lower corporate income tax rates, which would lead to greater capital investment, increasing worker productivity, raising long-run aggregate supply and economic growth.

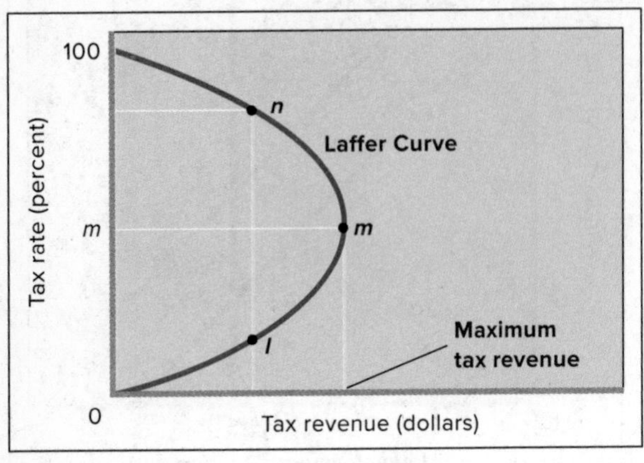

The **Laffer curve,** popularized by American economist Arthur Laffer, illustrates the relationship between the tax rate and tax revenue received by the government. At a 0% tax rate, the government receives no revenue. As the tax rate increases, government revenue increases. However, at some theoretical level, the tax rate becomes so high that it serves as a work disincentive. If the government takes 90% of a worker's paycheck in taxes, that worker loses the incentive to work. This backward bend continues until a 100% tax rate – where the government takes every penny of the worker's paycheck – the government receives nothing, because no one is willing to work. Throughout the early 1980s, Laffer argued that the US was on the upper section of the Laffer curve (such as Point n), and significant cuts in the marginal income tax rate would result in the double benefit of giving workers a greater incentive to work and significantly increasing the federal government's tax revenues (at Point m).

When President Ronald Reagan came into office in 1981, supply-side economics (also called "Reaganomics" or "the trickle-down theory" because benefits begin with the wealthy, with the idea of eventually trickling down to workers) began with major income tax cuts, primarily for the wealthy. Government revenue rose, but economists agree that it did not result from a movement from Point n to Point m on the Laffer curve; in fact, economists agree that the US economy is operating in the region below Point m. The tax cuts did not spur an increased work incentive; some found the extra take-home pay allowed them to work even fewer hours. Deficits significantly increased due to lower taxes and rising spending. So what increased the federal revenue when taxes were cut? An increase in aggregate *demand*, not aggregate *supply*.

When President Bill Clinton entered office in 1993, he reversed course, increasing the marginal income tax rates for those with the highest incomes in order to reduce deficits. His work with Congress in holding the line on spending while increasing revenues, paired with significant improvements in technology and productivity in the private sector, led to budget surpluses by the end of his administration. Even with the tax increases, the economy boomed, largely due to improvements in technology and productivity.

When President George W. Bush took office in 2001, he brought supply-side policy back into operation. He worked with Congress to again significantly cut marginal tax rates, targeting those with the highest incomes. The Fed reduced interest rates and the economy expanded, but did it expand as a result of a shift in aggregate *supply* or *demand*? Aggregate *demand* increased. By the end of Bush's presidency, the US economy had plunged into the Great Recession, and TARP spending was used to try to prevent collapse of the financial services industry. Tax cuts primarily targeted toward the wealthy and massive increases in spending led to unprecedented deficits during the Bush Administration, a repeat of the Reagan era.

When President Barack Obama came into office in 2009, he immediately faced a financial crisis and returned to Keynesian policy, using fiscal policy in the stimulus package to end the Great Recession and put the economy back onto the path of sustained growth. Massive government spending, along with some tax cuts in the stimulus package, significantly increased aggregate demand.

While economists today recognize a relationship between tax rates and government revenue, because the economy operates on the bottom side of the graph, it is not believed that reducing taxes directly increases government revenue via work incentives. While tax cuts can stimulate aggregate demand, they are not as effective as increases in government spending. However, the battle of the economists over appropriate economic policy has only begun and will be discussed in detail in Chapter 33.

PRACTICE The Laffer Curve

1. ________ According to supply-siders, the most effective factor for increasing economic growth is to reduce *what*?

2. ________ According to the Laffer curve, if the marginal tax rate becomes too high, will work incentive *increase* or *decrease*?

3. ________ According to mainstream economists, did supply-side tax cuts in the Reagan and Bush Administrations increase aggregate *supply* or aggregate *demand*?

Make sure to return to the AP Key Concepts section to check your understanding of the chapter's concepts important to AP coursework.

Economically Speaking

- **Aggregate Supply Shock** a sudden increase in resource costs that reduces aggregate supply
- **Full-Employment Output** real output produced when all resources are fully employed
- **Laffer Curve** illustrates the relationship between the tax rate and tax revenue
- **Long Run** period of time when input prices are flexible
- **Long-Run Aggregate Supply Curve** vertical curve at full-employment output
- **Natural Rate of Unemployment** the unemployment rate when the economy is producing at full potential output
- **Phillips Curve** illustrates the short-term tradeoff between unemployment and inflation rates
- **Short Run** period of time when input prices are fixed
- **Short-Run Aggregate Supply Curve** upward-sloping curve showing that at lower price levels, real output falls; at higher price levels, real output increases
- **Stagflation** a stagnant economy, high inflation, and high unemployment occurring together
- **Supply-Side Economics** theory that advocates lower taxes to support economic growth

33 Chapter

Current Issues in Macro Theory and Policy

What causes economic instability? Will the economy self-correct? Should the government intervene to stabilize the economy? If so, how? These questions are central to differences among macroeconomic theories. Chapter 33 introduces and explores differences among prominent economic theories.

Material from Chapter 33 may appear in a few multiple-choice questions on the AP Macroeconomics exam.

Key Concepts

Below is a summary of the chapter's concepts important to AP coursework. Upon completing the lessons that follow, return to these concepts to make sure you understand them and how the practice exercises you completed relate to them.

- Keynesians believe the economy is generally unstable, due to demand shocks.
  - GDP = Consumer + Investment + Government + Net Export spending
  - The investment sector is the most volatile.
- Monetarists believe the economy is stable, performing at full-employment output.
  - Wage and price flexibility allow the economy to self-correct.
  - Government attempts to stabilize the economy only make it more unstable.
  - Money Supply × Velocity = Price Level × Quantity of Goods Sold (P × Q = Nominal GDP)
  - Velocity and quantity are stable; therefore money supply increases only cause inflation.
- Classical economists believed the economy was stable at full employment until shocks occurred.
  - Flexible wages and prices would help the economy to self-correct.
- Rational expectations theorists believe people know about economic conditions and policies.
  - People will act quickly to counteract policies, making changes nearly instantaneously.
  - Government should not use stabilization policies because they will be ineffective.
- Monetarists argue that while the economy will self-correct, it will do so more slowly over years.

- Keynesians argue that the economy *can* self-correct, but it will require years of unemployment.
  - Workers and firms will resist the wage reductions necessary for self-correction.
  - Keynesians call for the use of fiscal and monetary policy to correct the economy.
- Monetarists advocate a monetary rule, requiring the Fed to increase the money supply at the rate of average annual real GDP growth.
- Monetarists also oppose the use of expansionary fiscal policy because it causes crowding out; some promote a balanced budget requirement to prevent its use.
- Keynesians promote the use of fiscal and monetary policy to avoid leaving people languishing in recessions for years while waiting for the economy to slowly self-adjust.
- Keynesians cite evidence that velocity is variable, so changes in money supply do not automatically cause inflation and can instill business confidence to invest and grow.
- Keynesians oppose mandatory balanced budgets because they make recessions worse; when revenue falls in a recession, government must raise taxes or cut spending, the wrong policies.
- Keynesians argue that crowding out during recession is minimal, because households and firms are already borrowing less due to lack of confidence during a recession.

Now, let's examine more closely the following concepts from your textbook:

- **What Causes Macro Instability?**
- **Does the Economy "Self-Correct"?**
- **Rules or Discretion?**
- **Summary of Alternative Views**

These sections were selected because a deeper understanding of the theories helps to explain why economists who study the same data promote diverse policy prescriptions for the economy.

What Causes Macro Instability?

Refer to pages 677–681 of your textbook.

A CLOSER LOOK Mainstream View and Monetarist View

Mainstream (**Keynesian**) economists believe the economy is generally unstable, with most instability resulting from unexpected demand shocks; wage and price stickiness divert changes into output and employment. The GDP formula from consumer, investment, government, and net export spending:

$$GDP = C + I + G + X_n$$

If spending rises in any one of these four sectors, aggregate demand increases, raising real output, the price level, or both. Keynesians argue that the investment sector is the most volatile. Because of the multiplier effect, an increase in aggregate demand can cause demand-pull inflation, while a decrease in aggregate demand can cause a recession. Keynesians also recognize supply shocks as a cause of economic instability, because such shocks significantly increase the cost of production for firms. As aggregate supply shifts to the left, higher unemployment combines with inflation to create stagflation.

Monetarism is a school of economic thought developed from the work of American economist Milton Friedman. **Monetarists** believe that the macroeconomy is generally stable at full-employment output because competitive markets and flexibility in prices and wages promote stability. Monetarists argue that changes in aggregate demand cause changes in wages and prices rather than output and employment. While Keynesians see government policy as the *answer* to economic instability, monetarists instead see government intervention as a *cause* of economic instability. Monetarists argue that minimum wage laws, pro-union legislation giving workers bargaining power to settle multi-year contracts, crop price supports, and pro-business monopoly laws have created the sticky prices and wages central to Keynesian theory. Even more importantly, monetarists argue that government attempts to stabilize the economy – especially through monetary policy – actually exacerbate the strength and duration of business cycles, rather than reducing them.

Monetarists do not view the economy through the Keynesian GDP formula, but instead focus on the **equation of exchange** (**quantity theory of money**) as central to their theory.

$$M \times V = P \times Q$$

M is the money supply, V is the **velocity** of money (the number of times a dollar turns over during a year), P is the price level, and Q is the quantity of goods sold during a year. PQ is the nominal GDP. The money supply, multiplied by the velocity, equals the value of the output on which it is spent.

Monetarists argue that the velocity is stable because people tend to hold the same amount of money over time. Therefore, according to monetarists, an increase in the money supply will directly lead to an increase in nominal GDP. Because the economy consistently produces at full-employment output, Q is also stable. So according to monetarists, an increase in the money supply only causes inflation. Higher prices may temporarily cause firms to increase output to get higher profit. But once wages and other production costs begin to rise, firms will return to full-employment output, but at the higher price level.

Monetarists view the use of discretionary monetary policy as a primary cause of economic instability. Because changes in the money supply and interest rates take so long to take effect, monetarists argue that they actually exacerbate cycles! If a significant increase in the money supply finally takes full effect just as inflation is increasing, it will only make the inflation worse. Changes in the money supply can also be ineffective if banks choose not to make loans or if customers do not redeposit funds to allow multiple expansion. For these reasons, monetarists oppose the use of discretionary monetary policy.

Caution

It is important not to confuse monetarism with the similar term "monetary policy." While monetarists and Keynesians both recognize the importance of money to the economy, monetarists *oppose* government attempts to stabilize the economy – especially those involving monetary policy. Monetary policy is instead associated with Keynesian theory.

PRACTICE Mainstream View and Monetarist View

Indicate which theory supports each statement: Keynesian or Monetarist.

1. ________ Government should not attempt to stabilize the economy, because changes in monetary policy only make business cycles more extreme.

2. ________ The investment sector is the most sensitive because firms make investment decisions based almost exclusively on interest rates and return on investment.

3. __________ A lack of consumer demand frequently results in macroeconomic equilibrium at less than full-employment output.

4. __________ Changes in the money supply primarily cause inflation and have little or no effect on output.

Does the Economy "Self-Correct"?

Refer to pages 681–684 of your textbook.

A CLOSER LOOK New Classical and Mainstream Views of Self-Correction

Classical economists believed that the economy was inherently stable, operating at full-employment output until some shock created temporary instability. But they believed that in the long run, the economy would self-correct to full-employment output due to flexible wages and prices. In the same way, neoclassical economists believe the economy will self-correct over time. Neoclassical economists tend to be either monetarists or believers of the **rational expectations theory.** This theory holds that consumers and firms are knowledgeable about economic conditions and fiscal and monetary policy. When faced with certain economic conditions, firms and consumers anticipate the policies Congress and the Fed will undertake, and then take action to protect themselves from the effects of those policies.

For example, during a recession, workers and banks may anticipate that the Fed will increase the money supply in order to increase aggregate demand. But because such an action can create inflation in the long run, workers will immediately negotiate higher wages to protect real wages, and banks will add the higher expected inflation rate in determining the nominal interest rate for loans. Higher wages and interest rates then dampen the growth that would have occurred as a result of the Fed's action. As a result, rational expectations theorists, like monetarists and classical economists, argue government should not engage in stabilization policy, and instead advocate waiting for the economy to self-correct.

Because the rational expectations theory holds that consumers and firms anticipate government policy and act even before it is enacted, adjustments occur instantaneously or very quickly. Under this theory, if price and policy changes are anticipated, firms and consumers react instantly, so output does not change. If an unexpected increase in demand for exports increases aggregate demand, workers almost instantly recognize prices will increase and begin to demand higher wages, very quickly increasing the cost of production and dissipating anticipated profit, so production returns to full-employment output.

Monetarists differ from rational expectations theorists regarding the speed at which adjustments occur. Monetarists believe that people and firms react to changes in the economy after they have begun to occur rather than anticipating them, so long-run adjustments may require two years or even longer.

Keynesians agree that quick adjustments occur in markets that move rapidly, such as stock, foreign exchange, and commodity markets. But they do not believe that such adjustments occur quickly across the broader economy. Empirical evidence has shown that prices and wages are indeed downwardly sticky, and recessionary and inflationary expectations of consumers and firms may linger for long periods of time, proving the economy does *not* quickly self-adjust. When aggregate demand falls, workers do not readily accept the wage cuts necessary to shift the short-run aggregate supply curve back out and return the economy to full-employment output. Instead, workers resist wage cuts, and the minimum wage and long-term contracts even prevent wage cuts in many cases. Firms may also resist wage cuts due to concerns about worker morale, shirking, and increased job turnover as workers quit to find jobs with higher pay. So, aggregate demand remains low, possibly for a long time. Keynesians argue that the economy will not self-adjust quickly – maybe not for years – so government action is necessary.

PRACTICE **New Classical and Mainstream Views of Self-Correction**

Indicate which theory supports each statement: Classical, Keynesian, Monetarist, or Rational Expectations.

1. ________ Flexible wages and prices allow the economy to self-correct when unexpected shocks occur.
2. ________ If the Fed announces it will increase the money supply, output will not rise, though prices will, because workers will act quickly to demand higher wages.
3. ________ Recessionary gaps can remain in place for years, so it is important for government to intervene to stabilize the economy.
4. ________ It may take a few years for the economy to emerge from a severe recession, but the government should not intervene in the self-adjustment process.

Rules or Discretion?

Refer to pages 685–688 of your textbook.

A CLOSER LOOK **In Support of Policy Rules and In Defense of Discretionary Stabilization Policy**

Monetarists and other neoclassical economists are convinced that government attempts to stabilize the economy instead actually further destabilize it. They point to monetary policy, concerned that attempts to reduce unemployment by increasing the money supply will create inflation instead.

Monetarists call for a **monetary rule,** requiring the Fed to increase the money supply at the rate of average annual real GDP growth, regardless of the state of the economy. Monetarists contend that if the money supply grows at a steady rate, money will be available in the economy in times of recession. The limit on growth will prevent overstimulation in times of inflation, thereby stabilizing economic growth. In addition, the increase in money supply would reduce interest rates, fueling investment in plant

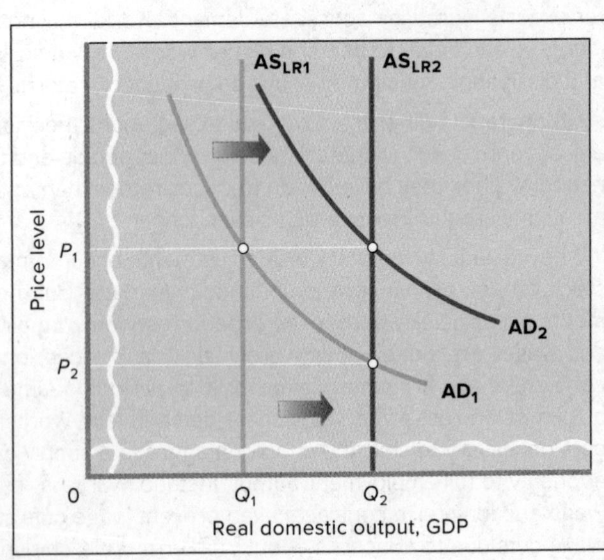

and equipment and further promoting steady annual economic growth. Rational expectations theorists argue monetary policy is simply ineffective because people will anticipate it and counteract it.

Monetarists also oppose the use of fiscal policy to stabilize the economy. Because expansionary fiscal policy requires the government to run deficits, the increased demand for money in the loanable funds market forces up interest rates and crowds out private investment – so while government spending may be increasing, it is offset by a decline in private sector spending. Further, the increase in interest rates negatively affects long-run economic growth, as firms reduce investment in plant and equipment. Rational expectations theorists instead argue that fiscal policy simply doesn't work; people anticipate the policy and act to counter it. Therefore, monetarists and other neoclassical economists oppose the use of fiscal policy to stabilize the economy, and some go so far as to advocate an annually balanced budget requirement, in an effort to restrict the use of fiscal policy.

Keynesians argue that because serious harm can befall firms and households in periods of deep recession and inflation, government intervention and stabilization are necessary to limit swings in the business cycle. Through fiscal policy, consumers and firms respond to tax and spending incentives, which directly affect aggregate demand. Through monetary policy, the Federal Reserve changes the money supply and interest rates, affecting aggregate demand more indirectly through interest rate incentives. Further, policies can be developed to promote long-run economic growth that might not otherwise exist in an economy constrained by monetary rules and balanced budget requirements.

Regarding the equation of exchange, Keynesians cite evidence that while the money supply and nominal GDP do correlate over the long run, in the short run, velocity actually is variable. While the money stock may remain the same, if it turns over faster and faster, it creates inflation. So a strict monetary rule may not limit changes in aggregate demand as effectively as monetarists contend it will. If firms increase investment and the velocity is increasing, limitations on the growth of the money supply will not be effective. But discretionary monetary policy allows the Fed to restrict the growth of the money supply and change interest rates in ways that discourage firms from overinvesting to the extent that they cause inflation. In the same way, business pessimism may reduce investment, and the Fed's failure to act reduces confidence that the economy will emerge soon from a recession. However, the right incentives to invest – through lower interest rates and the ability to earn a profit on capital investment – can spur an economic recovery.

Keynesians also oppose a mandatory balanced budget, arguing that such a requirement would significantly worsen economic instability. Because the federal government receives the largest percentage of its revenue from individual income taxes, when unemployment increases during a recession, government revenues fall. A balanced budget amendment would require the government to do one of two things to avoid unconstitutionally falling into a budget deficit: increase taxes or reduce government spending. Either action is precisely the *wrong* policy to invoke during a recession. Such policies only further reduce aggregate demand – and as even more workers lose jobs, tax revenues fall further, requiring repeated policy actions to lessen the recession. Discretionary fiscal policy allows government to work in a counter-cyclical fashion, to try to close recessionary and inflationary gaps.

Further, Keynesians argue that the problem of crowding out during a recession is likely to be minimal, if it occurs at all. During a recession, business optimism is low and firms are less likely to invest in plant and equipment because of excess capacity and reduced return on investment. Because firms' demand for loanable funds is already falling due to poor business conditions, Keynesians argue that increased government demand for loanable funds to finance deficits is not likely to crowd out new investment.

Keynesians also point to decades of historical use of fiscal and monetary policy to effectively limit periods of inflation and recession, allowing the economy to recover more quickly than would be anticipated if the economy were left alone to self-correct. It is important to note the actions of the Federal Reserve, Congress, and Presidents George W. Bush and Barack Obama in dealing with the worst financial crisis to strike the US in decades. In 2008, the Federal Reserve moved to reduce key interest rates to the 0-0.25% range, while providing loans to financial institutions facing a solvency crisis. In late 2008, Congress passed a $700 billion bill to bail out financial institutions and later auto manufacturers. In early 2009, Congress passed a fiscal stimulus package of nearly $800 billion in increased spending and tax cuts. The steep decline of aggregate demand was stopped and reversed. Without question, economists of all theoretical backgrounds will closely examine these policy actions to learn how we can more effectively address changes in our economy.

PRACTICE **In Support of Policy Rules and In Defense of Discretionary Stabilization Policy**

Indicate which theory supports each statement: Keynesian or Monetarist.

1. __________ If government uses a restrictive fiscal policy, aggregate demand, output, and employment will decrease.

2. __________ The government should not attempt to stabilize the economy; it should only change the money supply at a rate consistent with real GDP.

3. __________ Expansionary fiscal policy crowds out private investment, so it is ineffective in increasing aggregate demand.

4. __________ A balanced budget requirement would be good for the economy, because it prevents the government from using expansionary fiscal policy.

Summary of Alternative Views

Refer to pages 688–689 of your textbook.

A CLOSER LOOK **Summary of Alternative Views**

The table that follows summarizes the philosophies and policy prescriptions of Keynesian, monetarist, and rational expectations theorists. While economists of different schools of thought disagree about many things, they are destined to continue their research to find answers to our economic questions.

Issue	Mainstream Macroeconomics	New Classical Economics: Monetarism	New Classical Economics: Rational Expectations
View of the private economy	Potentially unstable	Stable in long run at natural rate of unemployment	Stable in long run at natural rate of unemployment
Cause of the observed instability of the private economy	Investment plans unequal to saving plans (changes in AD); AS shocks	Inappropriate monetary policy	Unanticipated AD and AS shocks in the short run
Assumptions about short-run price and wage stickiness	Both prices and wages stuck in the immediate short run; in the short run; wages sticky while prices inflexible downward but flexible upward	Prices flexible upward and downward in the short run; wages sticky in the short run	Prices and wages flexible both upward and downward in the short run
Appropriate macro policies	Active fiscal and monetary policy	Monetary rule	Monetary rule
How changes in the money supply affect the economy	By changing the interest rate, which changes investment and real GDP	By directly changing AD, which changes GDP	No effect on output because price-level changes are anticipated
View of the velocity of money	Unstable	Stable	No consensus
How fiscal policy affects the economy	Changes AD and GDP via the multiplier process	No effect unless money supply changes	No effect because price-level changes are anticipated
View of cost-push inflation	Possible (AS shock)	Impossible in the long run in the absence of excessive money supply growth	Impossible in the long run in the absence of excessive money supply growth

PRACTICE Summary of Alternative Views

1. Monetarists argue that if the money supply increases:

   A. __________ Will velocity remain *stable*, or does it *vary*?

   B. __________ Will the price level *increase*, *decrease*, or remain *stable*?

   C. __________ Will output *increase*, *decrease*, or remain *stable*?

   D. __________ The money supply increase will only cause *inflation* or greater *output*?

2. Keynesians argue that if the money supply increases:

   A. __________ Will velocity remain *stable*, or does it *vary*?

   B. __________ Will the price level *increase*, *decrease*, or remain *stable*?

   C. __________ Will output *increase*, *decrease*, or remain *stable*?

   D. __________ The money supply increase mostly causes *inflation* or greater *output*?

3. Indicate which theory supports each statement: Classical, Keynesian, Monetarist, Rational Expectations, or Supply Side.

   A. __________ The government should primarily lower taxes for corporations and the wealthy to promote investment and raise aggregate supply.

   B. __________ During a recession, the government should increase spending and the money supply and lower taxes in order to increase aggregate demand.

   C. __________ Fiscal and monetary policies are ineffective because people anticipate them and protect themselves from the policy effects.

   D. __________ If the Federal Reserve simply increases the money supply at the average rate of economic growth, the economy will remain relatively stable.

   E. __________ If the government does not intervene, flexible wages and prices will restore the economy to full-employment output in a fairly short time.

4. __________ If crowding out only partially reduces the effect of expansionary fiscal policy, overall, will expansionary fiscal policy *increase* or *decrease* aggregate demand?

Make sure to return to the AP Key Concepts section to check your understanding of the chapter's concepts important to AP coursework.

Economically Speaking

- **Equation of Exchange (Quantity Theory of Money)** economic theory that holds that an increase in the money supply will only cause the price level to increase
- **Keynesian Theory** economic theory that supports government intervention to stabilize the economy
- **Monetarist Theory** economic theory that calls for steady growth of the money supply to stabilize the economy
- **Monetary Rule** requires the Fed to increase the money supply at the rate of annual average real GDP growth
- **Rational Expectations Theory** economic theory that households and firms will adjust quickly to economic shocks, so government should not attempt to stabilize the economy
- **Velocity** the number of times a dollar turns over during a year

International Trade

Opening an economy to trade brings us full-circle to rediscover Chapter 1 concepts: comparative advantage, production possibilities, and gains from trade. Chapter 34 then extends the discussion of international trade, contrasting the gains from trade with the arguments for protectionist trade barriers.

Material from Chapter 34 is likely to appear in a few multiple-choice questions and a free-response question on both the AP Microeconomics and Macroeconomics exams.

Key Concepts

Below is a summary of the chapter's concepts important to AP coursework. Upon completing the lessons that follow, return to these concepts to make sure you understand them and how the practice exercises you completed relate to them.

- A trade deficit occurs when imports > exports; a trade surplus occurs when exports > imports.
- Land-, labor-, and capital-intensive industries develop based on a region's best resources.
- A nation has an absolute advantage when it can produce more products than another nation.
- Comparative advantage occurs when one country produces more efficiently than another.
- The nation with the lower opportunity cost should specialize to produce and export that good.
- If the question is set up using resources, find a common denominator to determine output.
- Terms of trade will always fall between the two opportunity costs of the countries.
- Benefits of trade include increases in efficiency, real incomes, standards of living, employment, output, economic growth, variety of products, and peaceful solutions to international conflicts.
- If the world price is lower than the domestic price and a country opens itself to trade, domestic quantity supplied will decrease while quantity demanded rises; imports will fulfill the shortage.
- Trade barriers are policies designed to limit trade; tariffs are taxes, while quotas limit quantities.
- Trade barriers decrease supply, raising import prices so consumers substitute domestic goods.
- Protectionists support trade barriers, making national security, diversification, infant industry, dumping, job- and firm-saving, and wage-protecting arguments.

- Free traders oppose widespread trade barriers, arguing targeted barriers are more effective.
- NAFTA removed trade barriers among the US, Canada, and Mexico to increase trade.

Now, let's examine more closely the following concepts from your textbook:

- **The Economic Basis for Trade**
- **Supply and Demand Analysis of Exports and Imports**
- **Trade Barriers and Export Subsidies**
- **The Case for Protection: A Critical Review**
- **Multilateral Trade Agreements and Free-Trade Zones**

These sections were selected because the calculations and concepts can be confusing.

The Economic Basis for Trade

Refer to pages 696–703 of your textbook.

A CLOSER LOOK Comparative Advantage and Specializing Based on Comparative Advantage

The US is the world's largest trading nation in combined imports and exports, but exports are only 13% of US total output. Imports and exports have both doubled as a percentage of GDP since 1980. Canada is our most important trading partner in the volume of goods and services traded. A **trade deficit** occurs when imports exceed exports, while a **trade surplus** is the result of exports exceeding imports. The US has experienced trade deficits in goods for decades, while we continue to hold trade surpluses for services. US net exports result in trade deficits in the hundreds of billions of dollars per year.

Because land, labor, and capital resources are distributed unequally, countries and firms must specialize to make the most of their available resources: **land-intensive industry, labor-intensive industry,** or **capital-intensive industry.** Countries are not permanently limited by their resources; investment broadens production possibilities. In the circular flow model, imports are a leakage as money leaves the country, while exports are an injection into the flow when foreign firms buy American products.

Countries gain from trade by specializing in the products they produce most efficiently, and then trading for products they can't produce as efficiently. To illustrate this reason for trade, we will return to the production possibilities curve from Chapter 1. We assume that there are only two nations, each nation only makes two products, the nations have equal amounts of resources and technology, and the opportunity costs associated with making each product are constant as production output changes.

Assume the table below illustrates the maximum production possibilities for the US and Mexico.

	Vegetables	Beef
United States	30 tons	30 tons
Mexico	20 tons	10 tons

A nation that is able to produce more of a product has an **absolute advantage.** In this case, the US can produce more vegetables and beef than Mexico, so the US holds absolute advantage in both products. It is possible for a nation to hold an absolute advantage in both products, one, or neither product.

But *comparative* advantage is the basis for determining specialization. **Comparative advantage** tells us which country is more *efficient* in producing each of the products. We must calculate each country's opportunity cost to produce each product. To do this, equate the products a country can produce. Reduce one side of the equation to one, and then perform the same operation on the other side of the equation. In this example, for Mexico, 20 tons of vegetables = 10 tons of beef. Divide the right side of the equation by 10 to get 1 ton of beef, and then divide the left side of the equation by the same 10 to get 2 tons of vegetables. Now the equation reads: 2 tons of vegetables = 1 ton of beef. So now you know that the opportunity cost for Mexico to produce 1 ton of beef is 2 tons of vegetables.

For every ton of beef produced, the US must give up producing one ton of vegetables. Therefore, in the US, 1 ton of beef = 1 ton of vegetables. But for every ton of beef produced, Mexico must give up producing two tons of vegetables. Therefore, in Mexico, 1 ton of beef = 2 tons of vegetables, and 1 ton of vegetables = ½ ton of beef. If both countries were self-sufficient and did not engage in trade, they would have to make a choice between the tradeoffs on their own production possibilities curves, shown below. But if countries are willing to trade, they can gain from the other country's production efficiency.

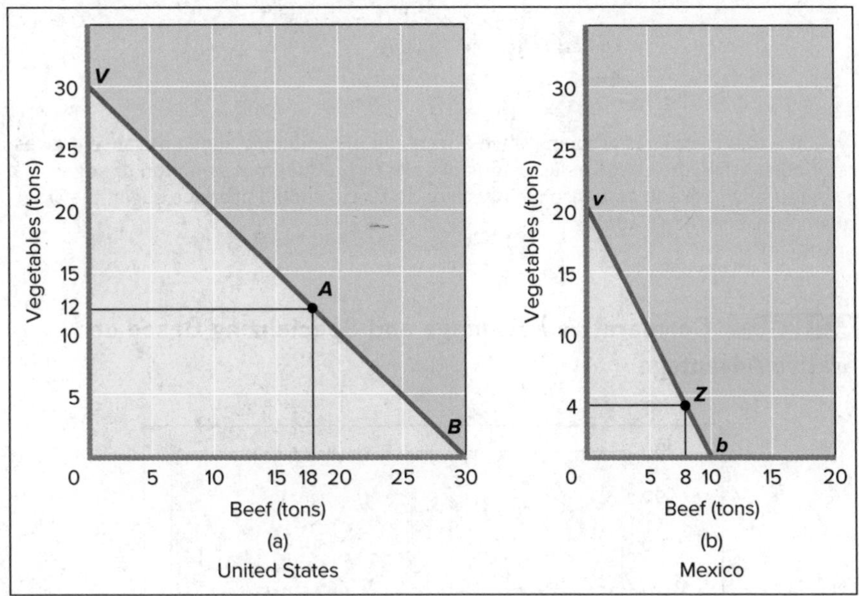

The **Law of Comparative Advantage** says that the total output in the world economy is highest when each country produces the good for which it has the lowest opportunity cost. In this case, to produce 1 ton of beef, the US must give up 1 ton of vegetables, while Mexico must give up 2 tons of vegetables. Because the US has the lower opportunity cost, it has the comparative advantage and should produce beef. At the same time, to produce 1 ton of vegetables, the US opportunity cost is 1 ton of beef, while Mexico's opportunity cost is ½ ton of beef. Because Mexico is the lower-cost producer of vegetables, Mexico should specialize in vegetables, the US should specialize in beef, and the two countries should trade. It is not possible for one country to hold the comparative advantage in both products.

Keep in Mind

AP Economics exam writers frequently set up the table in a different fashion. Rather than noting the quantity produced (output), they may note the amount of resources needed (input) to produce the products. The table would look more like this, in the number of labor hours to produce 1 ton:

	Corn	Sugar
United States	10 labor hours	30 labor hours
Brazil	20 labor hours	40 labor hours

To convert the data to the number of products produced, find a common denominator for the two products produced by one country. (Usually the problems are set up so that the larger number works as a common denominator.) In this example, use 30 hours for the US. In 30 hours of time, the US could produce 3 tons of corn or 1 ton of sugar. Then use 40 hours for Brazil. (It is fine to use different denominators, because you are only finding the ratio *within* each country.) In 40 hours of time, Brazil could produce 2 tons of corn or 1 ton of sugar. Put these new numbers into a new table like this:

	Corn	Sugar
United States	3 tons	1 ton
Brazil	2 tons	1 ton

Now you see that Brazil has a comparative advantage in producing sugar, because it gives up 2 tons of corn, while the US gives up 3 tons of corn to produce the same ton of sugar. The US has a comparative advantage in producing corn. So Brazil should produce sugar, the US produces corn, and they trade.

PRACTICE Comparative Advantage and Specializing Based on Comparative Advantage

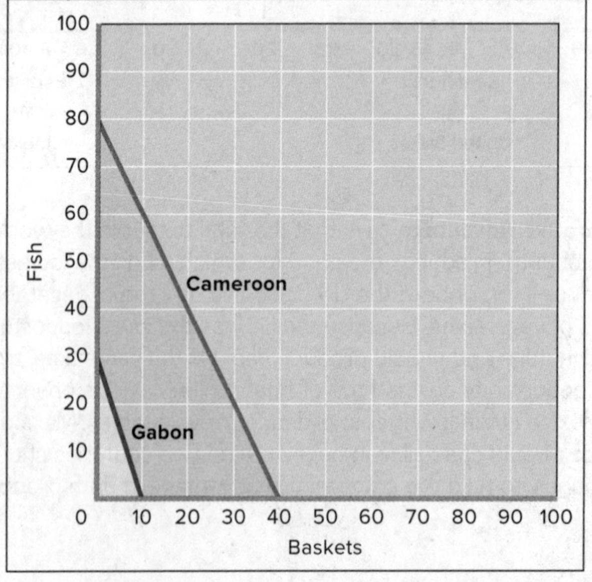

The graph above illustrates the production possibilities curves for Cameroon and Gabon.

1. __________ Which country has the absolute advantage in producing baskets?

2. __________ Which country has the absolute advantage in catching fish?

3. __________ What is Cameroon's opportunity cost for producing one basket?

4. __________ What is Cameroon's opportunity cost for catching one fish?

5. __________ What is Gabon's opportunity cost for producing one basket?

6. __________ What is Gabon's opportunity cost for catching one fish?

7. __________ Which country has the comparative advantage in producing baskets?

8. __________ Which country has the comparative advantage in catching fish?

The table below shows resource units each country requires to make products (remember to convert!).

	Televisions	Radios
Country A	12 resource units	4 resource units
Country B	8 resource units	2 resource units

9. __________ What is Country A's opportunity cost for producing one television?

10. __________ What is Country B's opportunity cost for producing one television?

11. __________ Which country should specialize in producing televisions?

12. __________ Which country should specialize in producing radios?

A CLOSER LOOK Terms of Trade and Gains from Trade

Terms of trade is the exchange ratio of products to be traded. For simplicity, we will assume a barter economy, with beef traded for vegetables. The terms of trade will always fall between the two countries' opportunity costs, because if either country did not gain from the trade, it would not choose to trade. In the case we explored earlier, the US is producing each ton of beef at an opportunity cost of 1 ton of vegetables, so it will not accept less than 1 ton of vegetables from Mexico in trade for beef. At the same time, Mexico will not pay more than 2 tons of vegetables for a ton of American beef, because it could have produced its own supply of beef at that price. Therefore, the price of 1 ton of beef will be between 1 and 2 tons of vegetables, with the final price of beef determined by supply and demand.

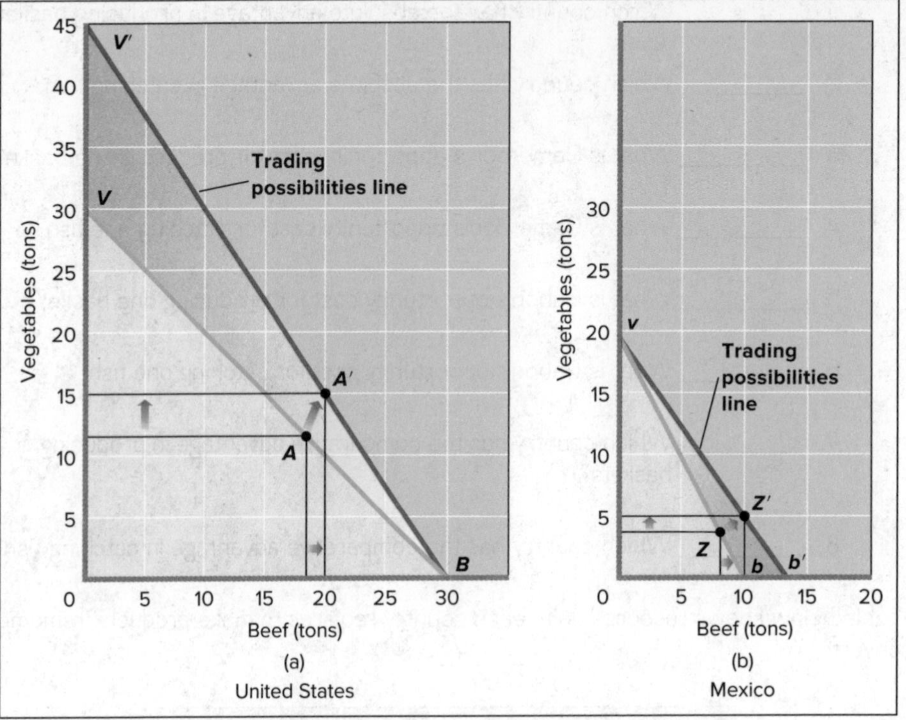

Assume the terms of trade are set at 1 ton of beef = 1.5 tons of vegetables. We can now draw new production possibilities curves called consumption possibilities frontiers, if each country completely specialized in the product for which it had a comparative advantage. Both countries can now reach beyond their domestic production possibilities curves, and both countries can have more beef and more vegetables than if they depended entirely on domestic production. Therefore, both countries gained from the trade. In Graph (a), the US moved from Point A (12 tons of vegetables and 18 tons of beef) to Point A′ (15 tons of vegetables and 20 tons of beef), gaining 3 tons of vegetables and 2 tons of beef. In Graph (b), Mexico moved from Point Z (4 tons of vegetables and 8 tons of beef) to Point Z′ (5 tons of vegetables and 10 tons of beef), gaining 1 ton of vegetables and 2 tons of beef. While the production possibilities curve can shift out domestically as the result of increases in the amount and quality of resources and technology, we now see that the consumption possibilities curve exists to the right of the production possibilities curve.

In reality, international trade is not so neatly done. Countries differ significantly in resources, far more than two countries are involved in cross-trade, countries do not exclusively specialize in one product, and the Law of Increasing Opportunity Costs causes the production possibilities curves to bow outward. Still, the basic principles of comparative advantage and gains from trade are true, and they explain why countries trade – because all countries involved benefit from that trade.

PRACTICE Terms of Trade and Gains from Trade

In India, the opportunity cost for producing one pound of spices is 5 flowers. In Pakistan, the opportunity cost for producing one pound of spices is 4 flowers.

1. __________ What is the opportunity cost for producing one flower in India?

2. __________ What is the opportunity cost for producing one flower in Pakistan?

3. ________ Which country has the comparative advantage and should produce spices?

4. ________ What are the terms of trade (range of acceptable prices) for spices?

5. ________ Which country has the comparative advantage and should produce flowers?

6. ________ What are the terms of trade (range of acceptable prices) for flowers?

7. ________ If the terms of trade are 1 spice = 4.2 flowers, who will benefit from this trade: *India, Pakistan, both,* or *neither*?

8. ________ If the terms of trade are 1 spice = 3 flowers, will India and Pakistan trade?

A CLOSER LOOK The Case for Free Trade

Free trade results in benefits for individual consumers and society as a whole. Because trade relies on comparative advantage, resources are allocated more efficiently. With specialization and trade, resources flow to the lowest-cost producers, and nations and consumers can import products at a lower price than they can produce them domestically. As a result, real income increases and standards of living rise, so material well-being also increases for the citizens of nations involved in the trade.

Exporting nations also gain, because other nations can buy their exports at a lower cost than they can produce domestically. As demand increases for those exports, firms expand and hire more workers to produce those exports, increasing both employment and output.

Free trade also deters monopolies by providing competition, which requires domestic firms to use more efficient production methods in order to compete. This competition promotes quality and encourages innovation, further supporting economic growth. In addition, free trade provides a wider variety of goods and services for consumers to choose from, improving the quality of life for consumers.

Free trade also has important political implications. As nations are linked by international trade and multinational corporations, they forge relationships and trade agreements. When faced with political disagreements, arguably, such nations are more likely to seek peaceful solutions rather than resorting to war.

PRACTICE The Case for Free Trade

Identify the ideas supporting free trade from the pairings below. Does free trade facilitate:

1. ________ *Efficiency* or *inefficiency*?

2. ________ *Higher* or *lower* prices?

3. ________ *Improved* or *reduced* standards of living?

4. ________ A *greater* or *lesser* number of monopolies?

5. ________ *Improved* or *reduced* rates of economic growth?

6. _________ A *greater* or *lesser* variety of goods for consumers?

7. _________ *Better* or *worse* relations among nations?

Supply and Demand Analysis of Exports and Imports

Refer to pages 703–706 of your textbook.

A CLOSER LOOK Supply and Demand in the United States

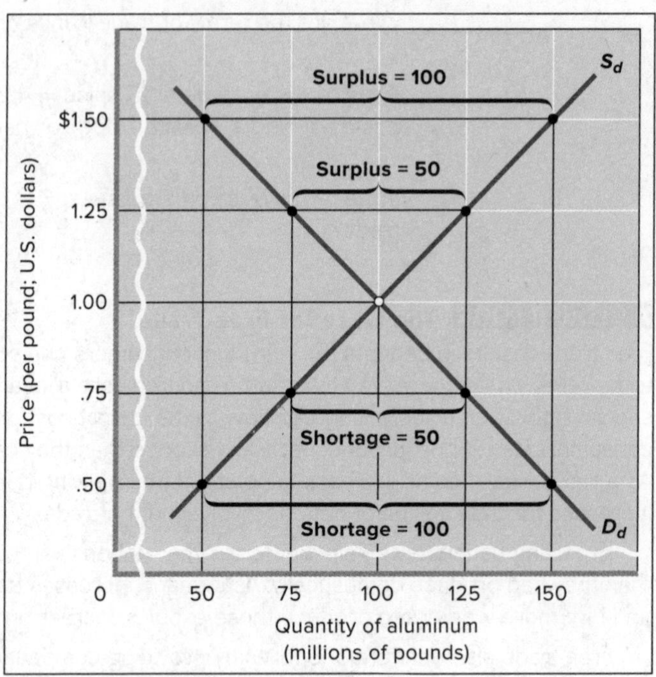

In a closed economy, supply and demand within a single country determine the **domestic price** and quantity. In the graph to the right, at a price of $1 per pound, 100 million pounds of aluminum will be produced and sold within the US. The **world price** is set by supply and demand among all countries that engage in trade of that product. If the world price is higher than the US price and the US opens its borders to trade, domestic firms are willing to produce more, while US consumers demand a lower quantity, resulting in a surplus of products. In the example in our graph, at a world price of $1.25 a pound, US firms increase production to 125 million pounds, while US consumers demand only 75 million pounds. The surplus of 50 million pounds is sold as exports in the world market. If the price were $1.50 a pound, domestic consumers would purchase even less, while US firms would produce even more, thus creating a 100 million pound surplus which could be exported to other nations.

Conversely, if the world price is 75¢ per pound and the US opens its economy to imported aluminum, the price of aluminum in the US market will also fall to 75¢ per pound. At the lower price, US consumers increase the quantity demanded to 125 million pounds, but domestic producers are only willing to produce 75 million pounds, leaving a 50 million pound shortage. The US will import the 50 million pounds of aluminum from other world producers who are willing to sell it at that price. If the world price fell to 50¢ per pound, US producers would reduce production to 50 million pounds as consumers increased their quantity demanded to 150 million pounds. The 100 million pound domestic shortage would be filled by imports to meet consumer demand. When the world price is higher than the domestic price, US firms increase production and export the additional products. When the world price is lower than the domestic price, US firms reduce production and the US imports additional products. After trade, the world and domestic prices of a product will be equal.

PRACTICE **Supply and Demand in the United States**

The graph to the right illustrates the US market for pork.
Pw indicates the world price of $2 per pound.

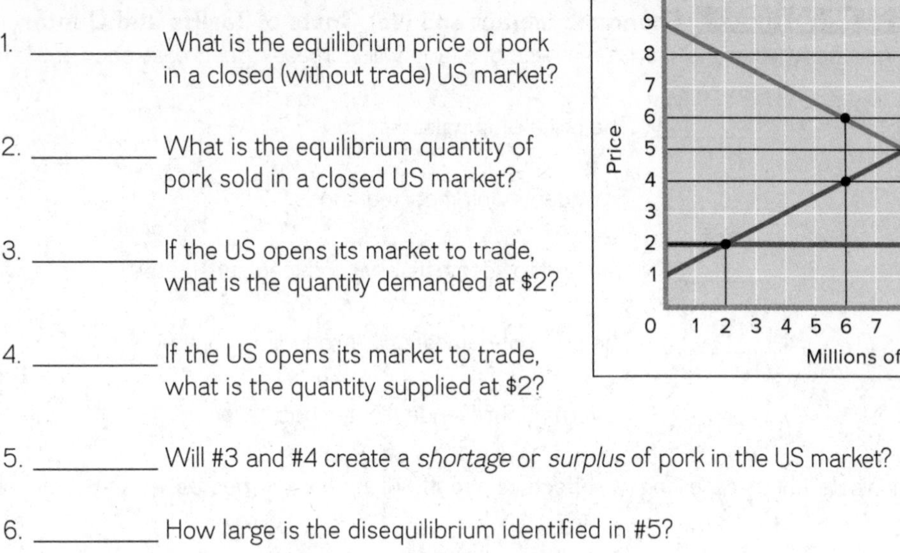

1. __________ What is the equilibrium price of pork in a closed (without trade) US market?

2. __________ What is the equilibrium quantity of pork sold in a closed US market?

3. __________ If the US opens its market to trade, what is the quantity demanded at $2?

4. __________ If the US opens its market to trade, what is the quantity supplied at $2?

5. __________ Will #3 and #4 create a *shortage* or *surplus* of pork in the US market?

6. __________ How large is the disequilibrium identified in #5?

7. __________ How will the US market fulfill the consumer demand identified in #5?

Trade Barriers and Export Subsidies

Refer to pages 707–709 of your textbook.

A CLOSER LOOK Economic Impact and Net Costs of Tariffs and Quotas

Trade barriers are policies intended to limit the amount of international trade. A **tariff,** an excise tax on imports, can be used to earn government revenue and to increase import prices to protect domestic producers from lower-cost import competition. A **quota** limits the number of imports allowed into a country. Non-tariff barriers include licensing agreements and quality controls. "Voluntary" export restrictions are "agreed to" by foreign producers when an importing nation threatens more direct trade barriers (such as tariffs) if the firms don't "voluntarily" reduce exports to that country.

Trade barriers reduce the supply of products within the importing country, increasing price and reducing the quantity sold. These actions hurt the foreign producer through lower sales and hurt the consumer through higher prices. Now that the market price is higher, domestic firms increase production at the higher price, so both the output and price increase for the domestic firm – which explains why firms lobby Congress so hard for trade barriers to protect them from competition. The other winner from trade barriers is government, which collects revenue from the tariffs, fees, and licenses. It is important to note that these increased costs are paid by American consumers, not the foreign producer.

There are other important negative effects of trade barriers to consider. Because less efficient firms are increasing production while the most efficient producers are reducing production, scarce resources are flowing away from efficient producers. Therefore, world output begins to fall. Further, because we are now buying fewer products from other countries, reducing output and incomes in *those* countries, foreigners now have less income available to purchase our products, reducing US exports, employment, and GDP. Numerous studies have shown that the costs of trade barriers to the consumer are substantially greater than the gains to domestic producers and the government. As a result of efficiency reductions and the millions of dollars invested in lobbying Congress to create such trade barriers, output, consumption, and the standard of living all fall.

PRACTICE **Economic Impact and Net Costs of Tariffs and Quotas**

Indicate whether the short-run effects of a tariff will *increase* or *decrease* each of the following.

1. _________ The price of imported goods
2. _________ The quantity of imported goods
3. _________ Demand for domestically-produced substitutes
4. _________ The price of domestically-produced substitutes
5. _________ Government revenue from import taxes

Indicate whether the long-run effects of a tariff will *increase* or *decrease* each of the following.

6. _________ Quantity produced by corporations in other countries
7. _________ Employment and wages of workers in other countries
8. _________ International demand for US export products
9. _________ American production of goods to be exported to other countries
10. _________ Employment and wages of US workers who produce export products
11. _________ Government revenue from income taxes

A Case for Protection: A Critical Review

Refer to pages 709–712 of your textbook.

A CLOSER LOOK **Arguments**

Protectionists, who support trade barriers, argue that we must protect US firms that produce goods necessary for national security, so we do not rely on foreign firms for our self-defense. **Free traders,** who oppose the use of significant trade barriers, agree that national security is a priority, but argue that non-defense firms will abuse the protections, claiming their products are also necessary for defense. Free traders instead propose direct subsidies to domestic producers of vital defense products.

Protectionists also argue we must use trade barriers to promote production of a variety of domestic goods, so we don't rely on strict specialization. Free traders agree that diversity in an economy is important, but note the US economy is already diverse, so this is not a relevant argument for the US.

The infant industry argument states that new domestic firms cannot immediately compete with established, efficient foreign firms. So protectionists argue that temporary tariffs should be placed on imports that compete with new domestic firms until those new firms get on their feet; then the tariffs can be removed to allow competition. Free traders argue that determining which new firms deserve protection is difficult. Further, firms that receive such protection will resist *ever* dropping the trade barrier. Free traders argue that targeted direct subsidies for protected firms are more effective.

Dumping is the practice of selling a good abroad at a price lower than the firm's cost of production, either as price discrimination or in an attempt to run domestic producers out of business. Protectionists argue we should use widespread tariffs to protect US firms. Free traders caution that what may look like dumping may really be a strong comparative advantage. They argue that targeted tariffs can be used to punish the few firms that use this unfair trade practice.

A popular protectionist argument is that trade barriers will save US jobs and firms. They argue that if imports are limited, consumers will buy domestic products instead, increasing domestic output and employment. Free traders point out that while imports may cost some domestic jobs, others emerge in the transportation and sale of imports. Trade barriers eliminate these jobs, as well as jobs in the other countries where the imports are produced. Lower incomes abroad reduce the demand for US exports, reducing US output and employment in our export industries. Countries are likely to retaliate, leading to large-scale trade wars. In the long run, trade barriers do not effectively increase domestic employment, and instead result in inefficiency and reduced output. International trade may reduce output and employment in less efficient domestic industries, but long-run gains in output and employment among more efficient producers outweigh these costs. Therefore, most economists support increased trade.

The final protectionist argument is that US workers must be protected from the low wages paid by firms abroad. Protectionists contend that if US firms are forced to compete with lower-priced imports, US firms must cut wages, reducing US standards of living. Free traders argue that US standards of living are higher due to consumers' ability to buy lower-priced imports rather than more expensive domestic products. Further, because US workers are more productive than workers in many other countries, US workers are paid higher wages. But if trade is limited and the US must allocate resources to inefficient producers, output and standards of living will fall. Finally, free traders argue that protectionists make the mistake of focusing on the differences in wages per hour, rather than labor cost per unit of output. US productivity is higher, leading to a similar labor cost per unit produced.

PRACTICE Arguments

Identify whether each of the following arguments would be made by a *protectionist* or a *free trader*.

1. __________ We must use widespread tariffs to prevent dumping.

2. __________ Differences in wages per hour do not threaten the jobs of US workers.

3. __________ Trade barriers do not save American jobs in the long run.

4. __________ If imports are limited, consumers will buy domestic products as substitutes.

Multilateral Trade Agreements and Free-Trade Zones

Refer to pages 712–715 of your textbook.

A CLOSER LOOK GATT, WTO, EU, NAFTA, and Recognizing Those Hurt by Free Trade

The General Agreement on Tariffs and Trade (GATT) reduced trade barriers among 128 nations from 1947 to 1993. In 1993, it was succeeded by the World Trade Organization (WTO), which continues to reduce trade barriers and resolve trade disputes among its 161 members. In 1958, European countries created a free-trade zone that eventually became today's European Union. These 28 nations trade without barriers, most of them with the common currency of the euro. In 1993, the US put into effect the **North American Free Trade Agreement (NAFTA)**, which removed trade barriers among the US, Canada, and Mexico. Opponents feared NAFTA would create massive unemployment if US firms moved to Mexico, but instead, employment, trade, and standards of living increased in all three countries.

While trade has increased world output and efficiency and improved the standards of living for export workers and consumers, **offshoring** of jobs and closing of domestic firms cause unemployment for American workers. In many cases, workers who have lost jobs to automation mistakenly believe it is due to international trade. While government officials have developed policies to help with the adjustment of workers and communities that have lost jobs and firms, the very real losses associated with trade lead to continued disputes over the wisdom of international trade.

PRACTICE GATT, WTO, EU, NAFTA, and Recognizing Those Hurt by Free Trade

1. __________ What agreement removed trade barriers among the US, Canada, and Mexico?

2. __________ What organization works to reduce trade barriers around the globe?

Make sure to return to the AP Key Concepts section to check your understanding of the chapter's concepts important to AP coursework.

Economically Speaking

- **Absolute Advantage** one country is able to produce more than another
- **Capital-Intensive Industry** industries primarily focused on the use of capital resources
- **Comparative Advantage** one country is able to produce more efficiently than another
- **Domestic Price** the product price set by supply and demand within a country
- **Dumping** selling a good abroad at a price lower than the firm's cost of production
- **Free Trader** a person who opposes the use of significant trade barriers
- **Labor-Intensive Industry** industries primarily focused on the use of labor resources
- **Land-Intensive Industry** industries primarily focused on the use of land resources
- **Law of Comparative Advantage** world output is highest when countries produce the goods for which they have the lowest opportunity cost
- **North American Free Trade Agreement (NAFTA)** agreement removing trade barriers among the US, Canada, and Mexico
- **Offshoring** moving work previously done by Americans to other countries
- **Protectionist** a person who supports the use of trade barriers
- **Quota** limit on the number of imports allowed into a country
- **Tariff** excise tax on imports
- **Terms of Trade** the exchange ratio at which products are traded
- **Trade Barrier** policy intended to limit the amount of international trade
- **Trade Deficit** imports exceed exports
- **Trade Surplus** exports exceed imports
- **World Price** the product price set by global supply and demand

Chapter 35

The Balance of Payments, Exchange Rates, and Trade Deficits

This study of economics concludes with the examination of how money moves between nations. Changes in the demand for imports, relative inflation and interest rates, and other factors such as tourism, international aid, and speculation can change the relative values of national currencies. Chapter 35 examines the causes and effects of changes in the supply and demand for currency in international exchange markets and the effects of such changes on imports and exports, as well as current and financial account balances.

Material from Chapter 35 appears in several multiple-choice questions and is a frequent free-response question on the AP Macroeconomics exam.

Key Concepts

Below is a summary of the chapter's concepts important to AP coursework. Upon completing the lessons that follow, return to these concepts to make sure you understand them and how the practice exercises you completed relate to them.

- To buy imports, one must first buy the nation's currency in the foreign exchange market.
- The balance of payments is the total value of transactions between two countries.
  - The current account primarily calculates the trade of products between countries.
    - If exports exceed imports, the country has a current account surplus.
    - If exports are less than imports, the country has a current account deficit.
  - The financial account calculates the flow of funds for investment in financial assets.
    - If capital inflow exceeds outflow, the country has a financial account surplus.
    - If capital inflow is less than outflow, the country has a financial account deficit.
  - The current and financial accounts *must* balance. One minus the other equals zero.
  - If a country has a current account deficit, it *must* have a financial account surplus.
- Fixed exchange rates were tied to gold; flexible exchange rates are set by supply and demand.
  - If a currency appreciates, its value increases; it takes more of another currency to buy it.
  - If a currency depreciates, its value falls; it takes less of another currency to buy it.
  - Because the values are related, as one currency appreciates, the other depreciates.

- Demand for a foreign currency changes due to changes in tastes, incomes, inflation rates, interest rates, expected return on investment, and speculation.
- If a currency appreciates, the products purchased with that currency become more expensive.
- Importers prefer a strong dollar to buy imports at a lower price.
- Exporters prefer a weak dollar to sell exports at what looks like a lower price to other countries.
- The US has consistently experienced trade deficits since the 1980s; they peaked in 2007.
- If Congress uses expansionary fiscal policy, interest rates rise in the loanable funds market. Foreigners increase demand for dollars to invest in US bonds, raising the value of the dollar. Imports look less expensive to Americans, so US imports rise; at the same time, US exports look more expensive to foreigners, so US exports fall, increasing the trade deficit.
- If the Fed uses expansionary monetary policy, interest rates fall in the money market. Foreigners demand fewer dollars to invest in the US, while Americans demand more foreign currency to invest abroad. The US dollar depreciates while the foreign currency appreciates.

Now, let's examine more closely the following concepts from your textbook:

- **The Balance of Payments**
- **Flexible Exchange Rates**
- **Recent US Trade Deficits**

These sections were selected because an understanding of currency values and financial and product flows completes the picture of the world economy.

The Balance of Payments

Refer to pages 721–724 of your textbook.

A CLOSER LOOK Current Account, Capital and Financial Account, and Why the Balance?

International trade for goods, services, or financial assets depends on the exchange of currencies. In order for a buyer in one country to buy products or assets from another country, the buyer must first buy the other nation's currency in the **foreign exchange market**. If a US firm wants to buy tomatoes from Mexico, it must buy pesos to pay for them. With an exchange rate of $1 = 20 pesos, US importers would pay a price of 5¢ per peso. If the price of a shipment of tomatoes were 10,000 Mexican pesos, US importers would have to pay $500 (.05 × 10,000) to buy the pesos necessary to buy the tomatoes.

The **balance of payments** is the total of all financial transactions that take place between the people of one country and the people of another country. Most of these financial transactions are for the purpose of buying goods, services, or financial assets. But other financial activities are included, such as tourism, the payments of interest and dividends, gifts, loans, and humanitarian aid. The balance of payments is divided into two major categories: the current account and the financial account.

The **current account** primarily calculates the amount of trade in goods and services. The balance of trade in goods and services is the difference between exports and imports. If exports exceed imports, the country has a trade surplus; if imports are greater than exports, the country experiences a trade deficit.

The **financial account** is the international flow of funds for investment in financial assets. When **capital inflows** from other countries (to invest in US assets) exceed **capital**

outflows from the US (to invest in assets abroad), the US experiences a surplus in the financial account. If US outflows are greater than inflows of funds from other nations into the US, the US would experience a financial account deficit.

In the balance of payments, the current and financial accounts *must* balance; the sum of the accounts must be zero. Countries can only trade products (goods and services) or assets. If a country imports more than it exports, the only way it can make up for that current account deficit is to transfer more assets to the country through a financial account surplus. So if a country has a current account deficit it *must* have a financial account surplus, to balance the trade accounts to zero.

Keep in Mind
Recent AP Macroeconomics exams have asked questions requiring knowledge of the differences between current and financial accounts and the effects of policies on their balances. It is important to be able to distinguish between the two accounts.

PRACTICE Current Account, Capital and Financial Account, and Why the Balance?

1. __________ If the exchange rate is $1 = 50 Philippine pesos and the price of a container of coconut oil is 4,000 Philippine pesos, what is the price in US dollars?

2. Indicate whether each of the following would count in the *current* account or *financial* account.

   A. __________ The US buys oil from Saudi Arabia

   B. __________ Colombian investors buy US bonds

   C. __________ The US sells computers to Australia

   D. __________ South Korean firms sell cars to US dealerships

3. If the US increases its imports from Kenya, indicate whether it will cause a *surplus* or *deficit* in:

   A. __________ The US current account balance

   B. __________ The US financial account balance

Flexible Exchange Rates

Refer to pages 724–729 of your textbook.

A CLOSER LOOK Depreciation and Appreciation

Before 1934, countries used the gold standard to set **fixed exchange rates,** with each currency worth a set amount of gold. From 1944 to 1971, the Bretton Woods system set relative values of international currencies in terms of other currencies or gold. Over time, countries began to use trade policies or affect currency values to manipulate markets, which distorted trade, reduced efficiency, and created international tensions. In 1971, **flexible exchange rates**, also known as the "managed float," became the norm for foreign exchange markets. The relative values of currencies are determined by supply and demand, with occasional interventions in crises by governments and the International Monetary Fund.

When the demand for British pounds increases, the quantity of US dollars required to buy a pound increases, and the value of the pound **appreciates** (rises). If the demand for British pounds falls, it takes fewer US dollars to buy them, and the value of the British pound **depreciates** (falls). It is important to recognize that the values of the two nations' currencies change relative to one another. If the British pound is appreciating against the US dollar, the US dollar must be depreciating. This occurs because Americans use US dollars to buy British pounds, changing the relative values of both currencies.

Let's say a new British band becomes an instant success, and American fans want to buy the band's music, T-shirts, and posters. American stores want to sell these products to consumers, so they order the products from British manufacturers. But to buy British products, the American stores must buy British currency first – and they buy those pounds with US dollars. When demand for British pounds increases, American stores must increase the supply of US dollars in the foreign exchange market in order to buy the pounds, simultaneously reducing the value of the dollar. So while the pound appreciates (requiring $2.50 rather than $2.00 to buy the British pound), the dollar depreciates (requiring the British to pay only 0.4 pounds, rather than 0.5 pounds, to buy one US dollar).

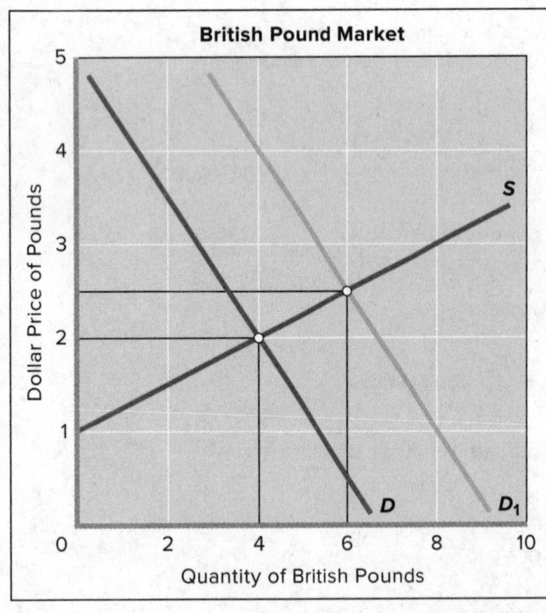

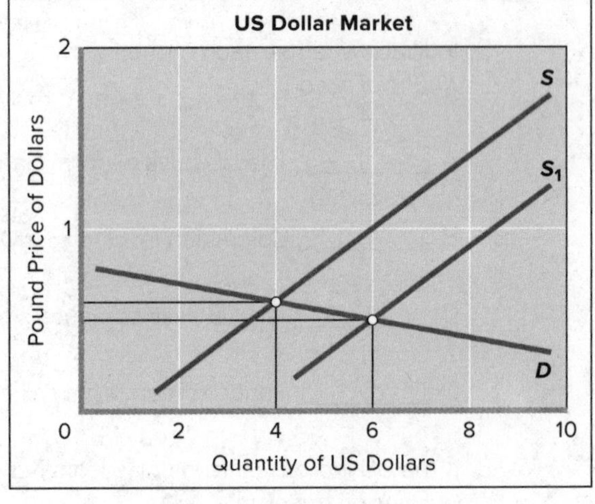

Keep in Mind

It is very important to understand how these two markets are linked. Some questions on the AP Macroeconomics exam only ask you to draw the graph for one market, but may still ask what is happening at the same time in the other market. Keep in your mind the image of the "teeter totter" or "see saw." If one end is going up, the other end *must* be coming down!

PRACTICE Depreciation and Appreciation

Draw graphs illustrating the international markets for Japanese Yen and US Dollars. Assume that US incomes fall, so consumers cannot afford to buy as many Japanese imports. Illustrate the changes in demand or supply in both the yen and dollar markets. Then answer the questions below.

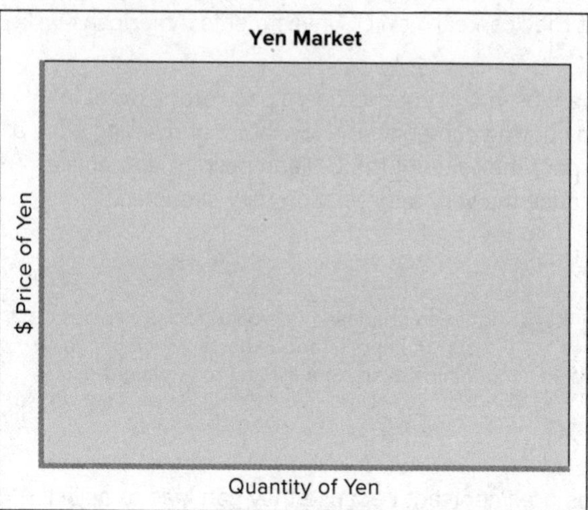

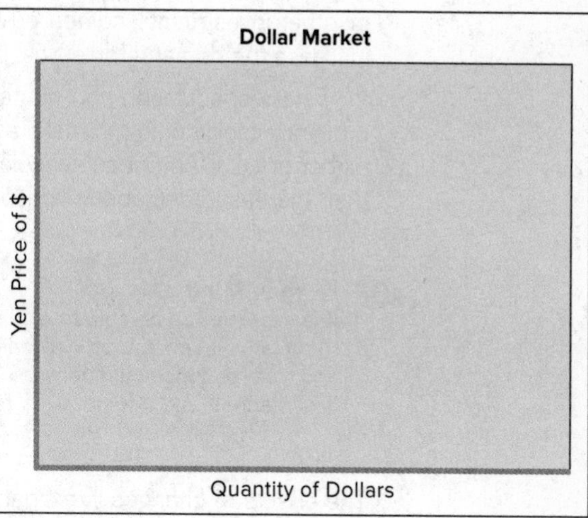

1. __________ Did the demand for Japanese imports *increase* or *decrease*?
2. __________ Did the demand for Japanese yen *increase* or *decrease*?
3. __________ Given #2, did the value of the yen *appreciate* or *depreciate*?
4. __________ Given #3, will imports look *more* or *less* expensive to American consumers?
5. __________ Given #2, did the supply of US dollars *increase* or *decrease*?
6. __________ Given #5, did the value of US dollars *appreciate* or *depreciate*?
7. __________ Given #6, will US exports look *more* or *less* expensive to Japanese buyers?

A CLOSER LOOK Determinants of Flexible Exchange Rates

Several factors can cause a change in the demand for a foreign currency. First, a change in consumer tastes affects consumer demand for imports. If a Japanese firm develops a popular new video game, US consumer demand for the product increases US demand for Japanese yen to pay for the product.

Second, a change in relative incomes changes the demand for currency. If US incomes rise, Americans buy more domestic products *and* imports. The rise in imports increases demand for foreign currency.

Third, changes in relative inflation rates affect import demand. If US prices rise more quickly than prices abroad, US consumers will buy more imports as substitutes, increasing demand for those currencies.

Fourth, changes in relative interest rates are an important factor in determining demand for currency. If South African interest rates paid on bonds are higher than interest rates in the US, Americans will see South African bonds as an attractive investment and increase demand for South African rand.

Fifth, differences in the expected return on investment can affect demand for currency. If US investors expect a greater return on their investments in German stocks, real estate, or other investments, compared to what they can earn on US investments, Americans will increase the demand for euros.

Finally, speculation contributes to changes in currency values. Speculators invest in currency itself, hoping to make a profit by buying currency at a low price and selling it for a higher price. If American speculators expect the value of the Chilean peso to appreciate, their increased demand for pesos can cause the very appreciation they expected.

Keep in Mind
It is important to be able to explain the linkages between changes in demand for currencies, the relative appreciation/depreciation, and the effects on imports and exports. Multiple-choice and free-response questions on the AP Macroeconomics exam require you to explain those links, causes, and effects.

The effects of changes in exchange rates are important because they can lead to adjustments in deficits or surpluses in the balance of payments. Assume we start with our equilibrium exchange rate, where $2 = 1 British pound. If consumer tastes change to desire more British imports, an increase in demand for British pounds increases the price of pounds for American consumers. However, because pounds are now more expensive, the prices of British products purchased with those pounds become more expensive. For example, a book worth 10 British pounds in the United Kingdom costs Americans $20 at the original exchange rate. But if it now costs $2.50 to buy 1 British pound, the price of the book has increased to $25. At higher prices, Americans will begin to reduce the quantity of imports demanded, reducing the demand for British pounds until their value falls. Where at one point the US had a deficit in the balance of payments, the change in exchange rates again returned to balance.

From the British side of the same equation, the increasing value of the British pound makes American products seem less expensive, and the quantity demanded increases. As the British demand more US products, the demand for US dollars to pay for those products increases, which increases the value of the dollar. As the price of the dollar increases, American products become more expensive and British citizens reduce the quantity demanded, bringing their earlier surplus in the balance of payments back into equilibrium. So while currencies may appreciate for a number of reasons, the flexibility of the exchange rate eventually reverses the process and leads the balance of payments back to equilibrium.

As a result of this exchange rate flexibility, changes in currency values can destabilize the domestic economy. Assume the US has an open economy and begins at full-employment output. If the US dollar appreciates, imports increase and exports decrease, creating a trade deficit. This reduction in net exports reduces aggregate demand, potentially reducing US output and employment. Conversely, a depreciated US dollar reduces US demand for imports because of the increase in import prices. But the increase in demand for the substitute US products increases the price of those US products. In addition, the increased foreign demand for US goods due to the cheaper US dollar further increases aggregate demand.

So which is better for the US: a **strong dollar** which has appreciated in value, or a **weak dollar** which has depreciated in value? The answer is: it depends. A company that is importing resources or products (such as a gas station or grocery store) would prefer to have a strong dollar, because import prices are cheaper, allowing importers to increase profits. But a company that is exporting products (such as a farmer or an auto manufacturer) would rather have a weak dollar, because foreign customers can buy more products at a lower price – even though the exporter hasn't changed its price.

PRACTICE Determinants of Flexible Exchange Rates

1. __________ Would a restaurant chain that imports coffee prefer a *strong* or *weak* dollar?

2. __________ Would a manufacturer that exports airplanes prefer a *strong* or *weak* dollar?

3. __________ If US incomes fall, will demand for foreign currency *increase* or *decrease*?

4. If the inflation rate is higher in the US than in Peru, indicate which would *increase* or *decrease*:

   A. __________ US exports to Peru

   B. __________ US demand for Peruvian products

   C. __________ US demand for the Peruvian sol and the value of the sol

   D. __________ The supply of US dollars in the foreign exchange market

   E. __________ The international value of the US dollar

Recent US Trade Deficits

Refer to pages 736–737 of your textbook.

A CLOSER LOOK Causes of US Trade Deficits and Implications of US Trade Deficits

US trade deficits increased dramatically 2002–2007. The US economy experienced greater growth in that period, and increased incomes allowed consumers to buy more imports than foreign consumers were buying from the US. In addition, the US opened a wide trade deficit with China. Low-priced Chinese products have dramatically increased US demand for imports, but because Chinese officials have pegged the yuan to the dollar, the increased demand doesn't raise the price of the yuan, so the trade deficit is perpetuated. Finally, the high interest rates and low saving rate of Americans opened a door for those abroad to invest in American stocks, bonds, and real estate. Trade deficits were cut nearly in half during the Great Recession and remain significantly lower than they were in 2007.

The concern with US trade deficits is that they come at the expense of increased borrowing from other nations or the sale of US assets. Remember, a deficit in the current account is accompanied by a surplus in the financial account. Foreigners own trillions of dollars more of US assets than Americans own of foreign assets. This foreign investment provides money for the purchase of capital, which can improve economic growth. To reduce the trade deficit, the US would have to reduce imports and increase exports – which would reduce foreign investment and could reduce potential growth.

One final important consideration is how changes in economic stabilization policies can affect exchange rates and international trade. When Congress uses expansionary fiscal policy by reducing taxes and increasing government spending, consumers have more income available to buy imports. At the same time, expansionary fiscal policy requires the government to borrow from the loanable funds market to finance deficit spending, increasing interest rates. The higher interest rates attract foreign investment as a capital inflow, increasing the demand for US dollars and causing them to appreciate. As US dollars appreciate, imports look less expensive, so imports increase; at the same time, the high value of US dollars makes US exports look expensive to foreigners, so exports decrease, increasing the trade deficit.

The Fed can also use expansionary monetary policy to stimulate economic growth, though its policies will have the opposite effect on capital flows. If the Fed increases the money supply, interest rates fall. Foreigners demand fewer dollars for investment, while Americans demand more foreign currency to invest in other countries that are paying higher interest rates on investment. As a result, a capital outflow develops. The increased demand for foreign currency increases its value, eventually causing imports to fall and exports to increase.

Changes in supply and demand for currencies and the resulting changes in currency values bring about impacts on production and employment in countries that trade. Globalization has increased the interdependence of nations, meaning we are no longer alone in our achievements – or our problems. As we see the effects of worker strikes, crop failures, or increasing incomes a world away affecting our own economy, we come to realize how important an understanding of economics is for us all.

PRACTICE Causes of US Trade Deficits and Implications of US Trade Deficits

Assume the US enters a recession and the government uses expansionary fiscal policy, causing a budget deficit. Answer the questions below to see the cause-and-effect chain of events that will result from the budget deficit.

1. ________ Will the interest rate in the loanable funds market *rise* or *fall*?
2. ________ Given #1, will Italian investors' demand for US bonds *rise* or *fall*?
3. ________ Given #2, will Italian investors' demand for US dollars *rise* or *fall*?
4. ________ Given #3, will the international value of the US dollar *rise* or *fall*?
5. ________ Given #4, will US imports of Italian products *rise* or *fall*?
6. ________ Given #4, will the international value of the Italian euro *rise* or *fall*?
7. ________ Given #6, will US exports of products to Italy *rise* or *fall*?
8. ________ Given #5 and #7, will the US trade deficit *rise* or *fall*?